THE SPIRITUALITY
OF THE
LATER ENGLISH PURITANS

THE SPIRITUALITY
OF THE
LATER ENGLISH PURITANS

AN ANTHOLOGY

Edited, and with an Introduction
by
Dewey D. Wallace, Jr.

MERCER

ISBN 0-86554-275-9

Library of Congress Cataloging-in-Publication Data
The Spirituality of the later English Puritans.
Bibliography: p. 245
    1. Spirituality—Early works to 1800. 2. Puritans—
Doctrines—Early works to 1800. I. Wallace, Dewey D., Jr.
II. Title.
BV4500.S67   1987   248.4'859   87-24692
ISBN 0-86554-275-9 (alk. paper)

Contents

PREFACE vii

INTRODUCTION xi

HOLY LIVES AND HOLY DEATHS 1
    Thomas Manton, "To the Reader" 2
    Edmund Trench, *Some Remarkable Passages in the Holy Life and Death*
        of the Late Reverend Mr. Edmund Trench 4
    Samuel Clarke, *The Life and Death of Mrs. Katherine Clarke* 17
    James Janeway, *A Token for Children* and *Invisibles, Realities* 32
    Theodosia Alleine, *A full Narrative of his Life* 53
    James Janeway and others, *A Murderer Punished and Pardoned* 79

HOLY MEDITATIONS 99
    William Bates, *A Discourse of Divine Meditation* 100
    Benjamin Keach, Poems from *The Glorious Lover*
        and from *War with the Devil* 108
    Ralph Venning, *A Spiritual Garden of Sweet-smelling Flowers* 113
    John Flavel, *Husbandry Spiritualized* and *Navigation Spiritualized* 119
    Thomas Vincent, *God's Terrible Voice in the City* 141
    Thomas Doolittle, *A Treatise Concerning the Lord's Supper* 145

HOLY COMFORTS FOR THE AFFLICTED AND UNCERTAIN 155
    Edmund Calamy, *The Godly Man's Ark* 156
    Benjamin Keach, *The Travels of True Godliness* 173
    Joseph Alleine, *Christian Letters* 179
    William Bates, *The Danger of Prosperity* 194
    Thomas Brooks, *A Cabinet of Choice Jewels* 196
    Walter Marshall, *The Gospel-Mystery of Sanctification* 208

HOLY EXPECTATIONS 219
    Edward Pearse, *The Great Concern* 220
    Theophilus Gale, *A Discourse of Christ's Coming* 231
    William Bates, *The Four Last Things* 239

SUGGESTED READINGS 245

To the memory of my great-grandfather,
Marcus Jediah Wallace
(1819–1878),
faithful Presbyterian pastor in Arkansas,
for whose family
the Puritan divines were required reading

Preface

The purpose of this anthology of Puritan spiritual writings is to establish the importance of spirituality in the Puritan movement and to define and illustrate the character of that spirituality, especially for the second half of the seventeenth century in England when devotional writing flourished. The selections chosen follow an introductory essay that portrays the themes and techniques of Puritan spirituality.

A word may be in order as to how I am using those much-debated terms *Puritan* and *Puritanism*. Of course, the adjective and noun may be employed to refer to a movement of militant, Reformed Protestants in (and at the edges of) the Church of England who sought further reform in that church from the time of Queen Elizabeth I (if not from the time of Edward VI) until the exclusion of Nonconformists from the established church in 1662. But the persons who led and constituted that movement shared a common configuration of religious attitudes, especially about the spiritual life; and the impulse or tradition carrying these attitudes can be properly denominated Puritanism up to the end of the seventeenth century in both England and colonial America. Thus I consider the Calvinistic, dissenting Protestants of the generation after the restoration of the monarchy in 1660 (to whom this volume mainly pertains) as both the children of the Puritan movement and as the upholders and continuators of the Puritan tradition as it dealt with the spiritual life. While it is true that terms such as *Dissenters* or *Nonconformists,* or denominational labels such as Baptist, Congregationalist, or Presbyterian are more precise, the general term *Puritan* is necessary for my purposes in this anthology. And overuse of denominational labels risks portraying these groups as being more distinct and coherent than they were.

Some who look at this anthology may wonder why several of the best-known Puritans of the Restoration era—notably Richard Baxter, John Owen, and John Bunyan—have been omitted; but they are already familiar names, and many of their writings are available in reprints of various sorts. My aim was to present examples from some significant, but relatively unknown, Puritan devotional writers. The important but lesser-known Puritan mystic Peter Sterry is another omission; but his often-strange writings have been well anthologized by Vivian De Sola Pinto's *Peter Sterry: Platonist and Puritan,* and no single or even several selections can quite capture the range of that remarkable writer. In the case of Joseph Alleine, where I have included a fairly well-known Puritan devotional writer, I have avoided excerpting his best-known, and often reprinted, *An Alarm to the Unconverted.*

In making selections for this collection I have chosen to include a small number of longer selections that truly represent the works from which they have been taken. In several cases an entire sermon, chapter, or other unit has been included either with no excisions or very brief ones.

The anthologized selections have been organized around four main topics. First, a number of items appear that illustrate the Puritan use of biographical and autobiographical materials to further the spiritual life. Second, selections that illustrate either instructions about meditation, meditations in verse and aphorism, or meditations on creatures and providences have been placed under the heading of "Holy Meditations." Pieces that wrestle with providence, suffering, and persecution, or that exemplify the Puritan occupation with assurance and other dilemmas of the spiritual life are included under "Holy Comforts for the Afflicted and Uncertain." And "Holy Expectations" brings the reader to the subject of death and the eschatological topics of the return of Christ and the beatific vision.

Inevitably, such an arrangement is somewhat arbitrary since some texts could have been classified differently. For example, Thomas Doolittle's meditation on the Lord's Supper might have been placed under comfort for the uncertain rather than meditation, for clearly it illustrates both. But all topics and selections carry the reader to the heart of Puritan spirituality.

In choosing texts for my selections, I have preferred the first or first extant edition of a selection, although because of availability I have sometimes used a later edition, usually the last printing during an author's lifetime. In editing the texts I have employed the following practices: I have transposed "j" to "i" and "u" to "v" and have changed to the modern "s". Contemporary spellings and apostrophes of omission have been left intact, except for a very few cases where the seventeenth-century spelling rendered a word incomprehensible. The capitalization of the edition I followed for any particular work has been left unchanged. Only a very few putative errors or misprints have been emended. Supplied words have been indicated by brackets. Some abbreviations have been spelled out fully. Quotation marks have replaced italics for quotations, and italics have generally been changed to roman type. Apostrophes, where lacking (their use was catching on in the latter part of the seventeenth century), have been supplied for possessives. And punctuation has been changed only where absolutely necessary to avoid confusion. It is my hope that following these principles results in an accurate yet readable text that retains something of the distinct flavor of the seventeenth-century pages.

Biblical quotations and allusions confront the editor of texts such as these with special problems. Since the pages of Puritan authors are sometimes pastiches of biblical references, it is impractical to identify every allusion in the notes. The method of citing chapter and verse has been regularized according to modern usage. A special problem has been caused by the penchant of Puritan authors to quote Scripture from memory rather than look up the exact wording. Where such quotations are only slightly inaccurate, I have sometimes supplied missing words in brackets or followed incorrect forms of a word with the correct one in brackets; where the inaccuracy is extensive, the footnote citation indicates that the verse is paraphrased. This accounts for the omission of quotation marks from some references that look like biblical quotations. With respect to non-biblical quotations, it has proved impossible to locate specifically every classical or patristic allusion; still the authors, where known, are identified.

Many debts have been incurred in the process of preparing this anthology. A grant from the University Research Committee of The George Washington University provided support for the collection and transcription of some of the materials needed. The staffs of the Folger Shakespeare Library and the microform reading room of the Library of Congress were always helpful in accommodating my requests. The resources of the Speer Library of Princeton Theological Seminary were an additional help. Charles Hambrick-Stowe read an early draft of the introduction and suggested many improvements. Richard Greaves read the entire manuscript with painstaking care, made many valuable suggestions, and helped me to avoid numerous errors. Robert G. Jones, John Ziolkowski, and Robert W. Kenny—my colleagues at The George Washington University—provided help on various difficult points related to the notes. The editorial staff of Mercer University Press supplied encouragement and assistance as the manuscript was readied for publication. My thanks are also due to Cheryl Matcho, James Estes, and Tina McAdams; they helped me with a number of the miscellaneous tasks involved in the preparation of the final typescript. But my deepest gratitude must go to Cynthia Gaizband, who typed most of the textual material, often deciphering it from blurred copies of sometimes nearly inscrutable seventeenth-century pages.

Dewey D. Wallace, Jr.
The George Washington University
October 1986

Introduction

Spirituality is the communion of persons with the divine, with emphasis on the nature of the devotion by which the divine is approached. It should be distinguished on the one hand from morality and dogma and on the other from religious institutions, though it is intertwined with both of these: patterns of moral behavior and belief are closely related to spirituality as cause or consequence, and such institutional religious realities as worship and fellowship may be regarded as aspects of spirituality. Perhaps the most similar concept is that of piety, when the latter is understood not in the classical sense of reverence for the gods but is taken instead to designate a whole style or manner of "being religious." In any case, spirituality is an aspect of much religious experience, and it has been an integral element of the Christian religion throughout its history, though various Christian times and places have been characterized by distinct spiritualities.

Puritanism—which in the historiography of the last century has been variously viewed as being primarily a social, political, ecclesiastical, moral, or theological movement—can be seen with greater plausibility as being at its core a piety (without denying the importance of these other factors). While this aspect of Puritanism was not ignored in the earlier literature (Perry Miller discussed Puritanism as Augustinian piety; William Haller described it as a brotherhood of preachers detailing the spiritual life for their auditors; and Geoffrey Nuttall defined it as "a movement towards immediacy in relation to God"), the most recent generation of Puritan scholarship—especially with regard to English Puritanism—has given it more emphasis. Gordon Wakefield, Horton Davies, Irvonwy Morgan, C. John Sommerville, and Gordon Rupp have written specifically on English Puritan piety, and a recent book by Charles Hambrick-Stowe has revised the understanding of American Puritanism by calling attention to it as piety, arguing that "at its heart . . . Puritanism was a devotional movement, rooted in religious experience," and that "the rise of Puritanism and the settlement of New England ought to be understood as a significant episode in the ongoing history of Christian spirituality."[1]

---

[1] Perry Miller, *The New England Mind: The Seventeenth Century* (Cambridge: Harvard University Press, 1954) ch. 1; William Haller, *The Rise of Puritanism* (New York: Columbia University Press, 1938) ch. 2; Geoffrey Nuttall, *The Holy Spirit in Puritan Faith and Experience* (Oxford: Basil Blackwell, 1946) 134; Gordon Wakefield, *Puritan Devotion: Its Place in the Development of Christian Piety* (London: Epworth Press, 1957); Horton Davies, *Worship and Theology in England from Andrewes to Baxter and Fox, 1603-1690* (Princeton: Princeton University Press, 1970) 117-32; Irvonwy Morgan, *Puritan Spirituality Illustrated from the Life and Times of the Rev. Dr. John Preston* (London: Epworth Press, 1973); C. John Sommerville, *Popular Religion in Restoration England* (Gainesville: University of Florida Press, 1977); Gordon Rupp, "A Devotion of Rapture in English Puritanism," in R. Buick Knox, ed. *Reformation, Conformity, and Dissent: Essays in Honour of Geoffrey Nuttall* (London: Epworth Press, 1977) 115-31; Charles Hambrick-Stowe, *The Practice of Piety: Puritan Devotional Disciplines in Seventeenth-Century New England* (Chapel Hill: University of North Carolina Press, 1982) vii, 25; Cf. Richard F. Lovelace, *The American Pietism of Cotton Mather: Origins of American Evangelicalism* (Grand Rapids: Christian University Press, 1979) 36, who says: "Recent scholarship has increasingly concluded that throughout most of its history English Puritanism can

As a chapter in Christian piety, or in the more current term, spirituality, Puritanism was not an isolated phenomenon. It derived from the spirituality of the Reformation, shaped by Luther's rediscovery of a gracious God, and more particularly from the spirituality of the Swiss Reformation and Calvin, which had distinctive emphases on union with Christ, disciplined Christian living, and sanctification as the purpose of God's gracious dealing with humankind. Insofar as Protestantism experienced an era of consolidation in the late sixteenth and seventeenth centuries, Puritanism can be seen as an important (perhaps the most important) phase in the development of a distinctly Reformed piety and spirituality. And this era of Protestant consolidation that defined and refined Protestant theology and devotion was in its turn only one part of a general revival of interest in the devotional and spiritual side of religion that swept across European Christendom as a whole, as a more settled Protestantism turned to the cultivation of the implications of its teaching for piety, while a resurgent Roman Catholicism applied religion to the everyday life of the laity. To recognize this seventeenth-century revival of spirituality belies that vision of church history that regards the evangelical revivals of the eighteenth century as a new departure after generations of religious deadness. In fact, the evangelical revivals were continuations (and simplifications) of seventeenth-century developments in piety and spiritual life.

The earliest English reformers were occupied with questions of theology, liturgy, and church reform; but some among them, such as Thomas Becon, found time for the production of devotional literature. The special hortatory and emotional tone that was later characteristic of Puritan spirituality was clearly adumbrated by John Bradford,[2] one of the Marian martyrs. By the mid-Elizabethan period there was a substantial clientele among English Protestants for the "affectionate divinity" of spiritual writers that outlined the steps of the Christian life and exhorted persons to proceed along its path. Such persons, lay and clerical, thought of themselves as "the godly," and both avidly listened to sermons and bought and read them when printed. That the largest portion of early Puritan and English Protestant devotional literature consisted of published sermons has misled those who have restricted notions of devotional literature to contend that Protestantism was remiss and late in producing such a literature. But this attitude fails to recognize that one of the distinctions of Protestant spirituality was a focus on sermons—spoken, heard, printed, and read—that articulated the ways of the spiritual life. By the end of the Elizabethan period, there were also many English Protestant examples of more traditional devotional literature.

Some of the Puritan preachers described by William Haller—such as Richard Greenham, Richard Rogers, Arthur Hildersam, Laurence Chaderton, and Richard Sibbes—were important writers about spiritual life in the late Elizabethan and Jacobean ages. So also were figures such as Edward Dering, whom Patrick Collinson has identified as a fountainhead of much practical divinity.[3] Although many of these Puritan leaders were in-

---

best be understood by examining its predominating stress on Christian experience''; and my own *Puritans and Predestination: Grace in English Protestant Theology, 1525-1695* (Chapel Hill: University of North Carolina Press, 1982) esp. 43-55 and 182-90, which deal with Elizabethan Protestant and Restoration Puritan piety, respectively.

[2]Wallace, *Puritans and Predestination*, 22-24.

[3]Patrick Collinson, *The Mirror of Elizabethan Puritanism: the Life and Letters of "Godly Mr. Dering"* (London: Dr. Williams's Trust, 1964).

volved in Nonconformity, most of them thought that pastoral work and spiritual concerns had primary importance. They sought to work within the structures of the Church of England, some of whose bishops they regarded as their allies in the promotion of piety.

The production of spiritual literature grew in the generations after these first Puritans, as a further development and refinement of what had begun earlier. After emigration to the shores of North America, Puritans continued these spiritual traditions with some modifications special to their new condition, though perhaps fewer than has sometimes been portrayed. Even the embittering disruptions of mid-seventeenth-century England—including civil war and controversy over episcopacy, ceremonial, and Arminian theology—did not stanch the flow of books concerned with the spiritual life.

However, after the middle of the century, Puritan spirituality experienced some change, resulting partly from altered conditions in church and state. Puritan spirituality after 1660 exhibited a sharpened focus and an amazing productivity. The Puritan spirituality of the second half of the seventeenth century provides the subject of this introductory essay and the material for this anthology.

The changed situation was the consequence of the collapse of Puritan rule in England in 1660. With the restoration of the monarchy, the position of most Puritans within the Church of England became difficult. After the St. Bartholomew's ejections of August 1662, the majority of those clergy to whom the term Puritan can be applied were to be found outside the Church of England, even though many of them still hoped for eventual reunion with the state church. The term *Dissenters* is often used to refer to the Puritans and their successors after the Restoration.

Not only were these clergy ejected from the Church of England, but the Clarendon Code made their activities in preaching and gathering congregations of followers illegal. Thus these later Puritans or Dissenters carried on their religious life under the shadow of persecution as well as under the burden of community opprobrium from persons of wealth and station who scorned them as rebels. They were also subject to mobs, which vented their hostilities against them. Dissenters often had to be clandestine in their preaching and congregating, and this sharpened their sense of distinctive identity. There were brief respites from persecution, especially with the royal Indulgence of 1672; but not until the Toleration Act of 1689 could their religious life be fully open. Even then, Dissenters felt insecure in their rights for another generation.

These events had important consequences for the Puritan impulse and the character of Puritan spirituality. First, many Puritans abandoned theocratic ideals for the shaping of a unified Christian society, and retreated into the confines of sectarian conventicle life. In the context of the gathered congregation threatened by persecution, the main consequences of these events for Puritan spirituality emerged: concentration on the spiritual life within the small fellowship and on the individual soul. This was a withdrawal from the more expansive and world-conquering zeal of an earlier day. In such a situation the struggles over the proper ecclesiology or liturgy for the Church of England receded as Dissenters found themselves free within their own conventicles to shape things as they wished. Church government or theology occasionally divided the subvarieties of the Dissenters, sometimes in bitter internecine quarrels; but the protracted struggle to remake the English national church was largely a thing of the past. Thus the piety and spirituality that had always been at the core of Puritanism, and from which other Puritan concerns had radiated, could now become the point of concentration for the still-considerable Puritan energies. Thus there ensued a period of great productivity in the creation of a literature of the spiritual life, and a sharpening of the focus of spirituality upon the drama of the individual soul, in the context of the withdrawn and faithful remnant community. The result was not a new Puritan spirituality but a shift in emphasis and a reduction of scope.

The Puritan Dissenters were for the most part united in their ecclesiology of the gathered church, though some of the Presbyterians still hankered after inclusion in the Church of England. They were also united in their Calvinism, except for followers of Richard Baxter with their moderating of Calvinist distinctives, and the Arminian General Baptists. Thus Puritan energies turned to the cultivation of the religious life and the refinement of devices for its maintenance and propagation. Alert to the situation, a new generation of leaders came to the fore who often set aside the more polemical concerns of the past and concentrated on the spiritual life. For example, Richard Alleine declared his desire to stress those "fundamental practical truths" of godliness upon which all Christians agreed. Thomas Cole said that he did not write for the "captious" but "to speak to the experience of humble Christians." John Howe described his treatise on *The Blessedness of the Righteous* as "wholly practical," having "little or nothing to do with disputation."[4] Many such Restoration Puritan divines are represented in this anthology: Joseph Alleine, Walter Marshall, Ralph Venning, Thomas Doolittle, James Janeway, and others. Richard Baxter professed to despise controversy, but was continually embroiled in it. Others, including the Baptists John Bunyan and Benjamin Keach, seemed to relish a good dash of theological conflict. The Congregationalist Thomas Gale was a devotional writer as well as a doughty and tenacious disputant. Many of these persons had been too young to play major roles in the years of the earlier Puritan struggles and spent most of their pastoral lives in the years between the great ejection and the Toleration Act. These divines constituted a transition to the devotionalism of such Dissenters of the next century as Matthew Henry, Philip Dodridge, and Isaac Watts, and to the evangelicalism of the awakenings. John Wesley drew extensively upon the writings of this generation of Puritan Dissenters.[5] Richard Lovelace has demonstrated the relation between the New Englander Cotton Mather's style of piety and the later awakenings, portraying Mather as a transitional figure between earlier Puritanism and later evangelicalism,[6] paralleling many of these English Puritans in the years after 1662. With the evolution of Puritan spirituality in this period towards the more emphatically personal and individual, it is a mistake to treat the evangelical awakenings as totally new departures.

The remainder of this essay surveys the themes and devices of English Puritan spirituality in the second half of the seventeenth century. The focus is on Puritan religious experience, not the theology related to it; consequently, when topics such as justification or sanctification are discussed, it will not be as doctrine, but as experiences of the Christian life. This methodological distinction was not usually made in the Puritan literature, though it is clear that significant differences exist between works of systematic theology and practical divinity.

---

[4]Richard Alleine, *A Letter to a Friend* (London, 1661) sig. A3; Thomas Cole, *A Discourse of Christian Religion* (London, 1692) v-vi; John Howe, *The Blessednesse of the Righteous* (London, 1668) sig. A2v.

[5]Robert C. Monk, *John Wesley's Puritan Heritage* (Nashville: Abingdon Press, 1966) 23, 39, 96.

[6]Lovelace, *The American Pietism of Cotton Mather*, vii, 4, 5, 33, 35, 38.

The Puritan spirituality of the latter seventeenth century was less a new departure than it was the refinement, intensification, and sometimes narrowing of earlier themes of Puritan piety. One of these themes was that true religion must be an inner, spiritual experience. As Matthew Mead noted, the inner life, rather than external duties, makes a Christian. "A man may profess religion, and yet never have his heart changed."[7] Real religion involved what Richard Alleine called "heart-work," a true change of the person.

Inner religion and personal change began with conversion. This experience, whether sudden or gradual, was a point of entry into the Christian life. Benjamin Keach said, "All true believers have passed through the Pangs of the New Birth." The theme of conversion appeared in two ways: in the many sermons and books that exhorted one to believe, be converted, or undergo the new birth, often detailing the stages entailed therein, and in the importance placed upon soul winning, or the conversion of others, as one of the manifestations of a truly spiritual life. So far as the first of these is concerned, Puritans after 1660 had no new doctrines to offer, though perhaps they intensified the new birth as an individual experience. The discussions of conversion exhorted the careless to press beyond mere outward religion and to realize the perilous state of their precious souls. Theophilus Gale's treatise *The Anatomie of Infidelitie* was about neither immorality nor intellectual unbelief, but aimed to awaken those who neglected religion, that they might "embrace Evangelic offers of Life, and Grace, before it be too late."[8]

With regard to soul winning, Puritan spirituality after 1660 placed emphasis on sermons, but also on the personal exhortations of faithful Christians, whether lay or clerical. Here one sees a gradual transition to the evangelicals of the eighteenth century. In biographies of devout persons the theme of soul winning is prominent. It was the principal aim of Joseph Alleine's ministry according to those who recorded his life, and it appears repeatedly in his letters of spiritual advice. John Janeway, whose short life was memorialized by his brother James, was a paragon of soul winning. No sooner had he undergone conversion than he turned to unconverted members of his family, pleading with them through "pathetical expressions" to be converted; he was also concerned about the souls of his fellow students at Cambridge, "desiring to carry as many of them as possibly he could along with him to Heaven." Joseph Alleine even considered going to China to preach the gospel, since preaching was closed to him in England—a most unusual proposal for his time. Such soul winning directed at the young and at foreign lands was typical of later evangelicalism.[9]

These elements of the Puritan discussion of conversion were repeated in many works. Among them, Richard Baxter's *A Call to the Unconverted* (1658), and Joseph Alleine's *An Alarme to the Unconverted* (1671), have pride of place. Both were frequently reprinted down to recent times.

The books on conversion also discussed justifying faith and its relation to conversion. Faith was obviously an important emphasis of Puritan spirituality. But while faith alone

---

[7]Matthew Mead, *The Almost Christian Discovered* (London, 1700) 25.

[8]Benjamin Keach, *A Golden Mine Opened* (London, 1694) 25, Theophilus Gale, *The Anatomie of Infidelitie* (London, 1672) sig. A3r.

[9]James Janeway, *Invisibles, Realities, Demonstrated in the Holy Life and Triumphant Death of Mr. John Janeway* (London, 1674) 8, 16-17; *The Life and Death of that Excellent Minister of Christ, Mr. Joseph Alleine* (London, 1677) 63.

was sufficient for justification in the Puritan view, simple believing was by no means the totality of the Christian life. Faith itself was considered more as personal trust and commitment than as intellectual assent to notions.

"Such as are made free by Christ, are delivered from the reigning power of sin," declared Thomas Doolittle.[10] The main focus of Puritan spirituality was not on conversion, but upon that which followed in the sanctification (the theological term) and holiness (the spiritual term) of the believer. This process was variously described as spiritual warfare and pilgrimage. Both images are the very stuff of the greatest Puritan spiritual allegory, John Bunyan's *Pilgrim's Progress*. In that work, Bunyan distilled the thousands of mundane homiletic exhortations about pilgrimage and spiritual combat into a powerful, imaginative synthesis. The theme of spiritual warfare reappeared in even more concentrated fashion in another of Bunyan's allegories, *The Holy War*. The pilgrimage theme was dealt with, albeit far less creatively, in the allegory of another Baptist spiritual writer, John Keach, author of *The Travels of True Godliness*. Richard Alleine wrote about the spiritual life under the title *The World Conquered*, an illustration of the combat theme. So prominent was the pilgrimage theme in Puritan spirituality that Charles Hambrick-Stowe regards it as "the principal metaphor running through Puritan spirituality and devotional practice."[11]

"You must despair of ever seeing the face of God without holiness," said Joseph Alleine, underlining the insistence of Puritan spirituality that the converted soul must go beyond conversion to actual holiness of life. In *The Gospel-Mystery of Sanctification Opened in Sundry Practical Directions*, Walter Marshall outlined fourteen directions on how to proceed to holiness. It would be impossible to exaggerate Puritan spirituality's concern with the growth of actual holiness of life. However, a discussion of the moral duties incumbent upon the converted would be to go into Puritan moral theology and beyond the scope of this essay. Puritans assumed that holiness of life was not just an affective state; it involved charitable activities without which any claim to spirituality was vain. For example, Edmund Calamy the elder exhorted his readers to "Joyn works of mercy and charity together with your profession of piety and holiness," and John Owen, the greatest of the Puritan theologians of the second half of the seventeenth century, declared that without the "grace" of charity to the poor, all religion was vain.[12] But holiness was not all grim seriousness and moral striving. For Richard Baxter it included "delighting in God, His Word and Works, and in His joyful praise."[13]

The holy person was a spiritual person. As John Owen explained, to be spiritually minded is in earthly existence the nearest one comes to heaven and blessedness. The holy and spiritually minded person was to think much of heaven, for he or she already lived

---

[10]Thomas Doolittle, *Captives Bound in Chains, Made Free by Christ their Surety* (London, 1674) 180.

[11]Hambrick-Stowe, *The Practice of Piety*, 54.

[12]Joseph Alleine, *An Alarm to the Unconverted* (London: Banner of Truth Trust, 1971) 59; Edmund Calamy, *The Godly Mans Ark* (London, 1657) sig. b4r; John Owen, "To the Reader," in Thomas Gouge, *The Surest and Safest Way of Thriving* (London, 1676).

[13]John T. Wilkinson, ed., *Richard Baxter and Margaret Charlton: A Puritan Love-Story, Being the Breviate of the Life of Margaret Baxter, by Richard Baxter, 1681 With Introductory Essay, Notes, and Appendices* (London: George Allen & Unwin Ltd., 1928) 128.

there within the soul. Accordingly, "heavenly mindedness" was one of the most prominent themes of Puritan spirituality in this era. Perhaps it was a more important theme than
in earlier Puritan piety as a result of the dashing at the Restoration of so many Puritan
hopes for the reconstitution of this world. Treatises were increasingly devoted to the subject of meditation on heaven. Bartholomew Ashwood's *The Heavenly Trade* recommended that the devout set aside some time each day for the "work" of "divine and
heavenly meditation," so that one might gain a "heavenly heart" to "perfume" all one's
earthly work. The justly famous and often reprinted book of Richard Baxter, *The Saints'
Everlasting Rest,* is considered by Helen White, in her study of English devotional prose,
to be one of the four masterpieces of English devotional literature in its century. William
Bates, a younger man often associated with Richard Baxter, who preached the sermon at
Baxter's funeral, was the author of *A Short Description of the Blessed Place* (1687). John
Bunyan introduced a character named Mr. Heavenly-Mind into his allegory on *The Holy
War,* and much of the discussion of the pilgrims with each other in *Pilgrim's Progress*
pertains to this subject. Popular Puritan biographies repeatedly praised their subjects for
heavenly mindedness. It was said of Joseph Alleine that his conversation was "always
mingled with Heavenly and Holy Discourses," and of John Rowe that he was "eminent
for his Heavenly mindedness," accounting himself "but a Pilgrim and Stranger upon
Earth."[14]

Heavenly mindedness was the spiritual person's foretaste of the joys of heaven through
meditation. This not only strengthened the soul for earthly trials but was one place in Puritan spirituality where the mystical element entered. The heavenly minded person was
absorbed in divine things, weaned from earth, and advanced in communion with God because proleptically transported into that blessed state where the saints see God and enjoy
his presence forever. John Howe, in his treatise on *The Blessedness of the Righteous,* discussed the manner and nature of this vision of God promised to the just. To meditate on
that state, binding one's heart so closely to God that all else paled into insignificance, was
the aim of the heavenly minded.

Equally prominent with heavenly mindedness as a locus for Puritan affective mysti-
cism was the theme of union with Christ. It was related to heavenly mindedness, as John
Owen noted: "One of the greatest privileges and advancements of believers, both in this
world and unto eternity, consists in their beholding of the glory of Christ."[15] But Puritans
spoke not only of union with Christ by anticipation but also by a present conjoining of the
soul with Christ in the process of the renovation and regeneration of a sinner. Union with
Christ thus was a reality for believers, but also an experience to be cultivated or antici-
pated. As such, it was described in detail by devotional writers. Walter Marshall said that
this union of Christ with the souls of believers was without parallel except in the union of

---

[14]John Owen, *The Works of John Owen, D.D.,* ed. William H. Goold, 24 volumes (London & Edinburgh:
Johnstone and Hunter, 1850-1855) 7:497; Barbara Kiefer Lewalski, *Protestant Poetics and the Seventeenth-
Century Religious Lyric* (Princeton: Princeton University Press, 1979) 165; Bartholomew Ashwood, *The
Heavenly Trade, or the Best Merchandizing* (London, 1678) 267, 276; Helen C. White, *English Devotional
Literature (Prose), 1600-1640* (Madison: University of Wisconsin, 1931) 257-62; *The Life and Death of that
Excellent Minister of Christ, Mr. Joseph Alleine,* 45; *The Life and Death of Mr. John Rowe of Credition in
Devon* (London, 1673) 70, 112.

[15]Owen, *The Works of John Owen,* 1:286.

the persons of the Trinity and in the union of the human and divine in the Incarnate Christ. This way of depicting it enabled Marshall to argue that there was both a true and effectual union of the soul with Christ and yet that they remained separate as persons.[16]

Puritan spirituality became most affectively mystical with regard to such topics as heavenly mindedness and union with Christ. In this context one encounters many of the more rapturous statements in Puritan devotion. Souls nearing death often received raptures of heavenly mindedness, although the experience was not restricted to that time. Those who had rapturous union with Christ often described these experiences in the language of human love. John Rowe's biography described him as having "an amorous union" with Christ. The same author, Theophilus Gale, elsewhere termed the soul's union with Christ as conjugal: "That soul who admits any other but Christ, to share in the same kind of conjugal Affection, which it owes to Christ, is guiltie of spiritual adulterie." Gale further depicted union with Christ sensuously as a "spiritual taste which savors and relisheth those incomparable sweetnesses that are in Christ."[17] Of the Puritan writers of this era none reveled in this kind of mystical language as fully as Peter Sterry or went so far in its expression as a Puritan leader of the previous generation, Francis Rous, author of *The Mysticall Marriage: Experimentall Discoveries of the heavenly Marriage between a Soule and her Saviour,* first published in 1631. Rous drew striking analogies between human, physical love and the love of the soul for Christ. Such sensuous language also often represented experiences of taste, smell, and sight.

The use of sensuous language to portray mystical experience had a long history and was very common among medieval mystics. Often it was presented, both in the Middle Ages and later, in commentaries upon the spiritual meaning of the physical imagery of the Old Testament book of Canticles (Song of Solomon). In the early eighteenth century it reappeared in the evangelical piety of Jonathan Edwards. Describing the pleasant sensations of soul he had when contemplating redemption in Christ, he observed that at such times "the whole book of Canticles used to be pleasant to me, and I used to be much in reading it."[18] Edwards also depicted the higher spiritual life as a "delectation."

Neither heavenly mindedness nor union with Christ should be considered apart from the Puritan view of the Holy Spirit. As G. F. Nuttall pointed out in his classic study of Puritan views of the Holy Spirit, this doctrine was for them a practical one,[19] closely related to conversion and holiness. John Owen wrote several large works on the Holy Spirit. However technical and scholastic, their ultimate focus was on the spiritual life made possible by the Holy Spirit. Puritan theologians and devotional writers believed that everything in their spirituality resulted from the work of the Holy Spirit—faith in believers, holiness in the sanctified, and the soul's union with Christ. Heavenly mindedness was one of the fruits of this work of the Spirit. In Puritan belief (as in Reformed theology gener-

---

[16]Walter Marshall, *The Gospel-Mystery of Sanctification Opened in Sundry Practical Directions* (London, 1692) 43-44.

[17]*The Life and Death of Mr. John Rowe,* sig. A8r; Theophilus Gale, *Theophilie: Or a Discourse of the Saints Amitie with God in Christ* (London, 1671) 34, 37.

[18]Clarence H. Faust and Thomas H. Johnson, eds., *Jonathan Edwards: Representative Selections, With Introduction, Bibliography, and Notes,* rev. ed. (New York: Hill and Wang, 1962) 60.

[19]Nuttall, *The Holy Spirit in Puritan Faith and Experience,* 7.

ally, though in greater practical detail) the Holy Spirit was the divine instrumentality by which the objective transactions in the divine economy of redemption—such as God's decrees, Christ's incarnation and atonement, or the justifying and adopting of sinners—were made effective in the lives of believers. Since the Holy Spirit was that aspect of the divine triad concerned with these applications of divine benefits to humankind, the practical theology and personal devotion of the Puritans concerned themselves extensively with the Spirit's work in religious experience.

The recognition that the religious life was effected by the work of the Holy Spirit meant that it was an activity initiated from God's side. Spirituality was the work of grace. Accordingly, the theme of God's grace was always present in Puritan writings on the spiritual life. Everything effected by the Holy Spirit—faith, holiness, union with Christ, heavenly mindedness—as well as the transactions of the plan of salvation, was ultimately a consequence of the free mercy of God, poured out upon his undeserving children. In response to this, human recipients of grace must be ever mindful of the obligation continually to thank God for unmerited favor and gracious condescension, remembering that persons make no contribution to their own redemption except willingly to receive the grace that God prepares and enables the will to receive. No wonder that Puritan writings on spirituality were filled with exclamations about the surpassing grace of God. The believer could only stand in awe, amazement, and gratitude before this miracle of redemption, giving God all the glory.

This leads to the one undertone of polemical theology that runs through the Puritan spirituality of the latter seventeenth century—unease about the rise and spread of moralism in Christian piety. Reacting to an Arminianism that taught that grace was given to those who exercised freedom of choice in seeking it and to a Latitudinarianism that taught that Christianity was primarily a new moral law given with clearer incentives than those of the Old Testament, Puritan spiritual writers responded that such an outlook destroyed the very character of Christian spirituality as something unattainable by human powers. Puritan piety was not a morality tinged with emotion, but something they believed to be on a plane of existence beyond natural capacities. It involved new birth and personal transformation, both supernatural, the work of a power of renovating grace that came from beyond human experience. As Owen put it, "That our affections may be spiritual and the spring of our being spiritually minded, it is required that they be changed, renewed, and inlaid with grace, spiritual and and supernatural." Benjamin Keach argued that "those who preach no other gospel than Morality, do but go about to make the People good Heathens; for what is this but the Religion of the Heathen Philosophers?" Bunyan continually insisted upon the qualitative difference between nature and grace and the absolute necessity of grace for the true spiritual life. Gale, a vigorous controversialist on behalf of supernatural grace, embodied his argument in the person of John Rowe, whom he described as showing how far beyond "the highest Attainments of the most Refined Morality" grace could carry those renewed by its power. The same battle cry was sounded throughout David Clarkson's *A Discourse of the Saving Grace of God* (London, 1688) and in the major theological works of John Owen and Thomas Goodwin. To make the point unmistakable, Gale asserted that "the Grace of the Covenant expects no foundation in us, no Condignitie, no Congruitie, no moral Capacitie, or Condition in us, but what itself intends to confer. The Covenant informs us, that Free-grace is moved by nothing without itself."[20]

Perhaps one reason why echoes of controversy over the theology of grace are to be found in the spiritual writings of Dissenters in the latter part of the seventeenth century is that the controversy had become acute among the dissenters themselves, especially over the issue of antinomianism. This issue, much debated during the 1640s, appeared again in the 1690s and drove a wedge between the more moderate Puritan devotional writers such as the Presbyterians Richard Baxter, William Bates, and John Howe, who had adopted some modifications in their Calvinism, and the more strictly Calvinist Particular Baptists and Congregationalists led by Benjamin Keach and John Owen, respectively. Suffice it to say here that the former party thought that the latter did not guard against that kind of Christian piety that allowed devout states of feeling to supplant rules and objective criteria in the spiritual life, while the latter accused the former of succumbing to moralism. In any case, this controversy over grace was the one discordant note often heard in works of late Puritan spirituality.

Consideration of the theme of grace in Puritan spirituality leads to the subject of predestination. This doctrine seems forbidding when discussed in terms of God's eternal will and decrees. In Puritan piety, however, it expressed the gratuitousness of God's dealings with persons and the steadfastness of God's purposes towards those who love him. In these guises predestination appears as a theme of Puritan spirituality, reminding believers that they were to give God all the praise for their spiritual lives, and that they were secure in God's hands. As Benjamin Keach explained, the nature of predestination is such that it secures believers from "final falling." Yet there was some unease about a doctrine so difficult to explain to outsiders. Spiritual writers such as Howe and Baxter discussed grace in the spiritual life without reference to predestination. Sometimes the subject appeared in the devotional literature in a context that suggested that spiritual directors were confronted with persons who reasoned from predestination to the uselessness of believing. (Bunyan's *Grace Abounding* and other autobiographies show this to have been the case). Thus Joseph Alleine tried to put predestination in proper perspective when he maintained, "You begin at the wrong end if you first dispute about your election. Prove your conversion, and then never doubt your election."[21] Perhaps when piety became more individualistic the doctrine of election came to be more of a personal problem than it had been in earlier Protestantism. If so, this led those of evangelical piety to instruct the faithful to consider it only after believing, not before. In this fashion predestination was brought back into contact with religious feeling and was separated from abstract systematizing, and it tended to be in this way that evangelicals looked upon it in the later awakenings, when they both exhorted perons to be converted and to acknowledge that their conversion was God's work. They thus insisted that redemption was a gratuitous, supernatural renewal that came from God at the same time that they bypassed intricate discussion of the implications of free will and foreordination. Sometimes later evangelicals have been ac-

---

[20]Owen, *The Works of John Owen,* 7:411; Benjamin Keach, *A Golden Mine Opened,* 437; Gale, Preface to *The Life and Death of Mr. John Rowe,* sig. A3v; Theophilus Gale, *The Anatomie of Infidelitie,* 107.

[21]Keach, *A Golden Mine Opened,* 177; J. Alleine, *An Alarm to the Unconverted,* 30.

cused of anti-intellectualism in their simplifying of theology, but perhaps they were returning a doctrine to the existential core from which it first arose.

Predestination in Puritan spirituality was not intended as an inducement to speculation but was considered a source of comfort and assurance. Much of the discussion of Puritan religiosity has centered on the question of assurance, and it too was a theme of Puritan spirituality. Many devout persons in the seventeenth century sought the assurance that they were in divine favor and a state of grace. An extensive Puritan casuistry, to which Richard Baxter among others contributed, developed around this question. Various spiritual conditions and "cases" were analyzed as to whether or not they indicated a real work of grace. Books with such titles as Richard Alleine's *Instructions about heart-work . . . that we may live in the Exercise and Growth of Grace here, and have a comfortable Assurance of Glory to Eternity* were avidly scrutinized for the answer to the most important question a person could ask—the fate of the soul for eternity. But the gist of reams of paper and gallons of ink expended in giving advice about assurance was that persons should trust and believe in the grace of God in Christ. However sinful one had been, grace was sufficient. Beyond that, Joseph Alleine recommended self-examination in order to find assurance.[22] Such examination involved looking for the fruits and effects of spiritual renewal. Holiness, real believing, a sense of union with Christ, and heavenly mindedness were evidences that a work of grace had been wrought in the soul, since all of these things came only by the Holy Spirit. On the other hand, one had to be on guard against mistaking the shadows of these things for the substance. Consequently, directions about assurance could take on great complexity though it was always acknowledged that many truly godly and regenerate persons never attained a sense of assurance.

Eschatology appeared in Puritan spirituality in heavenly mindedness, which was a foretaste of things to come. It also came into spiritual treatises under the topic of glorification, the theological assertion that the justified and sanctified would come finally to the beatific rest and glory. Another eschatological motif that regularly appeared in Puritan spiritual writings was the expectation of Christ's Second Coming, although in Puritan treatments of this subject after 1660 millenarianism diminished as expectations of a renewed earth were replaced by an understanding of the Second Coming that was more relevant to personal piety. This can be seen in Gale's *A Discourse of Christ's Coming: And the Influence, which the Expectation thereof hath on al manner of Holy Conversation and Godlinesse.* The title indicates the practical nature of the work. For Gale the Second Coming of Christ had lost its sense of the shaking of kingdoms the mid-century Puritans had often connected with it and had become primarily a matter of personal hope for the individual believer, and an incentive to a more ardent piety. The uses of this doctrine outlined by Gale included the awakening of "sleepy" and "secure" believers to watch and pray, preparing for the great day. Consideration of the Second Coming of Christ, he thought, would also emphasize the need for self-examination so that devout hearts might be ready.[23]

---

[22]*Remaines of That Excellent Minister of Jesus Christ, Mr. Joseph Alleine, . . . All tending to promote Real Piety* (London, 1674) 27.

[23]Theophilus Gale, *A Discourse on Christ's Coming* (London, 1673) 195, 197, 203.

Meditation on death is a hoary theme in Christian spirituality, but it seems to have taken on a new life in the spirituality of the Dissenters after the middle of the seventeenth century, as Daniel Defoe's story "The Apparition of Mrs. Veal" might suggest. This motif in Puritan spirituality drew on a long heritage of Christian treatises on dying well, and much of what Puritans said on that subject reproduced commonplaces of Christian piety. One of the early English Protestants, Thomas Becon, produced an oft-reprinted treatise, *The Sicke Mans Salve,* which influenced later Puritan versions of the art of dying. Gordon Wakefield, writing on Puritan devotion, says that the purpose of Puritan guides to the holy life was to prepare persons for a holy death. A comment from John Owen's sermon on "The Christian's Work of Dying Daily"—"It is the duty of all believers to be preparing themselves every day to die cheerfully, comfortably, and if it may be, triumphing in the Lord"—bears this out. Puritan devotional literature was studded with conventional reminders of the inevitability of death. Edward Pearse admonished his readers to "be much and frequent in the contemplation of death and the grave," and "in the midst of all your Enjoyments, expect Death's approach daily." Joseph Alleine exhorted his readers to "look often into Coffins, and behold your bones and dust, as shortly others shall, when turned out of your Graves." Thomas Vincent thought, after the fire and plague of London in 1665-1666, that the city "should have death in continual remembrance." Biographers of holy Puritans invariably recounted the deaths of their subjects so that, as one biographer put it, others might behold "how peaceably and comfortably they dye." James Janeway's account of the short life of his brother John devoted more attention to his death, its comforts and last words, than to his life. Young Janeway, a university student preparing for the ministry, eagerly looked forward to dying, and in his last few days uttered rapturous words of spiritual wisdom. Even as his body grew cold, he still had "fits of joy unspeakable, that he seemed to be in one continued act of Seraphick Love, and praise." James Janeway is best known for his treatise on the deaths of pious children.[24]

In the Puritan understanding of the life of the spirit it was expected that a dying person would have last moments of great clarity of vision and thus utter words of wisdom. As a consequence, the dying person was listened to attentively and the last words recorded for posterity's benefit. Leading spiritual writers especially were noted for dying words of wisdom. The last words of Joseph Alleine and others were treasured. But even ordinary persons might be expected to say profound things at death, as when the Altham Church Book recorded the death of a person who "poured out a flood of choice matter in his last minutes."[25]

The medieval treatises on dying portrayed Satan as making a last assault at this vulnerable moment, and Bunyan wrote that "sick Bed Temptations are oft-times the most violent, because then the Devil plays his last game with us." In Puritan spirituality, Satan's assault often took the form of tempting the dying to doubt their salvation. When

----

[24]Nancy Lee Beaty, *The Craft of Dying: Study in the Literary Tradition of the Ars Moriendi in England* (New Haven: Yale University Press, 1970) 108ff.; Wakefield, *Puritan Devotion,* 143; *The Works of John Owen,* 9:336; Edward Pearse, *The Great Concern; or a Serious Warning to a Timely and Thorough Preparation for Death* (Belfast, 1700) 83-84; *Remaines of Joseph Alleine,* sig. A5r; Thomas Vincent, *God's Terrible Voice in the City* (N.p., 1667) 254; Robert Bragg, *The Life and Death of the Godly Man* (London, 1676) 2; James Janeway, *Invisibles, Realities,* 40, 92, 98-100, 102, 105, 107, 119.

[25]Henry Fishwick, ed., *The Note Book of the Rev. Thomas Jolly,* Chetham Society, n.s. 33 (1894):135.

Samuel Clarke wrote about the life of his wife Katherine, he noted that at the end "Satan had no power to molest her." Joseph Alleine had to struggle with the Tempter at his death, but he rebuked Satan by telling him, "Away thou foul Fiend, thou Enemy of Man-kind . . . trouble me not, for I am none of thine! I am the Lord's, Christ is mine, and I am his. . . . Therefore be gone!" Clearly Satan and his host of demons were a very present reality for Puritans at the end of the seventeenth century. Thomas Jollie, one of the Puritan clergy at the time, was involved in a notorious case of exorcism.[26]

However much Puritan spirituality focused on individual experience, the spiritual life was lived in fellowship with other Christians and especially within the community of faith constituted by the congregation. The importance for Puritans of the proper form of church government should be traced to the experience of the Christian life occurring within a group of like-minded persons. Christian fellowship—more than just friendship—was a walking together in godliness, hence the importance of church covenants and the gathering of churches. With the issue of church government more or less settled after 1662 so far as the conflict between Church and Dissent was concerned, the Dissenting groups could turn to the task of building up the fellowship of the saints walking together. Nowhere is this seen more clearly than in the fellowship of Christiana, her children, and their associates in the second part of *Pilgrim's Progress*. (In the first part Christian's path is much more lonely.)

The importance of spiritual fellowship was magnified in the spirituality of the English Puritan generation after 1662 by the continual threat of persecution that loomed over the gathered churches of the Dissenters. Gerald R. Cragg has written of this period that "for the Puritans persecution was essentially a spiritual experience," as they found comfort and courage in their faith in God. The threat of persecution winnowed out the nominal adherents, as Benjamin Keach put it, separating "sincere Believers from drossy and chaffy Professors." Contemporary church records indicate how often members lapsed because of persecution. The community that remained was bound tightly in the consciousness of standing fast against a hostile world, and in such a situation there developed a strong sense of the distinction between the sheep and the goats. In this environment a very intense emotional piety flourished. Persecution carried theological meaning, as when the Baptist Keach maintained that Christ used "the Fan of persecution" to purge and purify his churches.[27]

Puritans were alert for signs of God's providence in the world. They took the untimely deaths of persecutors as signal instances of that providence. Thus Thomas Jollie commented in his notebooks on a persecutor who fell down some stairs and died, "a remarkable hand of God," and on "an awfull providence" that happened to one Laurence Heap, "who in his drunkenness fell from his horse and was found dead in a ditch." Bunyan depicted the "Saints of the Lord" as being "for the most part a poor, despised contemptible people," but he expected that the tables would be turned at judgment day, when "they

---

[26]Richard Greaves, ed. *Instruction for the Ignorant, Light For Them That Sit in Darkness, Saved by Grace, Come, and Welcome, to Jesus Christ: The Miscellaneous Works of John Bunyan*, 13 vols. (Oxford: Clarendon Press, 1979) 8:178; Samuel Clark, *The Lives of Sundry Eminent Persons in this Later Age* (London, 1683) pt. 2: 157; *Life and Death of Joseph Alleine*, 100; Thomas Jollie, *A Vindication of the Surey Demoniack as no Imposter* (London, 1698).

[27]Gerald R. Cragg, *Puritanism in the Period of Great Persecution, 1660-1688* (Cambridge: Cambridge University Press, 1957) 66; Keach, *A Golden Mine Opened*, 17.

that are the persecutors of the Saints of the Lord now in this world, shall see the Lord's persecuted ones, to be they that are so highly esteemed by the Lord as to sit, or to be in Abraham's bosome."[28]

Not only persecutors, but also those who scoffed at religion were frequently mentioned by spiritual writers as one of the trials of the godly. In Keach's allegory *The Travels of True Godliness,* the protagonist comes upon Scoffer and Scornful, who "loll'd out their Tongues at Godliness, jearing and deriding him shamelessly." In his autobiography George Trosse recorded it as one of the most grievous sins before his conversion that he had scoffed at godly persons.[29]

The persecution of the godly raised serious problems about the workings of God's providence. Puritan spiritual writers, especially after 1660 with the failure of Puritan hopes, devoted considerable attention to the afflictions of the godly. Dissenters repeatedly stated that while the afflictions visited upon the ungodly represented God working their destruction, the afflictions of the godly were sent by God as trials from which one must draw the right lessons. As J. Sears McGee has written, the doctrine "that God afflicted his children in love and his enemies in anger" was a commonplace of Puritan teaching throughout the century. Even before the disappointments of 1660 and 1662, Jeremiah Burroughs had written that "God's ordinary course is that his people in this world should be in an afflicted condition." Bartholomew Ashwood observed pithily that "afflictions are Christ's clay and spittle to open his people's eyes," and that "afflicting Providences are God's dieting his racers, that they may be more long-breath'd, and swift in their run towards glory."[30]

Judging from the frequent reprintings, Edmund Calamy's *The Godly Mans Ark* had one of the best and most popular treatments of this subject. He presented the doctrine that "the best of God's Saints are in this life subject to many great and tedious afflictions." He contended that the more saintly the person the greater the afflictions, noting that even Christ was not exempt from suffering. Afflictions were part of God's predestination: "That God which hath elected us to salvation, hath also elected us unto afflictions." But these afflictions were for the benefit of the saintly, who must prepare for them by gathering in a supply of "self-denial, humility, repentance, contempt for the world, and heavenly-mindedness." And so Calamy concluded that "whenever God brings us into the School of Affliction, let us labour to be good Schollars in it."[31]

---

[28]Henry Fishwick, ed., *The Note Book of the Rev. Thomas Jolly,* 52, 56; T. L. Underwood, ed., with the assistance of Roger Sharrock, *Some Gospel-Truths Opened, A Vindication of Some Gospel-Truths Opened, A Few Sighs From Hell: The Miscellaneous Works of John Bunyan,* (Oxford: Clarendon Press, 1980) 1:255, 272.

[29]Benjamin Keach, *The Travels of True Godliness, From the Beginning of the World to this present Day: in an apt and Pleasant Allegory,* 3d ed. (London, 1684) 59; *The Life of the Reverend Mr. George Trosse, Written by Himself, and Published Posthumously according to his Order in 1714,* ed. A. W. Brink (Montreal: McGill-Queen's University Press, 1974) 48.

[30]J. Sears McGee, *The Godly Man in Stuart England: Anglicans, Puritans, and the Two Tables, 1620-1670* (New Haven: Yale University Press, 1976) 25; Bartholomew Ashwood, *The Heavenly Trade,* 328, 330; Jeremiah Burroughes, *The Rare Jewel of Christian Contentment* (1648; rpt., London: Banner of Truth Trust, 1964) 115.

[31]Calamy, *The Godly Mans Ark,* 6, 21, 24, 28, 32, 35, 45-46.

The theme of the suffering of the godly is thus common in Puritan spiritual writers. Far from prosperity being equated with godliness in this literature, the opposite is the case: affliction is the lot of the godly while prosperity often accompanies the ungodly. Calamy considered that as long as the saints live on earth, their lives would be filled with many afflictions. Bunyan thought that saints should remember that their afflictions would only last as long as their lives. Calamy warned his readers against the error of Job's friends—censuring the afflicted as sinners—rather, they should censure those who lived without affliction! Such persons would rarely repent of their wickedness. Calamy added that "there is no surer sign of God's reprobating anger, than to suffer a man to prosper in wicked courses." Bartholomew Ashwood went farther in asserting that "God may prosper in the world those he hates." As C. John Sommerville has concluded of the devotional literature of later seventeenth-century England, "Popular authors did not suggest that earthly prosperity or the businessman's virtues were any sign of God's favor."[32]

The major themes of late Puritan spirituality were expressed and cultivated in many ways. Important among these means for the stimulation of the spiritual life were reading, attendance at sermons, conferring with the spiritually mature, partaking of the sacrament of the Lord's Supper, prayer, and meditation.

The primacy of the Bible as an authority was a cardinal principle of Protestantism. The Bible was that upon which all doctrine was to be based and by which it was to be tested. But as Charles Hambrick-Stowe has said, "The Bible was for Puritans above all a devotional book."[33] One result of this was that Puritan spirituality was expressed both in speech and writing in the idiom of the Bible, which was sometimes referred to as the "language of Canaan." So absorbed were devout Puritans in biblical language that they quite naturally expressed their deepest spiritual yearnings in it and almost unconsciously identified themselves with its characters, situations, and stories.

While the Puritans drew upon the whole of the Bible in their spirituality, their devotional literature showed a special affinity for certain portions of it, the Psalms and the Pauline epistles in particular. They sang the Psalms in public worship and even in private. The Puritans probably also liked them because so many of them expressed an embattled piety similar to their own under persecution. The attraction of the Pauline epistles was no doubt their representation of the steps of redemption—election, calling, faith, sanctification, and glorification—that were so important in their own outlook. Paul Coolidge has recently argued that Puritanism was a revival of the Pauline outlook.[34]

Puritans not only expressed their spirituality in biblical idiom, but also engaged in continuous reading and meditation upon the Bible. John Janeway, for example, was said by his biographer to have found the words of Scripture to be "sweeter to him than his food." Calamy, in discussing afflictions, exclaimed: "How sweet is a Text of Scripture to a childe of God in the hour of his distresse!" Bible reading was a central device of Puritan piety, serving as a reminder of how important literacy was to Protestants. The ability to read was almost a sine qua non of the spiritual life, quite unlike medieval spirituality.

---

[32]Ibid., 6, 8, 22-23; *Works of Bunyan,* 1:295-96; Ashwood, *The Heavenly Trade,* 361; Sommerville, *Popular Religion in Restoration England,* 101.

[33]Hambrick-Stowe, *The Practice of Piety,* 8.

[34]John S. Coolidge, *The Pauline Renaissance in England* (Oxford: Clarendon Press, 1970).

In addition to the Bible there was an enormous body of devotional literature available for the use of devout persons in Restoration England, and authors and publishers continually produced new works. Much of this appropriately consisted of biblical exposition, whether in printed sermons or commentaries. Often printed sermons included additional expository matter that limitations of time had not allowed in the pulpit. The printed versions of these sermons became long expositions of a passage, intended for devout reading and meditation. Many commentaries were not just works of biblical scholarship, but were intended for edification. Indeed, the greatest bulk of Puritan devotional literature consisted of such biblical expositions, and it is an error to exclude this material from consideration when analyzing Puritan spirituality since it was especially by such biblical exposition that the spiritual life was portrayed and stimulated. Those for whom the medieval mystical literature or the manuals of the Counter-Reformation are the models of devotional literature apply an alien standard in their determination of what among the productions of the Puritans belongs to the devotional genre. In so doing, they also miss the richness of the Puritan devotional output.

But Puritan devotional literature also included works of the more traditional kind. Francis Rous's book on the mystical marriage of the soul and Christ as well as some of the treatises of Peter Sterry might be considered mystical writings of an almost medieval kind. Puritans produced books of prayers and meditations, treatises on dying, and consolations directed to the bereaved, along with manuals on the spiritual life. These constitute a more conventional kind of pious literature. Books treating cases of conscience, related especially to the anxious search for assurance, were a specialty of some Puritan writers and would have been read not only by pastoral directors but by devout laypersons looking for their "case." Dialogues were popular as works of Puritan piety and had been produced since the Elizabethan age, as the works of George Gifford and Arthur Dent testify. A large amount of hagiographical literature, most of which began as funeral sermons with short biographies appended, also sprang up to nourish Puritan spirituality. Nothing more winsomely urged persons to the spiritual life than these concrete depictions of holiness. Samuel Clarke provided important collections of this sort of literature, but many edifying biographies of holy Puritans never found their way into his compilation. These biographies usually had prefaces that expatiated upon the importance of this way of inculcating and imbibing piety. Allegories were also popular, and the famous ones of John Bunyan are brilliant expositions of the perils and glories of the spiritual life. Some devotional works took poetic form. Benjamin Keach produced books that were mixtures of poetry, dialogue, and allegory. Other forms, such as emblem books or collections of aphorisms, will be described later in relation to Puritan meditation.

In sum, Puritans both before and after 1660 produced an enormous literature of "affectionate divinity," far outweighing their works of formal theology. Put simply, its volume testifies to the ardency, energy, and productivity with which they wrote about the spiritual life. Testimonies from the Puritan age reveal the importance that was attached to the reading of such literature: Richard Baxter remembered that he had begun the serious consideration of religion after reading a devotional book and recommended to pastors that they insure that each family in their charge was equipped with at least one other holy book besides the Bible. John Bunyan noted in his autobiography that while his wife had brought him no dowry, she did own a few devotional books that became important to his spiritual search.[35]

The word heard was even more important in Puritan piety than the word read. Those who could not read or had little leisure for it, or little access to books, could hear the spiritual life proclaimed and analyzed in sermons. Attendance at sermons is often mentioned in Puritan biographies as instrumental in the spiritual lives of their subjects, as skilled preachers summoned persons to conversion and holiness. The devout were encouraged to hear the sermons they needed for the spiritual life: Thomas Doolittle exhorted the reader to "set thyself under the preaching of the word." The biography of John Rowe mentions that that devout man once moved in order to be under the ministry of "an able preacher," so significant was this for the nourishment of the soul. The relationship of people to preacher in the fervent spirituality of the Dissenting congregation was important. In preaching the funeral sermon for a pastor, Robert Bragg reminded the weeping auditory that they had lost a preacher who had been one in a thousand as an interpreter of the spiritual life.[36] Not only did the devout hear sermons, but they spent the week afterwards reflecting on what they had heard. The devout often took notes on the sermon. Especially in New England, one pastoral activity was to call on families and examine them on the sermon of the previous Sunday, applying its lessons to them particularly.

The great weight given to preaching in Puritan cultus and spirituality has led some to consider the Puritans as little interested in sacramental piety. But recent scholars, notably E. Brooks Holifield, have documented the importance of sacramental theology in Puritanism. Holifield concluded that "sacramental piety found an increasingly secure place in the spirituality of many churches and ministers of the Puritan tradition." Many Puritan treatises exhorted the faithful to scrupulous preparation for receiving the sacrament and offered encouragement to the overscrupulous. "Affective" references to the sacrament of the Eucharist are frequent in Puritan books: Keach called it "precious soul-food." Thomas Doolittle's *A Treatise Concerning the Lord's Supper* went through numerous editions in the years after its publication in 1667, and it ranked as one of the most popular devotional books of its age.[37]

Insofar as sacramental piety focused on baptism, it was usually, among those English Puritans that practiced infant baptism, centered on the duty of "improving" one's baptism. Such "improvement" meant drawing lessons of duty and spirituality out of the remembrance of one's baptism and meditation upon it. They thought, as had Martin Luther, that baptism should be a ground for the believer's confidence in the promises of God.[38]

---

[35]John Bunyan, *Grace Abounding to the Chief of Sinners,* ed. Roger Sharrock (Oxford: Clarendon Press, 1962) 8; Richard Baxter, *The Autobiography of Richard Baxter,* ed. J. M. Lloyd Thomas (New York: E. P. Dutton, 1931) 7.

[36]Doolittle, *Captives Bound in Chains,* 183; *The Life and Death of Mr. John Rowe,* 20-21; Bragg, *The Life and Death of the Godly Man,* sig. 3.

[37]E. Brooks Holifield, *The Covenant Sealed: The Development of Puritan Sacramental Theology in Old and New England, 1570-1720* (New Haven & London: Yale University Press, 1974) ix, 127-28, 138, 197ff.; Keach, *A Golden Mine Opened,* 133.

[38]Wakefield, *Puritan Devotion,* 41-42.

Pastoral labors did not end with preaching and sacramental administration. They also involved the personal care of souls. In later Puritanism, exhortations to undertake this kind of ministry towards those under one's spiritual care increased. Baxter's *Reformed Pastor* was full of such advice, as were the works of Joseph Alleine. Thus Puritan pastors provided opportunities for persons to confer with the spiritually mature. This conferring could also be done with laypersons (the layman John Rowe was "abundant in holy counsells and exhortations") and in groups of godly persons. The importance of this to the soul, as Puritans saw it, can be glimpsed in *The Pilgrim's Progress,* where such conference is crucial to the lives of the pilgrims. The force of such spiritual counsel, whether given by clergy or laypersons, was that it was drawn from actual experience with troubles and temptations and thus could help others in their spiritual pilgrimage. Such conference called for sensitivity, too: Bunyan in the early phases of his search was deeply discouraged after seeking advice from one whom he eventually judged to be "a stranger to much combat with the devil" and thus of no help to his tortured soul.[39]

Some examples of this Puritan spiritual counsel have survived in letters and other forms. Correspondence was a common way that such advice was given. For example, many letters between Richard Baxter and Mrs. Katherine Gell, in which she worried about her despairing melancholy, are extant. Baxter suggested that she pray and avoid excessive self-scrutiny.[40]

Evidence of the Puritan effort to give personal, spiritual advice can also be seen in treatises directed to particular ages or classes of persons. Among these, books directed to the young stand out, such as Doolittle's *The Young Man's Instructor, and the Old Man's Remembrancer: or Controversies and Practical Truths, fitted to the capacity of Children, and the more Ignorant sort of People* (1673), Keach's *War with the Devil: or the Young Man's Conflict with the Powers of Darkness: In a Dialogue* (1673), and Matthew Mead's *The Good of Early Obedience: or the advantage of bearing the Yoke of Christ betimes* (1683).

Prayer is central to spiritual experience, and Puritans spent long hours in prayer. Some of the eminent ministers memorialized by biographers would rise at three or four in the morning in order to begin hours of prayer, and similar prayerfulness was recorded of devout laypersons as well. Ministers and layfolk kept special days of prayer, often accompanied by fasting. The New Englander Cotton Mather often lay in prayer for hours on his study floor, with his face in the dust as a token of humility before God. David Clarkson argued that prayer was such an acknowledgment of God's reality that no religion was even possible without it.[41]

Richard Alleine gave advice about prayer in his brief *Companion for Prayer* that typifies the Puritan outlook. He insisted that only those who reform their lives will have their prayers avail. Furthermore, prayer should quicken the devout to the fulfillment of their whole duty to God. One should pray with the "eye and heart" upon God and the other world. He also advocated prayer for the removal of a person's special corruptions, whether

---

[39]*The Life and Death of Mr. John Rowe,* 111; John Bunyan, *Grace Abounding,* 56.

[40]Quoted in William M. Lamont, *Richard Baxter and the Millennium: Protestant Imperialism and the English Revolution* (London: Croom & Helm, 1979) 34-36.

[41]David Clarkson, *A Discourse of the Saving Grace of God* (London, 1688) 77.

pride, sensuality, or slothfulness, and for the gift of the graces the person most needed, such as love, peaceableness, or meekness. He warned strongly against hypocrisy: "Let not the spirituality of your mornings and evenings, countenance or encourage you in your all-day carnality."[42]

"Thoughts," wrote Bartholomew Ashwood, should be held "to their work in divine and heavenly meditation every day." By means of "very careful self-scrutiny and scrupulous spiritual auditing," as Horton Davis has put it, Puritan meditators furthered their spiritual lives. This was often done by keeping a diary. John Janeway's biographer said "he kept a Diary, in which he did write down every evening what the frame of his spirit had been all the day long, especially in every duty. He took notice what incomes and profit he received in his spiritual traffique . . . what answers of prayers, what deadness and flatness, and what observable providences did present themselves, and the substance of what he had been doing." The Puritan spiritual life was a thoroughly self-examined one. William Haller aptly paralleled the diary keeping of the Puritans with the Roman Catholic confessional.[43]

Many Puritan spiritual autobiographies were printed or have survived in manuscript, providing us with a picture of conversion experiences and daily spiritual struggles. These autobiographies when published were useful to readers in distilling much of the personal experience of grace so important in that age. They especially flourished in the second half of the seventeenth century. The most important examples of this genre are *Grace Abounding to the Chief of Sinners* by Bunyan and Baxter's *Reliquae Baxterianae*, but many others—including those by George Trosse, Edmund Trench, or Hannah Allen—also illustrate this kind of literature. Baxter's account is one of a rather serene spiritual experience, but those by Bunyan, Trosse, and Allen portray tortured spiritual experiences. Bunyan thought he had committed the unpardonable sin, Trosse underwent temptations to blasphemy and suicide, and Hannah Allen seems to have been completely out of her mind for a long period of time prior to her conversion.[44]

Puritans meditated upon the Bible, devotional books, and sermons, using meditation to apply personally the lesson read, but certain other techniques and literary genres stand out as particularly characteristic, including meditation on aphorisms, "spiritualizing the creatures," the use of emblem books, and reflecting upon God's providences.

Collections of aphorisms or spiritual sayings of noted preachers or of others reputed for spiritual wisdom were popular. Sometimes these aphorisms were the last words of some notable individual; but whatever the source, the principle was that devout persons should continually have before them terse gems of wisdom on the spiritual life. Meditation on Bible verses was common, but the aphorisms of contemporary spiritual writers could have more direct application to the common spiritual problems of the seventeenth century. In

---

[42]Richard Alleine, *A Companion for Prayer* (London, 1684) 3-6, 9.

[43]Ashwood, *The Heavenly Trade*, 276; Janeway, *Invisibles, Realities*, 58-59; Haller, *The Rise of Puritanism*, 98.

[44]Owen C. Watkins, *The Puritan Experience* (London: Routledge and Kegan Paul, 1972) 28-29; *The Life of the Reverend Mr. George Trosse, Reverend Mr. Edmund Trench; Most of them drawn out of his own Diary* (London, 1693); Hannah Allen, *Satan his methods and malice baffled. A Narrative of Gods gracious dealings with that choice Christian Mrs. Hannah Allen* (London, 1683).

the Puritan's view, not only was great spiritual wisdom distilled into such sayings, which could speak directly to one's own spiritual experience, but also the mind was kept on the straight and narrow path by being continually filled with such matter. An unoccupied or wandering mind could easily be an occasion for sin, but a mind crammed with the wise saws of the spiritually mature was protected from Satan's assaults.

Many spiritual writers of the age became known for their aphorisms. Joseph Alleine's sayings were treasured by his posterity. Books were published with such titles as *Saint's Memorials: or Words fitly spoken, Like Apples of Gold in Pictures of Silver. Being, A Collection of Divine Sentences Written and Delivered by those late Reverend and Eminent Ministers of the Gospel, Mr. Edmund Calamy, Mr. Joseph Caryl, Mr. Ralph Venning, Mr. James Janeway* (1674). Ralph Venning was especially renowned for spiritual wisdom in pithy form, and he made a career of producing it. One collection, first published in 1658, bore the title *Canaan's Flowings, Or Milk and Honey. Being a collation of many Christian Experiences, Sayings, Sentences, Etc., which were formerly miscellaneously but are now Alphabetically Printed for the benefit of the Readers.* The book began with a short dialogue between God and Abraham called "Abraham's Faith and Fear," and then alphabetized topics under which the aphorisms were collected followed—with such headings as "Afflictions," "Anger," and "Atheism," among the first. Appended at the end was a collection of the wise spiritual sayings of ancient pagan authors, drawn from the classics, under the title of "The Heathen Improved. Or the Gibeonites hewing of wood, and drawing of water for the Sanctuary." A typical item is this: "Numa held, that the service of God was a greater honour than to be a king; and shall not Christians think so?"[45]

Spiritualizing the creatures was another popular device for Puritan meditation. This referred to the practice of finding a moral or spiritual lesson in objects of the natural world or in incidents of daily experience. Barbara Lewalski has traced this back to Godfrey Goodman's 1622 treatise *The Creatures Praysing God;* as a practice it received impetus from the *Occasional Meditations* of the Anglican bishop Joseph Hall. It was later strongly recommended as a device of meditation by Baxter. Probably many such "improvements" or lessons became clichés. Many Puritan spiritual writers of the generation after 1660 employed the method, perhaps because it bore some relationship to the new vogue for natural theology and the scientific observation of nature. Examples can be taken from many sources: Bartholomew Ashwood commented that "every herb in thy Garden preaches God to thee," and he recommended such herbal meditation; Thomas Doolittle combined improving the creatures and natural theology when he maintained that "a good going watch" leads to the conclusion that "some workman" is behind the natural world.[46] The master at the art of spiritualizing the creatures, however, was John Flavel, whose best-known titles were *Husbandry Spiritualized* and *Navigation Spiritualized.*

Emblem books were similar to this. These books used pictures, inscriptions, and epigrammatic verse in order to encourage the spiritual life, and the Puritan examples included "improving" the creature as well as interpreting the symbolism and complex

---

[45]Ralph Venning, *Canaan's Flowings* (London, 1658) 267.

[46]Lewalski, *Protestant Poetics and the Seventeenth-Century Religious Lyric,* 165; N. H. Keeble, *Richard Baxter: Puritan Man of Letters* (Oxford: Clarendon Press, 1982) 108-13; Holifield, *The Covenant Sealed,* 134; Ashwood, *The Heavenly Trade,* 308; Thomas Doolittle, *The Young Man's Instructor* (London, 1673) 32.

emblematic pictures. This kind of meditation could be simple and homely, as in Bunyan's *Book for Boys and Girls*. Among the creatures improved or spiritualized here, usually under appropriate pictures were the fatted swine, the beggar, an hourglass, the disobedient child, and even a "stinking breath," which reminded Bunyan of foul thoughts.[47]

Another important focus for Puritan meditation was on the workings of providence, broken down into disparate providences or particular events in which God's special hand toward persons or nations could be perceived. This had some similarities to improving the creatures except that it is not a matter of spiritualizing commonplace things and events but special events, regarded as particular signals from God. That the Puritans were on the lookout for such things suggests that they—unlike some of the emerging theological liberals of their day—continued to believe that God interfered with the regular flow of things in order to summon persons and nations in special ways. They also felt that the spiritually acute should seek skill in interpreting such events. Bartholomew Ashwood advised his readers to "get all the good you can from Providence; from favourable Providences, and from frowning Providences." It has already been noted that the untimely deaths of persecutors were seen as special providences. Often dangerously political meanings were given to prodigies, as in the *Mirabilis Annus* tracts of the early 1660s. Puritan biographies and spiritual diaries were filled with notation of these providences as they pertained to the spiritual life: Thomas Jollie in his private notebooks interpreted storms and rainfall in this way; John Rowe thought that the burning to the ground of his house was a warning to him of neglect of duty (he was "a curious observed of every passage of Providence," his biographer says); and George Trosse felt that "many Providences attended me which should have caution'd me; but I would take no notice of God in them, or Warning by them. Once, when I had greatly besotted my self by an Excess of Drinking, I rode into the Country, and fell from my Horse."[48] A later echo of narratives of going astray by refusal to heed providences can be found in Daniel Defoe's *Robinson Crusoe*.

Many sermons and treatises were devoted to the explication of providences, especially catastrophic ones, such as Thomas Vincent's treatment of the fire and plague of London in 1665 and 1666, or Benjamin Canfield's sermon *Of God Almighty's Providence Both in the Sending and Dissolving Great Snows and Frosts, and the Improvement, we ought to Make, of it. A Sermon, Occasioned by the Late Extreme Cold Weather* (1684). Vincent catalogued London's sins for which God had sent fire and plague as retribution, summoning both "sleepy sinners" and "drowsie saints" to awaken, and he "improved" the fire by noting that it should remind persons of what the fires of hell would be like. Thomas Doolittle, in *Earthquakes Explained and Practically Improved*, commented on the 1692 London earthquake, rather quixotically mixing geology and piety. Acknowledging that some earthquakes arose out of natural causes, he nonetheless felt that many were a warning to the wicked to forsake their sins. A collection of "improved" provi-

---

[47]Lewalski, *Protestant Poetics and the Seventeenth-Century Religious Lyric,* 179ff.; Bunyan's work is reprinted in *The Poems: The Miscellaneous Works of John Bunyan,* ed. Graham Midgley (Oxford: Clarendon Press, 1980) 6:197-269.

[48]Ashwood, *The Heavenly Trade,* 292; Richard Greaves, *Deliver Us From Evil: The Radical Underground in Britain, 1662-1663* (New York: Oxford University Press, 1986) 211-16. *The Note Book of the Rev. Thomas Jolly,* 27, 31, 52; Gale, *The Life and Death of Mr. John Rowe,* 63, 66; *The Life of the Reverend Mr. George Trosse,* 75.

dences by James Janeway was published posthumously as *Twenty-Seven Famous Instances of God's Providences in and About Sea-Dangers and Deliverances.*[49]

Surveying the themes and techniques of Puritan spirituality in the latter seventeenth century makes clear that the Puritan movement had at its core an interest in the development of the Christian spiritual life. Puritanism became important as a chapter in the unfolding development of Christian spirituality especially in the generation after 1660 as it matured the themes and techniques of earlier Puritan writers.

---

[49]Thomas Vincent, *God's Terrible Voice in the City,* 193, 195, 198, 256; Thomas Doolittle, *Earthquakes Explained and Practically Improved* (London, 1693) sig. A4, 15, 25, 97; James Janeway, *Mr. James Janeway's Legacy to His Friends: Twenty-Seven Famous Instances of God's Providence in and about Sea-Dangers and Deliverances* (London, 1683).

Holy Lives and Holy Deaths

A holy death was for the Puritans the culmination of a holy life, and both were fit objects of reflection for the development of the spiritual life. The late-seventeenth-century Puritan literature of spiritual autobiographies and biographies of saintly persons was extensive, and both familiarized the seeker with the kinds of spiritual struggles to be expected in the pursuit of conversion and holiness, and set forth concrete depictions of Christian virtue. Details about how these exemplary persons faced death and fared in their dying had an especial fascination for the devout.

In the selections that follow, Thomas Manton explains briefly the benefits to be derived from reading about holy persons; Edmund Trench exemplifies the genre of spiritual autobiography while revealing a characteristic Puritan spiritual struggle; Samuel Clarke portrays the ideal holy woman; James Janeway does the same for children and also shows what a holy death could be like; and Theodosia Alleine describes her husband as the ideal pastor. In the final selection a group of Puritan ministers chronicle the dramatic repentance of a notorious sinner. In all these variations of conversion and holiness, the aim of edification was paramount.

Introduction to Thomas Manton, "To the Reader," from Ferdinando Nicolls, *The Life and Death of Mr. Ignatius Jurdain*

Thomas Manton (1620-1677) was a prominent leader of the Presbyterians in the Cromwellian years. He was a scribe for the Westminster Assembly and often preached before the Long Parliament. In 1656 he became the rector of St. Paul's, Covent Garden, London, but was ejected in 1662. He had favored the return of the monarchy in 1660 and was honored by being made chaplain to King Charles II (though he never took up any related duties), but nonetheless could not accept all the terms of the Act of Uniformity. He was associated with Richard Baxter as a Presbyterian leader during the years following the Restoration. He often preached illegally, for which he suffered a brief imprisonment in 1670. He was awarded a doctorate in divinity from Oxford in 1660. Many of his sermons were published, and he was the author of many biblical commentaries.

The selection from Manton that follows is a brief epistle to the reader in which he maintains the importance of memorializing holy lives. It is taken from Ferdinando Nicolls, The Life and Death of Mr. Ignatius Jurdain, One of the Aldermen of the City of Exeter: Who departed this Life July 15th, 1640 *(London, 1654; Wing N1139) sigs. a1ʳ-a2ʳ. There is a rather full biographical notice of Manton by Charlotte Fell-Smith in the* Dictionary of National Biography.

Thomas Manton, "To the Reader"

Good Reader, It is a truth which alwaies God hath made good in his providence, that the memorial of the just shall be blessed; therefore since the Canon and rule of faith, or those Authentick records which we call The Scriptures, have been closed up: The Lord hath stirred up in every age some that could handle the pen of the writer, to continue the memory of his eminent and faithful servants to posterity with praise and honour. It would be vain in a case so known, to tell you particularly what hath been done in this kind, by Dorotheus, Sophronius, Jerome, Gennadius, Epiphanius, etc.[1] and by modern Writers without number; the Ancient Church had her Diptychs[2] or publick Tables, wherein the names of persons most noted for piety were recorded; and though the modern Canonization used among the Romanists

[1]Dorotheus, a sixth-century Palestinian ascetical writer; Sophronius, a seventh-century Patriarch of Jerusalem; Jerome, the fourth-century translator of the Bible into Latin; Gennadius of Marseilles, a fifth-century Christian writer; and Epiphanius, fourth-century bishop of Salamis—all wrote lives of saintly persons.

[2]Diptychs are lists of names of living and dead Christians for whom special prayers were made in both the Greek and Latin liturgies of the Eucharist. The term is taken from the two-leaved folder within which the lists of names were written.

be ridiculous, and some Sainted that were scarce men, and their legends bundles of lyes the very stain and infamy of Christianity; yet there is no reason that the true Saints, God's Worthies, should be defrauded of their publick honour, and buried in obscurity and silence without any Monument of their worth, and religious eminency: especially when we do consider how much God's glory is concerned in the credit of his servants, as also the profit of others; partly that they may be acquainted with the ancient wayes of the Spirit, and those Good old pathes wherein the Children of God walked and enjoyed communion with him: partly that they may be provoked by their examples to follow them in faith and patience, and heavenlinesse and strictnesse of conversation; we see many times that examples wake more than precepts, not onely as they convince, but as they do encourage: they convince more, because they are real; we look upon precepts as words spoken of course, wherein Religion may be counterfeited at a cheaper rate; therefore Noah, though a Preacher of righteousnesse, is said to convince the world by preparing an Ark, Heb. 11:8, and they incourage, because in them we see, that the exercise of godlinesse, though difficult, yet is possible, when men that are subject to like passions, and have the same interests and Concernments of flesh and blood that we have, can be thus mortified, self-denying, heavenly, holy: now examples have this force, not onely when the Saints are alive, and liable to present notice and observation, but after their death, when transmitted to posterity by faithful records; yea then many times they work more, their infirmities being buried with them, and their lives do then rather instruct then [than] Exasperate; living Saints standing in the way of interests[3] are more hated, and looked upon with prejudice, but usually there is great esteem of the dead; how often do God's Children live envied, and die Sainted! . . .

---

[3]Standing in the way of interests: running afoul of the selfish and powerful.

Introduction to Edmund Trench,
Some Remarkable Passages
in the Holy Life and Death
of the late Reverend Mr. Edmund Trench

Edmund Trench (1643-1689) was educated at Magdalen College, Oxford, where he received the B.A. in 1661. He was not beneficed in 1662, so he was not among the ejected ministers with whom he sympathized. He lived at Hackney in Middlesex from 1670 to 1674, and then at several places in Kent. He was an occasional preacher and an active spiritual director.

Several years after his death, in 1693 in London, was published Some Remarkable Passages in the Holy Life and Death of the late Reverend Mr. Edmund Trench; Most of them drawn out of his own Diary *(Wing T2109). What follows is taken from 18-29, 30-33, 37-40, 40-42, 50, 51-52, 52-54, 74-76, 77-88, 93-95, and 97-98. These passages from his diary and autobiographical fragments illustrate the Puritan penchant for keeping a close watch over the spiritual and moral life.*

Some Remarkable Passages
in the Holy Life and Death
of the late Reverend Mr. Edmund Trench

From such[1] I entred on my earthly Pilgrimage, Octob. 6, 1643, about 5 in the Evening, after my Mother had been 3 Days in painful dangerous Travail. I was born with a great Wound in my Head, suppos'd by a blow of a great boss'd Bible, as my Mother came out of Church: That was heal'd, and afterwards many Diseases and hurts in my Childhood, both Thigh-bones dislocated together: Afterwards an Arm broken, well set, no harm remaining. During my tender years, I was in my Parent's immediate Care in London and Hackney, from whom, and my good Grandfather, (whose Diversion I often was) I wanted not Instruction, Example, and Encouragement; and so far I seem'd to answer their Endeavours, that they delighted much in me. But I well remember, and thou, O Lord, much more, abundance of Wickedness I was guilty of, Disobedience to Parents, indulging my Appetite to excess, taking or stealing what was not allow'd; quarrelling especially with my next Brother Samuel, whom I shou'd have born with, considering his woful Affliction by the King's Evil;[2] Pride in Apparel, or what Abilities and Acquirements I had; Envy,

---

[1]The earlier part of the account told about his parents and ancestry.

[2]The King's Evil: scrofula, so called because it was believed that it could be cured by the touch of the king. Charles II still practiced this healing office after the Restoration.

mispence[3] of Time in Romances, Plays, idle Stories, &c. too much play and lying. All aggravated by so many and great Mercies and Means, such singular Love and Light, that I have often thought my Sins more hainous than theirs that I have seen going to Execution: They were never so engag'd, never enjoy'd such helps as I. Have mercy upon me, O Lord, according to thy great goodness, and blot out my Transgressions, for my Saviour's sake.

Towards the end of my 15th Year, I was sent to Cambridge with Mr. Samuel Jacomb, and by him plac'd in Queen's Colledge, under the Tuition of Mr. Andrew Paschall: There I got the Love and good Report of my Tutor and others, but was far from deserving it: I made a shift to do the Exercises required, but wofully neglected my Studies; sadly addicted to Tennis, Cards, and other expensive forbidden Sports, to reading Romances, Plays, and smutty Poets; and at length more entangled with bad Company, especially in the absence of my studious and loving Chamberfellow, (afterwards Sir J. K. an eminent Lawyer of the Inner-Temple, taken off when rising in Riches and Honour.) By them I was drawn once and again to Gluttony and Drunkenness, Swearing and Cursing, and at last to making (as they call'd it) indeed to stealing of Hankerchiefs, Knives, Books, or what else we cou'd lay our hands on. This was a common shameless practice: and suffering thereby from others, I thought I might right my self. It was God's goodness that I went no farther, having been tempted to go with 'em to naughty Women, which (my Inclination consider'd) I wonder I never did. Blessed be God who still restrained me, till my Chamber-fellow leaving the Colledge, and some other Obstacles being happily remov'd, when I was most in danger: My

Father who suspected nothing, but thought too well of me, thought fit for other Reasons I should remove to Oxford; Thither I went towards the end of 1660, to Magdalen-Hall: Before that Year expired, I proceeded Batchelor, which to Doctor's Sons (at least the eldest) was then permitted at 12 year's standing: Performing the usual Exercises[4] on that occasion, I was unexpectedly engag'd among some who were too excessively debauch'd for me. They stirr'd in me some abhorrence, as bad as I was, and drove me to better Acquaintance, and God cast me on such as were not only of a better temper, but really Pious, for whom I think my Parent's tincture had in some measure prepar'd me. I thought such Company wou'd please them, and (praised be God) it soon grew pleasant to my self also. By their Converse especially, and reading good Books, (though I also heard the best Ministers) those good Principles were awaken'd, which my Parents had sown, and they soon became vigorously active for Repentance and fruitful Obedience. I reflected on my Sins with shame and sorrow; I oft confess'd and bewail'd 'em before God with bitter Anguish and detestation: They soon turn'd my laughing into weeping, my usual chearfulness into a very sorrowful melancholy, and fill'd me with Self-abhorrence, Dread, and Horrour. In such a Condition I continued, though mercifully supported a long time, getting by degrees more gleams of light and intervals of Hope and Comfort. The Sin that was most troublesom to undo, was my taking (as before) several Things from others: I thought Restitution my Duty, though I thought I might take as I did to right my self, St. Austin's saying, *Non remittitur*

---

[3]mispence: misspending.

[4]Exercises: the public debates that preceded the awarding of degrees.

peccatum, nisi restituatur ablatum,[5] struck me like Thunder, and I had no rest till I parted with all, even with what I had from them that had wrong'd me. But shame and inconsideration betray'd me to a course that afterwards encreas'd my trouble: I wrote to one too guilty himself, and that had made me worse: He profess'd Repentance, and readiness to assist and imitate me in Restitution: and upon his repeated Engagements, I sent him all I cou'd think of, not my own in kind or value, and then was quiet as to that matter. (How his Friend serv'd him, you'll hear anon.) As to other Faults, my way was plain: I left off every course of Sin and Folly, those defended Games which had so wasted my time, fine and fashionable Clothes, and all bad and vain Company. I grew constant in secret and publick Duties of Religion, and convers'd with and imitated those I thought most strictly good. God's Service was my Design, doing good my Work, and in order thereto, I grew more and more inclin'd to the study of Divinity, and had more delight in the beginnings thereof. Many Favours I received from God, among which a signal Deliverance of my Chamber-fellow Mr. Foley, and my self, ought not to be forgotten: Washing in the River, he who cou'd not swim, desir'd me to hold him by the Hair, which while I did, swimming with my other Arm, we were gotten out of our depths, so that at length seeking for ground, we both sunk under water; my escape seem'd easie, but then I lost him; therefore I clasp'd as I cou'd his middle with my right Arm, and so made a shift to reach the Shallows. God gave me strength, and kept him, tho' his Head was under water, from laying hold or struggling, which might have destroyed us both. To thee, O Lord, the praise; To us thankfulness in a fruitful Life.

After almost two Years abode at Oxford, I left that University also, being sent about 7 Months after to Leyden by my good Father, who was willing I should study Physick.[6] Before I went, I understood his unfaithfulness whom I had trusted to right those I had wrong'd; and left with a better Man more than I could think due to any, except those my self righted.

In Holland I enjoy'd good Company, good Ministery, and my more intimate Converse with P.C. was useful: We only were together in a Dutch Papist's House, where he labour'd exceedingly under great Terrours and Sorrows for Sin; having many bitter Pangs and long Agonies, with plenty of Tears and Cries: which the Papist taking notice of, charg'd our Religion as uncomfortable. I help'd him as I could: He recovered by degrees, yet not fully till after our return to England. My Affection encreas'd with his Seriousness, deadness to this World, and vigour for a better, with the Thoughts whereof he seem'd wholly taken up. His Friends and himself at length inclining to his Marriage, at their desire, I recommended him to a Gentlewoman wish'd[7] to me: He was not then accepted, but afterwards reviv'd his Suit, and by other help obtain'd her. I refus'd to act farther, being disatisfied with that change of his Company, Garb, and Carriage, &c. that followed his Father's death, and his own remove to Grey's-Inn.[8] I had Reason to be glad, I did no more: for having obtained the Gentlewoman, (who prov'd desirable, so

---

[5]The Latin of St. Augustine means, "There is no remission of sins, except by the cleansing of restitution."

[6]Leyden is a city in the Netherlands where many Puritans had gone into exile (see Keith Sprunger, *Dutch Puritanism* [London: E. J. Brill, 1982]). It had a notable university. Physick: medicine.

[7]wish'd: intended.

[8]One of the Inns of Court in London where law was studied.

inclin'd to Vertue, that he profess'd he must be very faulty, if she prov'd not very good.) He brought her to Lincoln's-Inn Fields, engag'd her in vain Company, carried her to Plays, Entertainments, &c. I lovingly though plainly represented his Faults and Duty, and pray'd for him not without appearance of Success; he removing into the Country and living more restrainedly. But he grew strange to me, and I have some reason to fear the worst. Thou, O Lord, hear and help, and recover out of the Snare of the Devil. Keep me (though believing the best) from confidence in Man, and from making of Matches, seeing one, of whose Piety I had such assurance, hath so grosly fail'd; and let all make me more humble and watchful.

I saw at Leyden and other places, (notwithstanding their reformed Discipline)[9] reason enough to love my own Country still better; and therefore my inclination to Divinity still continuing, though I had made some progress in Physick, after about a year's absence, I return'd, 1664, continuing with my Parents at London, till the Plague and Fire[10] for awhile removed us. Midsummer, 1668, we came to Crouched-Fryars, and with my Brother was happy in comforting and diverting my Father, till we were Witnesses of his blessed Departure.

He left beside my self, dear Brother Thomas, born April 14, 1648. We always lov'd, and can hardly remember any quarrel between us. The youngest Sister Sarah also survived, born May 23.—May we see her New-born; May I do my Duty to promote it!

Soon after my Father's death, I was seiz'd by a Feavourish Distemper, accompani'd with Hypochondraic winds,[11] &c. which continued, and enforc'd serious Consideration: I found in my self a great change; Prayer and Reading had above 7 Years been my constant practice: I was temperate in Meats, Drinks, Apparel, &c. I hope truly humble; scrupulously careful to do no wrong, losing rather.[12] I gave the Poor constantly[13] the 10th, and of late the 7th part of my Income. Oaths and Curses which once and again I had been guilty of, I long since abhorr'd, and could not hear without trouble. Yet I was dejected, that though I had pleas'd and rejoyc'd my Parents, I had not been in all things so complying as I should; and yet more, because I had not so diligently improv'd my Time for God as I might; I hope I heartily repented, denying my self, and bearing Inconveniences for my good Mother, and resolving on greater Diligence in doing & getting good. I was likewise anxious whether Restitution were certainly made for the wrongs I had done in Cambridge 10 Years before; and determin'd to enquire and do what was further requisite. I was sensible of the kindness of this Affliction in the afore-said search and resolves, and in a farther change of my Temper, growing more meek, humble, and charitable: I felt more my own vitious Impotence, and the necessity of Divine Grace, as being, having, and doing nothing good, but as the Spirit makes me every moment.

Before I recovered from this Sickness, I was forsaken by my thoughts of Conforming (to the establish'd Church, by submitting to the Terms impos'd on Ministers)[14] to which I had been sufficiently inclin'd by the Reasons and Examples of several pious and judicious Persons. The

---

[9]Reformed Discipline: Presbyterian government, which many Puritans favored.

[10]The plague struck London in 1665; the great fire destroyed much of the city in 1666.

[11]hypochondriac: abdominal.

[12]i.e., suffering loss rather than doing wrong.

[13]constantly: continually.

[14]i.e., by the terms of the 1662 Act of Uniformity.

formidable Horrours of my Conscience, the dread of their return by reason of some doubts I could not well remove, determin'd me rather to a private Life, which I desir'd to render as useful as I might. . . .

I return'd from Deal after 3 Days stay with my dear Brother going to Aleppo:[15] I parted sadly with one so dear in the strictest bands of Love and Nature; yet we encourag'd our selves in our good God, whose Favour we had so experienc'd together, and hop'd we should still enjoy when so far asunder. I desired all might make me more long and labour after, and prepare for Heaven, where Friends part not bitterly any more, and where God is All in All for ever.

> Hackney, Octob. 11. 1670.

I grew ill of a Quartan Ague,[16] as it quickly proved: My Prayers were for Christian Patience and Wisdom to bear the worst, and make a good Improvement of all, that God might be glorified, my self and others bettered, and Christ more comfortably in life and death Advantage.[17]

> June 20. 1671

Trying Enfield-Air, for removing my Ague, I rode into the Chase,[18] and being among the Trees thoughtful[19] and careless, my Horse by a great and sudden start, turn'd me first on his Crupper, and ere-long on the ground; yet only tore my Clothes among the Trees and Bushes. I was forc'd to walk back to Coz. Farrington's, in the

heat, which turn'd my expected Cold into a violent Sweat. I desired thankfully to remember that Preservation in such apparent danger, and to be sensible of God's good Providence, as oft as I ride, and no such danger appears; and to be still as careful to perform, as I was ready to resolve and vow.

> Hackney, Apr. 22. 1672.

Scorbutick Pains and melancholy Fumes[20] much discompos'd me, though I had no more Ague-fits, &c. Yet they were not so much my trouble, as the Diseases of my Soul: My Prayers were for more Grace, that I might not relapse, but grow my self, and make others also more holy; that my Charity might be greater, the Defects thereof pardon'd; that my own Sins might lye heavier, and Afflictions lighter:
—*Ure, seca, Domine, modo non in aeternum.*[21]

> July 26. 1672.

Melancholy Fumes exceedingly disturbed and unfitted my Mind for any Service: I doubted[22] I should live useless, and apprehended God was taking the forfeiture of those Parts and Abilities I had abus'd. I prayed for Health, and Powers, and Opportunities to serve God, and be useful to Men, vouching the sincerity of my Heart; yet presently retracting, having found it so deceitful, and beseeching Mercy and help for my Saviour's sake.

Though urg'd, and on some accounts dispos'd to Marry, I chose rather to continue single, because I feared such a change would rather hinder God's chearful faithful Service; I should have less Time, less Mony [*sic*] for good Uses, and not be in a capacity to embrace some mean[23] Oppor-

---

[15]Deal is a borough in Kent; Aleppo is in Syria and was a major center of commerce under the Ottoman empire. His brother was evidently going abroad as a merchant.

[16]Quartan ague: severe fever and chills, recurring every fourth day.

[17]i.e., that in life and death Christ be an advantage to him.

[18]chase: an unenclosed tract of private land, reserved for hunting.

[19]thoughtful: absent-minded, preoccupied.

[20]scorbutic: caused by scurvy; melancholy fumes: abdominal gas.

[21]The Latin means: "purge and judge, O Lord, but not to eternity."

[22]doubted: feared, thought.

[23]mean: plain, common.

tunity of serving God in Publick, like what some had, who could not go farther than my self. I appeal to God, begging his Blessing according (as I hop'd) to the uprightness of my Heart.

Decem. 30. 1672. . . .

I had groaned many Days under great trouble of Mind, occasion'd at the first by some discourse about Sacriledge, and a Story of Dr. Holdsworth,[24] who hearing one express great hopes of good from the long Parliament;[25] he reply'd, He wou'd have none expect it, since Parliaments so sacrilegiously alienated Church-Lands.[26] I think I had heard as much formerly without being concern'd, but now I immediately apprehended, If the Alienation were sinful, so was the detention; and thence I might become guilty of Sacriledge, if I should enjoy an Estate taken long since from the Hospital of St. Bartholomew the Less, in Smithfield, bought by my Father at above 20 Years purchase, after divers preceding Alienations, and left by him after my Mother's Life to me.

My Terrours encreas'd by reading about Sacriledge, the Forms of ancient Dedication, with Curses, &c.

Thence Conscience ran backward, examin'd the material Passages of my Life, rack'd me with tormenting Scruples about Matters of *Meum & Tuum*,[27] and fill'd me with frightful Representations not only of my quondam[28] Cambridge Sinful-follies, but of my following Actions, for Father and Self, (in reference to the forementioned Estate:) So that I was strangely jealous I had some way done amiss, tho' very confident that since my Repenting and Restoring (1661, 12 Years before) I had ever studiously and scrupulously endeavour'd to do as I wou'd be done unto. Nor could I fix on any particular Failure, unless on selling two Horses last Year. Then I question'd whether my Attempts to satisfie such as I had wrong'd (while at Cambridge) had succeeded; and St. Austin's Saying, *Non remittitur, &c.* made me tremble. I also fear'd I had profan'd the Lord's Supper: and when on search I began to hope I had not, I charg'd my self with rash presumption, in thinking of so high and holy a Calling (as the Ministry) which such base former Sins wou'd disgrace. My Perplexities were lamentable: I had recourse to God by Prayer, though not sufficiently frequent and fervent; and I consulted his Word and Servants.

I could not find it was any Sin for me who had sinned so much, and perhaps hardned some, to endeavour the reclaiming of others: I found great Sinners had been (after Conversion) us'd by the Holy God as chosen Instruments of his Grace; and remembred many late Examples guilty of Sins materially equal, if not greater than mine, whom yet God blest with eminent Success and Comfort.

My fear of disgracing Religion seemed very unreasonable; the Sins known to few, very few and far off, so many Years since repented of and forsaken! and my Conversation (though needing manifold pardon from God) having long gain'd too favourable a Repute among Men. Therefore though most unworthy to be honoured by

---

[24]Richard Holdsworth (1590-1649) was a Cambridge-educated theologian who was also a well-known London preacher. He chose the royalist side in the civil wars and was ejected from office by the Long Parliament.

[25]The Long Parliament sat from 1640 until 1648. After the purge of 1648 it was known as the Rump Parliament. It was briefly reconvened in 1660.

[26]alienate: divert from rightful use. Various church lands had been so treated, especially during the civil wars. The question was whether or not it was sacrilege to alienate Church of England properties.

[27]Meum & Tuum: Latin for mine and thine, used especially with reference to ownership of property.

---

[28]quondam: former.

God, to do him any Service towards the Salvation of any poor Creature; yet I could not but think it lawful, yea my Duty to endeavour it to the utmost of my Capacity and Power; and thereon resolv'd to reject and resist such Suggestions as Temptations to Sin against my Duty. . . .

Thus for less than 4£ at the utmost value, I paid with a great deal of shame and trouble about 15£ and I gave 20£. extraordinary to the Poor. I would all that wrong'd me knew I forgave them, though none made me Satisfaction, except 3£ from one that desir'd to be conceal'd, were on that account.

Some Advantage I found by my Troubles in this Affair.[29]

1. I found much Pride within me, and was hereby made base and vile in my own Eyes, and willing to be so in others.

2. I minded too much what was less needful, and these Distractions drave me to the Essentials of Religion, and made me mind them more.

3. I was more convinc'd of my own Impotency and Nothingness, and of my constant dependence on God for Duty and Comfort: I found Reasons and Arguments nothing till God enabled me after another manner to apply them.

4. I was more sensible of the Necessity and Use of Prayer.

5. I understood better the condition of the Scrupulous, that their Troubles were not to be slighted as proceeding from Weakness and Folly; but to be tenderly manag'd: and that the withdrawings of the Spirit are something beside Melancholy, though that may be joyn'd with them.

6. I was warn'd by all to walk more circumspectly, that I might not provoke my Heavenly Father thus to chasten me: and instead of Controversies, especially about small and mysterious Matters, to study more the practical Life of Faith in nearer Communion with the blessed Fountain of Holiness, Peace, and Joy.

My Scruples about the Horses I sold had as little grounds as almost any other. I repeated my Charge to those that sold them, to speak truth, neither denying nor using any means to conceal any Fault: Only I doubted I was not sufficiently careful to have the Buyers acquainted with all I knew my self. It being the Rule of an Heathen, Tully: *Ne quid omnino quod venditor novit, emptor ignoret.*[30] Yet I could not learn the Buyers were damag'd, nor say they paid too dear; and good Men laugh'd at my Scruples, professing themselves would do as I had done. . . .

My Days were checquer'd with Duties and Failings, Hopes and Fears, Joys and Griefs: My Desires, and, I hope, sincere Endeavours, were for stronger Resolutions, more vigorous and lively Affections, ardenter Love, and sweeter Joy in a holy dependance on, Resignation and Obedience to my God, that I might through Grace write down more matter of Praise and Joy in perpetual well-doing; for my dearest Saviour's sake.

Hackney, July 28. 1674. . . .

Having on repeated Invitation taken a Journey to Glastenbury [Glassenbury] near Cranbroke in Kent; I had there proposed for a Wife, Mrs. Bridget Roberts, Daughter to the Lady of that Name. I was little (if at all) affected with the Honour, nor was the Portion[31] so great as I had been tempted with elsewhere: But there was desirable assurance of Piety, Humility, good Temper, Industry, and Frugality, and withal a

---

[29]i.e., his going about to make restitution for stolen items.

[30]Tully is Marcus Tullius Cicero, a Roman orator and author of the first century B.C. The Latin means: "the buyer shall not be ignorant of anything at all that the seller knows."

[31]portion: dowry.

fairer Opportunity of inoffensive Usefulness than had yet offer'd in my Circumstances. . . .

Tuesday, Octob. 5. 1675. we were Married in Glastenbury-Chappel, my self at the end of my 32d. Year, my Wife not 18, by Mr. Monckton, Vicar of Brenchly, Sir Thomas giving her, her Mother, other Brother and Sister, and a few besides present. I praised God who had enabled us to follow him our Ruler, Guide, and End; and had at length clear'd our way, and brought us into that near relation. I pray'd it might be sanctified and improv'd to the great ends which I hope we sincerely aim'd at.

All this while I endeavour'd, not without some success, that others might be the better, not the worse for me.

May 29, 1676. Glastenbury.

On my return, I set about doing good in the Family and Neighbourhood, having seriously consider'd my Duty to God, my Superiours, and others, and likewise their Circumstances among whom I was then to live.

The Family and others accustom'd to the old Chappel at Glastenbury, being two Miles or more from the Church, prejudic'd against the establish'd Worship, and the next Minister, the Vicar of G _____, especially Th., a drunken impertinent Sot, that distasted many conformable enough,[32] and made 'em approve more private Help. I still dealt openly as I had done before Marriage, declaring my desire of more publick Service, readiness to read Common Prayer,[33] almost all, going sometimes to the neighbouring Churches, and joyning in the Liturgy; and letting them know my practice of Communicating, and that kneeling.[34] I drew none to our private Meeting, but blam'd such as came from good Ministers,[35] professing I would not keep up a separate Congregation, but only while it appear'd expedient help for such as were so ill provided.[36] I proceeded with more Confidence and Comfort, because I had no trouble, nor heard of any dislike from the more comfortable Neighbours, and was more confirm'd in the moderate course I had taken by the impotent Censures of some uncharitable Persons. My Prayers were to know my Duty, and do it, pleasing God, though I displeas'd Man.

Glastenb. Sept. 20, 1676. . . .

I find it most difficult to get and keep an Heavenly Frame without Distraction: I am oft discompos'd by worldly Concerns, vex'd by the Sins and Weaknesses of others; and too easily diverted from my Studies, Meditations, and Prayers, by vain, impertinent, unsuitable, and unseasonable Thoughts: I labour and groan under them as my great Burden and Sin, and strive alas too ineffectually against them. What would I give, yea, what would I not give, do, or suffer, that my Soul were fix'd on God; that I could serve him without Distraction? That my Studies, Meditations, and Converse with God in his Word, Prayer, and Praise, were more free from wandring, more affectionate, spiritual and heavenly? Yet I'm sure I long and desire to labour more effectually that God may fill and possess my Soul; that his holy enjoying Service, (the perfect Happiness of Heaven) may be more

---

[32]i.e., that led many who otehwise would have conformed to dislike the established church.

[33]i.e., he was willing to conform to the use of the *Book of Common Prayer,* the liturgy of the Church of England. Many Puritans objected to parts of it.

[34]communicating: receiving communion. Many Puritans objected to receiving communion while kneeling, arguing that this implied the Roman Catholic dogma of transubstantiation.

[35]i.e., he did not encourage those who had good parish ministers to come to his private meetings.

[36]i.e., by a drunken Church of England clergyman.

and more begun on Earth. I value and breath[e] after the Divine Image as the greatest good, esteeming, and desiring to be rid of Sin as the greatest Evil; and Heaven is therefore most amiable, because there I hope to be wholly freed from Sin, and to serve and enjoy my God and Saviour in sinless Holiness.

O Lord help me to do as I profess, promise, and bind my self; That my Conversation may be more in Heaven: That thy Will may be more done by me on Earth, as 'tis in Heaven! That I may more comfortably hope and long to be in Heaven! And, O remember thy Churches and Children, and the whole World; Let my concern for them all be more according to thy Will, more pure and intense for thy Glory. Amen, for our Lord Jesus' sake.

My worldly Circumstances are not without Difficulties and Temptations; considerable Losses I have had, yet continued giving largely to the Poor: My Children dying, I did not think it my Duty to encrease my Estate. I have now Two likely to live, and may have more; so that my Charge rises, when what should maintain it falls. I resolve to cast my Care on God in well-doing, to exercise my self more than ever, to keep a Conscience void of offence, impartially to study and do my Duty, and pray continually.

Brenchley, Octob. 23. 1685.

My Practice hath in some measure answer'd my renewed Resolutions; I have employed my time better, pray'd harder, and endeavoured when call'd abroad to do some good, by good Discourse, when I thought it seasonable, and by making peace. God hath comforted me in the kindness of Friends; His Spirit, I hope, is with me: May I more abundantly find it, as I am call'd to do or suffer, for my Jesus's sake!

Brenchley, Feb. 25. 1686. . . .

April 26. Our younger Child Thomas died at the end of a Convulsion-Fit, about an Hour long, &c. May we more practically believe we must also die, and not cease preparing for it, till we come to desire it, and live in the constant joyful expectation of Eternity: We are many ways shamefully faulty that we do not: Pardon and help us for thy Mercies' sake. Amen.

Brenchley, May 29, 1686.

On the 23d. I solemnly remembered my Saviour's Passion, and renewed my Covenant with God thorow him; My Prayers and Vows were principally for encrease of Holiness in Heart and life. God graciously made use of a mean Affliction, (as others count it) to quicken both[37] the Day following; so that the past Week my Watch hath been more constant, my Recollections more frequent, at least every Evening: And I find to my comfort my Converse both with God and Man, hath been in some good measure, (if I mistake not) according to the Gospel. I have had many Reflections on God's manifold Goodness, many Abhorrings of my sinful Vileness: I desire my Actions, and (as God pleaseth) my Sufferings may be answerable, that I may glorifie him more on Earth, and help others to do so; and become very ready and willing to serve him better in Heaven. Amen, for my Saviour's sake.

June 5. [1686]

I praise God, I have liv'd this Week also as the former; My Soul hath been daily first and last with God: My Thoughts have very frequently return'd unto him, and my Time hath been improv'd with some diligence for his Glory. My Converse with others & in my own family, hath in some measure exprest the sense of those great Things that ought always above all to be minded. My Prayers and Resolves have

---

[37]i.e., his prayers and vows.

been and are for constancy and progress. Amen, for my Lord Jesus' sake.

June 12. [1686]

I hope I am still getting nearer Heaven; I have continued my Converse with God, and endeavoured to quicken others with my self to his blessed Service. Afflictions are much abated, but not my Fervor. O may Love be an abiding Principle thereof, acting[38] me with Vigour and Constancy for the Glory of God, and the good of all with whom I have to do. Amen, for my Lord Jesus' sake.

June 19, 1686.

Praised be God, I have endeavoured another Week to speak, and think, and act for him: His Mercies further engage me daily.

July 3. [1686]

I have thought oft daily of God and Heaven, and oft pray'd that I might please him better, and be more fit to be with him there: But I have not been so serious and warm, and earnestly desirous of getting and doing good as I was before, and yet I was last Lord's-day at the Sacrament: I hope God knows that I desire nothing in comparison with Holiness, that I may be at a greater distance from the Defilements of Sin, and have deeper and more abiding Impressions of his purifying Light and Love, and be more constant and successful in communicating thereof to others. I proceeded not so successfully in my Studies as I would, and I think sometimes have. I hope to pray and strive that I may be and do better. Impertinent Discourses, (the too common bane of Converse) have been my trouble. May I be able to oppose them with Christian Prudence, and to perfume every Place and Company with somewhat truly good; for his sake, who purchas'd and pleads for Grace to help in time of need.

July 10. [1686]

An indisposed Body and several incumbring Diversions have hindred me from serving God as I would; yet I hope my main design has not been wholly neglected.

I was faithful to two Persons in dealing plainly with them about some matters that had occasion'd several to speak evil of 'em. But I was so with abundance of tenderness, and therefore cannot but think one of them blame-worthy for the bad return he made. My Conscience bears me witness, I did what I did meerly from sense of Duty, having great reluctances; which only fear of God, and the love he commands to my Fellow-servants, overcame.

July 17. [1686]

I endeavoured to serve my good God, of whose kindness I have still more experience; but alas I have wanted that warmth and pleasure I have sometimes had: I long and desire to labour for it more than ever.

July 31. [1686]

I want the Aids of the Holy Spirit, because I doubt I do not seek and labour for and with them as I ought: I walk heavily, yet I hope in the right way. O for more Grace, or rather for better improvement of what I have, that I may have more; for Jesus's sake!

Aug. 7. & 14. [1686]

To the like purpose.

My Watch[39] has not been so constant, nor my Converse so useful as it should; Less profitable Discourses and Books have taken up too much time: I am not prepared as I would for the Lord's-Day approaching. I need and beg pardon, that I delight no more in the more spiritual heavenly Duties and Studies, and am as desirous, (O may I be as laborious) to do better; for, &c.

---

[38]acting: motivating, moving.

[39]Watch: often prayers and meditations, but here probably examination of one's life.

Brenchley, Aug. 31. [1686]

I have not been what I would, yet I hope I am in no way to be what I wish, in Heaven. O may I be much better on Earth! To Morrow I design to take a Journey with my Brother, &c. O may I be able to reflect with comfort at my return on what I was and did.

Sept. 21. [1686]

God's Goodness accompanied me in my Journey, shin'd in Relations Loveliness,[40] and Love, preserv'd my Family, and has brought us together in safety. May all be crown'd with encrease of Holiness and fruitful Gratitude, &c.

Octob. 16. [1686]

Four Fits of a Tertian Ague had much weaken'd and indisposed me; God then took it off, and I seem recovering my former State of Health: I thought of Death with little or no fear, and hope I should have been happy if I had died, though now my Reflections are not so comfortable. I have sometimes thought I was beyond what I wrote: but now I am down again. Bodily indisposition dulls me; But why is not my Soul more vigorous? Had I comply'd with the Holy Spirit, and convers'd with God as I ought, I might have had more of his comforting, strengthning Influences and helps. I desire to qualifie my self for them by a far better improvement of all Aids vouchsaf'd. Help, heavenly Father, for thy Son's sake, Amen.

Nov. 8. [1686]

Our Seventh Son was Baptiz'd and Nam'd Edmund; May we and ours be still more our God's, agnizing[41] his Supream Right, and living more in the lively sense

and active acknowledgements thereof. Amen; for, &c.

Decemb. 11. [1686]

My God has continued to engage me by his kindness to my whole Self and ours, and to our Relations who are so pleasant and useful to us. I have proceeded in my course of Duty, but alas too heavily without such Diligence, Life, and Chearfulness, as become so excellent a Service. I desire to be what I wish, and to endeavour with all my might: When shall I write that I am and do so? Lord, help me to help my self! and suffer me not to forfeit the Aids thou vouchsafest. May I improve 'em all with greater watchfulness, alacrity, and success! And may I do utmost for all that I am concern'd to help; for, &c.

Decem. 31. [1686]

The 25th I remembered my Saviour, and renew'd my Covenant at the Holy Table,[42] and before and after have taken some pains in his Service, sincerely (I hope) desiring and endeavourig to please him my self, and to help others to joyn with, yea, exceed me. May I still do better, and in the revolutions of Time, think more of, and prepare better for Eternity. Amen; for, &c.

Brenchley, Jan. 29, 1687

I hope I have been crawling upwards, though somewhat unevenly, and attempted to do good as I had occasions to converse with Men, and prepar'd my self, (at least sometimes) for Visits, that they might be useful, and not, as alas, too often lost in Impertinences. Many come and partake of what I customarily do in my Family on the Lord's Days, after publick Service. I may not exclude 'em, though uninvited.[43] I hope, and pray, and endeavour,

---

[40]Obscure, though perhaps the meaning here is that God's goodness shone through his family relationships.

[41]agnizing: acknowledging, recognizing, apprehending.

[42]i.e., he received communion.

[43]After the regular service in the parish church, many persons came to his private family prayers, making them a clandestine religious meeting of the sort that had been illegal.

that God may honour me to do their Souls some lasting good. I am sensible of God's goodness as to my private Concerns and publick Circumstances, and desire Heart and Life may be answerable; for my Saviour's sake. Amen.

I have been also disturb'd with the Extreams of some censorious Dividers; I have no Enmity against the Men, but can by no means approve their ways, nor concur as I am desir'd with 'em.

Apr. 25. 1687.

I have been doing my Duty, to the wearying and wasting of my flesh, I have been twice feasted by my Lord at his Table, I hope not without some advantage.

May 16. [1687]

The different Opinions, and especially the very indecent heats[44] of good men, to which the present liberty[45] gave vent, were no small disturbance to me.

July 2. [1687]

I desire to lay to heart the Condition of the Church of God; the woful neglects of Christian Love in all Parties, and the strange furious Heats that prey on the vital fervour of Religion, provoke God, and threaten destruction. Pity and help, O Lord; for vain is the help of man.

July 20. [1687]

(Speaking of a very deep and cutting Affliction that had often return'd.) I am far from entertaining hard thoughts of God; I heartily submit to his Soveraign Pleasure: I acknowledge his Justice might be far severer; and I am sensible of abundance of Mercy, and that I want Thankfulness, which I often beg of him. I'm still more confirm'd in the ways of Love that I have chosen, and abhor Love-killing Principles and Practices in all Parties.

Octob. 6. [1687]

Ending the 44th Year of my earthly Pilgrimage, I review'd what I wrote, Octob. 7, 1685 and found my Apprehensions of my own Condition much the same. I have continued taking pains in my Studies for the Service of Souls, to the wearying if not wasting of the Flesh; yet my Spirit hath not attain'd the frame I wish: impertinent Thoughts, wandring Imaginations, inordinate Affections, are my great and culpable Troubles. When shall I find and be able to write better! God grant that I may, whatever I suffer for't.

Decemb. 31. [1687] . . .

Yesterday I return'd from Hackney, having had a pleasant Converse with my Mother, Brother, and other dear Relations and Friends, and our pleasure was not, I hope, without some profit, though not so much as I hop'd. Growing Wickedness and approaching Sufferings we could too easily discern, and were in some measure affected with. We desire, and O may we strive more effectually to know and do our Duty how difficult soever; and Lord, pity, pardon, help and encrease thy People, and prepare us for thy blessed Will in all things; for our Lord Jesus's sake. Amen.

Aug. 6. [1688]

The 3d. my Mother came to us, and we may be longer together than we are like to be again on Earth. May our Discourses speak our sense hereof, and further our preparation for that blessed state, where parting of Friends will be no trouble.

Sept. 26. [1688]

I Yesterday assisted at the Fast in Horsmonden,[46] and being indispos'd in Body, and having too many Distractions in my Mind, I fear lest I spake unadvisedly in

---

[44]heats: fits of temper.

[45]In April 1687 a Declaration had given liberty to the dissenting Protestants.

[46]Fast in Horsmonden: such a fast was an all-day public service of prayer and fasting; Horsmonden is near Brenchley, east of Royal Tunbridge Wells.

Prayer; and yet my Head is so disturb'd, that I cannot recollect in what words I exprest my self. I have begg'd pardon of God, and the prevention or removal of offence, if any were taken, and resolv'd as Opportunities offer'd to be better prepar'd, as God shall enable by Prayer and Meditation. I am even forc'd to remove to Cranbroke, from which yet I cannot but be averse, particularly for fear of discord with ———. Lord, direct us not to neglect Holiness for Peace, nor yet to violate Peace through mistakes about Holiness. Amen; for, &c.

Octob. 11. 1688. [1688]

Last Week we remov'd from Brenchley to Cranbroke: Praised be God I came away desir'd at both Places. I had the blessing of the Poor I left, and the thanks of the publick Minister, for furthering his Work, and promoting Union among his People. Lord, make me more useful here, direct in Difficulties, support under Afflictions, and enable in all to honour thy Majesty, and effectually to promote the Salvation of others with my own. Amen; for, &c.

Nov. 29. [1688] . . .

I have been above two Months under the Chirurgeon's[47] hands for a sore Leg and Thigh. Pains have been sometimes very great; Relapses from Feavers, &c. several; Apprehensions of Death frequent: I have not, I think, been impatient; I have been without anxious Thoughts of Eternity; and willing, if God pleas'd, to leave my Body but fixedly desirous not to continue in it, unless I be and do the better for this Affliction. Twice as my ill Circumstances permitted, I view'd the Account of my self, Oct. 7, 1685. and still hope it is not false.

Of all Men, I could think only of Mr. ————, betwixt whom and my self there was any unkindness, but I think none sinful on my part. I was advis'd against meddling with him on that Subject, because I could not see it was my Duty, and it might do more harm than good.

Lord, pity me in my wearisom Condition, help me according to thy great Goodness; Refine me for thy better Service on Earth, or perfect in Heaven.

---

[47]chirurgeon: surgeon.

Introduction to Samuel Clarke,
The Life and Death
of Mrs. Katherine Clarke

Samuel Clarke (1599-1683) was the son of a clergyman and was educated at Emmanuel College, Cambridge. He was several times in trouble during the 1630s for his Nonconformity. In 1642 he became curate of St. Bennet Fink in London and during the 1640s he was prominent among the London clergy. In 1660 he joined Richard Baxter and other ministers in welcoming the king's return, but was none-theless ejected in 1662. Thereafter he lived in retirement, attending the parish churches of the Church of England and devoting himself to writing.

Early in his career as an author Clarke found a successful formula in produc-ing the lives of the pious and famous. Thus he produced The Marrow of Ecclesi-astical Historie, conteined in the lives of the fathers, and other learned men, and famous divines, which have flourished in the church since Christs time, to this present age *(London, 1650). There was a second edition of this in 1654 and a third in 1675. In 1650 he also brought out* The Second part of the Marrow of Ecclesi-astical History. *These works were followed with more biographical compilations:* A General Martyrologie *(London, 1651);* A Martyrologie *(London, 1652);* A Col-lection of the Lives of Ten Eminent Divines *(London, 1662); and* A General Mar-tyrologie . . . Whereunto is added the Lives of Thirty Two English Divines *(London, 1677) combined most of his earlier biographies. His final compilation came out in 1683—the year of his death—and bore the title* The Lives of sundry Eminent Persons in this Later Age *(London, 1683). Clarke was the author of some of these biographies, abbreviated others that had already appeared as separate works or as funeral sermons, and gained access to manuscript accounts from cor-respondents for yet others.*

He was the author of the life of his wife, Katherine Clarke, drawing on au-tobiographical fragments and devotional papers that she had left at her death as well as on his perhaps somewhat idealized memories. The account stresses her piety as the ideal Puritan wife and woman, but also portrays her as undergoing the same spiritual struggles as Puritan men.

The text is taken from The Lives of sundry Eminent Persons in this Later Age *(London, 1683; Wing C4538), sigs. Hh4ᵛ-Kk1ᵛ. (The pagination is confused, so the signatures provide more accurate guidance). For an interesting account of Samuel Clarke as a biographer, see William Haller,* The Rise of Puritanism *(New York: Columbia University Press, 1938) 102-108.*

The Life and Death of Mrs. Katherine Clarke

who Died, Anno Domini 1671.

Katherine Overton (for so was her Virgin Name) was born at Bedworth in the County of Warwick, four miles from Coventry, February the Twenty fifth, Anno Christi, 1602, of Godly, and Religious Parents. Her Father was Mr. Valentine Overton, Rector of Bedworth, where he lived a constant, and painful Preacher of God's Holy Word, till he was almost Eighty two years old. Her Mother was Mrs. Isa. Overton, a gracious Woman, and an excellent Huswife, who took off the whole burden of Family affairs, both within, and without Doors from her Husband, that he might with the more freedom attend his Holy Calling.

Our Katherine was, by these her Parents brought up Religiously, and it pleased God betimes to plant the seeds of Grace in her Heart, which first discovered themselves, when she was about fifteen years Old; At which time God was pleased to discover unto her the corruption of her nature, and some common miscarriages which are incident unto youth: And these made such a deep impression upon her tender years, that whereas she was naturally of a chearful Sanguine Constitution, she now became serious, and somewhat Melancholy. Hereupon Satan, that Old Serpent, and Enemy to our Souls, assaulted her with many, and various Temptations, whereby he sought to quench these Heavenly Sparks, to stifle this New Creature in its first Conception. But by frequent reading the sacred Scriptures, diligent attending to the Word Preached, and secret Prayer, it pleased the All-wise God to support, and strengthen her against him, and all his Devices. Yet did these conflicts continue the longer, because she had none to whom she durst unbosom her self, and make her Case known.

When she was about seventeen years old, she was by her Parents sent to Siwel [Sywell] in Northampton shire to wait upon a young Lady, that was somewhat Related to her.

Yet this kind of life was so tedious and irksome to her, that at the end of Six Months she prevailed with her Parents to send for her home again. Hear the Narrative of it in her own Words as they were found Written in her Cabinet after her Decease: "When (saith she) I was but young, my Father being at Prayers in his Family, I many times found such sweetness, and was so afflicted therewith, that I could not but wish that my Heart might oftner be in such a frame. But Childhood, and the Vanities thereof soon cooled these Heavenly Sparks. But my Father caused me to write[1] Sermons, and to repeat the same; As also to learn Mr. Perkins his Catechism,[2] which I oft repeated to my self when I was alone; And therein especially I took notice of those places wherein he had set down the Signs and Marks of a strong, and weak Faith, being convinced in my Conscience that without Faith I could not be saved; And

---

[1] write: write out, i.e., copy.

[2] William Perkins (1558-1602) was perhaps the outstanding English Calvinist theologian during the reign of Elizabeth I. Active at Cambridge and sympathetic to the Puritan movement, he wrote books that were widely used in the seventeenth century. His catechism, *The Foundation of Christian Religion* (London, 1592) influenced many later Puritan catechisms.

that every Faith would not serve turn to bring me to Heaven.

"Hereupon I fell to Examination of my self, and though I could not find the Marks of a Strong, (through God's Mercy) I found the marks of a true, though but weak Faith, which was some Comfort, and support to me. And that God which began this good work in me, was pleased to quicken and stir me up to a diligent use of such means as himself had ordained and appointed for the encrease thereof: As hearing the Word Preached, Receiving the Sacrament of the Lord's Supper, and use of other private Duties.

"But when I was about seventeen years old my Parents sent me to wait upon a Young Gentlewoman in Northampton-shire, the only Daughter of Sir W. W. At which time being sent so far from my near and dear Relations, and meeting with some other discouragements in the Family, through want of the means of Grace, which I formerly enjoyed, I grew very Melan-choly.

"I began also to have great workings of Conscience in me, and Satan (that deadly Enemy to the health, and welfare of our Souls, who like a Roaring Lion walks about continually seeking whom he may de-vour)[3] took his advantage (through my Ignorance of his devices) to raise up fears, doubts, and terrors of Conscience in me, by reason of my manifold Sins, and for walking so unworthy [of] God's Mercies whilst I did enjoy them, and for being so unfruitful under the means of Grace, and so unable to obey God, and to keep his Commandments.

"And by reason hereof I had no Peace, nor rest in my Soul, Night nor Day, but was perswaded that all the threatnings contained in the Book of God against Wicked and Ungodly men, did belong unto me, and were my Portion, as being one of them against whom they were denounced; Insomuch as when I took up the Bible to read therein, it was accompanied with much fear and trembling; Yet being convinced that it was my Duty frequently to read God's Word, I durst not omit, or neglect it.

"Thus I continued a great while, bearing the burden of grievous Temptations, and inward Afflictions of Conscience, yet durst I not open the wound, nor reveal my condition to any, as thinking and judging my condition and case to be like no Bodies else: But God who is rich and infinite in Mercy, and Jesus Christ, who bought his Elect at so dear a rate, would not suffer any of his to be lost, and therefore he was graciously pleased to preserve, strengthen, and uphold me by his own power from sinking into Hell through Despair, and from running out of my Wits.

"Thus by reason of my continual grief and anguish of Heart Night and Day, I was so weakned and changed within the compass of these six Months, that when I came home my Dear Parents they scarce knew me."

Some years after her return, she (for the most part) continued in her Father's Family, where by a diligent and conscientious use of the means, both publick and private, she did thrive and grow in Grace and in the knowledge of our Lord and Saviour Jesus Christ, as she increased and grew in Days and Years; and therewith also learned and exercised all parts of Huswifry, which might fit her for the Government of a Family, when God should call her thereunto.

February 2, Anno Christi, 1625, Which was the same Day on which King Charles the first was crowned, she was, with the consent of Parents on both sides, married to Mr. Sa[muel] Clark, who at that time was Minister at Shotwick, four miles beyond West-Chester, who looked upon this Match as the greatest outward temporal

---

[3]Allusion to 1 Peter 5:8.

Blessing that ever God bestowed upon him; whereby he could experimentally[4] say, That a Prudent Wife is the Gift of God: And that in the enjoyment of her, he enjoyed more Mercies than he could well enumerate. But to descend to particulars, and to take notice of some of these Virtues and Graces wherewith God had beautified, and adorned her Soul:

First her Piety was signal and exemplary from her first Conversion to the Hour of her Death: Her life was not stained with any scandalous Sin, which might be a blemish, either to her Person, Profession, or Relations. She was a constant, and diligent attender upon the publick Ministry of God's Holy Word; And when she lived where she had the opportunity of hearing Lectures in the week day, she made choice to attend upon those who were most plain, practical, and powerful Preachers, from whose Sermons, and God's blessing upon them, she always sucked some spiritual nourishment and came home refreshed from them. And when days of Humiliation, or Thanksgiving came, she never failed to make[5] one among God's People in the Celebration of them.

The Lord's Days she carefully Sanctified, both in publick and in private; rising earlier upon them than upon other's, especially when she had many young Children about her, that so she might have opportunity, as well for secret, as for Family duties, before she was called away to the publick. She was like unto David's Doorkeeper, One of the first in, and last out of God's House. Her constant Gesture at Prayer was Kneeling, thinking that she could not be too humble before God. Her usual manner was to write Sermons to prevent drowsiness and distractions, and to help Memory, whereof she hath left many

Volumes, and her practice was to make good use of them, by frequent reading and Meditating upon them; And if at any time she was cast into such Places, and Company as were a hinderance unto her in the strict Sanctification of this Holy Day, it was a grief and burden to her.

There was no Day that passed over her head (except Sickness, or some other unavoydable necessity hindred) wherein she did not read some portions of the Sacred Scriptures, both in the Old, and New Testament, and of the Psalms; and in Reading she took special notice of such passages as most concerned her self. She was frequent, and constant in Secret Prayer, and Meditation. She also read much in other good Books, especially, in the works of those Eminent, and excellent Divines, Mr. Ambrose, and Mr. Reynor:[6] And in reading of them she used to transcribe such passages as most warmed her heart.

She never neglected any opportunity of receiving the Sacrament of the Lord's Supper, and before her coming to it, was very strict, and serious in the Duty of Self-Examination, and for her furtherance therein, at those times she read some of those Books that treated upon that subject. And the Fruits of her holiness manifested themselves in the exercise of those Graces which God required of her. She was not a Wordy, but a Real Christian: A true Israelite, in whom was no guile.[7] Her endeavour was

---

[6]Isaac Ambrose (1604-1664) was educated at Oxford and became the vicar of Preston in Lancashire, from which he was ejected in 1662. He was highly reputed among the devout for secluding himself for prayer for a whole month (May) out of each year. He was the author of a book on the ministrations of angels. Edward Reyner was born in 1600 and educated at Cambridge. For forty years he was lecturer at St. Benedict's Cathedral, London. He wrote many books on the spiritual life. Contrary to the entry in the *Dictionary of National Biography*, he died before 1662.

[7]Allusion to John 1:47.

---

[4]experimentally: by experience.

[5]make: be.

to yield universal, constant, cheerful, and sincere Obedience to all God's Commandments, and wherein she failed, and came short, it was her grief, and Burden. Her Meditations upon what she heard and read were frequent: And her heart having indited[8] a good matter, her tongue was as the Pen of a ready Writer, taking opportunities to speak to the Edification of those with whom she conversed.

She filled every Relation with the Exercise of such Graces, and Duties as were suitable thereunto, knowing that where Relative duties are neglected, and not made Conscience of, there also our pretended Religion is in Vain.

First, As a Wife: She was singular, and very Exemplary in that reverence and obedience which she yielded to her Husband, both in Words, and Deeds. She never rose from the Table, even when they were alone, but she made courtesie.[9] She never drank to him without bowing. His Word was a Law unto her: she often denied her self to gratifie him: And when in her sickness, and weakness he mentioned her Case in particular unto God in his Prayers, the Duty being ended, she would make him courtesie, and thank him. In case of his absence she would pray with her Family Morning, and Evening: The like she would do in his presence, in case of his Sickness, and inability to perform the Duty himself. Her Modesty, and Chastity were rare, and remarkable: But fitter to be conceived by those which know what belongs to them, than to be expressed in words. For there is a conjugal, as well as a Virginal, and Vidual[10] Chastity.

In Case of her Husband's Sickness, she was a tender, diligent, and painful[11] Nurse

about him; Skilful, and careful in making him Broths, and what else was needful for him. If at any time she saw him in passion, with sweet and gentle words she would mollifie and moderate it. She was often a Spur, but never a Bridle to him in those things which were good.

She was always well pleased with such Habitations, as (in their many removes) he provided for her; And with such Apparel, and Diet as his means (which was sometimes short) would allow. She never grutched,[12] nor grumbled at any of those Dispensations which God's All-wise Providence carved out unto them.

Secondly, As a Mother to her Children (whereof God gave her nine, four Sons, and five Daughters) she nourished them all with her own breasts; was very handy and handsome about them in their minority; Kept them sweet and cleanly; In neat and modest Habits;[13] Knew how to order them both in Health and Sickness. She loved them dearly without fondness;[14] Was careful to give them Nurture as well as Nourishment, not sparing the Rod when there was just occasion. And as soon as they were capable, she was vigilant and diligent to season their tender years with Grace and Vertue, by instilling into them the first grounds, and Principles of Religion; And as they grew up, she did more freely discover her tender Affections to them, by Instruction, advice and good Counsel as there was occasion; And when they were disposed of abroad, by her gracious letters, and hearty Instructions at their meetings, she laboured to build them up in grace and godliness: And God was pleased to let her see (to her great joy and comfort) the fruits of her prayers and pains in keeping them from scandalous Courses in these corrupt times, and in

---

[8]indited: declared, uttered.

[9]courtesie: curtsy.

[10]Vidual: pertaining to widowhood.

[11]painful: painstaking.

[12]grutched: complained.

[13]Habits: clothes.

[14]Fondness: foolishness, overindulgence.

working Grace in most of their Hearts. When they were married, and had Children, she was frequently making one thing or other for them.

Thirdly, As a Mistress to her Maids: She was careful (so far as she could) to bring such as were Religious, at least, seemingly, into her Family; And having occasion to be much in their Company, she would take all occasions, and opportunities to manifest her love and care of their Souls, by frequent dropping in good Counsel, and wholesome Instructions; By Chatechising; Enquiring what they remembred of the Sermons they heard; Reading her Notes to them; Encouraging them in what was good, and with the Spirit of meekness blaming them for what was evil. And for Huswifery, and Houshold Affairs, she instructed their Ignorance, commended and incouraged what they did well, and her self (being of an active, and stirring disposition, and having her hand in most businesses) set them a Pattern, and gave them an Example how to order the same. She was careful (so far as possibly she could) to prevent all spoil, and to see that they did not eat the Bread of Idleness.

Towards her friends, and her own, and her Husband's Relations she was courteous and amiable in her deportment, free and hearty in their entertainment. She would have plenty without want, and competency without superfluity; And all so neatly and well ordered, that none which came to her Table (whereof some were Persons of Honor and Quality) but Commended her Cookery, and were well pleased with their entertainment.

In her Houshold Furniture she loved not to want, nor desired more than was needful. It was, though not costly, yet cleanly, and she was frequent in repairing and mending decays, and what was amiss, both in Linnens, and Woollens.

For her Apparel, she was never willing to have that which was costly for the matter, or gairish for the manner: Rather under than above her Rank. For the Fashion of it, was grave and Exemplary, without Newfangledness and Levity. She followed Peter's directions which he gave to Christian Women in his time (1 Pet. 3:3, &c.) "whose adorning, let it not be that outward adorning of plaiting their Hair, and of wearing of Gold, or of putting on of Apparel. But let it be the hidden man of the Heart, in that which is not corruptible, even the Ornament of a meek and quiet Spirit, which is in the sight of God of great price. For after this manner in old time, the holy Women who trusted in God adorned themselves being in subjection unto their own Husbands."

And whatsover Apparel she had, she was careful to keep it from stains, and rends, and so soon as any thing was amiss, presently to amend it, insomuch as she made it last long, and yet it was always whole and neat. All her own, and Husband's linnens, she made her self, and much of her other Apparel: And at leisure times she imployed her self in knitting Stockings for her self and Grand Children; and was as careful, and handy in mending her Husband's Cloaths, as her own.

She was very Charitable to the Poor where ever she lived, according to that Estate wherewith God had entrusted her. She was ready to relieve such as were Objects of Charity, with Meat, or Drink, and to lend them Mony, and to minister some Phisical things (whereof her Closet was never empty) according as their necessities required.

She had a very melting Heart, and truly Sympathized with the Church and People of God, whether at home or abroad, in all their sufferings, and rejoyced in their Prosperity. She was much affected with, and afflicted for that great loss which the Church of Christ had, when so many able,

Godly, faithful, and painful Ministers were ejected;[15] not thrust forth into, but thrust out from labouring in God's Harvest; wherein her Husband, and two Sons were co-sufferers, to the loss of their livelihoods; yet the loss of their Liberty lay nearer to her Heart, and was a far greater Grief to her than the outward wants they were exposed to.

Her Humility was not inferior to her other Graces. She had always a very low esteem of her self, and was ready to prefer others before her self, and would not take it ill when her inferiors were set above her; She well remembered the Apostle Peter's charge, "All of you be subject one to another, and be cloathed with Humility. For God resisteth the Proud, and giveth Grace to the Humble."[16] And that of S. Paul, Rom. 12:10, "In honour prefer one another."

Her Love to God, to his Ordinances, and to his Children was hearty, and without Dissimulation. She abhorred that which was evil, and clave to that which was good.[17] She was of so sweet and meek a disposition that she never used to speak evil of any, but was ever prone to forgive and forget wrongs.

She was very prudent in managing her Houshold affairs to the best advantage. She would have divers Dishes of Meat with little cost; yet so dressed and ordered as made them grateful and pleasing unto all: When they were alone, she had such variety of Dishes and Dresses as prevented nauseousness.[18] She was careful to see that nothing was lost or spoiled. By her wise and frugal managing her Houshold, though

her Husband had never much coming in, yet at the year's end he could always save something: So that her price to him was far above Rubies: His Heart trusted in her. For she did him good, and not evil all the Days of her Life, Prov. 31:10, 11, 12.

In her Younger Days she was healthful; Of a cheerful and active Spirit, and abhorring Idleness; She would have her Hand in every business. In her Old Age, though she was crazie,[19] yet whilst she could stand, she would be about one kind of work or other. She bore her weakness and Afflictions with much Patience and holy submission to the will and good pleasure of God; she was so uniform in the frame of her Spirit, and so maintained her Peace with God through her Holy and humble walking, that when Death, many times in her sickness, threatned to seize upon her, She feared it not, as knowing that it would be gain and advantage to her: Concerning which hear what she her self left in writing which was found after her Decease:

"In my younger Days (saith she) my spiritual Afflictions, and inward troubles continued long before I could attain to any assurance of my Salvation: But of late years it hath pleased God of his infinite Mercy, and Free Grace to give me more Assurance of his unchangeable Love to me through Faith in his Rich and free Promises of Life, and Salvation, through Jesus Christ, who is pretious to my Soul, and who is the Author and finisher of my Faith; God blessed for evermore: To whom be Praise and Glory World without end Amen."

In her converse with her Friends "She opened her Mouth with Wisdom, and in her Tongue was the Law of Kindness" (Prov. 31:26)[20] which made her Company grate-

---

[15]The St. Bartholomew's-day ejection of Puritan clergy who would not accept the terms of the Act of Uniformity (24 August 1662).

[16]1 Peter 5:5.

[17]Allusion to Romans 12:9.

[18]nauseousness: indigestion.

[19]crazie: weak.

[20]Here, as in other biblical allusions and quotations, Clarke changes the tense of verbs to fit the historical past of his own narrative.

ful unto all, and burdensom, or undervalued by none.

Divers years before her Death, upon catching Cold, she had many fits of sickness, and weakness, and some of them were so violent, as brought her near unto Death; Yet the Lord had mercy upon her Husband and Family in raising her up again almost beyond hopes, and expectation: And she was always a Gainer by her Afflictions, God making good that Promise to her, Rom. 8:28, "All things shall work together for good to them that love God, To them who are Called according to the [his] purpose." For after those fits she walked more humbly, holily, fruitfully, and faithfully, both in her General, and particular Calling, as one that waited daily for the appearing of her Lord, and Master. The Winter before her Death, she enjoyed better Health than she had done for some Winters before.

May the 25th, Anno Christi, 1675, Some Friends came from London to dine with her, and that morning (according to her usual custom in such Cases) She was careful, and busie in providing for their kind entertainment: But it pleased God whilst they were at Dinner to strike her with a kind of Shivering, which made her look paler than ordinary, and after Dinner her Distemper continued, so that she was soon confined to her Chamber, and not long after, for the most part to her Bed. But herein God shewed her great mercy, and had respect to her weakness, in that, during all the time of her languishing she was free from Sickness,[21] and pain, only sometimes she was troubled with some Stiches,[22] which yet were tolerable, not violent: She was also troubled with some Vapours which made her Breath very short; Yet had she a pretty good Stomach, and she relished her Food well till about two Days before her Death; But then, though she did eat, yet she found little tast in her Meat. Her sleep was pretty good, and always very quiet. She was never ill either after Food or Sleep. Only two Days before her Departure she slept little, by reason of the continual ratling of phlegm in her Throat, when she wanted[23] strength to expectorate it.

As for the State of her Soul during all the time of her sickness, she enjoyed constant Peace and Serenity, and had (through God's Mercy) much Joy, and Peace, by believing; Satan (that Roaring Lion) who uses to be most strong when we are most weak being so chained up by God, that he had no power to molest her. She often cryed out "Hold out faith and patience;" She told her nearest Relation, when she saw him mourning over her, that she was going to be joyned to a Better Husband.

Her youngest Son, taking his leave of her the Day before her Death, she gave him much Heavenly Counsel for the good of his Soul, and Blessed him, and all his, as she did the rest of her Children and Grand-Children. She earnestly desired to be Dissolved, and breathed after a fuller enjoyment of Jesus Christ, which she accounted best of all: She would sometimes say, that it was a hard thing to die: And this is a hard work. Her Understanding, Memory, and Speech continued till within two Minutes of Death; And a little before, her Daughter speaking to her of Jesus Christ, She replyed, "My God and my Lord:" And so June the 21, about five a Clock in the morning, She fell asleep, exchanging this Life for a Better, without any alteration in her Countenance, but only that her colour was gone. She closed up her Eyes herself, as who should say, It is but winking, and I shall be in Heaven. She changed her place,

---

[21]Sickness: vomiting.

[22]Stitches: sudden sharp pains.

[23]wanted: lacked.

but not her Company. She sickned May the 25th, *Anno Christi,* 1675. She concluded her Days June the Twenty First, being Monday, about five a Clock in the Morning; when having ended her last Sabbath upon Earth, she began to Celebrate an Everlasting Sabbath in Heaven. She was Aged Seventy three years and about four Months, and had been married almost Fifty years.

Thus did this Holy Woman wear out, not rust out: Burn out, was not blown out: Yea, she flamed, not smothered out, she served God in her Generation, and then retired into that Place where is health without Sickness: Day without Night: Plenty without Famine: Riches without Poverty: Mirth without Mourning: Singing without sighing: Life without Death: And these, with infinite more to all Eternity. There[24] is unspotted Chastity: Unstained Honor: Unparalleled Beauty. There is the Tree of Life in the midst of this Paradise. There is the River that waters the Garden: There is the Vine flourishing, and the Pomegranate budding: There is the Banqueting House where are all those Delicacies, and Rarities wherewith God himself is delighted. There shall the Saints be adorned, as a Bride, with rare Pearls, and sparkling Diamonds of Glory. A Glory fitter to be Believed, than possible to be Discoursed. An Exceeding, Excessive, Eternal weight of Glory (2 Cor. 4:17). Even such a weight, as if the Body were not upheld by the Power of God, it were impossible but that it should faint under it: as an eminent Divine speaketh.

After Mrs. Clarke's Decease, there was found in her Cabinet a Paper, which by frequent using, was almost worn out. It contained a Collection of these several Texts of Scripture which she had recourse unto in times of Temptation, or Desertion.

"Who is among you that feareth the Lord: That obeyeth the Voice of his Servant: That walketh in darkness and hath no Light: Let him trust in the Name of the Lord and stay upon his God,'' Isaiah 50.10.

For "the Name of the Lord is a strong Tower; The Righteous run unto it, and are safe,'' Prov. 18:10.

"Thou wilt keep him in perfect peace, whose Mind is stayed on thee, because he trusteth on [in] thee,'' Isaiah 26:3.

"Blessed is the Man that maketh the Lord his trust,'' Psa. 40:4. "Blessed is the Man [on] to whom the Lord imputeth not Sin,'' Psa. 32:2.[25]

Though our hearts may fail us, and our flesh fail us, yet God will never fail us, Psa. 73:26.

"For he hath said, I will never leave thee nor forsake thee,'' Heb. 13:5.

And again: I "will be a Father unto you, and ye shall be my Sons and Daughters, saith the Lord Almighty,'' 2 Cor. 6:18.

"I, even I am he that blotteth out thy Transgressions for mine own sake, and will not remember thy Sins,'' Isaiah 44[3]:25.

"My Grace is sufficient for thee: For my strength is made perfect in weakness,'' 2 Cor. 12:9.

"By Grace you are saved through Faith, and that not of yourselves,'' Eph. 2:8.

"I give unto them Eternal Life, and they shall not [never] perish, neither shall any man pluck them out of my Hand,'' Joh. 10:28.

"Who are kept by the Power of God, through Faith unto Salvation,'' 1 Pet. 1:5.

"The foundation of God standeth sure having this Seal; The Lord knoweth who [them that] are his,'' 2 Tim. 2:19.

"There is therefore now no condemnation to them which are in Christ Jesus,

---

[24]i.e., in heaven.

[25]"Iniquity" in the KJV has been changed to "sin."

who walk not after the Flesh, but after the Spirit,'' Rom. 8:1.

"Christ is the end of the Law for Righteousness to every one that believeth,'' Rom. 10:4.

"It is God that justifieth; who is he that condemneth?'' Rom. 8:33, 34.

"The promise is to you, and to your Children, and to all that are afar off; Even as many as the Lord our God shall call,'' Acts 2:39.

"The Gifts, and Calling of God are without Repentance,'' Rom. 11:29.

These Texts of Scripture having been as so many Cordials[26] unto her in Times of Temptation, it is hoped that they may prove so to others, and therefore for their sakes they are here set down. And hereby it appears that she was not without some shakings, but through God's Mercy, they were such as made her root the faster: And by her prudent, and seasonable holding forth the Shield of Faith, and the Sword of the Spirit, she became more than a Conqueror, through him that had loved her.

In another little Book, which was found after her Death, she gives this account of her self and of God's gracious dealing with her:

"From the beginning (writes she) of God's shewing me Mercy in my Conversion.

"I here set down God's gracious dealings with me, not for mine own Praise, but for the Glory of God, and to stir up my Heart unto true Thankfulness for such invaluable Mercies.'' And then she set down the time, manner, and means of her Conversion: And afterwards proceeds thus.

"What have been my Experiences of God's gracious dealings with me at several times under Afflictions: As

"First when Personal Afflictions have lain upon me, in regard of Bodily Sickness or Spiritual Distempers.

"Secondly. Or, Family Afflictions, when God hath taken away my dear Children.

"Thirdly: Or, when I have been under fears that God would take away my dear husband, by some dangerous sickness which he lay under.

"Fourthly, Or when I have been under great fears in the time of our Civil Wars.

"Fifthly, Or when I have been under spiritual Desertion, by God's hiding his Face, and Favour from me. Or by reason of weakness, and wants in Grace: Or by reason of strong, and prevailing Corruptions. Or by reason of Satan's Temptations:'' In all which Cases she left a memorial of God's gracious dispensations towards her. I shall set down only a few of them.

"It pleased God (saith she) for many years, to keep me (for the most part) in a sad and disconsolate Estate, and condition, not clearly Evidencing the certain Assurance of his Love to my Soul: So that many times I questioned whether I was a Child of God or no: Whether I had part in Christ Jesus or no: Whether I should ever attain to Life and Salvation or no: And this made me walk with a drooping, and disconsolate Spirit, so that I could take no true comfort in any thing: But though heaviness endured for a Night, Yet joy came in the Morning,[27] when the Lord caused the Light of his Countenance to shine upon me, which was better than Life.

"It pleased God upon the Death of my youngest Child, that it lay very heavy upon my Spirit, insomuch as I was brought oft upon my Knees to beg support from God and to crave his Grace and assistance that I might not break out to speak, or act any thing whereby God's Name might be dis-

---

[26]Cordials: ingratiating agents.

[27]Allusion to Psalm 30:5.

honoured, or the Gospel discredited: And that he would be pleased to make up this outward loss, with some more durable, and spiritual Comforts. And I found a seasonable, gracious, and speedy answer to these my Requests. For though I lay long under the burden of that loss, yet in this time did the Lord sweetly manifest his special Love to my Soul, assuring me that he was my gracious and reconciled Father in Christ; whereby my Love to him was much encreased, and even inflamed; so that, by his Grace, it wrought in me more diligence, and carefulness to maintain and preserve these Evidences of his Love, and to yield a holy submission unto his Will, as well in suffering, as in doing: As also by avoiding whatsoever might provoke him to withdraw the Evidences of his Love from me, without the sense whereof I could take little or no comfort in any thing.

"And furthermore, I bless God for it, and speak it to the praise and glory of his rich and free Grace, my Prayers, and earnest desires have been answered by God's giving me comfortable Assurance, both from the Testimony of his holy word, and the witness of his Blessed Spirit, of my Eternal, and Everlasting Salvation in, and by Jesus Christ. Yet have I not been without fears, and doubtings many times, through want of looking over my Evidences, or by neglecting to keep a narrow watch over my heart: Or from weakness of my Faith, and all through my own default and negligence. The Lord pardon it, and make me more circumspect for the time to come.

"By all these I have gained this Experience.

"First: That God is true and faithful in making good all his Promises seasonably unto us: As, That all things shall work together for our Good. And that God will never fail us, nor forsake us. &c.

"Secondly: That it is not in vain to wait upon God, and to seek unto him in our straits, who is more ready to hear than we are to ask.

"Thirdly: That I desire to see: Yea, and the Lord hath shewed me the vanity, and incertainty of the most satisfying Comforts this world can afford, and what an emptiness there is in them, that so I may, and I desire so to do, keep weaned affections towards them to sit loose from them, that I may be ready to part with them, when God calls them from me, or me from them.

"Again in regard of Bodily weakness and sickness, my Experiences have been these.

"First: That as a broken Shoulder can bear no burden; so the least Distemper, when the heart is not in an holy frame and temper is a burden insupportable. If God hides his Face from us, and withdraws the Evidences of his Love, and denies to assist us by his strength, we can neither do, nor suffer any thing. And on the Contrary, I found by Experience, that I could with much cheerfulness, holy submission and willingness, bear great Distempers, when I enjoyed the favour of God in them: So that then I could readily say, Good is the work of the Lord as well as is his Word. And, 'I will bear the Indignation of the Lord because I have sinned against him,' Mich. 7:9. And, 'Though he slay me, yet will I trust him,' Job. 13:15.

"Secondly, I found by experience also, that by my pains and sickness I was the better able to Sympathize with, and to pity and pray for others in the like case.

"Thirdly, Hereby I learned the more to prize Health: And that: First, Because in Health we have liberty, and opportunity to enjoy the Publick Ordinances with others of God's People, whereby the Graces of God's people are quickned, strengthened, and encreased in us, which otherwise (by reason of our corrupt natures) are apt to grow cold and languish, as will our bodies when they want food.

"Secondly, Because in health we injoy the benefit and the comfort of sweet, and quiet sleep, which much refreshes and cheers, and which commonly we want in sickness.

"Thirdly, Because in Health we find sweet satisfying comfort in the use of God's good Creatures, whereas in sickness the daintiest food is lothsome and troublesome. The consideration of these things made me the more to prize Health; To be very thankful for it, and the more careful to imploy, and improve Health and strength, to God's glory, and the furtherance of mine own salvation.

"In regard of Publick Dangers I have had a great deal of Experience of God's goodness towards me and mine several ways, and at several times. For

"First, When in the beginning of our Civil Wars and distractions I was sometimes overwhelmed with base and distrustful fears, occasioned by my not acting[28] faith upon the promises, and not remembring my former Experiences, nor considering God's love, power, and fidelity to his Children, in performing his so many gracious promises, made unto them in all estates, and conditions, and to me among the rest: Hereupon I resolved, by God's grace and assistance not to give way to this distrust and diffidence, praying God to assist me therein, and found more courage than formerly, so far as I know mine own Heart (though truly the Heart is very deceitful, as I have found by sad experience). The Lord teach and enable me to rely upon him with more courage and constancy, and more to live by faith upon his promises than formerly I have done.

"Indeed I have been apt to fall into new fears upon approaching dangers; Yet upon

---

[28]acting: exercising, causing to act.

successes, and glorious deliverances, I have oft resolved never to distrust God again, and yet my naughty heart hath deceived me, and made me ready to faint. But this I found by Experience, to the praise of my God's free grace, that as troubles have abounded, my consolations have much more abounded. For God brought seasonably into my mind many pretious promises, which were as so many sweet Cordials, which much supported and comforted my heart, and upheld my Spirit, when also new storms have arisen, and unexpected deliverances have followed, I have, and do resolve, by God's grace, not to distrust him any more. Yea, though more and greater dangers shall arise, yet will I trust in, and stay my self upon him, though (as Job said) he should slay me. The good Lord establish my heart in this good and holy resolution, who is able to keep us to the end, and hath promised that he will preserve us by his power, through Faith to the Salvation of our Souls.

"In regard of Satan's Temptations; Especially concerning my coming to the Sacrament of the Lord's Supper, my Experiences have been these:

"Finding often that I was very unable to sit and prepare my self for a comfortable approach to that Sacred Ordinance, I used to desire the Prayèrs of the Congregation unto God in my behalf, and I used the best endeavours I could in private, as God enabled me, though I came far short of what was required, and of what I desired: So that I did trust, and hope, through God's mercy, to find a comfortable day of it, and to have it a Sealing Ordinance to my Soul. But on the contrary, I found much deadness, and little spiritual tast, relish, and comfort in the use of it: So that my spirit was oft much troubled, and cast down in me; fearing lest I had some secret sin undiscovered, and unrepented of, which caused the Lord thus to hide his face from me.

"But then my gracious God brought this into my mind, that the Lord doth sometimes afflict us for the exercise, and improvement of our graces, as well as to humble us for our sins. I also considered, that as the Lord doth tender great Mercies to us in this Sacrament, renewing his Covenant of grace, and sealing unto us the Pardon of our sins in the blood of Christ: So he gives us leave to engage our selves (by renewing our Covenant with him) to believe in him, and to trust upon Christ for Life and Salvation: And it pleased God to give me faith to apply this in particular to my own Soul: And a while after, to shew me, and to make good to my Soul that pretious, and comfortable promise, That though he hide his face from us for a little moment, yet with Mercy, and Loving kindness he will return to us again. This was a wonderful comfort, and support to my dejected Heart: Blessed be the Lord forever, I desire to treasure up these Experiences, that for the future, I may resolve in the like case to put my whole trust and confidence in him, that so Satan may not entrap me in his snares through unbelief, but that I may resist him steadfast in the faith: For I am not altogether ignorant of his Devices. God's promise is that in all these things we shall be more than Conquerours, through him that hath loved us:[29] And hath said that 'this is the Victory which overcomes the World, even our faith,' I John 5:4.

"In the year 1669, There came to us the sad news of the Death of my second Son, Mr. John Clarke, a godly, faithful, and painful Minister, sometimes before ejected[30] out of the Rectory of Cotgrave in Nottingham-shire, who died the 18th, of September.

"Thus as the Waves of the Sea follow one another, so God is pleased to exercise his Children with one Affliction after another. He sees that whilst we carry about with us this Body of sin, we have need of manifold Trials, and Temptations, as saith the Apostle, I Pet. 1:6—'now for a season (if need be) ye are in heaviness through manifold Temptations;' to keep us under, and to make us the better to remember our selves.

"Indeed it hath been the Lord's course and dealing with me ever since he stopped me in the way as I was posting[31] to Hell, to raise up one Affliction or other, either inward or outward, either from Satan, the World, or from mine own corrupt Heart, and nature, not having Grace and Wisdom to behave and carry my self as I ought under his various Dispensations and Providences, as appeared at this time by his laying so great and grievous an Affliction upon me in taking away so dear a Son, from whom I had much Soul-comfort, and ardent Affections, which he manifested by his fervent Prayers for me, and by his spiritual Letters, and Writings to me, wherein he applied himself sutably [sic] to my Comfort in those inward troubles of Heart and Spirit which lay upon me. This caused my Grief and Sorrows to take the greater hold on me, upon the loss of one who was so useful to me: Yet hereby I do not derogate from my Elder Son, from whom I have the like help, and Comfort.

"Upon this sad occasion my Grief grew so great that I took no pleasure of any thing in the World: But was so overwhelmed with Melancholy, and my natural strength was so abated, that little Food served my turn, and I judged that I could not live long in such a condition.

"Hereupon I began to examine my Heart why it should be so with me, and

---

[29]Allusion to Romans 8:37.

[30]He was one of the ministers ejected by the Act of Uniformity.

[31]posting: hastening.

whether carnal and immoderate Affections were not the great Cause of my trouble, which I much feared; And having used many Arguments and laid down many reasons to my self to quiet and moderate my Passions, and yet nothing prevailed to quiet and calm my Heart, and to bow me to the Obedience of his revealed Will: And withal, considering that it was God only that could quiet the Heart, and set our unruly, and carnal Affections into an holy frame and order, and, That he was a present Help in times of trouble, I often and earnestly sought unto the Lord with many Prayers, and Tears, beseeching him to quiet my Heart, and to over-power and tame my unruly Affections, so as to be willing to submit unto him, and to bear his Afflicting Hand patiently and fruitfully, and to be ready and willing to submit (either in doing or suffering) to whatsoever he pleased to impose upon me: And to be ready to part with the best outward Comfort I enjoyed whensoever he should please to call for the same.

"And it pleased God seasonably to hear my Prayer, to regard my Tears, and to grant my Requests, by calming, and quieting my heart, and spirit, and by giving me much more contentedness to submit to his Holy Will, and good Pleasure, who is a God of judgment, and knows the fittest times and seasons to come in with refreshing comforts, and who waits to be gracious unto those that trust in him. Yet surely I was not without many Temptations in this hour of Darkness from that subtile Adversary who always stands at watch to insinuate and frame his Temptations answerable to our Conditions, and like a Roaring Lyon walks about continually, seeking to devour poor, yet precious Souls. Then I called upon the Lord in my distress, and he answered me and delivered me.[32]

" 'Bless the Lord O my Soul; and all that is within me Praise [bless] his Holy Name.'[33] For he hath remembered me in my low and troubled estate, and because his Mercy endureth for ever.

"Having thus had new experience of God's readiness to hear and help when I called upon him: And having found that it is not in vain to seek to, and to depend upon God in all our Straits, I could not but record these things, that so Every one that is Godly may seek unto him in a time wherein he may be found, who is a present help in times of trouble, and who doth for us abundantly above what we can ask, or think.

"The Lord knows that I write these things for no other end, but that God may have the Glory, and that others, especially my Relations, may be encouraged to seek God in their Straits, and to trust in him at all times. Amen."

After her Decease there was also found in her Cabinet a Paper with this Superscription:

"My Will and Desire is (with the leave of my Husband) to bestow upon my Children these things as tokens of my Motherly Affections, and that I may be remembered by them." She began with her Husband, and what she gave to him and all the rest, were all wrapped up in several Papers, and each Name endorsed on the outside to whom it did belong. And then concludes all thus:

"But above all, my Prayers unto God are, that he would especially bestow upon you, all needful Saving Graces, whereby you may be enabled to glorifie his Great Name, in those several places and callings wherein he hath set you. Amen. Amen."

She left also Legacies to some poor Neighbours: As also ten shillings to Mr. W.

---

[32]Allusion to Psalm 18:6.

[33]Psalm 103:1.

the Minister of the place, to buy him a mourning Ring: Concluding thus,

"If God shall please to bring me to my Grave in Peace, let this be the Text at my Funeral, Ephes. 2:8; 'For by Grace ye are saved, through Faith.' This Scripture I was oft put upon to have recourse to in times of Temptations, and Desertion."

In an other little Book she had collected sundry Texts of Scripture, which might minister grounds of great Comfort against Satan's Temptations, whereby he labours, by setting before us a black Bill of our Sins, and daily Infirmities, and our great inabilities to every Good Duty, to blot out our Evidences, to stagger our Faith, and to make us go heavily, and drooping in our way to Heaven.

Introduction to James Janeway,
A Token for Children
and *Invisibles, Realities*

James Janeway (1636-1674) was educated for the ministry at Oxford and was cited by Edmund Calamy—the historian of Nonconformity (d. 1732)—as one of the ejected clergy, though there is no record that he had been an incumbent minister. In the 1660s he was active as a Nonconformist preacher.

James Janeway was the author of a number of pious works, many of which focused on holy dying. Several of these went through many editions. In 1667 he published Heaven on Earth *(seven reprintings before 1700);* Death Unstung *followed in 1669 and was reprinted four times.* A Token for Children *came out in 1672 and was still being reprinted in the early nineteenth century. It is an example of Puritan literature intended for children and told the stories of devout children who had died young.* Invisibles, Realities *came out in 1673 and had seven printings by 1698. It tells the story, with an emphasis on his holy death, of James Janeway's younger brother John, who died in 1657 at the age of twenty-four, before he had entered into the ministry for which he had prepared at Cambridge. Imbedded in the narrative is also the deathbed scene of the Janeway brothers' father. Published after James Janeway's death was* Mr. James Janeway's Legacy to His Friends: Containing Twenty-Seven Famous Instances of God's Providences in and about Sea-Dangers and Deliverances *(London, 1683). This work was compiled by John Ryther, who appended a sermon of his own on the same subject. It was reprinted in an enlarged form in 1721 as* A Token for Mariners.

That which follows consists of Janeway's "Preface to Parents and School Masters" and two lives from A Token for Children: Being An Exact Account of the Conversion, Holy and Exemplary Lives, and Joyful Deaths, of several young children *(London, 1676; Wing J478), sigs. A3^r-A5^v, 27-38 and* A Token for Children. The Second Part *(London, 1673; Wing J480aA), 61-64. These are the first edition of the second part and the first available edition of the first part. (One copy of the first edition is extant, located in a Scottish library). The selections from* Invisibles, Realities, Demonstrated in the Holy Life and Triumphant Death of Mr. John Janeway, Fellow of Kings Colledge in Cambridge *(London, 1673; Wing J470) are from the first edition, 24-29, 39-42, 46, 58-60, 71-74, 91-93, 98-113, 118-120. For more detail on Janeway see the brief entry in* The Dictionary of National Biography, *by Alexander Gordon.*

A Token for Children:

Being
An Exact Account of the Conversion, Holy and Exemplary Lives,
and Joyful Deaths, of several young Children.

By James Janeway,
Minister of the Gospel.

TO ALL PARENTS, SCHOOL-MASTERS AND SCHOOL-MISTRESSES, OR ANY THAT HAVE ANY HAND IN THE EDUCATION OF CHILDREN.

Dear Friends,

I have oft thought that Christ speaks to you, as Pharaoh's Daughter did to Moses's Mother: Take this Child and Nurse It for me. O Sirs, consider what a precious Jewel is committed to your charge, what an advantage you have to shew your love to Christ, to stock the next Generation with Noble Plants, and what a joyful account you may make, if you be faithful: Remember, Souls, Christ, and Grace, cannot be over-valued. I confess you have some disadvantages,[1] but let that only excite your diligence: the Salvation of Souls, the commendation of your Master, the greatness of your reward, and everlasting glory, will pay for all. Remember the Devil is at work hard, wicked ones are industrious, and a corrupt nature is a rugged knotty piece to hew; but be not discouraged, I am almost as much afraid of your laziness and unfaithfulness, as any thing. Do but fall to work lustily, and who knows but that rough stone may prove a Pillar in the Temple of God? In the Name of the living God, as you will answer it shortly at his Bar, I command you to be faithful in Instructing and Catechizing your young ones; If you think I am too peremptory, I pray read the command from my Master himself, Deut. 6:7.

---

[1] disadvantages: hindrances.

Is not the duty clear? and dare you neglect so direct a Command? Are the Souls of your Children of no value? Are you willing that they should be Brands of Hell? Are you indifferent whether they be Damned or Saved? shall the Devil run away with them without controul? Will not you use your utmost endeavour to deliver them from the wrath to come? you see that they are not Subjects uncapable of the Grace of God; whatever you think of them, Christ doth not slight them; they are not too little to dye, they are not too little to go to Hell, they are not too little to serve their great Master, too little to go to Heaven; For of such is the Kingdom of God: And will not a possibility of their Conversion and Salvation, put you upon the greatest diligence to teach them? Or are Christ, and Heaven, and Salvation, small things with you? If they be, then indeed I have done with you: but if they be not, I beseech you lay about you with all your might; the Devil knows your time is going apace, it will shortly be too late. O therefore what you do, do quickly; and do it, I say, with all your might; O pray, pray, pray, and live holily before them, and take some time daily to speak a little to your Children, one by one, about their miserable condition by Nature: I knew a Child that was converted by this sentence, from a godly School-mistress in the Country: "Every Mother's Child of you are by Nature Children of wrath." Put your Children upon Learning their Catechism, and the Scriptures, and getting to pray and weep by themselves after Christ: take heed of their company; take heed of pardoning a lye; take heed of letting them mispend the Sabbath; put them, I beseech you, upon imitating these sweet Children;[2] let them Read this Book over an hundred times, and observe how they are affected, and ask them what they think of those Children, and whether they would not be such? and follow what you do with earnest cries to God, and be in travel[3] to see Christ formed in their Souls. I have prayed for you, I have oft prayed for your Children, and I love them dearly; and I have prayed over these papers, that God would strike in with them, and make them effectual to the good of their Souls. Incourage your Children to read this Book, and lead them to improve[4] it. What is presented, is faithfully taken from experienced solid Christians, some of them no way related to the Children, who themselves were Eye and Ear-witnesses of God's works of Wonder; or from my own knowledg[e], or from Reverend godly Ministers, and from Persons that are of unspotted reputation for Holiness, Integrity and Wisdom; and several passages are taken verbatim in writing, from their dying Lips. I may add many other excellent Examples, if I have any encouragement in this Piece. That the young generation may be far more excellent than this, is the Prayer of one that dearly loves little Children.

James Janeway

[2]i.e., those whose stories follow.

[3]travel: travail.

[4]improve: make good use of.

Example III

Of a little Girl that was wrought upon, when she was between four and five years old, with some account of her holy life and triumphant death.

1. Mary A. When she was between four and five years old, was greatly affected in hearing the word of God, and became very solicitous about her Soul and everlasting condition, weeping bitterly to think what would become of her in another World, asking strange questions concerning God and Christ, and her own soul: so that this little Mary, before she was full five years old, seemed to mind the one thing needful, and to choose the better part, and sat at the feet of Christ many a time and oft with tears.[5]

2. She was wont to be much in secret duty, and many times came off from her knees with tears.

3. She would chuse such times and places for secret duty, as might render her less observed by others, and did endeavour what possibly she could to conceal what she was doing when she was engaged in secret duty.

4. She was greatly afraid of hypocrisie, and of doing any thing to be seen of men, and to get commendation and praise; and when she hath heard one of her Brothers saying, that he had been by himself at prayer, she rebuked him sharply, and told him how little such prayers were like to profit him, and that was little to his praise

[5]Allusion to Luke 10:42.

to pray like a hypocrite, and to be glad that any should know what he had been doing.

5. Her Mother being full of sorrow after the death of her Husband, this Child came to her Mother, and askt her why she wept so exceedingly? her Mother answered, she had cause enough to weep, because her Father was dead: "No, dear Mother," said the Child, "you have no cause to weep so much, for God is a good God still to you."

6. She was a dear lover of faithful Ministers. One time after she had been hearing of Mr. Whitaker,[6] she said "I love that man dearly for the sweet words that he speaks concerning Christ."

7. Her Book was her delight, and what she did read she loved to make her own, and cared not for passing over what she learned without extraordinary observations and understanding; and many times she was so strangely affected in reading of the Scriptures, that she would burst out into tears, and would hardly be pacified, so greatly was she taken with Christ's sufferings, the zeal of God's Servant, the danger of a natural state.

8. She would complain oftentimes of the corruption of her nature, of the hardness of her heart, that she could repent no more thorowly, and be no more humble and grieved for her sins against a good God; and when she did thus complain, it was with abundance of tears.

9. She was greatly concerned for the souls of others, and grieved to think of the miserable condition that they were in; upon this account, when she could handsomly, she would be putting in some pretty sweet word for Christ; but above all, she would

do what she could to draw the hearts of her brethren and sisters after Christ; and there was no small hopes, that her example and good counsel did prevail with some of them when they were very young to get into corners to pray, to ask very gracious questions about the things of God.

10. She was very conscientious in keeping the Sabbath, spending the whole time either in reading or praying, or learning her Catechism, or teaching her Brethren and Sisters. One time when she was left at home upon the Lord's day, she got some other little children together with her brothers and sisters, and instead of playing (as other naughty children use to do) she told them, that that was the Lord's day, and that they ought to remember that day to keep it holy; and then she told them how it was to be spent in religious exercises all the day long, except so much as was to be taken up in the works of necessity and mercy; then she prayed with them her self, and among other things begged, that the Lord would give grace and wisdom to these little Children, that they might know how to serve him, as one of the little ones in the company with her, told afterwards.

11. She was a Child of a strange tenderness and Compassion to all, full of Bowels[7] and Pity: whom she could not help, she would be ready to weep over; especially if she saw her Mother at any time troubled, she would quickly make her sorrows her own, and weep for her and with her.

12. When her Mother had been somewhat solicitous about any worldly thing, she would, if she could possibly, put her off from her care one way or other. One time she told her, O Mother, grace is better than that (meaning something her Mother

---

[6]This would presumably not be the well-known Cambridge Calvinist theologian William Whitaker, who died in 1595, but either Jeremiah Whitaker (1599-1654), a Church of England clergyman of Puritan views who sat in the Westminster Assembly, or his son William Whitaker (1629-1672), one of the ministers ejected in 1662.

[7]Bowels: bowels of compassion, e.g., Colossians 3:12.

wanted) I had rather have grace and the love of Christ, than any thing in the world.

13. This Child was often musing and busied in the thoughts of her everlasting Work; witness that strange question: O what are they doing which are already in Heaven? And she seemed to be hugely desirous to be among them that were praising, loving, delighting in God, and serving of him without sin. Her language was so strange about spiritual matters, that she made many excellent Christians to stand amazed, as judging it scarce to be paralell'd.

14. She took great delight in reading of the Scripture, and some part of it was more sweet to her than her appointed food: she would get several choice Scriptures by heart, and discourse of them savourly,[8] and apply them sutably.

15. She was not altogether a stranger to other good Books, but would be reading of them with much affection; and where she might, she noted the Books particularly, observing what in the reading did most warm her heart, and she was ready upon occasion to improve it.

16. One time a woman coming into the house in a great passion, spoke of her condition, as if none were like hers, and it would never be otherwise; the Child said, it were a strange thing to say when it's night, it will never be day again.

17. At another time a near Relation of hers being in some streights made some complaint, to whom she said, ''I have heard Mr. Carter say, A man may go to Heaven without a Penny in his Purse; but not without Grace in his heart.''

18. She had an extraordinary love to the people of God; and when she saw any that she thought feared the Lord, her heart would e'n leap for joy.

19. She loved to be much by her self, and would be greatly grieved if she were at any time deprived of a conveniencey for secret duty; she could not live without constant address to God in secret; and was not a little pleased when she could go into a corner to pray and weep.

20. She was much in praising God, and seldom or never complained of any thing but sin.

21. She continued in this course of praying and praising of God, and great dutifulness and sweetness to her Parents, and those that taught her any thing; yea, she did greatly encourage her Mother while she was a Widow, and desired that the absence of a Husband might in some measure be made up by the dutifulness and holiness of a Child. She studied all the ways that could be to make her Mother's life sweet.

22. When she was between Eleven and Twelve years old, she sickned, in which she carried it with admirable patience and sweetness, and did what she could with Scripture arguments to support and encourage her Relations to part with her that was going to Glory, and to prepare themselves to meet her in a blessed Eternity.

23. She was not many days sick before she was marked;[9] which she first saw her self, and was greatly rejoyced to think that she was marked out for the Lord, and was now going apace to Christ. She called to her Friends, and said, ''I am marked, but be not troubled, for I know I am marked for one of the Lord's own.'' One asked her how she knew that, She answered, ''the Lord hath told me that I am one of his dear Children.'' And thus she spake with a holy confidence in the Lord's love to her soul, and was not in the least daunted when she spake of her death; but, seemed greatly delighted in the apprehension of her nearness to her Father's house. And it was not long

---

[8]savourly: savoringly.

[9]marked: i.e., as with a rash or pocks.

before she was filled with joy unspeakable in believing.

24. When she just lay a dying, her Mother came to her and told her she was sorry that she had reproved and corrected so good a child so oft. "O Mother," said she, "speak not thus, I bless God, now I am dying, for your reproofs and corrections too; for it may be, I might have gone to Hell, if it had not been for your reproofs and corrections."

25. Some of her Neighbours coming to visit her, asked her if she would leave them? She answered them, "if you serve the Lord, you shall come after me to glory."

26. A little before she died, she had a great conflict with Satan, and cried out, "I am none of his;" her Mother seeing her in trouble, asked her what was the matter? She answered, "Satan did trouble me, but now I thank God all is well, I know I am none of his, but Christ's."

27. After this, she had a great sense of God's love, and a glorious sight, as if she had seen the very Heavens open, and the Angels come to receive her; by which her heart was filled with joy, and her tongue with praise.

28. Being desired by the standers by to give them a particular account of what she saw: she answered, "you shall know hereafter;" and so in an extasie of joy and holy triumph, she went to Heaven, when she was about Twelve years old. Hallelujah.

A Token For Children.
The Second Part.

*Being a farther Account of the Conversion, Holy and exemplary Lives,
and Joyful Deaths of several other young Children,
not published in the First Part.*

by James Janeway,
Minister of the Gospel

Example XII.

*Of the excellent carriage of a Child
upon his death bed when but seven years old.*

Jacob Bicks, the Brother of Susannah Bicks, was born in Leiden in the year 1657, and had religious education under his godly Parents, the which the Lord was pleased to sanctifie to his Conversion, and by it lay in excellent provisions to live upon in an hour of distress.

2. This sweet little Child was visited of the Lord of a very sore Sickness upon the sixth of August, 1664, three or four weeks before his Sister, of whose life and death we have given you some account already:

in his disintemper he was for the most part very sleepy and drousie till near his death, but when he did wake he was wont still to fall a praying.

3. Once when his Parents had prayed with him, they asked him if they should once more send for the Physician? "No" (said he) "I will have the Doctor no more; the Lord will help me: I know he will take me to himself, and then he shall help all."

4. "Ah my dear child," said his Father, "that grieveth my heart:" "Well"

(said the Child) "Father let us pray, and the Lord shall be near for my helper."

5. When his Parents had prayed with him again, he said, "come now dear Father and Mother and kiss me, I know that I shall die."

6. "Farewell dear Father and Mother, Farewell dear sister, farewell all. Now shall I go to heaven unto God and Jesus Christ, and the holy angels: Father, know you not what is said by Jeremiah: Blessed is he who trusteth in the Lord: now I trust in him, and he will bless me. And in I John 2, it is said, Little Children love not the world, for the world passeth away."

7. "Away then all that is in the world, away with all my pleasant things in the world: away with my Dagger for where I go there is nothing to do with Daggers and Swords; men shall not fight there but praise God. Away with all my books; there shall I know sufficiently, and be learned in all things of true wisdom without books."

8. His Father being touched to hear his child speak at this rate could not well tell what to say, but, "my dear child, the Lord will be near thee and uphold thee."

9. "Yea Father" (said he) "the Apostle Peter saith, God resisteth the proud, but he giveth grace to the humble. I shall humble my self under the mighty hand of God, and he shall help and lift me up."

10. "O my dear child," said his Father, "hast thou so strong a faith?"

11. "Yea," said the Child, "God hath given me so strong a faith upon himself through Jesus Christ that the Devil himself shall flee from me, for it is said, He who believeth in the Son hath everlasting life, and he hath overcome the wicked one. Now I believe in Jesus Christ my Redeemer, and he will not leave or forsake me, but shall give unto me eternall life, and then I shall sing holy, holy, holy, is the Lord of Sabbaoth."

12. Then with a short word of Prayer, "Lord be merciful to me a poor sinner," he quietly breathed out his Soul, and sweetly slept in Jesus when he was about seven years old. He died August 8, 1664.

Hallelujah.

Invisibles,[10] *Realities,*

Demonstrated in the Holy Life and Triumphant Death
of Mr. John Janeway

CHAP. V.

His great love to, and frequency in the duty of
Prayers: with remarkable success.

He was mighty in Prayer, and his spirit was oftentimes so transported in it that he forgot the weakness of his own body and of others' spirits; indeed the acquaintance that he had with God was so sweet, and his converse with him so frequent, that when he was ingaged in duty he scarce knew how to leave that which was so delightful and suited to his spirit. His constant course for some years was this. He prayed at least three times a day in secret, sometimes seven times, twice a day in the family or Colledge. And he found the sweetness of it beyond imagination, and injoyed wonderful communion with God, and tasted much of the pleasantness of a Heavenly

[10]invisibles: spiritual things.

life. And he could say by experience that the waies of wisdom were waies of pleasantness, and all her paths peace. He knew what it was to wrestle with God and was come to that pass that he could scarce come off his knees without his Father's blessing. He was used to converse with God with a holy familiarity as a friend, and would upon all occasions run to him for advise, and had many strange and immediate answers of prayer. One of which I think it not altogether impertinent to give the world an account of.

His Honoured Father Mr. William Janeway Minister of Kelshall in Hartfortshire being sick, and being under somewhat dark apprehensions as to the state of his soul, he would often say to his son John: "O son! this passing upon eternity is a great thing, this dying is a solemn business and enough to make any one's heart ake, that hath not his pardon sealed, and his evidences for Heaven clear. And truly son I am under no small fears as to my own estate for another world. O that God would clear his love! O that I could say cheerfully I can die, and upon good grounds be able to look death in the face and venture upon eternity with well grounded peace and comfort!''

His sweet and dutiful Son made a sutable reply at present; but seeing his dear Father continuing under despondings of spirit (though no Christians that knew him but had a high esteem of him for his uprightness) he got by himself and spent some time in wrestling with God upon his Father's account, earnestly begging of God that he would fill him with joy unspeakable in believing, and that he would speedily give him some token for good that he might joyfully and honourably leave this world to go to a better. After he was risen from his knees he came down to his sick Father and asked him how he felt himself. His Father made no answer for some time

but wept exceedingly (a passion that he was not subject to) and continued for some considerable time in an extraordinary passion of weeping, so that he was not able to speak. But at last having recovered himself with unspeakable joy he burst out into such expressions as these. "O Son! now it is come, it is come, it is come. I bless God I can dye: The Spirit of God hath witnessed with my spirit that I am his child: now I can look up to God as my dear Father, and Christ as my redeemer, I can now say this is my friend and this is my beloved. My heart is full, it is brim full: I can hold no more. I know now what that sentence means, the peace of God which passeth understanding, I know now what that white stone[11] is wherein a new name is written, which none know but they which have it. And that fit of weeping which you saw me in, was a fit of overpowering love and joy, so great that I could not for my heart contain my self: neither can I express what glorious discoveries God hath made of himself unto me. And had that joy been greater, I question whether I could have born it, and whether it would not have separated soul and body. Bless the Lord, O my soul, and all that is within me bless his holy name that hath pardoned all my sins and sealed the pardon. He hath healed my wounds and caused the bones which he had broken to rejoice.[12] O help me to bless the Lord! he hath put a new song into my mouth: O bless the Lord for his infinite goodness and rich mercy! O now I can dye! it is nothing. I bless God I can dye. I desire to be dissolved and to be with Christ.'' You may well think that his son's heart was not a little refreshed to hear such words, and

---

[11]White stone: an allusion to Revelation 2:17 where a white stone upon which the believer's name is written is mentioned. White symbolizes the purity of the redeemed.

[12]Allusions to Psalms 51:8 and 103:1-2.

see such a sight, and to meet the messenger[13] that he had sent to Heaven returned back again so speedily. He counted himself a sharer with his Father in this mercy, and it was upon a double account welcome, as it did so wonderfully satisfie his Father and as it was so immediate and clear an answer of his own prayers, as if God had from Heaven said unto him thy tears and prayers are heard for thy Father: thou hast like a Prince prevailed with God: thou hast got the blessing: thy fervent prayers have been effectual: go down and see else.

Upon this, this pretious young man broke forth into praises and even into another extasie of joy that God should deal so familiarly with him; and the Father and Son together were so full of joy, light, life, love and praise that there was a little Heaven in the place. He could not then but express himself in his manner: "O blessed and for ever blessed be God for his infinite grace! O who would not pray unto God! verily he is a God that heareth prayers and that my soul knows right well!" And then he told his joyful Father, how much he was affected with former despondings and what he had been praying for just before with all the earnestness he could for his soul, and how the Lord had immediately answered him. His Father hearing this, and perceivig that his former comforts came in a way of prayer, and his own child's prayer too, was the more refreshed and was the more confirmed, that it was from the spirit of God, and no delusion. And immediately his Son standing by he fell into another fit of triumphing joy, his weak body being almost ready to sink under that great weight of glory that did shine in so powerfully upon his soul. He could then say, now let thy servant depart in peace, for mine eyes have seen thy salvation. He could now walk through the valley of the shadow of death and fear no evil. O how sweet a thing is it to have one's interest in Christ cleared, how comfortable to have our calling and election made sure! How lovely is the sight of a smiling Jesus when one is dying! How refreshing is it when heart and flesh and all are failing, to have God for the strength of our heart and our portion for ever! O did the foolish unexperienced world but know what these things mean, did they but understand what it is to be solaced with the believing views of glory, to have their senses spiritually exercised, could they but tast[e] and see how good the Lord is, it would soon cause them to disrellish their low and bruitish pleasures, and look upon all worldly joys as infinitely short of one glimpse of God's love! After this, his reverent Father had a sweet calm upon his spirits, and went in the strength of that provision that rich grace laid in, till he came within the gates of the New Jerusalem: having all his graces greatly improved, and shewed so much humility, love to, and admiring of God, contempt of the world, such prizing of Christ, such patience as few Christians arrive to, especially his faith by which with extraordinary confidence he cast his Widow and eleven fatherless Children upon the care of that God who had fed him with this manna in his wilderness state. The benefit of which faith all his children (none of which were in his life time provided for) have since to admiration experienced. And it is scarce to be imagined how helpful this his precious Son John Janeway was to his Father by his heavenly discourse, humble advice and prayers. After a four months conflict with a gainful consumption and hectick feaver,[14] his honoured Father sweetly slept in Jesus.

---

[13]Messenger: i.e., his prayers.

[14]hectic fever: lung congestion with fever.

CHAP. IX.

His Retire into the Country; and His first sick-ness.

He now leaves the Doctor's house,[15] and retires himself into the Country, to his Mother and eldest Brother; who did not spare to use their utmost diligence and tenderness to recruit the decays of nature,[16] but hard study, frequent and earnest prayers, and long, and intense meditations, had so ruinated this frail Tabernacle, that it could not be fully repaired: yet, by God's blessing upon care, and art, it was underpropped for some time.

Whilst he was in this declining condition, in which he could have little hopes of life; he was so far from being affrighted, that he received the sentence of death in himself with great joy; and wrote to his dearest relations, to dispose them to a patient compliance with such a dispensation, as might separate him and them for a while: And to wean their affections from him, he solemnly professed, that as for himself he was ashamed to desire and pray for life. "O," saith he, "Is there any thing here, more desireable than the injoyment of Christ? Can I expect any thing below, comparable to that blessed vision! O, that Crown! that Rest which remains for the people of God! and (blessed be God) I can say, I know it is mine. I know that when this tabernacle of clay shall be dissolved, that I have a house, not made with hands; and therefore I groan, not to be uncloathed, but to be cloathed upon with Christ. To me to live is Christ and to dye is gain."[17]

"I can now through infinite mercy, speak in the Apostle's language, I have fought the good fight, hence-forth there is laid up for me a crown incorruptible that fadeth not away."[18]

When he perceived one of his nearest Relations distressed at the apprehensions of his death; he charged him, not to pray for his life, except it were purely with a respect to the glory of God. "I wish" (said he) "I beg you, to keep your minds in a submissive frame to the will of God concerning me. The Lord take you nearer to himself, that you may walk with Him; to Whom if I go before, I hope you will follow after." Yet after this, he was through mercy finely recovered, and his friends were not without some hopes of his living to be eminently instrumental for God's glory, in his generation.

After he was recovered in some measure, he fell again to his former practice of ingaging deeply in the secret and great duties of Religion which he constantly practised (except when God discharged him by sickness): secret prayer, at least three times a day, sometimes seven times, yea more; besides family, and Colledge-duties, which were before hinted, he set a part an hour every day for set and solemn meditation; which duty he found unspeakably to improve his graces, and to make no small addition to his comforts: His time for that duty was most commonly in the evening, when he usually walked into the field, if the weather would permit; if not, he retired into the Church, or any empty solitary room. Where, (observing his constant practice, that, if possible, I might be acquainted with the reason of his retiredness) I once hid my self that I might take the more exact notice of the intercourse, that, I judged, was kept up between him and God. But, O what a

---

[15]He had lived for a while at the house of a Dr. Cox, whose children he tutored.

[16]He had become ill while at the Coxes'.

[17]Allusion to Philippians 1:21.

[18]Allusion to 2 Timothy 4:7-8.

spectacle did I see! Surely, a man walking with God, conversing intimately with his Maker, and maintaining a holy familiarity with the great Jehovah; Me-thought, I saw one talking with God; me-thoughts, I saw a spiritual Merchant in an heavenly Exchange, driving a rich trade for the treasures of the other world. O what a glorious sight it was! Me-thinks, I see him still; how sweetly, did his face shine![19] O, with what a lovely countenance did he walk up and down, his lips going; his body oft reaching up, as if he would have taken his flight into Heaven! His looks, smiles, and every motion spake him to be upon the very Confines of Glory. O, had one but known what he was then feeding on! Sure, he had meat to eat which the world knew not of! Did we but know how welcome God made him when he brought him into his banqueting-house. That which one might easily perceive his heart to be most fixed upon, was, The infinite love of God in Christ, to the poor lost Sons and Daughters of Adam. What else meant his high expressions? What else did his own words to a dear friend signifie, but an extraordinary sense of the freeness, fulness, and duration of that love. To use his own words, ''God'' (saith he) ''holds mine eyes most upon his Goodness, his unmeasurable-Goodness, and the Promises which are most sure, and firm in Christ. His love to us is greater, surer, fuller than ours to our selves. For when we loved our selves so as to destroy our selves, he loved us so as to save us.''

. . . Yet, for all this, he had his gloomy days and the Sun was sometimes overcast, his sweets were sometimes imbittered with dreadful, and horrid temptations. The Devil shot his poisonous arrows at him; yet, through the Captain of his salvation, he came, more than a conqueror, out of the field. He was, with Paul, many times lifted up into the third Heavens and saw and heard things unutterable: but, lest he should be exalted above measure there was a Messenger of Satan sent to buffet him.[20]

It would make a Christian's heart even ake to hear and read what strange temptations this gratious soul was exercised with. But he was well armed for such a conflict, having on the shield of faith whereby he quenched the fiery darts of that Wicked-One:[21] yet, this fight cost him the sweating of his very body for agonies of spirit; and tears and strong cries to Heaven, for fresh help. As for himself he was wont to take an arrow out of God's quiver and discharge it by faith and prayer, for the discomfiture of his violent enemy who at last was fain to fly.

These temptations and conflicts with Satan did not a little help him afterwards in his dealing with one that was sorely afflicted with temptations of the like nature. . . .

He was one that kept an exact watch over his thoughts, words and actions, and made a review of all that passed him, at least once a day, in a solemn manner. He kept a Diary, in which he did write down every evening what the frame of his spirit had been all the day long, especially in every duty. He took notice what incomes and profit he received in his spiritual traffique; what returns from that far-country; what answers of prayer, what deadness and flatness, and what observable providences did present themselves, and the substance of what he had been doing; and any wandrings of thoughts, inordinancy in any passion; which, though the world could not discern, he could. It cannot be conceived by them which do not practise the same, to what a good account did this return! This,

---

[19]Allusion to Moses, whose face shone after he had been with God, Exodus 34:29-35.

[20]Allusion to 2 Corinthians 12:2-7.

[21]Allusion to Ephesians 6:16.

made him to retain a grateful remembrance of mercy, and to live in a constant admiring and adoring of divine goodness; this, bought him to a very intimate acquaintance with his own heart; this, kept his spirit low[22] and fitted him for freer communications from God; this, made him more lively and active; this, helped him to walk humbly with God, this made him speak more affectionately and experimentally[23] to others of the things of God: and, in a word, this left a sweet calm upon his spirits, because he every night made even his accounts; and if his sheets should prove his winding-sheet, it had been all one: for, he could say his work was done; so that death could not surprize him.

Could this book of his experiences, and register of his actions have been read, it might have contributed much to the compleating of this discourse, and the quickning of some, and the comforting of others. But these things being written in characters, the world hath lost that jewel.[24]

He studied the Scriptures much, and they were sweeter to him than his food; and he had an excellent faculty in opening the mind of God in dark places.[25]

In the latter part of his life he seemed quite swallowed up with the thought of Christ, Heaven, and eternity; and the neerer he came to this the more swift his motion was to it, and the more unmixed his designs for it; and he would much perswade others to an universal free respect to the glory of God, in all things; and making Religion one's business, and not to mind these great things by the by.

---

[22]low: humble.

[23]experimentally: experientially.

[24]i.e., he wrote his diary in a secret code.

[25]i.e., in obscure passages of scripture.

CHAP. XIV.

His trouble at the Barrenness of Christians.

He was not a little troubled at the barrenness of Christians in their discourse, and their not improving their society for the quickning and warming of their hearts; the expence of pretious time unaccountably, the ill management of visits, and the impertinency of their talk, he oft reflected upon with a holy indignation. It vext him to the soul, to see what prizes sometimes, were put into the hands of Christians and how little skill and will they had to improve them, for the building up of one another in the most holy faith: and that they who should be incouraging of one another in the way to Zion, communicating of experiences, and talking of their Country, and of the glory of that Kingdom which the Saints are heirs of, could satisfie themselves with empty common vain stuff; as if Christ, Heaven and Eternity were not things of as great worth as any thing else, that

usually sounds in the ears and comes from the lips of professors. That the folly of common discourse among Christians might appear more, and that he might discover how little such language did become those that profess themselves Israelites, and that say, they are Jews; he once sate down silent and took out his pen and ink, and wrote in shorthand the discourses that passed for some time together, amongst those which pretended to more than common understanding in the things of God: and after a while he took his paper and read it to them, and asked them whether such talk was such as they would be willing God should record. This he did, that he might shame them out of that usual unobserved and unlamented unprofitable communication and fruitless squandring away that inestimable Jewel, Opportunity. "Oh, to spend an hour or two together, and to hear scarce a word for Christ or that speaks peoples' hearts in love with holiness; Is not this writing a brave rational divine discourse? Fie fie. Where's our love to God and souls all this while, where's our sense of the pretiousness of time, of the greatness of our account? Should we talk thus, if we believed that we should hear of this again at the day of judgement? And do we not know that we must give an account of every idle word? Is this like those that understand the language of Canaan? Did Saints in former times use their tongues to no better purpose? Would Enoch, David, or Paul, have talked thus! Is this the sweetest communion of Saints upon earth? How shall we do to spend eternity in speaking the praises of God, if we cannot find matter for an hour's discourse?''

''Doth not ths speak aloud our hearts to be very empty of grace, and that we have little sense of those spiritual and eternal concerns upon us?''

As the barrenness and empty converse of Christians was a sin that he greatly bewailed, so the want of love amongst Christians, and their divisions, did cost him many tears and groans; and he did what he could to heal all the breaches that he could, by his tender prudent and Christian advice and counsel; and if prayers, tears and intreaties and counsels would prevail and cement differences, they should not long be open. Nay if his letters would signifie any thing to make an amicable and Christian correspondencie, it should not be wanting. . . .

CHAP. XVI.

An account of the latter part of his Life.

For the latter part of his life; he lived like a man that was quite weary of the world, and that looked upon himself as a stranger here, and that lived in the constant sight of a better world. He plainly declared himself but a Pilgrim that looked for a better Country, a City that had foundations, whose builder and maker was God. His habit, his language, his deportment, all spoke him one of another world. His meditations were so intense, long and frequent, that they ripened him apace for Heaven; but, somewhat weakened his body. Few Christians attain to such a holy contempt of the world, and to such clear believing, joyful, constant apprehensions of the transcendent glories of the unseen world.

He made it his whole business to keep up sensible communion with God, and to grow into a humble familiarity with God, and to maintain it. And if by reason of company or any necessary diversions, this was in any measure interrupted; he would complain, like one out of his element, till his spirit was recovered into a delightful more unmixed free intercourse with God. He was never so well satisfied, as when he was more immediately ingaged in what brought him nearer to God; and by this he injoyed those comforts frequently, which other Christians rarely meet with. His graces and experiences, toward his end grew to astonishment. His faith got up to a full assurance; his desires into a kind of injoyment and delight. He was oft brought into the banqueting house, and there Christ's banner over him was love; and he sate down under his shadow with great delight, and his fruit was pleasant unto his tast[e]. His eyes beheld the King in his beauty, and while he sate at his Table, his spicknard[26] did spend forth its pleasant smell: he had frequent visions of glory, and this John lay in the bosom of his Master,

---

[26] An aromatic substance derived from an Oriental plant.

and was sure a very beloved Disciple, and highly favoured.[27] His Lord oft called him up to the Mount to him, and let him see his excellent glory, O the sweet foretasts that he had of those pleasures that are at the right hand of God. How oft was he feasted with the feast of fat things, those wines on the lees well refined; and sometimes he was like a Giant refresht with new wine, rejoicing to run the race that was set before him, whether of doing or of suffering. He was even sick of love,[28] and he could say to the poor unexperienced world, ''O tast[e] and see!'' and to Christians, ''come and I will tell you what God hath done for my soul. O, what do Christians mean that they do no more labour to get their senses

---

[27]Allusion to John 13:23.

[28]Sick of love: surfeited or made sick by an excess of love; allusion to Song of Solomon 5:8.

spiritually exercised? O, why do they not make Religion the very business of their lives? O, why is the Soul, Christ and Glory thus dispised? Is there nothing in communion with God? Are all those comforts of Christians, that follow hard after him, worth nothing? Is it not worth the while to make one's calling and election sure? O, why do men and women jest and dally in the great matters of eternity? Little do people think, what they slight, when they are seldom and formal in secret duties, and when they neglect that great duty of Meditation, which I have, through rich mercy, found so sweet and refreshing: O, what do Christians mean, that they keep at such a distance from Christ? Did they but know the thousandth part of that sweetness that is in him, they could not choose but follow him hard; they would run and not be weary, and walk and not be faint. . . . ''

CHAP. XVII.

His last Sickness, and Death.

And now the time draws nigh, wherein his longings shall be satisfied; he is called to his last work; and truly, his deportment in it, was honourable; his carriage so eminently gratious, so meek, patient, fruitful, joyful and thankful, that it made all his friends stand and wonder as being abundantly above their experience and reading; and those Christians that saw him, could not but admire God in him, and look upon him as one of the most singular instances of rich grace, and even bless God that their eyes ever saw, or their ears ever heard, such things; and had such a sensible demonstration of the reality of invisibles.

He falls into a deep Consumption.

His body is now shaken again, and he falls into a deep Consumption; but, this messenger of God did not in the least damp him. Spitting of blood, was no ghastly thing to one that had his eye upon the blood of Jesus; faint sweats did not daunt him that had always such reviving cordials at hand. It's matter of joy to him, that he was now in some hopes of having his earnest desires satisfied.

After he had been a while sick, a sudden dimness seized upon his eyes; by and by his sight quite failed; and there was such a visible alteration in him, that he and others judged these things to be the symptoms of death approaching. But when he was thus taken, he was not in the least surprized; but was lifted up with joy to think, what a life he was going to, looking upon death it self as one of his Father's servants, and his friend that was sent as a messenger to conduct him safely to his glorious palace.

When he felt his body ready to faint, he called to his Mother and said, ''Dear

Mother, I am dying, but I beseech you be not troubled; for, I am through mercy, quite above the fears of death, it's no great matter. I have nothing troubles me but the apprehensions of your grief. I am going to Him, whom I love above life."

But it pleased the Lord to raise him again a little out of this fainting fit, for his master had yet more work for him to do before he must receive his wages. Although his outward man decaied apace, yet he is renewed in the inward man day by day: his graces were never more active, and his experiences were never greater. When one would have thought he should have been taken up with his distemper, and that it had been enough for him to grapple with his pains, then he quite forgets his weakness; and is so swallowed up of the life to come, that he had scarce leisure to think of his sickness.

For several weeks together, I never heard the least word that savoured of any complaint or weariness under the hand of God; except, his eager desire to be with Christ, be counted complaining, and his haste to be in Heaven be called impatience. Now's the time when one might have seen Heaven and the Glory of another world realized to sense.[29] His faith grew exceedingly and his love was proportionable, and his joys were equal to both.

O the rare attainments! The high and divine expressions, that dropped from his mouth! I have not words to express what a strange, triumphant, angelical frame, he was in, for some considerable time together. It was a very Heaven upon earth, to see and hear a man admiring God at such a rate, as I never heard any, nor ever expect to hear or see more, till I come to Heaven. Those that did not see cannot well conceive, what a sweet frame he was in, for at least six weeks before he died. His soul was almost alwaies filled with those joys unspeakable and full of glory. How oft would he cry out; "O, that I could but let you know what I now feel! O, that I could show you what I see! O, that I could express the thousandeth part of that sweetness that I now find in Christ! You would all then think it well worth the while to make it your business to be religious. O my dear friends, we little think what a Christ is worth upon a death-bed. I would not for a world, nay for millions of worlds, be now without a Christ and a pardon. I would not for a world be to live any longer: the very thoughts of a possibility of recovery, makes me even tremble."

When one came to visit him, and told him, that he hoped it might please God to raise him again, and that he had seen many a weaker man restored to health, and that lived many a good year after: "And do you think to please me" (said he) "by such discourse as this? No, Friend, you are much mistaken in me, if you think that the thoughts of life, and health, and the world, are pleasing to me. The world hath quite lost its excellency in my judgement. O how poor and contemptible a thing is it in all its glory, compared with the glory of that invisible world which I now live in the sight of! And as for life, Christ is my life, health and strength; and I know, I shall have another kind of life, when I leave this. I tell you it would incomparably more please me, if you should say to me, You are no man of this world; you cannot possibly hold out long; before to morrow you will be in eternity. I tell you I do so long to be with Christ, that I could be contented to be cut apieces, and to be put to the most exquisite torments, so I might but die, and be with Christ. O, how sweet is Jesus! Come, Lord Jesus, come quickly. Death, do thy worst! Death hath lost his terribleness. Death, it is nothing. I say, Death is nothing (through grace) to me. I can as easily die as shut my

---

[29]realized to sense: experienced by the senses.

eyes, or turn my head and sleep: I long to be with Christ; I long to die;'' that was still his note.

His Mother and Brethren standing by him he said; ''Dear Mother, I beseech you as earnestly as ever I desired any thing of you in my life, that you would cheerfully give me up to Christ; I beseech you, do not hinder me, now I am going to rest and glory. I am afraid of your prayers, lest they pull one way and mine another.''

And then turning to his Brethren he spake thus to them, ''I charge you all, do not pray for my life any more: you do me wrong, if you do! O that glory, the unspeakable glory that I behold. My heart is full, my heart is full. Christ smiles, and I cannot choose but smile: can you find in your heart, to stop me who am now going to the compleat and eternal injoyment of Christ? Would you keep me from my Crown? The arms of my blessed Saviour are open to imbrace me; the Angels stand ready to carry my soul in his bosom. O, did you but see what I see; you would all cry out with me, how long, dear Lord, come Lord Jesus come quickly! O, why are his Chariot-wheels so long a coming!''

And all this while he lay like a triumphing conqueror, smiling and rejoicing in spirit.

There was never a day towards his end but (as weak as he was) he did some special piece of service in, for his great Master. Yea, almost every hour did produce fresh wonders.

A Reverend, Judicious and holy Minister came often to visit him, and discoursed with him of the excellency of Christ, and the glory of the invisible world. ''Sir,'' said he, ''I feel something of it; my heart is as full as it can hold in this lower state; I can hold no more here. O that I could but let you know what I feel!''

This holy Minister praying with him his soul was ravished with the abundant in-comes of light, life and love; so that he could scarce bear it, nor the thought of staying any longer in the world, but longed to be in such a condition, wherein he should have yet more grace and more comfort, and be better able to bear that weight of glory; some manifestations whereof did even almost sink his weak body, and had he not been sustained by a great power, his very joys would have overwhelmed him; and whilst he was in these extasies of joy and love, he was wont to cry out,

''Who am I Lord, who am I, that thou shouldst be mindful of me! Why me Lord, why me, and pass by thousands and look upon such a wretch as me. O, what shall I say, unto thee, O thou preserver of men? O, why me Lord, why me? O blessed, and for ever blessed, be free grace! How is it, Lord, that thou shouldst manifest thy self unto me, and not unto others, even so Father, because it seemeth good in thy eyes. Thou wilt have mercy because thou wilt have mercy. And if thou wilt look upon such a poor worm who can hinder! Who would not love thee! O blessed Father! O how sweet and gratious hast thou been unto me! O, that he should have me in his thoughts of love, before the foundations of the world.''

And thus he went on, admiring and adoring of God, in a more high and heavenly manner than I can clothe with words. Suppose what you can on this side Heaven; and I am perswaded you might have seen it in him. He was wonderfully taken with the goodness of God to him in sending that aged experienced Minister to help him in his last great work upon earth. ''Who am I,'' said he, ''that God should send me a messenger one among a thousand'' (meaning that Minister who had been praying with him with tears of joy).

Though he was towards his end, most commonly in a triumphant joyful frame; yet, sometimes, even then he had some small intermissions, in which he would cry out, "Hold out faith and patience; yet a little while, and your work is done." And when he found not his heart wound up to the highest pitch of thankfulness, admiration and Love; he would with great sorrow bemoan himself, and cry out in his Language,

"And what's the matter now, O my soul, what wilt thou, canst thou thus unworthily sleight this admirable and astonishing condescention of God to thee? Seems it a small matter, that the great Jehovah should deal thus familiarly with his Worm; and wilt thou pass this over, as a common mercy? What meanest thou, O my soul, that thou dost not constantly adore and praise this rare, strong, and unspeakable Love! Is it true, O my soul, doth God deal familiarly with man, and are his humble, zealous, and constant love, praise, and service too good for God? Why art not thou O my soul, swallowed up every moment with this free unparallell'd everlasting Love."

And then he breaks out again into another triumphant Extasie of praise and joy; and expressed a little of that which was unexpressible in some such words as these,

"Stand astonished ye Heavens, and wonder O ye Angels, at this infinite grace! Was ever any under Heaven more beholding to free grace than I? Doth God use to do thus, with his creatures? Admire him for ever and ever, O ye redeemed ones! O those joys, the tast[e] of which I have! Those everlasting joys, which are at his right hand for evermore! Eternity, Eternity it self, is too short to praise this God in. O bless the Lord with me, come let us shout for joy and boast in the God of our Salvation. O, help me to praise the Lord; for his mercy indureth for ever!"

One of his brethren (that had formerly been wrought upon by his holy exhortations and example) praying with him, and seeing of him, (as he apprehended) near his

Dissolution, desired, that the Lord would be pleased to continue those astonishing and soul supporting comforts to the last moment of his breath, and that he might go from one Heaven to another, from grace and joy imperfect, to perfect grace and glory; and when his work was done here, give him, if it were his will, the most easie and triumphant passage to rest; and that he might have an abundant entrance administred into the everlasting Kingdom of our Lord and Saviour Jesus Christ.

At the end of the Duty he burst out into a wonderful Passion of joy. (Sure that was joy unspeakable and full of glory!) O what an Amen did he speak, Amen, Amen, Amen, Hallelujah.

It would have made any Christian's heart to leap, to have seen and heard, what some saw and heard, at that time; and I question not, but that it will somewhat affect them to hear and read it; though it be scarce possible to speak the half of what was admirable in him; for, it being so much beyond president,[30] it did even astonish and amaze those of us that were about him, that our relation must fall hugely short of what was real.

I verily believe that it exceeds the highest Rhetorick, to set out to the life what this heavenly creature did then deliver. I say again, I want[31] words to speak, and so did he; for, he saw things unutterable: But yet, so much he spake as justly drew the admiration of all that saw him; and I heard an old experienced Christian and Minister say it again and again, That He never saw, nor read, nor heard the like: neither could we ever expect to see the glories of Heaven more demonstrated to sense, in this world. He talked as if he had been in the third Heavens, and broke out into such words as these,

---

[30]president: precedent.

[31]want: lack.

"O, He is come! He is come! O how sweet! How glorious is the blessed Jesus! How shall I do to speak the thousandth part of his praises! O for words, to set out a little of that excellency! But it is unexpressible! O how excellent, glorious, and lovely is the precious Jesus! He is sweet, He is altogether lovely! And now I am sick of Love, he hath ravished my soul with his beauty! I shall die sick of Love."

"O my friends stand by and wonder, come look upon a dying man, and wonder; I cannot my self but stand and wonder! Was there ever a greater kindness, was there ever sensibler manifestations of rich Grace! O, why me, Lord, why me! Sure this is akin to Heaven, and if I were never to enjoy any more than this; it were well worth all the torments that men and Devils could invent, to come thorow even a Hell to such transcendent joys as these. If this be dying, dying is sweet: let no true Christian ever be afraid of dying. O Death is sweet to me. This Bed is soft. Christ's Arms and Kisses, his Smiles and Visits, sure they would turn Hell into Heaven. O that you did but see and feel what I do! Come and behold a dying man more chearful than you ever saw any healthful man in the midst of his sweetest enjoyments! O Sirs, Worldly pleasures are pitiful poor sorry things, compared with one glimps[e] of this glory, which shines in so strongly into my Soul! O why should any of you be so sad, when I am so glad? This, this is the hour that I have waited for!"

About eight and forty hours before his Death, his eyes were dim, and his sight much failed; his Jaws shook and trembled, and his Feet were cold, and all the symptoms of Death were upon him, and his extream parts were already almost dead, and senseless, and yet even then, his joys were (if possible) greater still: He had so many fits of Joy unspeakable, that he seemed to be in one continued act of Seraphick Love

and praise. He spake like one that was just entring into the gates of the new Jerusalem: the greatest part of him was now in Heaven; not a word drop'd from his mouth but it breathed Christ and Heaven. O what incouragement did he give to them which did stand by, to follow hard after God, and to follow Christ in a humble, believing, zealous course of life, and adding one degree of grace to another, and using all diligence to make their Calling and Election sure; and that then, they also should find, that they should have a glorious passage into a blessed Eternity.

But most of his work was Praise, a hundred times admiring of the bottomless love of God to him. "O, why me, Lord, why me!" And then he would give instructions to them that came to see him. He was scarce ever silent, because the Love of Christ and Souls, did constrain him. There was so much work done for Christ in his last hours, that I am ready to think, he did as much in an Hour as some do in a Year.

Every particular person had a faithful affectionate warning. And that good Minister, that was so much with him, used this as an argument to perswade him to be willing to live a little longer, and to be patient to tarry God's leisure; sure God hath something for thee to do that is yet undone; some word of exhortation to come to some poor soul, that you have forgot.

The truth of it is, he was so filled with the love of Christ, that he could scarce bear absence from Him a moment. He knew that he should be capable of bearing of greater glory above, than he could here. It was the Judgement of some that were with him, that his heart was not only habitually, but actually set on God all the day long; and nothing of human frailty, that could be thought a sin, did appear for some time; except it were his passionate desire to die, and difficulty to bring himself to be willing to stay below Heaven.

He was wont every evening to take his leave of his friends, hoping not to see them, till the morning of the Resurrection; and he desired that they would be sure, to make sure of a comfortable meeting at our Father's house, in that other World.

I cannot relate the twentieth part of that which deserved to be written in letters of Gold. And one that was one of the weakest, said, that he did verily believe, that if we had been exact in our taking his sentences, and observing his daily experiences, he could not imagine, a Book could be published of greater use to the World, next the Bible it self.

One rare passage I can't omit, which was this, that when Ministers or Christians came to him, he would beg of them, to spend all the time that they had with him in Praise. "O help me to praise God, I have now nothing else to do from this time to Eternity, but to praise and love God. I have what my soul desires upon Earth, I can't tell what to pray for but what I have gratiously given in.[32] The wants that are capable of supplying in this World, are supplied. I want but one thing, and that is, A speedy lift to Heaven. I expect no more here, I can't desire more, I can't hear more. O praise, praise, praise that infinite boundless love that hath, to a wonder, looked upon my soul, and done more for me than thousands of his dear children. O bless the Lord, O my soul, and all that is within me bless his holy name.[33] O help me, help me, O my friends, to praise and admire him that hath done such astonishing wonders for my soul; he hath pardoned all my sins, he hath filled me with his goodness; he hath given me grace and glory, and no good thing hath he withheld from me."

"Come, help me with praises, all's too little: come, help me, O ye glorious and mighty Angels, who are so well skilled in this heavenly work of praise. Praise him, all ye creatures upon the Earth, let every thing that hath being, help me to praise him. Hallelujah, Hallelujah, Hallelujah: Praise is now my work, and I shall be engaged in this sweet imployment forever. Bring the Bible, turn to David's Psalms, and let us sing a Psalm of praise; Come let's lift up our voice in the praise of the most high, I will sing with you as long as my breath doth last; and when I have none, I shall do it better."

And then turning to some of his friends that were weeping, he desired them, rather to rejoyce than weep upon his account. It may justly seem a wonder, how he could speak so much as he did, when he was so weak; but the joy of the Lord did strengthen him.

In his sickness, the scriptures that he took much delight in, were the fourteenth, fifteenth, sixteenth, and seventeenth of John. The fifty fourth of Isay[34] was very refreshing also to him; he would repeat that word "with everlasting mercies will I gather" with abundance of joy.

He commended the study of the Promises[35] to Believers and desired that they would be sure to make good their claim to them, and then they might come to the Wells of Consolation, and drink thereof, their fill.

According to his desire most of the time that was spent with him, was spent in Praise; and he would still be calling out, "More Praise still. O, help me to Praise him: I have now nothing else to do; I have done with Prayer, and all other Ordinances; I have almost done conversing with mortals. I shall presently be beholding Christ himself, that dyed for me, and loved me, and washed me in his Blood."

---

[32]i.e., already prayed for.

[33]Psalm 103:1.

[34]Isay: Isaiah. The text alluded to is 54:7.

[35]i.e., God's promises of help and grace.

"I shall before a few hours are over, be in Eternity singing the Song of Moses, and the Song of the Lamb. I shall presently stand upon Mount Zion, with an innumerable company of Angels, and the Spirits of the just made perfect, and Jesus the mediator of the New Covenant, I shall hear the voice of much people and be one amongst them, which shall say Hallelujah, Salvation, Glory, Honour, and Power unto the Lord our God; and again, we shall say Hallelujah. And yet a very little while, and I shall sing unto the Lamb, a Song of Praise, saying, Worthy art thou to receive Praise who wert slain, and has redeemed us to God by thy blood, out of every Kindred, and Tongue, and People, and Nation, and hast made us unto our God, Kings and Priests, and we shall reign with thee for ever and ever."[36]

"Methinks I stand, as it were, with one foot in Heaven, and the other upon Earth; methinks, I hear the melody of Heaven, and by Faith, I see the Angels waiting to carry my Soul to the bosom of Jesus, and I shall be for ever with the Lord in Glory. And who can choose but rejoyce in all this."

In several times, he spake in this Language, and repeated many of these words often, over, and over again, with far greater affection, than can be well worded. And I solemnly profess, that what is here written, is no Hyperbole, and that the twentieth part of what was observable in him is not Recorded, and though we can't word it exactly as he did, yet you have the substance, and many things in his own words with little or no variation. . . .

Then that Godly Minister came to give him his last visit, and to do the office of an inferiour Angel, to help to convey this blessed soul to Glory who was now even upon Mount Pisgah,[37] and had a full sight of that goodly Land at a little distance. When this Minister spake to him, his heart was in a mighty flame of Love and Joy, which drew tears of Joy from that pretious Minister, being almost amazed to hear a man just a dying, talk as if he had been with Jesus, and came from the immediate presence of God; O the smiles that were then in his Face, and the unspeakable Joy that was in his Heart; one might have read Grace, and Glory, in such a man's countenance. O the praise, the triumphant praises, that he put up! And every one must speak praise about him, or else they did make some jar in his harmony.

And indeed most did, as well as they could help him in praise. So that I never heard, nor knew more praises given to God in one Room, than in his Chamber.

A little before he died, in the Prayer, or rather Praises, he was so wrapped up with admiration and joy, that he could scarce forbear shouting for joy. In the conclusion of the Duty, with abundance of Faith, and fervency, he said aloud, "Amen, Amen!"

And now his desires shall soon be satisfied. He seeth Death coming apace to do his office, his jaws are loosened more and more, and quiver greatly; his hands and feet are cold as clay, and a cold sweat is upon him: but, O how glad was he when he felt his Spirit just agoing! Never was Death more welcome to any mortal, I think. Though the pangs of Death were strong; yet, that far-more-exceeding and Eternal weight of Glory, made him indure those bitter pains, with much patience and courage. In the extremity of his pains, he desired his eldest Brother to lay him a little lower, and to take away one pillow from him, that he might die with the more ease; His Brother replied, that he durst not for a

---

[36]Allusions to Revelation 5:9-13.

[37]Mt. Pisgah: the mountain from which Moses viewed the promised land, Deuteronomy 34:1-4.

world, do any thing that might hasten his Death a moment. Then he was well satisfied, and did sweetly resign himself up wholly to God's disposal; and after a few minutes, with a sudden motion gathering up all his strength, he gave himself a little turn on one side; and in the twinkling of an eye, departed to the Lord, sleeping in Jesus.

And now blessed soul, thy longings are satisfied, and thou seest and feelest a thousand times more than thou didst upon Earth, and yet thou canst bear it with delight, thou art now welcomed to thy Father's house by Christ, the beloved of thy soul; now thou hast heard him say, Come, thou blessed of my Father, and, Well done good and faithful servant, enter thou into the joy of thy Lord, and wear that Crown which was prepared for thee, before the foundation of the World.

O that all the Relations which thou hast left behind thee, may live thy Life, and die thy Death, and live with Christ, and thee, for ever and ever. Amen, Amen.

Introduction to Theodosia Alleine,
A full Narrative of his Life

Theodosia Alleine was the daughter of Richard Alleine, one of the ministers who was ejected by the Act of Uniformity and an important figure among the spiritual writers. Theodosia was probably born in Somerset shortly after her father began preaching there. In 1655 she married Joseph Alleine, whose family—though bearing the same surname—was not related to hers. At the time of their marriage Joseph had recently joined George Newton as fellow pastor in the parish of St. Mary Magdalen, Taunton, Somerset. For a while Theodosia kept a school at Taunton, and the pupils boarded in their house. When her husband was imprisoned in 1663 at Ilchester for his illegal religious activities, she offered to remain with him in prison and stayed nearby in order to assist him. When his health failed as a result of imprisonment, she supervised his removal to Bath and his consultations with physicians. After his untimely death she assisted his former ministerial colleagues in putting out a volume that memorialized Joseph Alleine's faithfulness as a pastor. She was the author of a substantial part of the volume, an account of her husband's ministry and sufferings.

The memorial volume was entitled The Life and Death of that Excellent Minister of Christ Mr. Joseph Alleine, Late Teacher of the Church of Taunton in Somerset-shire; Assistant to Mr. Newton *(London, 1671). The text that follows, which is almost the whole of Theodosia Alleine's account, portrays Joseph as a saintly person and an ideal pastor; it is taken from the corrected edition of 1677 (Wing A1015), 62-78, 87-108. This edition made many corrections of the somewhat garbled earlier versions. The work was popular and had seven printings up to 1693. For more about Theodosia Alleine, one can consult the hagiographical C. Stanford,* Joseph Alleine: His Companions and Times *(1861).*

A full Narrative of his Life,

(from his Silencing till his Death)
by his Widdow Mrs. Theodosia Allein, in her own Words;
wherein is notably set forth
with what patience he ran the Race that was set before him,
and fulfilled the Ministry that he had received of the Lord.

Before the Act for Uniformity came forth, my Husband was very earnest day and night with God,[1] that his way might be made plain to him, that he might not desist from such Advantages[2] of saving Souls, with any scruple upon his Spirit: In which, when he saw those Clauses of Assent and Consent, and Renouncing the Covenant, he was fully satisfied:[3] But he seemed so moderate before, that both my self and others thought he would have Conformed: He often saying, He would not leave his work for small and dubious Matters: But seeing his way so plain for quitting the publick Station that he held, and being thoroughly perswaded of this, that the Ejection of the Ministers out of their Places, did not disoblige them from preaching the Gospel; he presently took up a firm resolution to go on with his work in private, both of Preaching and Visiting from House to House, till he should be carried to Prison, or Banishment, which he counted upon,[4] the Lord assisting him: And this Resolution, without delay, he prosecuted; for the Thursday after[5] he appointed a Solemn Day of Humiliation, when he Preached to as many as would adventure themselves with him at our own House; But it being then a strange thing to the most Professors to suffer, they seemed much afrighted at the threatnings of Adversaries; so that there was not such an appearance at such opportunities as my Husband expected; whereupon he made it his Work to converse much with those he perceived to be most timerous, and to satisfie the Scruples[6] that were on many amongst us; So that the Lord was pleased in a short time to give him such success that his own People waxed bold for the Lord, and his Gospel: and multitudes flocked into the Meetings, at whatsoever season they were, either by day or night; which was a great Encouragement to my Husband, that he went on with much Vigour and Affection in his work, both of Preaching, and Visiting, and Catechizing, from House to House.

He went also frequently into the Villages and Places about the Towns where the Ministers were gone, as most of them did flie, or at the least desist for a considerable time after Bartholomew day;[7] Where-ever he went, the Lord was pleased to give him great success; many converted, and the generality of those animated to cleave to the Lord and his ways.

But by this the Justices' rage was much heightned against him, and he was often threatned and sought for; but by the Power

---

[1] i.e., earnest in prayer.

[2] advantages: opportunities.

[3] i.e., satisfied that he could not subscribe to the terms of the Act of Uniformity and renounce the Solemn Language and Covenant, by which one swore allegiance to the parliamentary regime that had overthrown the king.

[4] counted upon: expected.

[5] i.e., after his ejection from the Church of England parish in Taunton.

[6] Scruples: misgivings, particularly about the morality of illegal meetings.

[7] The day of the ejections, August 24, 1662.

of God, whose Work he was delighted in, was preserved much longer out of their hands than he expected: For he would often say, ''If it pleased the Lord to grant him three months liberty before he went to Prison, he should account himself favoured by him, and should with more chearfulness go, when he had done some Work.'' At which time we sold off all our Goods, preparing for a Gaol, or Banishment, where he was desirous I should attend him, as I was willing to do, it always having been more grievous to me to think of being absent from him, than to suffer with him.

He also resolved, when they would suffer him no longer to stay in England, he would go to China, or some remote Part of the World, and publish the Gospel there.

It pleased the Lord to indulge him, that he went on in his Work from Bartholomew day till May the 26th after: Though often threatned, yet he was never interrupted, though the People both of the Town and Countrey were grown so resolute, that they came in great multitudes, at whatever season the Meeting was appointed, very seldom missing twice a Sabbath, and often in the week: I know that he hath Preached fourteen times in eight days, and ten often, and six or seven ordinarily in these Months, at home and abroad, besides his frequent converse with Souls. He then laying aside all other Studies which he formerly so much delighted in, because he accounted his time would be but short. And the Lord (as he often told me) made his Work in his Ministry far more easie to him, by the supplies of his Spirit both in Gifts and Grace, as did evidently appear, both in his Doctrine and Life; he appearing to be more Spiritual, and Heavenly, and affectionate than before, to all that heard him, or conversed with him.

He was upon a Saturday in the evening, about six a clock, seized on by an Officer of our Town, who had rather have been otherwise employed, as he hath often said, but that he was forced to a speedy execution of the Warrant, by a Justice's Clerk, who was sent on purpose with it to see it Executed, because he feared that none of the Town would have done it.

The Warrant was in the Name of three Justices, to Summon him to appear forthwith at one of their Houses, which was about two Miles from the Town, but he desired liberty to stay and Sup with his Family first, supposing his Entertainment there would be such as would require some refreshment: This would not be granted, till one of the chief of the Town was bound for his speedy appearance: His Supper being prepared, he sat down eating very heartily, and was very chearful, but full of Holy and gracious Expressions, suitable to his and our present state. After Supper, having prayed with us, he with the Officer, and two or three Friends accompanying him, repaired to the Justices' house, where they lay to his charge, that he had broken the Act of Uniformity by his Preaching; which he denied, saying; That he had Preached neither in any Church, nor Chappel, nor place of Publick Worship since the 24th of August, and what he did was in his own Family, with those others that came there to hear him.

Here behold how many Ministers have these eight or nine years been silenced in England, Scotland, and Ireland, whose Holy Skill and Conscience, Fidelity and Zeal, is such, as would have justly advanced most of the Antient Fathers of the Church, to far greater renown, had they been but possessed with the like: Of whom indeed The World is not worthy. O! how many of them am I constrained to remember, with joy for their great worth, and sorrow for their silence! But though Learning, Holiness, wonderful Ministerial Skill, and Industry, Moderation, Peaceableness, true

Catholicism, absolute Dedication unto Christ, Zeal, Patience, and Perseverance, did not all seem sufficient to procure his Ministerial or Corporal Liberty in his latter years; yet they did much more for him than that, in qualifying him for the Crown which he now enjoyeth; and to hear, Well done good and faithful Servant, enter into thy Master's Joy.[8]

But, alas, Lord! What is the terrible future evil, from which thou takest such men away! And why is this World so much forsaken? As if it were not a Prayer of Hope which thou hast taught us, Thy Will be done on Earth, as it is in Heaven.

He hath Printed a small Book, called, A Call to Archippus,[9] to perswade the silent Non-conformists, to pity Souls, and to be faithful in the Work to which they are Devoted and Consecrated, how dear soever it may cost them.

He held that Separation in a Church was necessary, many times from the known corruptions of it. But allowed not separation from a Church, where active Compliance with some sinful Evil, was not made the Condition of Communion. And in this way he frequently declared himself in Health and Sickness, and most expresly in my hearing on his Bed of Languishing, when he was drawing near his Long-Home.

And that the People were not disobliged from attending upon their Ministry, who were ejected out of their Places, as his Book entituled, A Call to Archippus, sheweth; after that Black and Mournful Sabbath, in which he took his farewel with much affection of his Beloved People.[10]

When he was taken up for Prison, he was not onely contented, but joyful to suffer for the Name of Jesus and the Gospel, which was so dear to him; Intimating, that God had given him much more time than he expected, or askt of him, and that he accounted it cause of rejoycing, and his honour, that he was one of the first called forth to suffer for his name.

Although he was very suddenly surprised, yet none could discern him to be in the least moved.

He pitied the condition of his Enemies, requesting for them, as the Martyr Stephen did for those that stoned him, That God would not Lay this sin of theirs to their charge.[11] The greatest harm that he did wish to any of them, was, That they might throughly be Converted and Sanctified, and that their Souls might be saved in the day of the Lord Jesus.

He was very urgent with those that were Unconverted, to look with more care after their Salvation, now they were removed from them that longed for it, and had watched for their Souls; using this as an Argument often, That now they were fallen into the hands of such, many of which, if not most of them, had neither Skill nor Will to save Souls; And setting home upon them with most tender Affections, what miserable Creatures they were while Unregenerate, telling them how his Heart did yearn for them, and his Bowels turned within him for them; how he did pray and weep for them, while they were asleep, and how willingly he had suffered a year's Imprisonment: Nay, how readily he could shed his Blood to procure their Salvation. His Counsels and Directions were many, and suited to the several states of those he thus Conversed with, both as to their degree and place, and their sins and wants, and would

---

[8]Allusion to Matthew 25:21.

[9]A Call to Archippus; or An Humble and earnest Motion to Some Ejected Ministers, (by way of Letter) to take heed to their Ministry, That they fulfil it (n.p., 1664).

[10]St. Bartholomew's day, 1662, was often called "Black Bartholomew's Day."

---

[11]Acts 7:60.

be too long to recite, though I can remember many of them.

To his fellow Prisoners, he said, "The Eyes of GOD and Angels are upon you, and the eyes of Men are upon you; now you will be critically observed. Every one will be looking that you should be more Holy than others, that are called forth to this his glorious Dignity, to be the Witnesses of Christ Jesus, with the loss of your Liberties."

He was eminently free from harsh censuring and judging of others, and was ready to embrace all in Heart, Arms, and Communion, Civil and Religious, any that professed saving faith in Jesus Christ, and did not overthrow that Profession by some Fundamental Error in Doctrine or Wickedness of life and conversation.

And yet they accused him of being at a Riotous Assembly, though there were no Threats, nor dangerous Words; no Staves, nor Weapons, no Fear so much as pretended to be struck into any man, nor any other Business met about, than Preaching and Prayer. Here he was much abused, receiving many scorns and scoffs from the Justices, and their Associates, who were met to hear his Examination, also from the Ladies and other Gentlemen, who called him often Rogue, and told him, he deserved to be Hang'd, and if he were not, they would be Hang'd for him: With many such like scurrilous Passages, which my Husband received with much patience; and seeming, as they apprehended by his Countenance, to slight their Threatnings, they were more inraged at him: They urged him much to accuse himself, which they seeing they could not bring him to; and having no evidence, as appeared after, yet did make his Mittimus[12] for to go to the Gaol on Monday Morning, after they had detained him till twelve at Night, abusing

[12]Mittimus: a warrant for being committed to prison.

him beyond what I do now distinctly remember, or were fit to express.

As soon as he returned, it being so late, about two a Clock, he lay down on the Bed in his Cloaths, where he had not slept above two or three hours at the most, but he was up, spending his time in Converse with God, till about eight a Clock; by which hour, several of his Friends were come to Visit him: But he was so watched, and the Officer had such a charge, that he was not suffered to Preach all that Sabbath, but spent the day in discoursing with the various Companies, that came flocking in from the Town, and Villages, to visit him; Praying often with them, as he could be permitted. He was exceeding chearful in his Spirit, full of admirations of the Mercies of God, and incouraging all that came to be bold, and venture for the Gospel, and their Souls, notwithstanding what was come upon him for their sakes: For, as he told them, he was not at all moved at it, nor did not in the least repent of any thing he had done, but accounted himself happy, and under the Promise Christ makes to his, in the 5th of Matthew, That he should be doubly and trebly blessed now he was to suffer for his sake: And was very earnest with his Brethren in the Ministry, that came to see him, That they would not in the least desist when he was gone, that there might not be one Sermon the less in Taunton; and with the People to attend the Ministry with greater Ardency, Diligency, and courage, than before; assuring them how sweet and comfortable it was to him to consider what he had done for God in the months past: And that he was going to Prison full of Joy, Being confident that all these things would turn to the furtherance of the Gospel, and the Glory of God.

But he not being satisfied to go away, and not leave some exhortations with his People, appointed them to meet him about one or two a Clock in the Night, to which they shewed their readiness, though at so unseasonable a time: There was of Young and Old, many hundreds; he Preached and Prayed with them about three hours.

And so with many yearnings of his Bowels towards them, and theirs toward him, they took their farewel of each other; a more affectionate Parting could not well be.

About nine a Clock, he with two or three Friends that were willing to accompany him, set out for Ilchester: The Streets were lined on both sides with People, and many followed him a foot some miles out of the Town, with such lamentations, that (he told me after) did so affect him, that he could scarce bear them; but the Lord so strengthned him, that he passed through them all with great Courage and Joy, labouring both by his chearful Countenance and Expressions, to encourage them.

He carried his Mittimus himself, and had no Officer with him; but when he came there, he found the Gaoler absent, and took that opportunity to Preach before he went into the Prison; which was accounted by his Adversaries, a great addition to his former Crime. As soon as the Gaoler came, he delivered his Mittimus, and was clapped up in the Bridewel Chamber, which was over[13] the common Gaol. When he came to the Prison, he found there Mr. John Norman,[14] late Minister of Bridgwater, who for the like cause, was Apprehended and Committed a few dayes before him (a Man, who for his singular Abilities in Preaching, his fervent Zeal, and Holy Boldness in the Cause of Christ, his Constancy to his Principles in the most Wavering and Shak-

ing Times, joyned with an exemplary Carriage and Conversation, was deservedly had in great repute among the People of God in these Western parts; and indeed there were very few that knew him, either among the sober Gentry, or Commonalty, but for his eminent Parts, and spotless Life, had great respects for him). There were also five more Ministers, with fifty Quakers,[15] which had all their Lodgings in the same Room, only parted with a Mat, which they had done for a little more Retirement. It was not long after before Mr. Coven, and Mr. Powel,[16] with eight more, were brought into the same place, being taken at Meetings; which made their Rooms very strait,[17] and it was so nigh to the upper part of the Prison, that they could touch the Tiles as they lay in their Beds, which made it very irksom, the Sun lying so hot on it all the day, and there being so many of them, and so much Resort continually of Friends, they had very little Air, till they were forced to take down the Glass, and some of the Tiles, to let in some Refreshment. But here they were confined to Lie, and eat their Meals, and had no place but a small Garden, joyned to the place where all the Common Prisoners were; which was no Retirement for them, they having there, and in their Chamber, the constant noise of those wretches, except when they slept; who lay just under them, their Chains ratling, their Tongues often Blaspheming; or else Roaring and Singing by Night, as well

---

[13]over: above, i.e., a second floor.

[14]John Norman (d. 1669) had been vicar of Bridgewater from 1647 until his ejection after the Restoration. Joseph Alleine's sister Elizabeth was Norman's wife. He remained in prison for eighteen months, and resumed private, illegal preaching after his release. He was the author of several works of spirituality.

[15]Many Quakers were arrested for their illegal meetings. But, as can be seen, the Puritans did not get along with them in prison.

[16]Stephen Coven (d. 1692) and Thomas Powel. Coven had been ejected in 1660 but continued to preach. He licensed a meeting-house under the Indulgence of 1672. Powel was ejected from an Exeter parish in 1662. In 1665 he was reported to be conducting illegal Congregationalist meetings. He too took out a license under the 1672 Indulgence.

[17]Straight: crowded.

as in the Day: And if they went into the Courts of the Prison, there was the sight of their Cloathes hanging full of Vermin, and themselves in their Rags and Chains: But that which was most grievous to them, they had no place to retire to God in, neither alone, nor together. They were also much molested by the Quakers, who would frequently disturb them by their Cavils, in the times of their Preaching, Praying, and Singing, and would come and work in their Callings[18] just by them, while they were in Duties,[19] which was no small disturbance to them: And the want of the Air was more to my Husband, than to most of them, because he always accustomed himself, both in Oxford, and after, to spend his most secret Hours abroad in by-places,[20] in the fields or woods.

As soon as he came into the Prison, he Preached and Prayed, that[21] he called the Consecration of it. After he had spent a day or two in the Prison, being willing to have me either in the Town, or there, to attend him, and to keep company with his Friends, who came frequently to visit him, he then began to fit up his Lodging; having prevailed with the Keeper for one Corner, which was more private than the rest, to set his Bed in, about which he made a little Partition by some Curtains, that so he might have conveniency for Retirement. This was much comfort to him, and after a few Weeks, he got leave of the Keeper to go out a Mornings and Evenings a mile or more, which he did constantly, unless the

Weather, or his Keeper's fury did hinder him.

Their Diet was very good and sufficient, and sometimes abundant, by their Friend's kindness. Here they Preacht once a day constantly, sometimes twice, and many came daily to hear them, eight or ten miles around about the Countrey; and Multitudes came to visit them, it being a strange sight to see Ministers laid in such a place. Their Friends were exceeding kind to them, endeavouring by their frequent visits, and provisions for Diet, and supplies of Money, to make their Prison sweet to them.

But my Husband's Labours were much increased by this, spending all the day in converse, he was forced to take much of the Night for his Studies, and secret Converse with God.

Thus he with my Brother Norman,[22] and his Company, with their fellow prisoners, continued in that place for four Months, being tossed from Sessions to Assizes.[23] On the 14th of July following, he was brought to the Sessions held at Taunton, and was there Indited for Preaching on May the 17th, but the Evidence against him was so slender, that the Grand Jury could not find the Bill, so that he was not brought to his Answer there at all: And his Friends hoped he should have been dismissed, it being the constant practice of the Court, that if a Prisoner be Indited, and no Bill found, he is Freed by Proclamation. But however my Husband was sent to Prison again until the Assizes; and to his Friends

---

[18]callings: occupations. Workmen in seventeenth-century English prisons were often allowed the tools of their or some other trade. Bunyan, for example, was a lace-maker during his long imprisonment.

[19]duties: prayers and devotions.

[20]by places: out-of-the-way places.

[21]that: which, i.e., he consecrated the prison by his prayers.

---

[22]brother: brother-in-law.

[23]Different courts of law where their cases were taken up. Sessions was a regional court that usually met quarterly. It was presided over by a justice of the peace and dealt with local cases. Assizes were regular courts meeting at stated intervals presided over by judges acting on a commission from higher courts. To go from sessions to assizes would indicate that the case was considered fairly important.

that earnestly expected his Inlargement,[24] he said, "Let us bless God that his Will is done, and not the will of such Worms as we."

August the 24th, He was again Indited at the Assizes, and though the Evidence was the very same, that at the Sessions was by the Grand Jury judged insufficient, yet now at the Assizes, the Bill was by them found against him. So was he had to the Bar, and his Indictment read, which was to this purpose: That he, upon the 17th day of May, 1663, with twenty others, to the Jurors unknown, did Riotously, Routously [sic][25] and Seditiously, Assemble themselves together, contrary to the Peace of our Soveraign Lord the King, and to the great Terrour of his Subjects, and to the evil example of others. Unto which, his Answer was, That as to Preaching, and Praying, which was the truth of the Case, of these things he was guilty, and did own them as his Duty; but as for Riotous, Routous, and Seditious Assemblies, he did abhor them with his Heart, and of these he was not guilty. At last he was found guilty by the Petty Jury, and was Sentenced by the Judge to pay an Hundred Marks, and to lie in Prison till payment should be made. Sentence being pronounced against him, he only made this brief Reply: That he was glad that it had appeared before his Countrey, That whatsoever he was charged with, he was guilty of nothing but doing his Duty, and that all did appear by the Evidence, was only that he had Sung a Psalm, and instructed his Family, others being there, and both in his own House: And that if nothing that had been urged would satisfie, he should with all chearfulness and thankfulness, accept whatsoever Sentence his

Lordship should pronounce upon him, for so Good and Righteous a Cause. Thus from the Assizes he was sent to Prison again, where he continued a whole Year, wanting but three days.

But the Winter coming on, they were willing to try if they could have the favour to be removed to the Ward,[26] this place being like to be as cold in the Winter, as it had been hot in the Summer, (there being no Chimney in the whole Chamber) which with some difficulty they obtained; and then had more comfortable Accomodations in all respects.

Here they had very great Meetings, Week-days, and Sabbath days, and many days of Humiliation, and Thanksgiving. The Lord's days many Hundreds came. And though my Husband, and Brother Norman, had many Threats from the Justices and Judges, That they should be sent beyond Sea, or carried to some Island, where they should be kept close Prisoners; yet the Lord preserved them by his Power, and thus ordered it, that their Imprisonment was a great furtherance to the Gospel, and brought much Glory to him, both by their Preaching and Conversing with Souls: In which they had great Success through his Blessing on their Labours. My Husband having here more freedom, made a little Book, Entituled *A Call to Archippus,* to stir up his Nonconforming Brethren, to be diligent at their work, whatsoever Dangers and Sufferings they might meet withal: And because he could not go to his Flock, he had prepared for them, *The Synopsis of the Covenant,* which was after placed into one of my Father's Books.[27]

---

[24]Inlargement: release, i.e., to be at-large.

[25]routously: disorderly, creating a "rout." The 1672 edition has "wantonly," but that does not conform with the repetition following.

[26]The Ward was probably a more comfortable part of the same prison.

[27]This was placed in Richard Alleine's *Heaven Opened; or, A Brief and plain Discovery of the Riches of God's Covenant of Grace* (London, 1665). In the edition of 1671 it runs from pages 215-273.

And for the help of the Governours of Families, in their Weekly Catechizing those under their charge, he explained all the Assemblie's shorter Catechism;[28] to which he annexed an affectionate Letter, with Rules for their daily Examination; which were Printed and Dispersed into all their Houses by his Order, while he was a Prisoner. He also writ many Holy, and Gracious, and affectionate Letters to all his Relations, and many other Friends, to many Churches of Christ in other parts and places, both far and near.

His Sufferings that he underwent for the sake of the Gospel, could neither remit his Zeal, not abate his Activity for God, but he would gladly imbrace all Opportunities of doing him Service. The Minister who was appointed to Preach at certain times to the Felons in the prison, being by sickness disabled for that Work, he freely performed that Office among them, as long as he was permitted; earnestly exhorting them by Repentance towards God, and Faith toward our Lord Jesus Christ, to secure the eternal welfare of their Souls; freely bestowing upon them, according to his Ability, for their Relief; that by doing good to their Bodies, he might win upon them to receive good for their Souls. He was very forward to promote the Education of youth, in the Town of Ilchester, and Country adjacent, freely bestowing Catechisms on those that were of poor Families, to instruct them in the Principles of Religion; stirring up the Elder to Teach, and incouraging the Younger to Learn. He was a serious and faithful Monitor to his fellow Sufferers, if he espyed any thing in any of them, that did not become the Gospel, for which they suffered.

Here, as else-where, he was a careful redeemer of his time; his constant practice was, early to begin with God, rising about four of the Clock, and spending a considerable part of the Morning in Meditation and Prayer, and then falling close to his study, in some corner or other of the prison, where he could be private. At times, he would spend near the whole night in these Exercises, not putting off his Clothes at all, only taking the repose of an hour or two in his Night-Gown upon the Bed, and so up again. When any came to visit him he did not entertain them with needless impertinent[29] Discourse, but that which was serious, profitable, and edifying; in which he was careful to apply himself to them, according to their several capacities, whether Elder or Younger; exhorting them to those gracious Practices, which by reason of their Age, or Temper, Calling, or Condition, he apprehended they might be most defective in, and dehorting[30] them from those Evils they might be most prone and lyable unto. He rejoyced that he was accounted worthy to suffer for the works of Christ; and he would labour to incourage the timorous and faint-hearted, by his own and others' experience, of the Mercy and Goodness of God in Prison, which was far beyond what they could have thought or expected. He was a careful observer of that Rule of the Lord Jesus, Mat. 5.44, "Love your enemies, bless them that curse you, do good to them that hate you, and pray for them that [which] despitefully use you, and persecute you." It was none of his practice to exclaim against those that were the greatest Instruments of his Sufferings.

In all his Imprisonment, at present, I could not discern his Health to be the least impaired, notwithstanding his abundant

---

[28]The "Shorter Catechism" was drawn up by the Westminster Assembly in 1647 (though largely the work of Anthony Tuckney) and approved by that body in 1648. It was a favorite among Presbyterians and Congregationalists and is still widely used.

[29]impertinent: irrelevant, i.e., not pertinent to their souls.

[30]dehorting: dissuading, advising against.

Labours; but cannot but suspect, as the Physicions judged, that he had laid the foundation for that Weakness, which suddenly after surprised him, and was his death.

At his return from the prison, he was far more earnest in his Work than before; yet willing to preserve his liberty among his people, who had no Minister that had the oversight of them, though some came and preached while he was absent. And the People flocked so greatly after him, that he judged it best to divide the Company in to four, and resolved to Preach four times each Sabbath to them: But finding sensibly that would be too hard for him, his strength much decaying, he did forbear that course, and preached only twice a Sabbath as formerly, and often on Week-dayes at Home and in the Country; and spent what time he had else from his studying, in private converse with God, as formerly he had done, pressing all that feared the Lord, especially those that were of a more weak and timerous Spirit, to a life of Courage and Activity for God, and to be much in helping one another, by their Converses, now Ministers were withdrawn, and to be much in the Work of Praises and Thanksgiving to God, rejoycing and delighting themselves in him; and with chearfulness and readiness, denying themselves for him: and resigning themselves, and all they did enjoy, to him: Letting the World know, they could live comfortably on God alone, on his Attributes and Promises, though they should have nothing else left.

But it pleased the All-wise God, to take him off from the eager pursuit of his Work, and designs for him, by visiting him in the later end of August, with much weakness, so that he had not above three months time after he came out of Prison: for he going about sixteen miles, at the request of a Society, whose Pastor was not able to come among them to Preach, and to Administer a more solemn Ordinance;[31] he was so disabled, that he was not able to perform the great and chief work, though he did adventure to preach, but with much injury to himself, because he would not wholly disappoint the People who came so far, as many of them did: with much difficulty, after three or four dayes, I made way to get him home to Taunton, where we then sojourned, and presently had the best Advice the most Able Physicions, both in and round the Town, could give; who advised together, and all judged it to be from his abundant Labours, and the preaching too soon after his Meals; as he did, when he Preached four times a Sabbath, whereby he had so abated the natural heat of his Stomach, that no Food would digest, nor oftentimes keep within him: He would assure us, he was in no pain, but a constant discomposure in his Stomach, and a failing of his Appetite, that he could not for many Weeks bear the scent of any Flesh-meat, nor retain any Liquors[32] or Broths, so that he consumed[33] so fast, that his Life seemed to draw to an end: But the Lord did so bless the means,[34] that he recovered out of this Distemper, after two Months' time, but so lost the use of his Armes from October till April, that he could not put off nor on his Cloathes, nor often write either his Notes, or any Letters, but as I wrote for him, as he dictated to me: He was by all Physicions, and by my earnest beseechings often diswaded from Preaching, but would not be prevailed with, but did go on once, and sometimes twice a Sabbath, and in his private Visiting all that Winter; in the Spring, the use of his Arms returned, for which he

---

[31]Presumably a baptism or, more likely, a celebration of the Lord's Supper—the Puritans often referred to these sacraments as ordinances.

[32]liquors: liquids.

[33]consumed: wore out.

[34]means: method of treatment.

was exceeding thankful to the Lord; and we had great hopes of his Recovering; and making use of further Remedies, he was able to go on with more freedom in his Work: And the Summer following, by the use of Mineral-Waters in Wiltshire, near the Devises, where he was born, his strength was much increased, he finding great and sensible good by them.

But he venturing too much on what he had obtained, his weakness returned frequently upon him the next Winter, and more in the Spring following, being seised as he was at the first: But it continued not long at a time, so that he did preach often to his utmost strength (nay, I may say, much beyond the strength he had) both at Home and Abroad; going into some remote parts of the Country, where had been no Meetings kept all that time the Ministers had been out which was two Years: And there he ingaged several of his Brethren to go and take their turns, which they did with great success.

He had also agreed with two of his Brethren to go into Wales with them, to spread the Gospel there; but was prevented in that, by his weakness increasing upon him: It was much that he did, but much more that he desired to do.

He was in this time much Threatned, and Warrants often out for him; and he was so far from being disturbed at it, that he rejoyced; that when he could do but little for God, because of his Distempers God would so far honour him, that he should go and suffer for him in a prison. He would often with chearfulness say, They could not do him a greater kindness. But the Lord was yet pleased to preserve him from their rage, seeing him not then fit for the inconveniences as of a Prison.

The five Mile Act[35] coming in force, he removed to a place called Wellington, which is reckoned five miles from Taunton, to a Dyer's House, in a very obscure place, where he preached on the Lord's Dayes, as he was able: But the vigilant Eyes of his old Adversaries were so watchful over him, that they soon found him out, and resolved to take him thence, and had put a Warrant into the Constable's hand to apprehend him, and sent for our Friend, and threatned to send him to Gaol for entertaining such persons in his House: So my Husband returned to the House of Mr. John Mallack, a Merchant, who lived about a mile from Taunton, who had long solicited him to take his House for his Home: We being in such an unsetled state, my Husband thought it best to accept of his courteous offer. But many of his Friends were willing to enjoy him in the Town, and so earnest, that he did, to satisfie them, go from one to another, staying a fortnight, or three weeks, or a month at each House; but still took Mr. Mallack's for his Home: This motion of his Friends he told me, (though it was troublesome for us to be so unsetled) he was willing to embrace, because he knew, not how soon he might be carried again from them to prison, and he should have opportunity to be more intimately acquainted with them, and the state of their Souls; and of their Children and Servants, and how they perform their Duties each to other in their Families.

He went from no House without serious Counsels, Comforts, or Reproofs, as their conditions called for; dealing with all that were capable, both Governours and others particularly, acquainting them faithfully and most affectionately, what he had seen amiss in any of them.

He went from no House that was willing to part with him; nor had he opportunity to answer the requests of half that invited us to their Houses: So that he would often bless God, and say with holy Mr.

---

[35]The Five Mile Act (October, 1665) was one of the penal statutes of the Clarendon Code directed against Puritan dissenters. It forbade any ejected or Nonconformist clergyman from coming within five miles of a town where he had formerly ministered.

Dod,[36] That he had a hundred houses for one that he had parted with; and though he had no Goods, he wanted nothing, his Father cared for him in every thing, that he lived a far more pleasant life than his Enemies, who had turned him out of all: He was exceedingly taken with God's Mercy to him, in Mr. Mallack's entertaining him and me so bountifully, the House and Gardens, and Walks, being a very great delight to him, being so Pleasant and Curious, and all Accommodations within suitable, so that he would often say, That he did as Dives,[37] fare deliciously every day: But he hoped he should improve it better than he did, and that God had inclined him to take care for many Poor, and for several of his Brethren in the Ministry; and now God did reward him by not suffering him to be at the least expence for himself or me.

He was a very strict observer of all Providences of every day, and did usually reckon them up to me before we went to sleep, each night after he came into his Chamber and Bed, to raise his own Heart and Mind, to praise the Lord, and to trust him, whom we had such experience of, from time to time.

The time of the Year being come for his going to the Waters,[38] he was desirous to set one day apart for Thanksgiving to God, for all his Mercies to him and them, and so to take his leave of them.

Accordingly, on the 10th of July 1665 divers of his Brethren in the Ministry and many of his Friends of Taunton, met together to take their leave of him before his

---

[36]John Dod (d. 1645) was parish minister of Hanwell in Oxfordshire from 1585 to 1604, when he was deprived by his bishop for Nonconformity. But he found other pulpits and kept preaching until his death. He was known for homely and vivid aphorisms.

[37]Dives is the name traditionally given to the rich man in the parable of Lazarus, Luke 16;19-31.

[38]The waters at Bath, supposedly restorative of health.

departure, at the House of Mr. Mallack, then living about a mile out of the Town. Where after they had been a while together, came two Justices, and several other Persons attending them, brake open the Doors by force, (though they might have unlatched them if they had pleased) and with Swords came in among them. After much deriding and menacing Language, which I shall not here relate, having taken their Names, committed them to the custody of some Constables, whom they charged to bring them forth the next day, at the Castle Tavern in Taunton, before the Justices of the Peace there. The next day the Prisoners appeared, and answered to their Names; and after two dayes tedious attendance, were all Convicted of a Conventicle, and Sentenced to pay three Pounds a piece, or to be committed to Prison threescore dayes. Of the Persons thus Convicted, but few either paid their Fines, or suffered their Friends to do it for them. My Husband, with seven Ministers more, and forty private Persons, were committed to the Prison of Ilchester: When he, together with the rest of his Brethren and Christian Friends, came to the Prison, his Carriage and Conversation there was every way as Exemplary, as in his former Confinement. Notwithstanding his weakness of Body, yet he would constantly take his turn with the rest of the Ministers, in preaching the Gospel in the prison; which turns came about the oftener, though there were eight of them there together, because they had Preaching and praying twice a day, almost every day they were in prison; besides other Exercises of Religion, in which he would take his part.

And although he had many of his Flock confined to the Prison with him, by which means he had the fairer opportunity of Instructing, and Watching over them, for their Spiritual good; yet he was not forgetful of the rest that were left behind, but would frequently visit them also, by his Letters full of serious profitable Matter, from which they might reap no small benefit, while they were debarred of his bodily presence. And how greatly sollicitous he was for those that were with him, (that they might be the better for their Bonds, walking worthy of the many and great Mercies they had enjoyed during their Imprisonment; that when they came home to their Houses, they might speak forth, and live forth the Praises of GOD, carrying themselves in every respect as becomes the Gospel, for which they had been Sufferers) you may clearly see by these parting Counsels that he gave them that Morning that they were delivered, which I shall recite in his own Words, as they were taken from his Mouth in Shorthand, by an intimate Friend, and fellow Prisoner, which you may take as followeth, etc. . . .

He was prevented of going to the Waters, by his last Imprisonment; for want of which, his Distempers increased much upon him all the Winter after, and the next Spring more; yet not so as to take him fully off from his Work, but he Preached, and kept many Days, and Administred the Sacrament among them frequently.

But going up to the Waters in July 1667, they had a contrary effect upon him, from what they had at first: For after three dayes taking them, he fell into a Feaver, which seised on his Spirits, and decayed his strength exceedingly, so that he seemed very near Death: But the Lord then again revoked the Sentence passed upon him, and enabled him in six Weeks to return again to his People, where he much desired to be: But finding, at his return, great decay of his strength, and a weakness in all his Limbs, he was willing to go to Dorchester, to advise further with Doctor Lose, a very Worthy and Reverend Physitian, from whom he had received many Medicines, but never conversed with him, nor had seen him,

which he conceived might conduce more to his full Cure.

The Doctor soon perceiving my Husband's weakness, perswaded him to continue for a fortnight or three weeks there, that he might the better advise him, and alter his Remedies as he should see occasion; which motion was readily yielded unto by us.

But we had not been there above five days, before the use of all his Limbs was taken away on a sudden; one day his Arms wholly failing, the next his Legs; so that he could not go, nor stand, nor move a Finger, nor turn in his Bed, but as my self and another did turn him night and day in a Sheet: All means failing, he was given over by Physicians and Friends, that saw him lie some weeks in cold Sweats night and day, and many times for some hours together, half his Body cold, in our apprehensions, dying: receiving nothing but the best Cordials that Art could invent, and Almond Milk,[39] or a little thin Broth once in three or four days. Thus he lay from September 28, to November 16, before he began to Revive, or it could be discerned that Remedies did at all prevail against his Diseases: In all this time he was still chearful, and when he did speak, it was not at all complaining, but always praising and admiring God for his Mercies; but his Spirits were so low,[40] that he spake solemn, and very softly. He still told us he had no pain at all, and when his Friends admired his Patience, he would say; God had not yet tryed him in any thing, but laying him aside out of his Work, and keeping him out of Heaven; but through Grace he could submit to his pleasure, waiting for him: It was Pain he ever feared, and that he had not yet

---

[39]Almond Milk: a mixture of blanched almonds and water, used medicinally.

[40]Here "low spirits" means lack of animal vitality, not depression.

felt; so tender was his Father of him; and he wanted strength (as he often told us) to speak more of his Love, and to speak for God, who had been, and was still so gracious to him. Being often askt by my self and others, how it was with his Spirit in all this weakness? he would answer: He had not those ravishing joys that he expected, and that some Believers did partake of; but he had a sweet serenity of Heart, and confidence in God, grounded on the Promises of the Gospel, and did believe it would be well with him to all eternity.

In all this time, I never heard one impatient word from him, nor could upon my strictest observation, discern the least discontent with this state; though he was a pitiful Object to all others that beheld him, being so consumed, besides the loss of the use of his Limbs: Yet the Lord did support and quiet his Spirit, that he lay as if he had endured nothing; breaking out often most affectionately in commending the kindness of the Lord to him, saying, Goodness and Mercy had followed him all his days.

And indeed the loving kindness and care of God was singular to us in that place, which I cannot but mention to his praise.

We came Strangers thither, and being in our Inn, we found it very uncomfortable; yet were fearful to impose our selves on any private House: But necessity inforcing, we did enquire for a Chamber, but could not procure one; the Small Pox being very hot in most Families, and those that had them not, daily expecting them, and so could not spare Rooms, as else they might. But the Lord who saw our affliction, inclined the heart of a very good Woman, (a Minister's Widdow) one Mrs. Bartlet, to come and invite us to a Lodging in her House; which we readily and thankfully accepted of; where we were so accommodated; as we could not have been any where else in the Town, especially in regard of the assistance I had from four young Women

who lived under the same roof, and so were ready, night and day, to help me, (I having no Servant nor Friend near me) we being so unsetled, I kept none, but had alwayes tended him my self to that time: And the Ministers and Christians of that place were very compassionate towards us, visiting and praying with and for us often: And Dr. Lose visited him twice a day for twelve or fourteen Weeks, except when he was called out of Town, refusing any Fees tendered to him: The Gentry, in and about the Town, and others, sending to us what-ever they imagined might be pleasing to him; furnishing him with all delicates that might be grateful to one so weak; So that he wanted neither Food nor Physick, having not only for necessity, but for delight; and he did much delight himself in the consideration of the Lord's kindness to him in the love he received, and would often say, "I was a Stranger, and Mercy took me in; in Prison, and it came to me; sick and weak, and it visited me." There were also ten young women, besides the four in the House, that took their turns to watch with him constantly; for twelve weeks space I never wanted one to help me: And the Lord was pleased to shew his power so in strengthening me, that I was every night (all these weeks in the depth of Winter) one that helped to turn him, never lying out of the Bed one night from him, but every time he called or wanted any thing, was waking to assist her in the Chamber, though as some of them have said they did tell,[41] that he did turn him more than 40 times a Night, he seldom sleeping at all in the Night, in all those Weeks: Though his tender affections were such, as to have had me sometimes lain in another Room, yet mine were such to him, that I could not bear it, the thoughts of it being worse to me than the trouble or disturbance he accounted I had with him,

---

[41]tell: count.

for I feared none would do any thing about him with such ease; neither would he suffer any one all the day to touch him but me, or to give him any thing that he did receive; by which I discerned it was most grateful to him, and therefore so to me; And I never found any want of my Rest, nor did get so much as a Cold all that winter, though I do not remember that for 14 or 15 years before, I could ever say I was one month free of a most violent Cough, which if I had been molested with then, would have been a great addition to his and my affliction; and he was not a little taken with the goodness of God to me in the time of all his sickness, but especially that Winter; for he being not able to help himself in the least, I could not be from him night nor day, with any comfort to him or my self.

In this condition he kept his Bed till December the 18th. And then, beyond all expectation, though in the depth of Winter, he began to revive and go out of his Bed; but he could neither stand nor go, nor yet move a finger, having sense in all his Limbs, but not the least motion: As his strength did increase, he learnt to go, (as he would say) first by being led by two of us, then by one; and when he could go one turn in his Chamber, though more weakly, and with more fear than the weakest Child that ever I saw, he was wonderfully taken with the Lord's Mercy to him: By February he was able, with a little help, to walk in the Streets; (but not to feed himself) nor to go up or down stairs without much help.

When he was deprived of the use of his Limbs, looking down on his Arms, as I held him by all the strength I had: He again lifted up his Eyes from his useless Arms to Heaven, and with a cheerful countenance said: "The Lord hath given, and the Lord hath taken, and blessed be the Name of the Lord."[42]

---

[42]Allusion to Job 1:21.

Being asked by a Friend, How he could be so well contented to lie so long under such weakness? He answered,

"What, is God my Father, Jesus Christ my Saviour, and the Spirit my sweet Friend, my Comforter, and Sanctifyer, and Heaven my Inheritance? Shall I not be content without Limbs and Health? Through Grace I am fully satisfied with my Father's pleasure."

To another that asked him the same, he Answers, "I have chosen God, and he is become mine, and I know with whom I have trusted my self, which is enough: He is an unreasonable wretch that cannot be content with a God, though he had nothing else: My interest in God is all my joy."

His Friends (some of Taunton) coming to Dorchester to see him, he was much revived, and would be set up in his Bed, and have all the Curtains drawn, and desired them to stand round about the Bed, and would have me take out his Hand, and hold it out to them, that they might shake him though he could not them; as he used formerly to do, when he had been absent from them. And as he was able thus he spake to them: "O how it rejoyces my heart to see your Faces, and to hear your Voices, though I cannot speak as heretofore to you: Methinks I am now like Old Jacob, with all his Sons about him: Now you see my weak estate; thus have I been for many weeks, since I parted with Taunton, but God hath been with me, and I hope with you; your Prayers have been heard, and answered for me, many wayes; the Lord return them into your own Bosoms. My Friends, Life is mine, Death is mine; in that Covenant I was preaching of to you, is all my Salvation, and all my desire; although my Body do not prosper, I hope through Grace my Soul doth.

"I have lived a sweet Life by the promises, and I hope through Grace can Die by a Promise: It is the Promises of God which are everlasting, that will stand by us: Nothing but God in them will stead us in a day of Affliction.

"My dear Friends, I feel the power of those Doctrines I Preached to you, on my Heart: Now the Doctrines of Faith, of Repentance, of Self-denial, of the Covenant of Grace, of Contentment, and the rest; O that you would live them over, now I cannot Preach to you.

"It is a shame for a Believer to be cast down under Afflictions, that hath so many glorious Priviledges, Justification, Adoption, Sanctification, and eternal Glory. We shall be as the Angels of God in a little while: Nay, to say the truth, Believers are, as it were, little Angels already, that live in the power of Faith. O my Friends! Live like Believers, trample this dirty World under your feet; Be not taken with its Comforts, nor desquieted with its Crosses, You will be gone out of it shortly."

When they came to take their leaves of him, he would Pray with them as his weak state would suffer him; and in the words of Moses and of the Apostles, Blessed them. The same he always used after a Sacrament: The Lord bless you and keep you, the Lord cause his Face to shine upon you, and give you peace. And "the God of Peace, that brought again from the Dead our Lord Jesus, . . . through the Blood of the Everlasting Covenant, make you perfect in every good work to do his Will, working in you that which is well-pleasing in his sight, through Jesus Christ, to whom be glory, for ever and ever. Amen."[43]

And then spake thus, "Farewell, farewell my dear Friends. Remember me to all Taunton; I beseech you and them, if I never see your faces more, go Home and live over what I have preached to you, and the Lord provide for you when I am gone: O! let not all my labours and sufferings, let not my wasted strength, my useless Limbs, rise up in judgment against you at the great Day of the Lord."

Another time, some coming to Visit him there, he spake thus to them: "O! my Friends, let your whole Conversation be as becomes the Gospel of Christ; whether I am present or absent, live to what I have spoken to you in the Name of the Lord: Now I cannot Preach to you, let my wasted strength, my useless Limbs, be a Sermon to you: Behold me, I cannot move a finger; all this is come upon me for your sakes, and the Gospel; It is for Christ and you that I have thus spent out my self: I am afraid of you,[44] lest some of you, after all that I have spoken to you, should be lost in the World. There are many Professors who can pray well and talk well, whom we shall find at the left hand of Christ another day: You have your Trades, your Estates, your Relations; be not taken with these, but with God: O live on him! For the Lord's sake go Home and take heed of the world, worldly Cares, worldly Comforts, worldly Friends, &c." saying thus:

"The Lord having given Authority to his Ministers to bless his People, accordingly I bless you in his Name," using the same words as before, and so parted with them; with many other dear Expressions of his Love to them and the Town.

And thus he was used to Converse with all that came to Visit him, as he was able, looking alwayes chearfully upon them, and never complaining of any Affliction He was under, except it were to excite his Taunton Friends to their Duties.

In February, he being very desirous to return among his People, he moved it to his Doctor, who consented to it, fearing that Air might be too keen for him in March.

---

[43]A paraphrase of Numbers 6:25 combined with Hebrews 13:20-21.

[44]afraid of you: afraid for you.

And hoping that it might much add to his Cure, to satisfie his mind.

In a Horse-Litter I removed him: He was much pleased at the sight of the place, and his people, who came flocking about him, and he seemed to increase in strength, so that he was able to feed himself the Week after he came Home: But I fearing the frequent Visits of his Friends might be prejudicial to him, perswaded him to remove to Mr. Mallack's House, which he was again invited to, and most courteously entertained.

And thus he continued increasing in strength, till the beginning of April, and he began to decline again, and was taken after some dayes with Convulsion Fits, as he sat in his Chamber one Afternoon, and had three or four more fits that Night: But in the use of Means, through God's Blessing, he had no more in three Weeks. One Evening being in his Chamber, he desired me to leave him a while alone; which I was very unwilling to do, but his importunity made me to go down from him: But in less than half a quarter of an hour, he was fallen to the Ground in one of his former Fits, and had hurt his Face; and from his Nose came much Blood, which was very clotted and corrupt, which Physicions seeing, did conclude (though it were grievous to me, that under such weakness, he should have so sad an Accident) that the fall saved his life. For had not that Blood come from his Head, he had, so far as they could rationally judge, died in that Fit, which took away his senses for the present; but he went to Bed, and slept so well that night, as he had not in many weeks before; so that my Self, and Friends, feared that he had been in an Apoplexy: But he awaked about six in the morning, much refreshed, and full of the Praises of God for his Mercies to him, being very sensible how suddenly he was surprised the Evening before. After this, he lived alwayes expecting Death,

saying often to me and his Friends, "It is but a puff, and I am gone." And therefore would, every Night after he had been at Prayer, bid all the Family farewel, telling them, He might be dead before the Morning, and droping [*sic*] some holy Counsels to them, would depart to his Chamber: All the while I was undressing him, he would be discoursing of Spiritual things, it being all his delight; and when we lay down to rest, his last words were usually, "We shall shortly be in another Bed, therefore it is good to mind it, and provide for it apace; farewel my Dear Heart, the Lord bless thee," and so he would go to his rest. In his Health and Sickness, his first Speeches in the Mornings would be, "Now we have one day more; here is one more for God; now let us live well this day; work hard for our Souls; lay up much Treasure in Heaven this day, for we have but a few to live."

After this, the strength of his Limbs, which were decayed, returned again, and he was, beyond all expectation, so far recovered, that we have no fears of his relapsing again: His Appetite, and Rest, and all repaired. But about the sixth of May, he began again to find weakness in his Stomach, which in a few dayes so grew upon him, that he lost his Limbs again; and on the 12th of May, in the Morning, having lain some dayes and nights in cold Sweats, as heretofore at Dorchester, he was again seised with Convulsions, first lying four hours with his eyes fixed to Heaven, not speaking one Word, nor in the least moving himself, my self and Friends weeping by him, at last he spake to us with a very audible Voice, "Weep not for me, my work is done," and seemed to be full of Matter to utter to us, but was immediately seised with a terrible Convulsion, which was sad to behold; it so altered his Countenance, and put him into such Sweats, that 'twas strange to see how the drops lay and run down his Face, and Hands, and Body:

This held him two hours or more, and ceased, but he was left by it without any sense; and in a quarter of an hour, or little more, fell into another, in which he rattled, and was cold, so that we apprehended every breath would be his last. The Physicion who was then by him, accounted his Pulse to be gone, and that he would be dead in a few minutes: But the Lord shewed his Power here once again in raising him, so that many came and saw him, that heard the next day he was alive, would not believe till they came and saw him again. These violent Fits went off about twelve a Clock, and he revived, but had no sense to converse with us till the next day, nor did he perfectly recover them four dayes after, and then was as before, and so continued very weak till July, no strength coming into his Hands or Legs; for the most part confined to his Bed, but still chearful in his Spirit, and free to discourse with any that came to visit him, as long as he was able.

But the Lord had yet more work for him to do: I seeing him lie so hopeless, as to his Life or Limbs, and considering the Winter was growing on apace, I proposed it to the Doctors to have him to the Bath; some were for it, others against it; acquainting my Husband with it, he was much pleased with it, and so earnest in it, that I sent immediately to Bath for a Horse-Litter, and the Lord was pleased strangely to appear in strengthening him for his Journey; so that he that had not in many weeks been out of his Bed and Chamber, was able in two dayes to reach near forty miles, (but when he came to Bath, the Doctors there seemed to be much amazed to behold such an Object, professing they never saw the like) much wondering how he was come alive such a journey, and doubted much to put him in: But he having tryed all Artificial Baths, and Oyntments, and Plasters before, he resolved, against their Judgements, to adventure himself.

At his first appearing in the Bath, being wasted to Skin and Bone, some of the Ladies were affrighted, as if Death had been come in among them, and could not endure to look toward him.

The first time he went in, he was able to stay but a little while, but was much refreshed, and had no Symptom of his Fits, which he feared the Bath might have caused again: Through the blessing of the Lord upon this means, without any thing else, except his drinking of Goat's-Milk, he that was not able to go nor stand, nor move a Finger, could in three Weeks time walk about his Chamber, and feed himself: his impaired Appetite was again restored, and his strength so increased, that there seemed no doubt to the Physicions of his full Recovery, he having not the least sign of any inclination to his Fits, from the twelfth of May till his Death drew nigh.

In this time of his being in Bath, his Soul was far more strengthened with Grace; so that my self, and all that beheld him, and conversed with him, discerned sensibly his growth; and he was in the Nights and Dayes, so frequently with God, and often in such ravishments of Spirit from the Joyes and Consolations that he received from the Spirit of God, that it was oftentimes more than he could express, or his bodily strength could bear; so that for my own part, I had less hopes of his continuance on Earth than ever before: For I perceived plainly, the Lord had spared him but to recover strength of Grace, and to make him a more evident instance of his singular Love, before he took him hence.

He being now more chearful than formerly, and more exceedingly affectionate in his carriage to me, and to all his Friends, especially with those that were most Heavenly, the Lord was pleased to order it in his Providence; that were many such then who came to use the Bath, as Mr. Fairclough and his Wife, Mr. How of Torrington, Mr.

Joseph Barnard and his Wife, and several of our Taunton Friends, and of Bristol Ministers and others,[45] which was a great comfort to us.

His parts seemed to be more quick in his Converses, whatever he put upon, either by Scholars, or those that were more Inferiour. He had many visitors there, both of strangers and Friends, who were willing to see him, and discourse with him, having heard what a monument of Mercy he was; and he would to all of them, so amplifie upon all the Passages of God's dealings with him, as was very pleasant to all that heard him; and did affect many that were strangers to God, and to Religion, as well as to him.

He found much favour, even among the worst; both Gentry and others (such as would make a scoff at Religion, or holy Discourse from others) would hearken to him, though he did often faithfully reprove many for their Oaths, and excess in Drinking, [and] their lascivious Carriages,[46] which he observed in the Bath; and there was none of them but did most thankfully accept it from him, and shewed him more respect after, than they had done before: In which he observed much of God's goodness to him, and would often say to me: ''O! how good is it to be faithful to God.'' The vilest of these Persons, as I was by several informed, said of him, That he never spake with such a man in his life.

His Reproofs were managed with so much respect to their Persons, and the honourable esteem he had of their Dignity, that they said, They could not but accept his Reproofs, though very close and plain: And his

way was, some time before he intended to reprove them, he would often in the Bath Converse with them, of things that might be taking with them;[47] and did so ingage their Affections, that they would willingly every day converse with him: He being furnished (from his former Studies) for any Company, designing to use it still for Holy ends; by such means hath he caught many Souls.

While he was in this place, though he had many Diversions, by his using the Bath constantly every day, and his frequent Visits, besides his Weakness, yet he kept his constant Seasons, four times a Day, for his Holy Retirements; waking in the Morning constantly at or before five a Clock, and would not be disturbed till about seven, when he was carried to the Bath. Having the Curtains drawn close, he spent his time in Holy Meditation, and Prayer, and Singing, and once again before Dinner, but then he spent less time; and about half an hour before two in the Afternoon, just before he went abroad.

For though he never attained to so much strength so to be able to walk abroad in the Streets without my leading him, or some other, yet he would be imployed for his Lord and Master. The Chair-men that used to carry him to the Bath, he appointed to fetch him about Three a Clock, who carried him to Visit all the Schools and Almes-houses, and the Godly Poor, especially the Widdows; to whom he would give Money, and with whom he would Pray; and Converse with them, concerning their Spiritual States, according as their Necessities required; engaging those that were Teachers, and Governours, to Teach the Assemblie's Catechism,[48] buying many Dozens, and giving them to distribute to their Scholars; and many other small Books which he thought might be useful for them; and then would come and see, in a Week or Fortnight, what progress

---

[45]Probably Richard Fairclough, who was ejected from a Somerset rectory in 1662 but remained nearby. By 1672, however, he was in London. Mr. Howe of Torrington is John Howe (1630-1705), one of the leading Presbyterians among the Dissenters.

[46]Carriages: behaviors.

---

[47]i.e., of their business.

[48]The ''Shorter Catechism''; see n. 28 above.

they had made: He also ingaged several to send their Children once a Week to him to be Catechised; which they did hearken to him in: And we had about sixty or seventy Children every Lord's Day to our Lodging, and they profited much by his Instructions, till some took such offense at it, that he was forced to desist, and the School-Master was threatned to be cited to Wells before the Bishop, and many others affrighted from it.

He also sent for all the godly Poor he could find in that place, and entertained them at his Chamber, and gave to them every one as he was able, as a Thank-Offering to the Lord for his Mercy to him, and desired them, with several others, to keep a day of Thanksgiving for him; Mr. Fairclough, Mr. How, and Himself, performing the duties of the day.

Thus though his Sickness had been long, and his Expences great, he thought he could never spend enough for him from whom he had received all: He constantly gave Money or Apples to all the Children that came to be catechized by him, to ingage them, beside all he gave to the Teachers, and Poor, which indeed was beyond his ability, considering his Estate: But I am perswaded, he did foresee that his time would be but short; and having made a competent and comfortable provision for me, he resolved to lay up the rest in Heaven; he did often say to me, If he lived never so long, he would never increase his Estate, now I was provided for; he having no Children, God's Children should have it.

But he was yet again designing what he might do before he took his leave of the World: And his next work was, to send Letters to all his Relations and intimate Friends, in most of which he urges them to observe his Counsels, for they were like to be his last to them. I always wrote for him, for he could not, by reason of his weakness, write a Line.

At this time he had a great desire to go to Mr. Joseph Barnard's, which was about Five Miles from Bath, there to finish his last Work for God, that ever he did on Earth; which was to promote the Exercise of Catechising in Somersetshire and Wiltshire: Mr. Barnard having had a great deliverance as well as himself, he proposed this to him as their Thank-Offering to God, which they would joyntly tender to him. They had ingaged one to another, to give so much for the Printing of six thousand of the Assemblie's Catechism, & among other Friends, to raise some Money, for to send to every Minister that would ingage in the Work and to give to the Children for their Incouragement in Learning: This Work was finished by Mr. Barnard, after my Husband was gone to his Rest.

He finding himself to decline again, apprehended it was for want of using the Bath, and therefore desired to return, and I being fearful he should ride home, seeing some Symptoms of his Fits, sent for the Horse-Litter, and so carried him again to the Bath: Where, by the Doctor's advice, after he had taken some things to prepare his Body, he made us of the Hot Bath (the Cross-Bath being then too cold) and so he did for four dayes, and seemed to be refreshed, and the strength that he had in his Limbs to recover, rather than abate; and two of his Taunton Friends coming to see him, he was chearful with them: But on the third of November, I discerned a great change in his Countenance, and he found a great alteration in himself, but concealed it from me, as I heard after: For some Friends coming to visit him, he desired them to pray for him, for his time was very short; But desired them not to tell me of it: All that day he would not permit me to move out of the Chamber from him, except once while those Friends were with him. After we had dined, he was in more than ordinary manner transported with Affection towards me;

which he expressed, by his returning me thanks for all my pains and care for him and with him, and putting up many most affectionate requests for me to GOD, before he would suffer me to rise as we sat together: At Night again, at the Supper, before I could rise from him, he spake thus to me:

"Well, now my dear Heart, my Companion in all my Tribulations and Afflictions, I thank thee for all thy pains and labours for me, at Home and Abroad, in Prison and Liberty, in Health and Sickness;" reckoning up many of the Places we had been in, in the dayes of our affliction: And with many other most endearing and affectionate Expressions, he concluded with many Holy Breathings to God for me, that he would requite me, and never forget me, and fill me with all manner of Grace and Consolations, and that his Face might still shine upon me, and that I might be supported and carried through all difficulties.

After this he desired me to see for a *Practice of Piety;*[49] and I procuring one for him, he turned his Chair from me, that I might not see, and read the Meditations about Death in the latter end of that Book; which I discerning, askt of him, Whether he did apprehend his end was near? To which he replyed, He knew not, in a few days I would see; and so fell into Discourse, to divert me; desiring me to read two Chapters[50] to him, as I used to do every night; and so he hasted to Bed, not being able to go to Prayer; and with his own hands did very hastily undoe his Coat and Doublet, which he had not done in many

months before: As soon as he was in Bed he told me, He felt some more than ordinary Stoppage in his Head; and I brought him something to prevent the Fits, which I feared: But in a quarter of an hour after he fell into a very strong Convulsion: Which I being much affrighted at called for help, and sent for the Doctors; used all former and other means, but no success the Lord was pleased to give then to any: But they continued for two days and nights, not ceasing one hour.

This was most grievous to me, that I saw him so like to depart, and that I should hear him speak no more to me; fearing it would harden the Wicked to see him removed by such a stroak: For his Fits were most terrible to behold: And I earnestly besought the Lord, that if it were his pleasure, he would so far mitigate the heavy stroak I saw was coming upon me, by causing him to utter something of his Heart before He took him from me; which he graciously answered me in; for he that had not spoke from Tuesday Night, did on Friday Morning, about three a Clock, call for me to come to him, speaking very understandingly, between Times,[51] all that day: But that Night, about nine a Clock, he broke out with an audible voice, speaking for sixteen hours together, those and such like words as you formerly had account of;[52] and did cease but a very little space, now and then, all the Afternoon, till about six on Saturday in the Evening, when he departed.

About three in the Afternoon he had, as we perceived, some conflict with Satan, for he uttered these words:

"Away thou foul Friend, thou Enemy of all Man-kind, thou subtile Sophister, art thou come now to molest me! Now I am just going! Now I am so weak, and Death upon me. Trouble me not, for I am none of thine!

[49]Lewis Baylie, *The Practice of Piety,* was a devotional favorite, with fifty-nine editions between 1613 and 1735. It was translated into many languages, including that of the Algonquian Indians of North America. Baylie had been the Anglican bishop of Bangor and died in 1631. John Bunyan came into possession of a copy through his wife, and it was one of two books instrumental in his conversion.

[50]i.e., of the Bible.

[51]between times: from time to time.

[52]Various collections of his last words were circulated after his death.

I am the Lord's, Christ is mine, and I am his: His by Covenant; I have sworn my self to be the Lord's, and his I will be: Therefore be gone.'' These last words he repeated often, which I took much notice of; That his covenanting with God was the means he used to expel the Devil and all his Temptations.

The time we were in Bath, I had very few hours alone with him, by reason of his constant using the Bath, and Visits of Friends from all Parts thereabouts, and sometimes from Taunton; and when they were gone, he would be either retyring to GOD, or to his Rest: But what time I had with him, he alwayes spent in Heavenly and Profitable Discourse, speaking much of the Place he was going to, and his Desires to be gone: One Morning as I was dressing him, he looked up to Heaven and smiled, and [when] I urged him to know why, he answered me thus,

"Ah my Love, I was thinking of my Marriage Day, it will be shortly; O what a joyful day will that be! Will it not, thinkest thou my dear heart?''

Another time, bringing him some Broth, he said, "Blessed be the Lord for these refreshments in the way home; but O how sweet will Heaven be!''

Another time, "I hope to be shortly where I shall need no Meat, nor Drink, nor Cloaths.''

When he looked on his weak consumed hands, he would say, "These shall be changed; This vile Body shall be made like to Christ's Glorious Body.

"O what a Glorious Day will the Day of the Resurrection be! Methinks I see it by Faith; How will the Saints lift up their heads and rejoyce, and how sadly will the wicked World look then!

"O come and let us make haste, our Lord will come shortly, let us prepare.

"If we long to be in Heaven, let us hasten with our Work; for when that is done, away we shall be fetch.

"O this vain foolish, dirty world, I wonder how reasonable Creatures can so dote upon it! What is in it worth the looking after! I care not to be in it longer than while my Master hath either Doing or Suffering work for me, were that done, farewel to Earth.''

He was much in commending the Love of Christ, and from that exciting himself and me to obedience to him, often speaking of his Sufferings and of his Glory.

Of his Love-Letters, as he called the Holy History of his Life, Death, Resurrection, Ascension, and his Second coming; The thoughts of which he seemed always to be much ravished with.

He would be frequently reckoning the choice Tokens Christ had sent him, which I remember he would frequently reckon up, 1. The Pardon of Sin. 2. A Patent for Heaven. 3. The Gift of the Spirit. 4. The Robe of his Righteousness. 5. The Spoiles of Enemies. 6. The Charter of all Liberties and Priviledges. 7. The Guard of his Angels. The consideration of this last he did frequently solace himself in, saying to me often, when we lived alone in the Prison, and divers other Places; "Well, my Dear, though we have not our Attendants and Servants as the Great Ones, and Rich of the World have, we have the Blessed Angels of God still to wait upon us, to minister to us, and to watch over us while we are sleeping; to be with us when journeying, and still to preserve us from the rage of Men and Devils.''

He was exceedingly affected with the three last Chapters of Saint John's Gospel, especially Christ's parting Words, and Prayer for his Disciples. But it is time for me to set a stop to my Pen, God did pour into him, and he did pour out so much, that it was scarce possible to retain the Converses of one day, without a constant Register: His Heart, his Lips, his Life was filled up with Grace; in which he did shine both in Health and Sickness, Prosperity and Adversity, in Prison and at Liberty, in his own House, and in the Churches of Christ, wherever he came: I never heard any that conversed with him, but would acknowledge it was to their advantage.

At my Husband's first coming to Taunton, he was entertained by Mr. Newton as a Sojourner, and after he was ordained in Taunton in a Publick Association Meeting, he administered all Ordinances joyntly with him; though he were but an Assistant, Mr. Newton would have it so, who dearly loved him, and highly esteemed of him; and seeing him restless in his Spirit, and putting himself to many tedious Journeys to visit me, (as he did once a Fortnight 25 miles) he perswaded him to marry, contrary to our purpose, we resolving to have lived much longer single. The 4th of October 1655, after a year and two Month's acquaintance, our Marriage was consummated.

And we lived together with Mr. Newton, near two years, where we were most courteously entertained, and then hoping to be more useful in our Station, we took a House, and I having been alwayes bred to work, undertood to teach a School, and had many Tablers, and Scholars,[53] our Family being seldome less than Twenty, and many times Thirty; My School usually fifty or sixty of the Town and other places. And the Lord was pleased to bless us exceedingly in our endeavours: So that many were converted in a few years, that were before Strangers to God: All our Scholars called him Father: And indeed he had far more care of them than most of their natural Parents, and was most tenderly affectionate to them, but especially to their Souls.

His course in his Family was Prayer, and reading the Scriptures, and singing twice a day, except when he catechised,

which was constantly once, if not twice a Week: Of every Chapter that was read, he expected an account of, and of every Sermon, either to himself or me: He dealt with them and his Servants frequently together, and apart, about their Spiritual states, pressing them to all their Duties, both of First and Second-Table,[54] and calling them strictly account, whether they did not omit them. He also gave them Books suitable to their Capacities and Condition, which they gave a weekly account of to him or me; but too often by publick Work was he diverted, as I am apt to think, who knew not so well what was to be preferred.

His Lord's-Days' Work was great, for though he Preacht but once in his own Place, yet he was either desired by some of his Brethren to supply theirs on any Exigency, or would go where was no Minister; and so was forced often to leave his Family to me, to my great grief and loss: In his Repetitions in publick, as well as Catechising, his own Family came all in their turns, to Answer in the Congregation, both Scholars and Servants.

When I have pleaded with him for more of his time with my Self and Family, he would answer me: His Ministerial Work would not permit him to be so constant as he would; for if he had Ten Bodies and Souls, he could imploy them all in, and about Taunton: And would say, "Ah my Dear, I know thy Soul is safe; But how many that are Perishing have I to look after? O that I could do more for them!"

He was a Holy, Heavenly, Tenderly-Affectionate Husband, and I know nothing I could complain of, but that he was so taken up, that I could have but very little converse with him.

His Love was expressed to me, in his

---

[53]Tablers and Scholars: those who ate at their table and were their school pupils.

[54]Duties drawn from the Ten Commandments, of which the first table outlines duties to God and the second covers duties to other persons.

great care for me, Sick and Well; in his Provision for me; in his Delight in my Company; saying often he could not bear to be from me, but when he was with God, or employed for him; and that often it was hard for him to deny himself to be so long absent: It was irksome to him to make a Meal without me, nor would he manage any Affair almost without conversing with me, concealing nothing from me, that was fit for me to know; being far from the Temper of those Husbands, who hide all their Concernes from their Wives, which he could not endure to hear of, especially in Good Men.

He was a faithful reprover of any thing he saw amiss in me, which I took as a great evidence of his real good will to my Soul; and if in any great thing he gave me offence, which was but seldom, so far would he deny himself, as to acknowledge it, and desire me to pass it by, professing to me he could never rest till he had done so; and the like I was ready to do to him, as there was far more reason; by which course, if any difference did arise, it was soon over with us.

He was a very tender Master to his Servants, every way expressing it to their Souls and Bodies, giving them that incouragement in their places they could desire; expecting from his whole Family that respect, and obedience to his Commands which their Rule required; reproving them that were careless and negligent in observing them.

He was frequent in keeping solemn dayes of Humiliation, especially against[55] a Sacrament.

He was a very strict observer of the Sabbath, the Duties of which He did perform with such joy and alacrity of Spirit, as was most pleasant to joyn with, both in Publick, and in the Family, when we could enjoy him: And this he did much press upon Christians, to spend their Sabbaths more in Praises and Thanksgivings, as days of holy rejoycing in our Redeemer.

All the time of his Health, he did rise constantly at, or before four of the Clock (and on the Sabbaths sooner, if he did wake) he would be much troubled if he heard any Smiths, or Shoomakers, or such Tradesmen at work at their Trades, before he was in his Duties with God: Saying to me often, O how this Noise shames me! Doth not my Master deserve more than theirs? From four till eight, he spent in Prayer, Holy Contemplation, and singing of Psalms, which he much delighted in, and did daily practise alone, as well as in his Family: Having refreshed himself about half an hour, he would call to Family-Duties,[56] and after that to his Studies, till eleven or twelve a Clock, cutting out his work for every hour in the day. Having refreshed himself a while after Dinner, he used to retire to his Study to Prayer, and so Abroad among the Families he was to visit, to whom he always sent the day before; going out about two a Clock, and seldom returning till seven in the Evening, sometimes later: He would often say, "Give me a Christian that counts his time more precious than Gold." His Work in his publick Ministry in Taunton, being to preach but once a Sabbath, and Catechise; he devoted himself much to Private Work, and also Catechised once a Week in Publick besides, and repeated the Sermon he Preached on the Sabbath-Day, on Tuesday in the Evening.

He found much difficulty in going from House to House, because it had not been practised in a long time by any Minister in Taunton, nor by any others of his Brethren; and he being but a Young Man, to be looked upon as singular, was that which called for much Self-denyal, which the

---

[55]against: before.

[56]Family-Duties: leading the whole family (including servants) in prayer and devotion.

Lord inabled him to Exercise: For after he had Preached up in Publick the Ministers' Duty to their People, and theirs to receive them, when they came to them for their Spiritual Advantage, he set speedily upon the Work.

In this Work, his course was, to draw a Catalogue of the Names of the Families in each Street, and so to send a day or two before he intended to visit them, that they might not be absent, and that he might understand who was willing to receive him: Those that sent slight Excuses, or did obstinately refuse his Message, he would notwithstanding go to them, and if (as some would) they did shut their Doors against him, he would speak some few affectionate words to them; or if he saw cause, denounce the Threatnings of God against them that despise his Ministers, and so departed; and after would send affectionate Letters to them, so full of love, and expressions of his great desires to do their Souls good, as did overcome their Hearts; and they did many of them afterwards readily receive him into their houses. Herein was his Compassion shewed to all Sorts, both Poor and Rich, not disdaining to go into such Houses amongst the Poor, as were often very offensive to him to sit in, he being of an exact and curious[57] temper: yet would he with Joy and Freedom deny himself for the good of their Souls, and that he might fulfil his Ministry among those the Lord had given him the oversight of.

I perceiving this work, with what he did otherwise, to be too hard for him, fearing often he would bring himself to distempers and diseases, as he did soon after, besought him not to go so frequently: His answer would be, "What have I strength for, but to spend for God? What is a Candle for, but to be burnt?" And he would say, "I was like Peter, still crying, O spare thy self; But I must not hearken to thee, no more

thou my Master did to him:" Though his Labours were so abundant, I never knew him, for nine Years together, under the least distemper one quarter of an Hour.

He was exceeding temperate in his Dyet, though he had a very sharp Appetite, yet did he at every Meal deny himself, being perswaded that it did much conduce to his Health: His converse at his Table was very profitable, and yet pleasant, never rising, either at home or abroad, without dropping something of God, according to the Rule he laid down to others. He was very much in commending and admiring the Mercies of God in every Meal, and was still so pleased with his provision for him, that he would often say, He fared deliciously every day, and lived far better than the Great Ones of the World, who had their Tables far better furnished: For he enjoyed God in all, and saw his Love and Bounty in what he received at every Meal: So that he would say, "O Wife! I live a voluptuous life; but blessed be God, it is upon Spiritual Dainties, such as the World know not, nor taste not of."

He was much in minding the Poor, that were in want of all things, often wondering that God should make such a difference between him and them, both for this World and that to come; and his Charity was ever beyond his Estate, as my self and many other Friends did conceive, but he would not be disswaded, always saying, If he were Prodigal, it was for God, and not for himself, nor sin.

There were but few, if any, Poor Families, especially of the godly in Taunton, but he knew their necessities, and did by himself or Friends relieve them: So that our Homes were seldom free of such as came to make complaints to him. After the times grew dead for Trade, many of our godly men decaying, he would give much beyond his ability to recover them: He would

---

[57]curious: fastidious, particular.

buy Pease and Flitches of Bacon,[58] and distribute twice a year, in the cold and hard Seasons. He kept several Children at School at his own Cost; bought many Books and Catechisms, and had many thousands of Prayers printed, and distributed among them: And after his Brethren were turned out,[59] he gave Four Pounds a Year himself to a Publick Stock for them, by which he excited many others to do the same, and much more, which else would never have done it: And on any other occasions as did frequently fall in, he would give even to the offence of his Friends: So that many would grudge in the Town to give him what they had agreed for; because he would give so much. Besides all this, the necessities of his own Father, and many other Relations were still calling upon him, and he was open handed to them all: So that it hath been sometimes even incredible to our selves to consider how much he did, out of a little Estate, and therefore may seem strange to others: Moreover, when he had received any more than ordinary Mercy at the Hand of GOD, his manner was, to set apart some considerable Portion out of his Estate, and dedicate it to the Lord, as a Thank-offering, to be laid out for his Glory in pious and charitable Uses.

When I have begged him to consider himself and me; he would answer me, He was laying up, and GOD would repay him: that by liberal things he should stand, when others might fall that censured him; that if he sowed sparingly, he should reap so; if bountifully, he should reap bountifully.

And I must confess, I did often see so much of GOD in his dealings with us according to his Promises, that I have been convinc'd and silenc'd; God having often so strangely and unexpectedly provided for us: And notwithstanding all he had done, he had at last somewhat to dispose of to his Relations, and to his Brethren, besides comfortable provision for me.

Thus his whole Life was a continual Sermon, holding forth evidently the Doctrines he Preached; Humility, Self-denyal, Patience, Meekness, Contentation,[60] Faith, and holy Confidence shining in him, with most dear Love to God, and his Church, and People; and where he longed and panted to be, he is now shining in Heaven, singing Praises to God, and to the Lamb, which Work he much delighted in whilst here on Earth.

---

[58]Pease: dried pease or beans; flitch of bacon: a cured side of bacon.

[59]By the Act of Uniformity.

[60]contentation: contentedness.

Introduction to
A Murderer Punished and Pardoned

A Murderer Punished and Pardoned, or a True Relation of the Wicked Life, and Shameful-happy death of Thomas Savage, Imprisoned, justly Condemned, and twice Executed at Ratcliff, for his Bloody Fact in Killing his Fellow-Servant was first published at London in 1668. Within three years it was in its thirteenth printing. It told the lurid story, summarized on the title page, which ended in the repentance of the malefactor after he had been frequently visited by Dissenting ministers concerned for his soul. Its popularity no doubt stemmed from its combination of sensational narrative with the lesson that there is the hope of grace for every sinner.

It was the composite work of five ministers, all of whom had some part in visiting Thomas Savage and encouraging his repentance. Three of them—James Janeway, Thomas Doolittle, and Thomas Vincent—appear elsewhere in this anthology. The other two were the otherwise unknown Hugh Baker, and Robert Franklin (1630-1684), a Suffolk vicar who moved to London after his ejection in 1662 and several times suffered imprisonment for illegal preaching.

What follows is taken from pages 4-20, 24-44, and 46-47 of the original edition (Wing A996). The Wing attribution of the work to Richard Alleine is without any basis.

A Murderer Punished and Pardoned

Thomas Savage was born in the Parish of Giles's in the Feilds, was put out Apprentice to Mr. Collins, Vintner, at the Ship-Tavern in Ratcliff,[1] where he lived about the space of one year and three quarters, in which time he manifested himself to all that knew him, to be a meer[2] Monster in Sin; in all that time he never once knew what it was to hear one whole Sermon, but used to go in at one Dore and out at the other, and accounted them fools that could

spare so much time from sin as two or three hours on a Lord's day, to spend in the Lord's Service: He spent the Sabbath commonly at the Ale-house, or rather at a Base house with that vile Strumpet Hannah Blay, which was the cause of his ruine; he was by a young man (now gone to Sea) first enticed to go drink there, and after that he went alone, and now and then used to bring her a Bottle or two of Wine, which satisfied not her wicked desires, but she told him, if he would frequent her house, he must bring money with him; he told her often he could bring none but his Master's, and he never wronged his Master of two pence in his life; still she enticed him to take

---

[1]Ratcliff was a parish within the environs of London and the jurisdiction of Middlesex county; vintner: a wine merchant.

[2]meer: very.

it privately; he replyed, he could not do it, because the Maid was alwayes at home with him; Hang her Jade,[3] saith this impudent Slut, knock her brains out, and I will receive the money. This she many times said, and that day that he committed the Murder he was with her in the morning and she made him drunk with burnt Brandy, and he wanted one Groat to pay of his Reckoning; she then again perswaded him to knock the Maid on the head, and she would receive the money; he going home, between twelve and one of the clock, his Master standing at the Street dore, did not dare to go in that way, but climbeth over a back dore, and cometh into the Room where his Fellow-Servants were at Dinner. O saith the Maid to him, Sirrah, you have been now at this Baudy house, you will never leave till you are undone by them; he was much vexed at her, and while he was at Dinner the Devil entred so strong into him, that nothing would satisfie but he must kill her, and no other way but with the hammer: to which end, when his Master was gone with all the rest of the Family to Church, leaving only the maid and this Boy at home, he goeth into the Bar, fetcheth the hammer, and taketh the Bellows in his hand, and sitteth down by the Fire, and there knocketh the Bellows with the hammer, the Maid saith to him, sure the Boy is mad, Sirrah, what do you make this noise for? he said nothing but went from the Chair and lay along in the Kitchen window, and knocked with the hammer there, and on a sudden threw the hammer with such force at the Maid, that hitting her on the head, she fell down presently, screeching out; then he taketh up the hammer three times, and did not dare to strike her any more, at last the Divel[4] was so great with him, that he taketh the hammer and striketh her many blows with all the force he could, and even rejoyced that he had got the victory over her; which done, he immediately taketh the hammer and with it strikes at the Cupboard dore in his Masters Chamber, which being but slit Deal[5] presently fell open, and thence he taketh out a Bag of Money, and putting it upon his arm under his Cloak, he went out at a back dore strait way to this base house again; when he came thither, the Slut would fain have seen what he had under his Cloak, and knowing what he had done, would very fain have had the Money; he gave her half a Crown and away he went without any remorse for what he had done; going over a stile, he sat down to rest himself, and then began to think with himself, Lord what have I done! and he would have given ten thousand worlds he could have recalled the blow; after this he was in so much horror that he went not one step but he thought every one he met came to take him, he got that night to Greenwich and lay there, telling the people of the house that he was to go down to Gravesend, that night he rose and walked about and knew not what to do, Conscience so flew in his face. The Mistress of the house perceiving the Lad to have Money and not sealed up, said, I wish this Lad came by this Money honestly; the next morning he going away towards Woollidge [Woolich], the Mistress of the house could not be satisfied, but sent for him back, and told him, Sweet heart, I fear you came not by this money honestly; yes, indeed Mistress (saith he) I did, for I am carrying of it down to Gravesend to my Master a Wine-Cooper, we live upon London-Bridge, and if you please to send any one to my Mistress, I will leave the Money with you; so there were some people going to London, and he writ a Note to send to his Mistress, and he left the money with the Woman of the

---

[3]Hang her jade: hang the jade!
[4]Divel: devil.

[5]Deal: fir or pine wood.

house, and went his way, wandring toward Woollidge, and there was in the Ship-yard, about which time news came to Greenwich of the Murther that was committed at Ratcliff by a youth upon his fellow-servant, and that a bag of Money was taken away; the Mistress of the house forthwith concluded that sure it was the same youth that was at her house, and that that was the money; where-upon she sent men out presently to seek him, who found him in an Alehouse where he had called for one pot of Beer, and was laid down with his head on the Table, and faln asleep: one of the men calling him by his name, Tom, saith he, did not you live at Ratcliff? he said yes, and did not you Murther your fellow-servant? he confessed it, and you took so much money from your Master, he acknowledged all; then said they you must go along with us, he said, yes with all my heart. So they went forthwith to Greenwich to the house where he lay that night, where when he came he met his Master with some friends, and when his Master spake to him of it, he was not much affected at first, but after a little while burst out into many tears; thence he was conveyed to the Justice Ratcliff, where he fully confessed the Fact again, and by him was committed close Prisoner in the Gaol of Newgate,[6] where Mr. H. B.[7] (who after some acquaintance with him, had this preceding Narrative from his own mouth) came to see and speak with him, and he seemed but little sensible of what he had done, are you (said he) the person that committed the Murther upon the Maid at Ratcliff? he said, yes, O what think you of your condition? what think you will become of your precious soul? you have by this sin not only brought your Body to the Grave, but your Soul to Hell, without in-

finite mercy: were you not troubled for the fact when you did it? not for the present Sir, said he, but soon after I was when I began to think with my self what I had done. The next time he asked him, whether he were sorry for the fact? he said, wringing his hands and striking his breast, with tears in his eyes, yes Sir, for it cuts me to the heart to think that I should take away the life of a poor innocent Creature, and that is not all, but for any thing I know, I have sent her soul to hell, O how can I think to appear before God's Bar! when she shall stand before me and say, Lord this wretch took away my life and gave me not the least space that I might turn to thee! he gave me no warning at all Lord! O then what will become of me!

Soon after the Imprisonment of this Thomas Savage in Newgate, upon the desire of one of his friends, Mr. R. F. and T.V.[8] went to him in the Prison, and had liberty, with much readiness, from the Keepers, to discourse with him; They asked him, if he were the person that had Murthered the Maid, he answered that he was; they did then open to him the hainous nature of that sin, endeavouring to set it home upon his Conscience, telling him of the express Law of God, Thou shalt not kill; and the express threatning, That whosoever sheddeth man's blood, by man shall his blood be shed. They spake to him of the Law of the Land, and the punishment of Death which would certainly be inflicted upon him, that he had but a few Weeks more to live, and then he would be Tryed, and Condemned, and Executed; but they told him that the punishment of temporal death was but small in comparison with the punishment of eternal death in Hell, which he had deserved, and was exposed unto. They told him, that so soon as Death should

---

[6]Newgate: a notorious poison in London.

[7]Hugh Baker, one of the authors. See the introduction.

[8]Robert Franklin and Thomas Vincent, two more of the authors. See the introduction.

make a separation between his Soul and body, that his Soul must immediately appear before the dreadful Tribunal of the Sin-revenging God, and there receive its final doom; and be irreversibly sentenced to depart from the presence of the Lord, into everlasting fire, if he were found under the guilt of this or any other sin. They asked him if he knew what Hell was? telling him what a fearful thing it would be for him to fall into the hands of the living God, how intollerable the immediate impressions of God's wrath would be upon his Soul! what horrour and anguish he would there be filled withal! and how he would be bound up in Chains of darkness until the judgment of the great day! and then told him of the Glorious Appearance of the Lord Jesus Christ to Judgment, that Soul and body should be then joyned together, and condemned together, and punished together with such exquisite torments as never entred into the hearts of man to conceive! declaring the extremity and the eternity of the Torments of Hell, which were the just demerit of his sins. Then they asked him, whether he had any hopes of escaping this dreadful punishment of hell? He answered that he had: They enquired into the grounds of his hopes, He told them that he repented of his fault, and hoped God would have mercy on his Soul. They asked him whether he thought his Repentance would procure for him a Pardon? He knew no other way. They told him that God was just, and his justice must be satisfyed, and there was no way for him to do it, but by undergoing the eternal torments of Hell, and did he know no way of satisfying God's Justice besides, and pacifying his anger that was kindled against him? No, he knew not any; and yet did he hope to be saved? he answered, yes. They enquired whether ever

he had experience of a gracious change wrought in him. Herein he could give no account, and yet hoped to be saved. Yes. They told him, his hopes were unsound, having no good foundation, and he would find himself disappointed; that it was not his repentance, his tears, and prayers (though he ought to use them as means) that would save him, if he fixed the Anchor of his hope upon them. That if he hoped to be saved in the condition which for the present he was in, he would certainly be damned. That he must cast away all those groundless hopes he had conceived, and endeavor to despair in himself, that being pricked and pained at heart, through the apprehensions of the wrath of God ready to fall upon him & seeing no possibility of flying and escaping if he looked only to himself, he might cry out, what shall I do to be saved?[9] and enquire after a Saviour; and then they spake to him of the Lord Jesus Christ: and the way of Salvation by him, which before he was sottishly ignorant of, as if he had been brought up in a Country of Infidels, and not of Christians. The words spoken to him by these two Ministers seemed to take little impression upon him, whilst they were present; yet after they were gone, the Lord did begin to work and he did acknowledge to Mr. B. that two had been with him (he knew not their names) whose words were like arrows shot into his heart, and he did wish that he had those words in writing, especially one expression of T.V. That he would not be in his condition for ten thousands worlds, did affect and so affright him that he said, it made his hair stand an [on] end.

---

[9]This allusion to Acts 16:30 is the question Christian asks himself at the beginning of John Bunyan's *Pilgrim's Progress*.

An account of a discourse between T.D.[10] and T.S.
about fourteen dayes after he was Prisoner in Newgate.

When I came in and saw him in Irons, I said, were these Fetters for the sake of the Gospel they would be farr more precious than Chains of Gold, but see here the cursed fruits of Sin, thou that shouldst all thy life time have been a faithful servant of God, hast neglected no time to serve the Devil.

I asked him, how old he was? he said, 16 years old; I told him he was a young man, but an old sinner; then I began to set my self to bring him to a sense of his sin, and of his miserable and lost estate; and asked him whether he believed there was a God? he answered, yes; and dost thou believe that this God is true, he said, yes, and taking up the Bible, I asked him, dost thou believe, that this is the Word of God, he answered, yes; Then I told him, according to this Word, he was a damned wretch, and God had past a Sentence of death upon him; and told him plainly that he should not enter into the Kingdom of God, but be a Companion of Devils in a lake of Brimstone to all eternity (meaning without repentance, conversion and faith in Christ). Then I turned him to several Scriptures, and told him this was the Word by which he must be judged at the bar of God, and be damned or saved according as then he should be found to be, converted, or unconverted; The Scriptures were these. 1 Cor. 6:9: "Know ye not that the unrighteous shall not inherit the Kingdom of God? be not deceived: neither fornicators, nor Idolators, nor Adulterers, not effeminate, nor abusers of themselves with Mankind;" verse 10: "nor Thieves, nor Covetous, nor Drunkards nor Revilers, nor Extortioners, shall inherit the Kingdom of God."

Another Scripture I read to him was Gal. 5:19: "now the works of the flesh are manifest, which are these: adultery, fornication, uncleanness, lasciviousness;" verse 20: "Idolatry, witchcraft, hatred, variance, emulations, wrath, strife, seditions, heresies;" verse 21: "Envyings, murders, drunkenness, revelings, and such like of the which I tell you before as I have also told you in time past, that they which do such things shall not inherit the Kingdom of God."

The next Scripture to the same purpose was Rev. 21:8: "But the fearful and unbelieving and the abominable, and murderers, and whoremongers and sorcerers, and idolaters, and all liars, shall have their part in the lake which burneth with fire and brimston[e]: which is the second death."

I told him these were the words, of the holy true and infallible God; this was the sentence which God had passed upon him, as the desert of those abominable Sins, which he was guilty of; so these Scriptures pointed at several of the sins which he confessed he had lived in, and had committed as drunkenness, lying, uncleanness and murder. I cryed, you confess your self guilty of these sins, and that God threatneth you with eternal death, with everlasting torments, and exclusion from his presence and Kingdom, not only God's justice, but God's truth also, stood betwixt him and eternal happiness, and I told him, that I spake it with reverence, that the holy God must be a lyar, or else he dying in the guilt of these sins must be certainly and eternally damned. I asked him, what do you think? how will you escape the damnation of hell, and the great wrath that is to come? you have heard what God saith, what do you say? what course will you take, and what means will you use, that you may not according to God's threatning be cast

---

[10]Thomas Doolittle, another of the authors. See the introduction.

among Devils into eternal devouring flames? to this, at present he made no reply, but did often shake his head, and lifted up his eyes towards heaven.

Next I endevoured to bring him to a sight and sense of the corruption of his nature, and of the sinfulness of his heart; and told him all those sins were in his heart, before they were actually committed; and turned him to the saying of Christ, Mat. 15:19: "for out of the heart proceed evil thoughts, Murders, Adulteries, Fornications, Thefts, False-witnesses, Blasphemies," and told him that in his repentance for those sins he must not only lay to heart and be grieved for the outward acts, but lament and bewail the inward principle of corruption, whereby he was so strongly inclined to such horrid abominations, according to the example of David after his sins of Adultery and Murder in his confession, did follow them up to the rise and original form whence they did spring, Psalm 51:5: "Behold I was shapen in iniquity, and in sin did my mother conceive me." By this time I perceived some workings of heart within him; and that he was in some measure sensible of his lost estate, and by his deportment and carriage, to be cast down, not knowing what to do; I was unwilling to leave him without some grounds of hope that it may be, he might be saved; that there was a possibility that he might obtain pardoning mercy, and be delivered from that great damnation that was due to him for his great transgressions. I began to open to him the readiness of Christ, the fullness and sufficiency of Christ to save the greatest Sinners, and that God (I hoped in mercy to his soul) had sent me one of his Embassadours to offer him a pardon, and eternal life, if he were but willing to accept of Christ upon the terms of the Gospel, for his Lord and Saviour, and did encourage and assure him upon repentance and faith in Christ, there was

mercy yet for him, though a Murderer, from these Scriptures. Isa. 1:18: "Come now & let us reason together, saith the Lord, though your Sins be as Scarlet, they shall be as white as snow, and though they be red as[11] Crimson, they shall be as wool." As I opened to him the great mercy of God in Christ towards Sinners, died in grain,[12] that were Sinners of a Scarlet colour, that had committed hainous transgressions, he brake forth into tears, and wept plentifully at the tidings of mercy and possibility that such a one as he might be saved. Besides, I turned him to some Scripture promises, that God would certainly forgive his sins, and save his soul if he could repent, and get faith in Christ, such as Prov. 28:13: He that confesseth and forsaketh his sin, shall find mercy,[13] and Isa. 55:7; "Let the wicked forsake his way, and the unrighteous man his thoughts: and let him return unto the Lord, and he will have mercy upon him, and to our God, for he will abundantly pardon." This Scripture he diligently heeded, and turned it down in his Bible;[14] and these two Scriptures, (the night before he suffered) amongst others he alleadged as the grounds of his hope of mercy.

I also gave him some Scripture instances of great Sinners that had obtained mercy, turned him to the example of Manasseh, 2 Chro. 33, to that of Mary Magdalen, Luke 7:37, 38, to that of the Jews, Acts 2:37, 38, that were guilty of the blood of Christ, that had murdered the Son of God; a greater Murther than which could not be committed; and yet upon Repen-

---

[11]"like" in the KJV.

[12]died in grain: dyed down into the grain of the wood, i.e., deeply tinted with sin.

[13]This is a paraphrase rather than a direct quotation.

[14]turned it down: marked the page by folding it over.

tance and Faith, many of them were pardoned and saved. To that of Paul (1 Tim. 1:13, 14, 15, 16): shewed him how God had set up Paul as a pattern of Free-Grace, towards great sinners, for the encouragement of such, that (although guilty of great sins) afterwards should believe. To all these he hearkened very carefully, and took notice of the places of Scripture for his Meditation after I left him.

And last of all, I endeavoured to set before him Jesus Christ, as the only remedy and Saviour for his Soul, and shewed him the insufficiency of all his Duties, Prayers, and Tears, to get off the guilt of the least sin; that if he could shed a thousand tears of blood for any one vain thought, it would be no better than puddle water to justify, or to save him. Much discourse I had with him at this time, besides what is here inserted, and several other times when I went to visit him in Newgate, which I willingly omit, because this book should not swell to too great a bulk.

After all, I went to Prayer with him; in which Duty he was much dissolved into tears, he seemed to me, and his faithful friend that was most with him above all others, to be very earnest in Prayer, and with weeping eyes to beg for pardon and for converting grace, and Christ to be his Saviour, which was much insisted on in the Prayer that was made for him.

After which, advising him to consider of what I said, for that time I took my leave of him.

The next time, after this Discourse, that Mr. Baker came to him, he enquired how it was with him; he said, what T.D. had said did very much startle him, that he knew not what to reply, and cryed out very much of the hainousness of his sin; that he should commit that horrid sin of Murder; and knew not what to do; for that left a deep impression upon his heart, that God must be a lyar, or else he (in that condition of impenitency) must be damned: yet he laid hold upon that promise that was unfolded to him, That if a sinner turn from his wicked wayes, God would abundantly Pardon: and afterwards read on the verse that followed, Isa. 55:8: "For my thoughts are not your thoughts, neither are your wayes my ways saith the Lord:" Upon which considering, said, Men cry out for death and vengeance, no mercy to be had from men, but God's thoughts to a repenting sinner were life, for he delighteth not in the death of a sinner.

About four or five dayes after this, he was puzled about his performing of Duties, and resting only upon Christ for Salvation, for he was tempted, if he perform duties to rest upon them; or to let them alone, and leave them off, if he must rest only upon Christ; at which time H.B. comming to him, enquired how it was with him now? and how he hoped to be saved? he answered, by Repentance and Faith; and I could easily tell you, to satisfy you, that I do repent, and do believe, but truly so to do as I ought, I find it the hardest thing in the world, I do believe, and I do not, I cannot tell how to believe that Christ dyed for sinners, so as to throw myself wholly and fully upon him, and to think my Tears and Prayers will do me no good.

But here, Reader, we must take notice of the unwearied diligence of the Devil, in using all means from time to time, to undo, ruine, and wound the soul of this poor Malefactor, who would not forbear to solicite him to sin, after he was cast into Prison for former Iniquities he had committed; for we cannot but judge that the Devil was loath to loose such a prey, as his Immortal soul, when he had brought him to the very mouth and gates of hell, to have him snatched out of his hands by the free grace of God the Devil did work the more (because he knew his time to tempt him was but short) to blemish and eclipse the gracious work of God upon his heart, and cloud the glory of God's mercy in saving such a sinner. He was by some former acquaintance visiting of him (who shewed their Love to a death-deserving sinner, no other way than by calling for drink, and desiring him to drink with them), overcome therewith, and after some former convictions of sin, and his lost estate, did twice relapse into the sin of drunkeness, whereby he caused many to fear that all this while he had no more than some common workings of the spirit; and put us to a stand, that we knew not what would be the issue of these things; but yet not daring to omit endeavours (if possible) as instruments under God to save his soul, we did after this, visit him again and again, and set forth unto him the greatness of his sin, that he should sin yet more against the Lord; and in his affliction and chains to provoke the Lord to greater wrath against his soul; with many words to that purpose.

After which his soul was wounded, his heart was pierced, he knew not what to do; he asked, may mercy be had for a backsliding sinner? to which were given him some Scriptures, where God called to backsliding sinners to return; and invited them to repent, and promised mercy to them if they did, even after they had done as wickedly as they could: and this was much enlarged upon before him from Jer. 3:11 to 19th verse. But God that had begun to awaken and to rouse his conscience, that he might set him up as a pattern of free grace, would not let the Devil go thus away with his soul, but brought him to a deep sense of his falling into sin, that he much lamented with many tears the sadness of his state; the misery of his soul, saying, what will become of my soul! my immortal soul! I cannot think what will become of my soul! I deserve hell ten thousand times over, and have I now but one grain of sand left in the glass to work for eternity! shall I neglect

God any longer? O I have neglected God too long already! striking his hand upon his brest, and wringing his hands, and shaking his head, and weeping abundantly, said, Lord, what shall I do? O God what shall I do? Lord, what will become of me? If God had dealt justly with me, I had now been in hell, I had been dashed into hell when I murthered that poor innocent creature: I wonder that I am not now in hell; that such a wretch as I am not in hell: God hath been pleased to manifest more mercy to me in sparing of me, and affording me so long time for repentance, but I have neglected time and relapsed into drunkenness and vain talking, time after time. I thought this place (meaning the hole in Newgate) a hell upon earth, and did account it a heaven to be among the other prisoners; but now, God hath tryed me, whether sin will be bitter and displeasing to me or not, I have this day (being Lord's day) been among the Prisoners, and they asked me to play at Cards, but instead of complying with them, I reproved them, and told them for my part, I had profaned Sabbaths enough already, I have but a little time to work for my soul, and I ought not to neglect time now, that they likewise (he told them) if they rightly considered had something else to do, and striking his hand upon his breast, with much earnestness he cryed out with tears, Now, now, I find that God hath been at work, that God hath been at work upon my soul, he hath, I am sure been at work, for now I see so much evil, and taste such bitterness in sin, that I am not so much troubled that I am to die, nor so much troubled that I am in danger of hell, as to think I should so dishonor God, That I should so offend so gracious and mercyful a God, and spurn against all his mercies. Oh my soul, my Immortal soul, I know not what will become of it to all eternity, It is the grief of my very soul that I have neglected time as I have done, now I see so much need of a

Christ, and so much preciousness and excellency in Christ; that if the greatest King in the world should come and throw his crown at my foot and tell me I should enjoy it, and all the glory of it for millions of years, and should have my liberty presently, and should say, but it must be without Christ, I would sooner choose to die this moment; nay, to be racked to pieces by ten thousand deaths, or burn ten years together, so I may have a Christ. I speak freely from my heart, so far as I know my heart, and now I find it is not only the Devil's tempting me, hath brought me to this, but this cursed, wretched, devillish heart of mine within. It is within me, so that it was in me before it was committed by me. I deserved hell ten thousand times over before I committed this horrid sin, well now I am resolved, I will pray as much as I can, and weep and wrestle with God, as if I were to have Heaven for it; but when I have done all, I will deny all, for my Prayers and tears cannot save me, and I will fully and wholly throw my self at the feet of Christ, and if I am damned, I will be damned there, and more he spake to this purpose in Mr. Baker's hearing.

About three dayes after Mr. B. comming to him, asked him how it was with him; He told him that the Devil was very busy with him, and did sollicit him grievously with his temptations, perswading him to have thoughts of escaping; these things (said he) hindred my minding of God one part of the day, the other part of the day the Devil fills me with drowsiness, that I can neither pray nor read, nor perform any duty, nor mind any one that prayes with me; sometimes he tempts me to delay, telling me that it is time enough for me to think of Repentance when I am Condemned, and that God is a merciful God; and sometimes

he tempted me to despair, telling me that it was impossible that so monstrous a sinner as I had been should be saved, but blessed be God that he made me to think that these were the but Devil's temptations, although I have been sadly hurried with them for some dayes; but that which did most fil[l] me with terror, was the frequent fears of the Devil's appearing personally to me, which did so exceedingly trouble me in Prayer, so that I could say nothing when I kneeled down, but was fain to see the Candle down before me, and didst not look one way nor other, for fear I should see him; and my thoughts have been so vain many times when you have been reading to me, that I have scarse heard a word of what you said.

. . .

On Saturday during the Sessions,[15] he was Arraigned, and pleaded Guilty, confessing with many tears, and wringing his hands, that he did through the instigation of the Devil, and enticement of that wretched creature (meaning his Harlot) that he had committed that bloody fact, which was such an horrour to his conscience that he would not do it again for ten thousand worlds; his carriage and confession was such, that he much moved the honourable Bench and Jury, and most of the beholders.

On Monday next, he received his sentence of death, after which time he was with the other condemned Prisoners, and did pray with them four times a day, and read to them, and sung Psalms with them. After the execution of the rest, he had time given or procured him by the honourable Sheriff of London for some dayes: which he improved to the great advantage of his soul.

---

[15]Sessions: a regional court usually held quarterly and conducted by a justice of the peace who adjudicated local cases.

On Friday night he uttered these expressions in Company with H. B.
being the day that the other Prisoners were executed:

I find, saith he, so much sweetness, and delight, and pleasure in God's ways, and so much folly in the ways of sin, that if there were no heaven to reward, nor any hell to punish, I could not but love the ways of God, and the people of God; O it is so sweet to be in company with them, praying and conversing with them, over what is in hearing others Swear and Curse, that I account it as great a mercy as any almost, that I may be in their company; O me thinks it is a heaven to me to be with God's Ministers and people, and prayer now is so sweet, that I grudge the time always when I am off from my knees, or go down to the Grate:[16] Now there is nothing in the world I prize like Christ, one Christ above ten thousand worlds; now I do repent, and I do believe through mercy; it is the Lord's work, but I earnestly beg and pray for a more humble, and a more broken heart, and a more thorough sense of sin, and a greater sorrow for it, and beg that God would enable me to come to him, to believe in him. Lord saith he, faith is thy work, repentance is thy work, do thou enable me to repent, nay, thou hast enabled me to repent, and I do from the very bottom of my heart, Lord, as far as I know my own heart: I repent that I should offend so gracious, and so merciful a God as thou art, Lord, and faith is thy work. Lord saith he, hast not thou said no man can come to thee except the Father draw him,[17] draw me O Lord, and I shall run to thee, enable me to believe Lord, and I shall believe; nay, I do believe Lord, that Jesus Christ his bloud was not shed in vain. Did Christ die for nothing, Lord, did he not die to save all repenting and believing sinners, of whom I am chief?

---

[16]Grate: window looking out of the prison.

[17]Allusion to John 6:44.

On Saturday at night in Company with Mr. Baker,
he discoursed thus:

O my dear friend, taking me by the hand, come hither, saith he, and opening the Coffin, look here is the ship, saith he, in which I must launch out into the Ocean of eternity: and is it not a terrible thing (saith he) to see one's own Coffin and burying cloaths, when at the same time I am as well as you; do you think it would not daunt you; and to go to the Gallows to have the halter, and to die there, were it ten hundred times a worse death, but to suffer this cursed death for such horrid sins, O this is sad! why said I, you have a greater mercy in some respect than those that die in their beds, for they are full of sickness and pain, and cannot so well mind repentance as you who are well and have nothing else to mind. Ah Sir, saith he, their sins are of a far less nature than mine, and so they do not need so much repentance as mine do; my doing for such horrid sins makes my repentance to be so much the more hard. O saith he, I believe it, it is a hard work to die, I could carry it out as bravely as any, (do you think I could not?) But to consider that as I die, and am sentenced from God's Bar, so I must be for ever, immediately either be everlastingly happy, or everlastingly miserable: To consider this, would make a stout heart to tremble; those poor creatures that were here the other night, (meaning the other condemned Prisoners) they know now that what it is to be in an eternal state, and if they are gone to hell, O Lord, how miserably are they disappointed, who hoped for to have gone to heaven and are sent from thy Bar to endless burning: Lord, what a mercy is it that I have a little time longer left, let it be improved to thy glory, and let my soul live, and I shall praise thee.

The last Lord's day he lived, he desired to be alone, and spent it in wrestling with God by prayer, and in other duties in order to his preparation for his great change by death, that then he expected the next day; in which duties he found so much of God, that he had some fore-tasts of the joys of heaven, and when we asked him what of God he had found that day, he replyed, that he had such pleasure and delight in mourning for sin, and praying unto God, that he was loth to come off from his knees; at night there were some Ministers that sate[18] up with him, and spent that night in prayer with him and for him, and in conference; on Monday morning came T.D. to him before day (thinking it was his last day, for an order was sent on Friday for his execution on Monday) and said to him, Thomas, how is it with you now, your last day begins to dawn; he said, blessed be God I am not afraid to die, because I hope I shall go to Jesus Christ; after sometime in prayer for him, we desired him to spend sometime in that duty, which he performed with so much affection, and earnest pleading with God, that all the company were exceedingly melted, and their hearts beyond ordinary measure warmed and raised, that the room did ring with sighs and groans; and there was such a mighty presence of the spirit poured out upon him, and on those that joyned with him, that we do not remember the time, whenever we had experience of the like; in which prayer, after the confession of his sins, he begged earnestly for pardon, and for an interest in Christ, saying, O Lord, wilt thou let me die without a Christ? shall I leave this world before thou smilest upon my soul? thou hast

promised pardon, and mercy, and salvation to those that do repent, and to those that do believe. Lord I do repent, I do believe if I know my own heart, I do repent; I do believe, Lord I roll my self upon thy Son, I cast my self at his foot for mercy; thou wouldest be just if thou dost damn me, but thou hast pardoned others, and it will be to the praise of thy free-grace to pardon me; Lord, shall those prayers that have been made, and all those tears that have been shed for me, and all those instructions which have been given me, be all in vain? with many other expressions in that prayer, which wonderfully affected the hearts of those that were with him; that afterwards we looked upon one another, wondring at the grace of God towards him, that one so wicked all his days, so young (being 16 years old), so lately acquainted with the ways of God, should have such a spirit of prayer poured out upon him: after this he prayed with more life and fervency than before, and the nearer he came to his end, the more we perceived God was ripening him for glory.

After this we took our leave of him, not knowing but that was the last day; for the Cart stood below, and the Coffin fetched down, and some of the honourable Sheriffs of London's men, came into the prison; but the Sheriff of Middlesex having not notice to be ready, his execution was deffered till Wednesday following.

Reader here take notice, that the report that the reason why he was not executed on Monday, was because he was drunk, is an abominable falshood, for to our knowledge, that were with him, he did not eat nor drink that morning. When we went up to him again, we told him we perceived he was not to die that day, giving him caution, not to think there was any pardon intended for him; and one came from the Sheriff to acquaint him with the reason of the delay of his execution.

---

[18]sate: sat.

When his Coffin was carryed up to him again, one asked what he thought, and what were the workings of his heart, when he saw his Coffin brought back, he said, he was much troubled, and it daunted him to see it; for he could willingly have dyed that day to go to Christ. On Monday in the afternoon he had an excessive pain in his Teeth (as we judge occasioned by his leaving off his cloaths, and putting on some thin apparal to die in;) and that evening he expressed great willingness to die and leave this world; he said, I see and find so much excellency in Christ, that he is so pure, pure in grace, pure in holiness, pure in all things, Lord, I count it an hell to be upon earth, I so long to be where I might enjoy thee: and he spent some time in prayer (notwithstanding his pain) with much affection, wherein he said, the pain of the Teeth was great, but the pain of hell was greater!

On Tuesday, the day before he dyed, after some time spent in prayer both by him and H.B. being full of joy, he expressed himself thus, O my dear friend, what a welcome shall I give you when you come to heaven; and say to you, come, see, come, see, this is the glory of that you told me of, but all that you ever told me, was nothing to what I have found, O what a place is this! O how shall we love one another then! sure it cannot be, but heaven must be a glorious place, where God, and Christ, and Angels be.

The night before he dyed a Minister came to Thomas Savage, and after other serious discourse, for satisfaction of a Christian friend that had seen him before, he demanded of him what were now the grounds of his hopes of salvation? He made this reply, God both in infinite mercy made me deeply sensible of great sins, and not only of them, but of the vileness of my heart and nature, and God hath made me to abhor my self for my sin[s], and I hope truely to repent of them, for that which hath

been the delight of my soul, is now as bad as Hell; and God hath given me to see that all my own Prayers and tears, and all the prayers of all the good people that come to me are not able to save: A Christ alone; I throw my self at the feet of Christ for mercy, and if I perish, I will perish there. I feel longings and breathings after Christ, and love him more than my life; I long to be with him, and I would not be to live any longer; this world is a little Hell because of sin. I fear not death, for I hope the sting of it is taken out for me.

This last night before his death, he desired us to sit up with him, in order to his better preparation for the great work he had to do the next day, that we might wrestle with God on his behalf, that when death approached so near unto him, he might have some nearer accesses of God into his soul, that when pale death stared him in the face, he might see God's smiling countenance; which opportunity we readily embraced, and spent the former part of the night in prayer, till two of the clock in the morning; about which time he desired us to go down into the Lodge, that he might have some part of the night for prayer and meditation alone, and to discourse a while with his friend Mr. Baker, to whom he most of all did open his very heart, and spake more freely to, than to any other (whom for that reason we left with him) and when we were gone down, his friend being with him, who told us afterwards, he fell into admiration;[19] and said, What a prodigy am I? What a wonder of mercy that God should incline the hearts of his Ministers to come and pray with me, and pour out their souls in prayer thus for me? For me a Murtherer; for me a Drunkard; for me so vile and sinful? Well, I cannot but love God, and though I go to Hell, yet I will love God for his goodness and graciousness to me already manifested

---

[19]admiration: a mood of wonder.

in this world; yea, though I should be damned for my sin, yet I could and would love God: What, would they venture to come and pray with me, a Murtherer? How did they know but I might have murthered some of them? Pray for me? wrestle for me! well, I know God loves me; I am sure God loves me.

When he was in prayer some of us heard him say: Now Lord I am coming to thee, thou art mine, and Christ is mine, and what need I be afraid of Death? Lord give me some sense, and some sign of thy Love, that when my soul shall be separated from my body, it might be received into glory.

Afterwards when he looked upon his cloaths he had put on to dye in, [he] said, What! have I got on my dying cloaths? dying cloaths did I say? they are my living cloaths, the cloaths out of which I shall go into eternal glory, they are the best cloaths that ever I put on.

About four of the clock in the morning we went up to him again, full of expectations what he would say to us, and what we should hear from him; and T.D. stood behind him and took his expressions as he spoke to them, from his own mouth; and first he told us, I account it a great mercy that God hath shewed me the evil of sin, before he cast me into Hell; sin hath not only brought my body to the grave, but my soul in danger of everlasting burnings.

The Lord will have mercy on me I hope; I am filled with joy, I am no more afraid to dye, than to stand in this place, the Lord make me thankful. The Lord hath been working on my soul; for it was not that I could pray, nor refrain from company, nor delight in any thing that is good; I have cause to bless God, that ever I was taken (and this we have heard him often say) for if I had escaped, I had gone on in my sin, and might have lost my soul for ever.

One asked him which he thought was worse, hell or sin? using some gesture of

body, [he] said, hell is very dreadful, but sin is worse than hell, because sin brings men's souls to hell, and sin is that which offendeth God.

One asked him, what he thought of heaven? with a smiling countenance [he] said, heaven! it cannot be, but heaven must be an excellent place, for it is an holy place. We spake to him concerning his Coffin, that was by him, whether it did not trouble, and amaze him to have it in his sight; he replyed, with all my soul I could go into my Coffin; oh it is a comfortable place. (He spake it with joy) I can comfortably die. I have found such a deal of joy and comfort, that I would not for a world have been without it.

We enquired, whether death did not afright him: morning Light will presently appear, he answered, death indeed did trouble me, but now not at all, I long for day, I am not daunted at death. Die! It is nothing: this Life is nothing: but to die eternally, and to loose[20] God, and Christ, and Heaven, that is death. Hell torments is not so much, as to be shut from the presence of God. Alas! who would not die this death to go to Jesus Christ? when my body is upon the Gibbet, my soul shall be carryed by Angels into heaven. My heart is so drawn out after God, that I could leave this world to be with him. This world is nothing, those that have the pleasures of it, they have nothing. I desire to die, because I long to be with Christ, there I shall never sin more; there is no sin, but joy, where I shall sing Hallelujahs & praise to God. We asked what he thought of the company of God's people, for he now had had experience of company good and bad. He said, I had rather be here (meaning the hole in Newgate) with bread and water with such company, than to have the company of wicked persons, with the greatest dainties.

---

[20]loose: lose.

It was wicked company that drew me away. I account it the greatest mercy, to have the prayers of God's people for me; had I had my deserts, I had been now in hell, where I should have had no prayers, no instructions; God doth love me, for he hath inclined the hearts of his people and Ministers to pray for me, and their prayers have prevailed.

Being asked, what promises he found to be his support against the guilt of sin, now he was to die, he alledged these, repeating the words himself: whosoever will, let him come and drink of the waters of life freely, and he that confesseth and forsaketh his sin, shall find mercy; and "let the wicked forsake his way & the unrighteous man his thoughts, and let him return unto the Lord, and he will have mercy on him, and to our God, for he will abundantly pardon."[21] This word (abundantly pardon) did often refresh his soul; I have sinned abundantly, but God will pardon abundantly. After these, he mentioned another, viz., "This is a faithful saying, and worthy of all acceptation," that Jesus Christ came to save sinners,[22] of whom I am chief: and said, I do rely and throw my self upon Jesus Christ, I do believe there is merit enough in him, and all sufficiency in him to save me; It is nothing that I can do, will save me.

He complained, that it was the grief of his soul, that he could love God no more, and love Christ no more for his mercy towards him, in giving him so much time, and so many helps, in sending so many Ministers to instruct him, but added, when several Ministers had been with me, I threw off all, and returned to sin, & did as vainly as any. I could not have repented, and believed of my self,[23] it is the work of God. He often said, I fear not death, it was nothing with him to die and go to Christ. He often said, that he had rather die immediately, having an interest in Christ, than to live a thousand years in this world, in the enjoyment of all the pleasures of it, without Christ.

And, this he had found more pleasures and delight in the ways of God since he came into Prison, than ever he found in all the ways of sin.

He confessed his sins, saying, he first neglected and profaned the Sabbath, & said this was the beginning of all his wickedness, that on the Sabbath morning, he studied what company to go into, in what place of sin he might spend the Sabbath: then to wicked Society, then to Alehouses, then to Brothel-houses, then to murder, then to theft, then to Newgate, and yet at last, he hoped, to heaven.

He lamented, saying, I have striven to dishonour God, and to run into sin; Oh that I should spend so much time in serving of the Devil, and now have but little moment of time to spend in the service of God, and to the glory of God.

This discourse being ended, we desired him now on his last morning before he went into eternity to pray with us, and he willingly consented, and his prayer was as followeth, being taken from his mouth by Thomas Doolittel, that also took in writing his preceding discourse, Verbatim.

---

[21]Isa. 55:7; Thomas Doolittle had earlier brought this text to the prisoner's attention.

[22]1 Tim. 1:15.

[23]of my self: by my self.

The Prayer of Thomas Savage in Newgate,
with those that sate up with him
all the night before his Execution:

O Most merciful and ever blessed Lord God, I beseech thee O Lord look down upon me, with an eye of pity if it be thy blessed will; it is thy infinite mercy that I am on this side the grave and out of hell: O Lord I have deserved to be cast into torments to all eternity. How have I offended thee, and run on in sin, and thought I could never do enough to abuse thy mercy! pardon the sins that I have committed, wash that bloud from off my soul, let not my soul perish to eternity. It was an horrid crime to shed innocent bloud. pardon that sin, O Lord, let the bloud of Christ cry more for mercy, than the bloud of that creature cry for vengeance. O Lord, thou hast been merciful to me in giving me time to repent, for ought I know her soul is undone for ever, Lord forgive me. Lord forgive me, I knew not what I did. Forgive my Sabbath breaking, lying, cursing, forgive my drunkenness, blot them out of the book of remembrance, turn them away behind thee. Lord I have repented of them from my soul, that ever I should offend God, so good, and so merciful and gracious, I do believe on thee, and do wholly throw my self upon thee. I acknowledge it would be just in thee to damn my soul, but it will be infinite mercy in thee to save me, and what free grace will it be in thee to pardon me! it is dreadful to loose the body, but how dreadful will it be to loose the soul to all eternity! Lord let it not be in vain that I have had so many instructions, O let me not go down to hell, let my soul bless and praise thy name for ever, for what thou hast done for me, thou hast been at work upon my heart, and thou hast helped me to repent, the Lord be praised. Lord I desire to be more and more humbled under the sense of my sins, for they are dreadful; there are many souls that have not committed those sins that are now in hell. O what mercy is it that I am not in those flames, in those devouring flames! Lord as thou hast spared me here, spare me to eternity. Let not my soul perish, Lord reveal thy self unto me, make known thy love unto me, tell me my sins are pardoned, tell me, that I have an interest in Christ before I go hence, and be seen no more, that I might leave some testimony behind me, that I might tell thy Ministers, what thou has done for me, and tell thy people what thou hast done for my soul, Lord this will not be only for my satisfaction, but for thy glory. Blessed Lord, pardon the sins that I am guilty of, and take away this cursed base heart of mine, break this rocky stony heart in pieces, these sins of Murder and Drunkenness, &c. were in my heart before, I thought no eye did see me commit those sins, but thou didst see me. Lord turn my heart to thee, and take away this heart of stone, and take away this cursed nature, for it was this cursed nature that brought me to these sins, and to this end, and I was in danger of losing my soul to all eternity, but Lord though I am a great sinner, Christ is a great Saviour, he is able to save me from my Sins, though they be never so great. I do believe Lord, I speak freely from my heart, so far as I know my heart I do believe. It is my grief I can sorrow no more for my Sins, which have been the cause of my offending thee so long and so much. One drop of thy blood sprinkled upon my soul will pardon all my Sins, Lord cross the black line of my Sins with the red line of thy blood: I am not able to answer for one vain thought, much less for all my horrid crimes, Lord save my immortal soul that I might sing praise to thee to all eternity. Thou hast pardoned Manasseh *that was a great sinner, and* Mary Magdalen *and* Paul, *that were great sinners, and the Thief upon the Cross, and thy mercies are as great, thy mercy and thy love to repenting Sinners is not shortned, though my sins be great, yet thy mercies are greater than my Sins; Lord be with me in my death, then let me have some comfortable assurance of thy love unto my Soul, of the pardon of my Sin, do thou be my God and my Guide now, and to all eternity.* Amen.

This prayer he put up with much earnestness, with great brokenness of heart for sin, that all that joyned with him, were exceedingly affected, and blessed God for the spirit of prayer, they discerned God had so plentifully poured out upon him.

After we had some other discourse with him, we took our leave of him, telling him we purposed to see him again at the place of Execution. After two or three hours, when the time of his going from Newgate drew near, we were willing to return to see him once more there, and the rather because one Minister that had not yet been with him,[24] was desirous to visit him; and

---

[24]Presumably James Janeway, the only one of the ministerial authors not yet introduced into the story. See the introduction. Janeway had a special interest in the death of the pious; this is illustrated by the selections from him above.

then again after some few words with him, we asked him to go to Prayer again, once more, saying now, this will be the last time, that we shall pray with you in this place. And he did perform this duty with great liveliness, that now he excelled himself, and the nearer he came to his end, the more fervently, we perceived he prayed; but we took notice, that in this last duty in Newgate he was much in praising God, and blessing God for his mercy to him, to our great astonishment.

After a few words, when this duty was over, we took some of us our final farewel of him; and he, expressing his thanks to God's people for their Prayers for him, and to the Ministers for their love and pains with him, was commended by us to the grace of God, saying, Thomas, the Lord be with you, the Lord of heaven be with you, O the Lord of mercy help you, and have compassion on you.

This morning he expressed himself to his friend H.B. thus, Oh my friend, we cannot tell how glorious a place heaven is, but if once I get thither, and could drop down a Letter to you and tell you of the glorious things I there shall find, how would it rejoyce your heart? and to this friend parting with him, said, I know God loveth me, and that I am going to the Kingdom of heaven.

The last Speech of Thomas Savage
at the place of his Execution at Ratcliff:

Gentlemen,

Here I am come to dye a cursed and ignominious Death, and I most justly deserve it, for I have Murthered a poor innocent Creature, and for ought I know, have not only Murthered her Body, but if God had no more mercy on her Soul, then I had of her Body, she is undone to all Eternity; so that I deserve not only death from men, but damnation from God. I would have you all that look upon me take

warning by me, the first sin I began with was Sabbath breaking, thereby I got acquainted with bad Company, and so we went to the Ale-house, from the Ale-house to the Bawdy-house, there I was perswaded to Rob my Master, as also to Murder this poor innocent Creature, for which I am come to this shameful end. I was drawn aside I say, by ill Company, pray take heed of that, for it will not only bring your Bodies to the Grave, but your Souls to Hell; have a care of neglecting the Sabbath, it is that which hath not only brought my body to the grave, but my soul in danger of eternal torments. And try the wayes of God, for the Lord be praised I have found so much of excellency and sweetness in God's wayes, that I bless God that ever I came into a Prison. And now though I am leaving this world, I know I shall go to a better place; for I have repented from my soul for all my sins, not because I am to dye for them, but to see that I should do that whereby I should deserve Hell ten thousand time over, and so dishonour God.

Now the Lord have mercy on my soul.

The Prayer of Thomas Savage
at the place of Execution:

O Most merciful and for ever blessed Lord God, I beseech thee look down upon my poor immortal soul which now is taking its flight into another world, which now is ready to appear before thy bar. Lord I beseech thee prepare me for it, and receive my soul into the arms of thy mercy, and though my body dye, and I come to dye this shameful death, yet let my soul live with thee for ever, Lord pardon all the horrid Sins that I have committed, the Sabbath-breaking, Lying, Swearing, Cursing, Uncleanness, and all the rest of my Sins that ever I have committed; Lord give me a new heart, and give me faith, that I may lay hold and throw my self fully and wholly upon thee; inable me, O Lord, give me saving repentance that I may come to thy Bar, and thence be received into glory, let me not be a prey to Devils to all eternity, let not my soul perish, though my body dye, let my soul live, Lord let me not be shut out from thy presence, and let not all the Prayers, and Tears, and Counsels, and Instructions that have been made and shed on my behalf, be in vain; pity my poor soul Lord, my immortal soul, Lord, it would be just with thee to cast me into everlasting burning. I have been a great sinner, but Christ is a great Saviour. O Lord thou hast pardoned great Sinners, and thou canst do it Lord, and Lord wilt thou not do it? Lord let me not be a fire brand of hell, and a prey to devils to all eternity, let me not then be shut up with devils and damned souls when my soul takes in flight into another world. Lord I have repented for what I have done, from the bottom of my heart I have repented, and Lord if thou wouldst damn me thou wouldst be just, but how infinitely more would it be for the glory of thy free grace to save such a Sinner as I am; good Lord pour down thy spirit upon my soul, O tell me that I have interest in Christ's blood, good Father, good Lord, before I go hence. Lord I am willing, I am willing to leave this world, I can prize thee above all, there is nothing I can prize like to thee, wilt thou not receive my soul? receive it into thy arms, and say, come thou blessed of my Father, good Father for Jesus Christ sake pitty my poor soul, for pittye's sake. Lord it is not my Prayers or tears will save my soul, but if ever I am saved it must be through free grace, and the blood of Christ, and if there be not enough in that blood, Lord I am willing to be damned. Lord look down upon my poor soul, and though I have been such a sinner thou art able to pardon me, and wash me, apply one drop of thy blood to my soul, Lord, my immortal soul, that is more worth than ten thousand worlds, it is true Lord, I confess I have taken a great deal of pleasure in sin, I have run on in sin, and could not invent where to go on thy day, and was wont to study into what place, and into what company I might go upon the Sabbath day: forgive me Lord, wash me, receive me into thy arms O lord. Oh for one glimps of mercy, Lord if thou wilt please to reveal thy self to me, I shall tell it to all that behold me, it is a mercy Lord that I am not in hell, and that thou showest me the bitterness of sin, before I come into hell, it is a mercy Lord that I have had the prayers, converse and instructions of so many of thy Ministers and people. Lord receive my soul, one smile Lord, one word of comfort for Jesus' sake, O let me not go out of this world, let not my soul perish, though I killed a poor innocent creature, Lord deal not with me as I dealt with her, but pitty me, pitty me for Jesus Christ's sake, Amen.

One asked him in the Cart, well now Thomas, how is it with your soul, what sense have you of God's love? He answered, Sir I thank God through infinite mercy, I find God loves me, and that now I can cheerfully go.

After his Cap was over his Eyes
he used these Expressions.

Lord Jesus receive my Spirit.
Lord one smile.
Good Lord one word of comfort
    for Christ's sake,
though Death make a separation
    between my soul and body, let nothing
separate between thee and my soul
    to all eternity.
Good Lord hear me.
Good Father hear me.
O Lord Jesus receive my soul.

Whilst he did thus pathetically express himself to the people especially to God in prayer, there was a great moving upon the affections of those who stood by, and many tears were drawn from their eyes by his melting Speeches. All this was the more remarkable in this young man, being under sixteen years of age when he was first apprehended.

After he was turned off the Cart he strugled, for a while, heaving up his body, which a young man (his friend) seeing, to put him quickly out of his pain, struck him with all his might on the breast several times together, then no motion was perceived in him, and hanging some considerable time after that, and as to all outward appearance dead, insomuch as one said to another friend of his, namely Mr. B., now he is in Eternity, and the people beginning to move away, the Sheriff commanded him to be cut down, and being received in the arms of some of his Friends, he was conveyed by them into a house not far distant from the place of Execution, where being layed upon a Table, unto the astonishment of the beholders, he began to stir and breath[e] and rattle in his throat, and it was evident his life was whole in him; from the Table he was carried to a Bed in the same house, where he breathed more strongly, and opened his eyes, and his mouth (though his teeth were set before) and offered to speak, but could not recover the use of his tongue; but his reviving being known, within 4 hours the Officers came to the house where he was, and conveyed him to the place of Execution again, and hung him up again, until he was quite dead, whence he was carried by his mourning friends to Islington, where he now sleepeth in the bed of his Grave, untill the morning of the Resurrection, from whence though buried in dishonour, he will then be raised in glory.

Thus you have had the Relation of one that was but young in years but old in wickedness: you have read of his Sabbath breaking, Prophaneness, Swearing, Lying, Stealing, Drunkenness, Fornication, and the like Sins, which he confessed himself frequently and deeply guilty of, and to compleat and fill up the measure of his Sins he added to the rest the Horrid sin of Murder. I believe you have scarcely heard of sin grown up to such maturity in so short a time, as it did in him, who when he was imprisoned was under sixteen years of age.

And what could any expect should be the issue and product of Sin arrived to such perfection, but Death, and wrath, and the vengeance of Eternal Fire?

But Behold here an instance of Free grace! His sins did abound, but God's grace did super-abound. Sometimes God doth sow the seed of grace in the heart that is most unlikely to receive it; and reapeth Great Glory to his name by pardoning Great Sins. . . .

Let not any from this example of God's free grace, presume to continue and indulge themselves in a sinful course, hoping to obtain mercy at the last as he hath done, and so turn God's glory into shame and his grace into wantonness; for it is a rare example, hardly again to be parallel'd: will a man run himself thorough the body, because some have been healed of such wounds? will a man drink down poyson, because some by an Antidote have expelled the poyson and escaped with life? is not presumption the bane and ruine of millions of souls? may not God cut you off in the act of some of your sins, and not give you time for repentance? and if life doth continue, may not he deny you the grace of repentance? doth not custome and continuance in sin harden your heart and fasten you in Satan's Chains? hath not God threatned that such who cry peace, peace to themselves though they walk after the immagination [*sic*] of their hearts, to add drunkenness to thirst, That he will not spare them, but his anger and his jealousie shall smoke against them, and that he will blot out their name from under heaven, Deut. 29:19, 20.

The great improvement which should be made of God's gracious dealings with this young man, is for all to admire God's free grace; and especially for poor distressed Souls, that are upon the brink of hell in their own apprehensions, and are ready to dispair of God's mercy, because of the greatness of their sins; to take encouragement from hence, and hope that there may be mercy in store for them; they have not been Murderers, whatever their sins have been; and if a Murderer hath been received into favour, why may not they hope? Let such think with themselves that it is free grace hath saved him, and let them sue out at the throne of grace for the same grace which is freely tendred unto them.

Holy Meditations

Along with prayer, Bible reading, and hearing sermons, meditation was an important device of Puritan spirituality. The first selection that follows—from William Bates—presents a general discussion of the duty and nature of meditation as Puritans conceived it. Such meditation often took the form of self-examination; and this has already been seen in the autobiographical materials from Edmund Trench, and in the meditative fragments embedded in the narrative about Katherine Clark. The writing of verse could be a meditative exercise for the author at the same time that it produced, in a winsome form, material for others to meditate upon. The examples of the verse of Benjamin Keach illustrate this. Aphorisms were also considered excellent material for meditation, since the mind could retain them and mull them over; the following selection from Ralph Venning exemplifies the work of one of the most accomplished authors of this genre. More prominent than either verse or aphorisms as subjects of meditation were the multifarious phenomena of nature which could be spiritualized, and the surprising and providential works of God, the meanings of which could be drawn out by the skilled preacher. John Flavel was the acknowleged champion of the first of these, as the selections from him that follow will show, while Thomas Vincent was a skilled practitioner of the latter, as his "improvement" of the plague and fire of London evidences. No form of Christian meditation was more traditional than that by which the Christian prepared for the sacrament; and the selection from Thomas Doolittle's classic illustrates how a Puritan spiritual writer handled that.

Introduction to William Bates,
A Discourse of Divine Meditation

William Bates (1625-1699) was educated at Cambridge and was a vicar in London until his ejection in 1662. The year before his ejection he had been awarded the degree of Doctor of Divinity by Cambridge. Bates was one of the moderate Presbyterians who worked closely with Richard Baxter. He had favored the restoration of the monarchy, even though he suffered by it. Bates was a moderate Calvinist who wrote such major theological works as The Harmony of the Divine Attributes in the Contrivance and Accomplishment of Man's Redemption *(1697). He also wrote many practical works that avoided controversy and presented the Christian life in a plain and direct style. He preached the funeral sermons for many notable Dissenters, including Baxter and Thomas Manton.*

What follows consists of most of several chapters taken from his treatise on meditation, in which he urges his readers to meditate on the "creatures" as well as on the scriptures, and in which he also gives practical directions about such matters as the proper times for meditation. The text is taken from The Works of the Late Reverend and Learned William Bates, D.D. *(London: for B. Aylmer and J. Robison, 1700; Wing B 1100), where* A Discourse of Divine Meditation, On Psal. CXIX. Ver. 97 *first appeared in print. According to the "Bookseller's Advertisement" the text was "Exactly taken in Short-Hand and Approved by the Author in his Life-time as Faithfully done for private Use" but never prepared for the press. The following excerpts are taken from 881-85 and 887-89. The* Dictionary of National Biography *has a brief life of Bates by A. B. Grosart.*

William Bates,
A Discourse of Divine Meditation

Chapter 1

Meditation is a Duty so Rare and unpractised, that I think the Knowledge of it is not among all Christians, [and] the exercise of it is among very few; and therefore if I should tell you that it is an Unaccustomed Duty, this might be an imperfect account of it.

In the general. Meditation is the vehement motion of the Understanding, for that is the leading faculty in this Duty. And that I may the more fully explain it to you, I will consider its Kinds: it is either speculative, or practical.

1. Speculative meditation is this: When there is a serious Inquiry made after some hidden Truth, when the Soul purposeth to enrich itself with the Treasures of Knowledge; And this is practised by many Rational Men; I mean those, whose Understandings are more refined and raised

than ordinary Peoples'. But if our Meditation be meerly Speculative, it is but like a Winter Sun, which shines but doth not warm. This therefore I shall not speak of.

2. Practical Meditation. The end whereof is to bring the Soul to a serious detestation of Sin, to a Closing with, and Imbracing of the Will of God: This is that I intend to treat of, and it is like blowing of the Coals to warm the Soul. This I shall Describe to you in this manner.

Meditation is the serious Exercise of the Understanding, whereby our Thoughts are fix'd on the Observation of Spiritual things in order to practice. To open the several parts of this Description:

First, then, here's the Act, 'tis the serious exercise of the Understanding. And in this respect, Meditation is an inward secret Duty; the Soul retires it self into its Closet, and bids farewel to the World. It is an Invisible Duty to the Eye of men; and therefore Carnal persons do not Relish it: It is an Exercise of the Understanding; it is that Duty wherein we do not converse with drossy outward things. And this is another Reason that renders it so difficult to the men of the World. You may observe this as a Rule, That every Duty the more Spiritual it is, the more Carnal men disrelish it; and therefore they will rather hear the Word than pray in their Families; and rather Pray than Meditate; and what's the reason? Because Meditation is a more Spiritual Duty. Nay further, because 'tis an exercise of the understanding, therefore it is one of the most Noble Works that a Christian can perform; Reason is then in its Exaltation. When the Soul doth meditate, it doth put forth the most Rational Acts, and then is the Soul most like to God; for God spends an Eternity in Contemplating his own Essence and attributes. That's the Act.

Secondly, the Quality of this Act, whereby the Thoughts are fix'd. There is a great inconsistency in the Thoughts of Men;

but Meditation doth Chain and fasten them to a Spiritual Object. The Soul then lays a Command upon it self, that the thoughts (which otherwise are very fleeting and feathery) should be fixed upon its Object.

This Duty upon this very account is very Advantageous: You know a Garden that is watered by sudden Showers, is more uncertain in its Fruit, than when 'tis refreshed by a constant Stream; so when our thoughts are sometimes upon good things, and then run off; when they do but take a Glance (as it were) upon holy Objects, and then run away; there is not such Fruit brought into the Soul as when our Minds by Meditation do dwell upon them. The Rayes of the Sun may warm us, but they do not Inflame unless they are contracted in a burning Glass; so some slight thoughts of Heavenly things may warm us a little, but will never inflame the Soul, till they be fixed by close Meditation. Therefore David (who was an excellent man at this Duty) tells us his Heart was fixed, and saith the same concerning the frame of a good man.[1]

Thirdly, Consider the Object of this Meditation; our thoughts are fix'd on the observation of Spiritual Things: all Spiritual Truths are Symbolical to a gracious Heart, and will yield some advantage to the Soul; but there are some particular Truths which may be of more usefulness. To Instance in two or three. Meditation fixeth it self upon the Joy and Glory of Heaven, that so the Soul may aspire and breathe after it; It fixeth itself upon the defiling nature of Sin, that so the Soul may for ever Renounce and Abhor it; It fixeth itself upon the never dying Worm and Fire of Hell, that a Christian may alwayes labour to eschew it, and run from it. Such objects as these the Meditation of a Christian is fixed upon.

Fourthly, Consider the End of Meditation. It is in order to Practice. There are

---

[1] Ps. 112:7.

many persons that fly over a Garden of Flowers, (I mean over many Spiritual Objects), their thoughts run and they gather no Honey, they bring no fruit to their Souls; but this is not the way of a Christian; and therefore Spiritual Meditation is thus described by God himself. "This Book of the Law shall not depart out of thy mouth, but thou shalt Meditate therein day and night, that thou mayest observe to do according to all that is written therein."[2] The end of it is to observe for Practice and Use. So in the Book of Job we have an Expression applicable to this Purpose; "lo this, we have searched it; so it is, hear it, and know thou it for thy good."[3] Some know things that they may know them, and some know things that they may be known, and taken notice of; but Spiritual Meditation draws forth the strength of an Object for a man's own Good.

Now this Practical Meditation, is either Occasional or Deliberate.

First, Occasional Meditation, that is, when the soul Spiritualizeth every Object, when the understanding is like a Limbeck[4] that distils something from every thing it sees and views for the good of the Soul. This is that Spiritual Chymistry that turns all Metals into Gold. Our blessed Saviour was a most eminent Example of this, he drew Spiritual matter from Natural Objects; the gospel is full of parables upon this Account.

A Christian should labour to see all things in God, and God in all things. Every stream should lead him to the Fountain. All things here below should be but a Ladder to raise up his Soul to God. I shall speak more of this occasional Meditation, because it is of great Use, and he that neglects it

1. Reflects Dishonour upon God.
2. Is Injurious to his own Soul.
3. Doth neglect the Creature.

I speak now of those Meditations that may be raised by those variety of Objects before us.

1. He doth Reflect dishonour upon God. The end of the Creature is this, that God may have and receive a Tribute of Honour and Praise; and therefore God hath infused a reasonable Soul into the Body of Man, that so Man might be a considering Creature, whereby he hath fitted man for Meditation: this Duty doth oblige all Rational Beings. See Job 38:7, Where the Lord speaks concerning the work of Creation, when "the morning stars sang together." As Birds sing at the break of Day, so in the morning of the Creation the Angels sang together; and God expects it from Man, because he hath given him a Reasonable Soul. Our Five Senses are so many Doors whereby the External Objects are conveyed to us, and the Soul is to take notice of them. Nay for this very end did God create man in the last day of Creation, when he had made a Feast he brought Man as the Guest, and when he had provided a Palace, he produced Man to dwell in it; and what's the Reason, but this, that he might glorifie the Creatour? When God had adorned the Heavens with Stars, and the Earth with Flowers; then he brought forth Man to give him the praise of all. The First Sabbath was Instituted for this end, that men might solemnly bless God for the Creation of the World.

2. He that doth not Meditate occasionally injures his own Soul. He that makes use of the Creatures, and doth not learn by them, robs himself of the best part of that which he should enjoy of them. The Creatures are but the Adumbrations of the Infinite Majesty that is above. Now will any Man content himself with painted Meat for

---

[2]Josh. 1:8.

[3]Job 5:27.

[4]limbeck: alembic, a distilling apparatus.

Food? So wilt thou content thyself with the bare enjoyment of the Creature; and not Ascend up to God? He hath given thee the Creatures upon this Account, that they might be Instruments to raise up thy Soul to himself.

3. He Neglects the Creature. There is nothing within the whole Circuit of Nature, but is of some use to raise up our Souls to God. From the Sun, to the Stone; from the Cedar, to the Violet; every creature hath a voice to teach us something of God. This whole World is a School for man. All the Creatures spell this to us, That there is a God. Now if we Neglect this use of it, by our Meditation, then we Neglect the Creature. The whole Creation is a well tuned Instrument, and Man is to make the Musick; and if we do not by Meditation raise up our Thoughts to God, we are in the fault. I will not Pass it over without reckoning what Advantages the Soul may get by it.

1. This will dispose and fit the Soul for Admiration and Praise of God. What's the Reason that men do rather wonder at the Effects of Art, than at the works of God in Nature? but this, because they do not Meditate upon them? So that many Persons set God beneath a Painter or Carver. Praise and Admiration is the going forth of the Understanding upon an Excellent Object. Now when you shall read the Book of the Creation, you will have reason to praise the Author of it. When you cast your Eyes upward and consider the Sun, O meditate and take notice of this, that Bright Sun is but a shadow of God! It is God that hath stretched forth that Rich Canopy over our heads. When you cast your Eye down, and consider the vast body of the Earth, it hangs in the Air, which is so weak a thing that it cannot hold up a Feather, it's founded upon the Power of God.

2. As it will dispose the Soul for Praise, so for Thanksgiving. Now this differs from Praise thus; When I praise a thing, I Re-spect the worth of it; When I am Thankful for a thing, I Respect my Interest in it. Now when a man shall Consider this great World, and [that] all things here below were made for the Glory of God and the use of Man, this will raise our thanksgiving to God, and Inflame our Love to him. What's the Reason that we are more Grateful for small Courtesies of Men, than for the Rich Benefits of God? But because we do not Meditate on them.

3. This Occasional Meditation upon the Creature without Us, will be an excellent Ground for our Faith and Dependance upon God. Our Lord Jesus doth urge his Disciples to believe upon this Account. Saith he, ''do you not see the Lillies, they neither sow nor spin, yet they are clothed with a richer garment than Solomon? Do you not see the Sparrows? there is not one of them falls to the ground without a Providence, and you are of more worth than many sparrows.''[5] When a Christian shall consider thus; God is the great Master of the Family of Heaven and Earth, he makes Provision for all his Creatures; and if my God takes Care of these things that are Inferiour to me, much more will he take care of me; for 'tis Christ's argument, ''ye are of more value that many sparrows.'' Nay,

4. This occasional Meditation, will be a means to cure the most vicious part of our Lives; for what is the wickedest part of a man's Life? it is his vain Thoughts. As in Nature there is no Vacuity or Emptiness, but a Vessel is either filled with Liquor or the Air; now the more Water you pour in, the more Air goes out. So if you would but store your Souls with these Occasional Meditations, it would thrust out vain and vile Thoughts. Oh 'tis a Rare Temper when a Christian is alwayes upon the Wing.

---

[5]This paraphrase is a conflation of Matt. 6:26, 28 and Matt. 10:29, 31 and adds the characteristically Puritan term ''providence'' to the mixture.

When he is like the Beams of the Sun, they touch the Earth, but the Body of the Sun is fixed in Heaven. So 'tis with a Christian when he converseth with the World, but enjoyes God.

5. This Occasional Meditation will enliven thy Obedience to God. When thou considerest thus with thyself, that thou art alwayes maintained by the Expences of his Providence, this will Encourage thee in his Service. A Master looks for the Service of him he feeds and maintains; so if you consider you are always supported by the Charges of Free Grace, and every good thing given, is the Fruit of God's Bounty; any, that all the Creatures observe God by a perpetual Law, this will likewise raise thy Obedience to him.

The Sun alwayes Runs his Course, without Errour or Alteration. All the Creatures here below will contradict their own proper Nature to be subservient to the Will of God; such Meditations as these will enliven your Obedience. To sum up all: Occasional Meditations brings this Advantage to us, The World, which is the House of Man, is made the Temple of God. And then are all the Creatures used according to the design and end of God, for which they were Created, when all these Beams of Goodness which shine from the Father of Lights, are Reflected upon him again.

Secondly, There is deliberate meditation, and that is Two-fold: it is either Direct or Reflexive.

1. Direct. When the Understanding fixeth it self upon some Truth, and draws from it those Advantages which may be proper to it self. We read of Isaac, that he went out into the field to meditate.[6] The Word in its primitive signification hath this Import; that he went forth to Confer with truth; When there is a mutual and reciprocal Discourse between Truth and the Soul, when the Soul meditates upon the Law of God, takes the Command of God, and speaks to it, and the Command speaks to the Soul, there's a mutual Conference. Therefore it is said, the Law "Shall talk with thee,"[7] it shall give thee direction how to manage the Course of thy Life.

2. Reflexive Meditation; and that is, when there is a Solemn discourse between the Soul of man, and himself; when there is a Colloquy or Soliloquy, an inward Conference between a man and his own heart, and he inquires how the state and case stands in reference to himself, whether or no reconciled to God? and puts Practical Questions concerning his Everlasting State.

---

[6]Gen. 24:63.
[7]Prov. 6:22.

Chapter III.

The time for this Duty; and there are three things I shall open to you in reference to that.

1. The Frequency of it;
2. The Continuance;
3. the Seasons when we may most for the advantage of our Souls draw forth our Meditations.

First, For the Frequency.

In the General you must know, the Scripture doth not Positively Determine any set times wherein we are Obliged to Meditate.

Spiritual Prudence and holy Affections should give Rules to us for the frequency of Meditation. The Scripture speaks in general Terms, David tells us of a Godly Man, that he Meditates in the Law Day and Night.[8] And as for his own Practice, although he had the Business of a Kingdom,

---

[8]Ps. 1:2.

and the Pleasure of the Court to divert him, yet saith he, it is my Meditation "all the day," which implies the Constant disposition of his Soul to this Duty, and likewise that Ordinarily he was wont to set apart some Portion of every Day for the Performance of it. There are two things which should persuade you to frequency in it.

1. By Frequency, you will make your thoughts more pliable for the Discharge of this Duty. Your Souls will be more accomplished and fitted for the Exercise of it. You know that Customary Running makes a person long breath'd. So when we often use ourselves to this Duty, our thoughts will be more Consistent, and we shall be more Improved and Ripened for the Exercise of it. Whereas he that long neglects it, will find that Meditation first is unpleasant, then unnecessary, at last Burthensome and Odious; and this proceeds from disuse.

2. Long Interruptions of it will hinder the fruit of it. When there are large Gaps and Strides between our performance of this Duty, we lose the benefit of our former Meditations. As it is with our Bodies, if a Man makes a Free, and Liberal Meale, this will not maintain his Body to Morrow, and a Day after, but he must have constant Food, else Nature languishes and decayes; so you Meditate to Day [sic], but if you should Neglect it for many days after, you will lose the Benefit of it, and the Soul decayes and Languishes. If the Bird leaves her Nest for a long space, the Eggs Chill and are not fit for production; but when there is a Constant Incubation, then they bring forth: So when we leave Religious Dutyes for a long Space, our Affections Chill, and grow cold; and are not fit to produce Holiness, and Comfort to our Souls; But when we are constant in this work, then shall we find the Advantage of it.

Secondly, For the Continuance of this Duty, How long must we continue in it?

I Answer, so long ordinarily till thou dost find some sensible Benefit Conveyed to thy Soul. The Nature of Man doth much disrelish this Duty, and we are apt to be soon weary of it; our thoughts are like a Bird in the Cage, which flutters the more because of its Confinement; so our thoughts are apt to run strayingly out, when we Confine them to such a Duty as this is; but he that begins and doth not proceed, loses the Benefit of the Duty. As it is in the kindling of a Fire in wet Wood, you know Continuance is that which must cause the Flame. When you blow at first, there's a little smoak arises, by holding on you raise Sparks, but he that goes forward at last brings it to a flame. So 'tis in the Duty of Meditation; When you begin to meditate upon Spiritual things, at first you raise a smoak [of] a few Sighs towards God; by continuance you raise some Sparks of Heavenly Desires; but at last there's a Flame of Holy Affections that goes up towards God. Now you should not ordinarily leave the work till the Flame doth so ascend. When a Man goes forth in a Calm and Serene Evening, and views the Face of the Heavens, he shall first see a Star or two twinkle and Peep forth; but if he continues, both their Number and Lustre is Increased, and at least he sees the whole Heaven is bespangled with Stars in every part; So when thou dost Meditate upon the promises of the Gospel; at first it may be one Star begins to appear, a little Light conveys itself to thy heart; but go forwards and then thou wilt find when thy thoughts are Amplyfied and Ripened, there will be a clear Light, more satisfaction conveyed to thy Soul; and in Continuance the Covenant of Grace, will appear Bespangled with Promises as Heaven with Stars, and all to give thee Satisfaction.

Thirdly, for the Seasons of Meditation.

To that I answer, there is no time in it self but is alike pleasing to God, and there are no hours that are Amiss to a Gracious Spirit. Yet nevertheless there are some particular Seasons, wherein our Affections are more Smart and Vigorous, wherein our thoughts are more lively, and more disposed for this duty of Contemplation. Now we should Chuse these Seasons. I will instance in some Seasons which the Scripture speaks of.

First, The Morning, after the Body hath been composed by the sweetness of Rest, then is a fit time for Meditation, and there's a double reason for it.

1. Because we should Consecrate the first Fruits to God. We should pitch our Virgin thoughts upon him, and upon Spiritual things, before they are opened to the Imbracements of Inferiour Objects. When you awake in the Morning you have many Suitors that attend your thoughts. Now have a care that it be not with you as it was in the Inn of Bethlehem; Strangers took up the Rooms in the Inn, and Christ was excluded, and put to a Manger. So in the Morning, vain Worldly thoughts take up the Room of your Souls, but God and Christ are excluded. We should honour the Lord with the first of our Substance, and with the first of our thoughts and Affections.

2. In the Morning Meditate upon this Account, because the Influence of the Duty will be visible in your Lives in the Succeeding parts of the Day. That wherewith a Vessel is first Seasoned conveys a lasting Savour and Tincture to it. So Holy Meditation, leaves an abiding Tincture upon our Hearts all the Day. 'Tis an excellent expression of Solomon (speaking of the Law of God) "When thou awakest it shall talk with thee."[9] What's the meaning? As Servants come to their Masters in the Morning, and receive Rules from them, how they shall direct their Business in the Day; so a Gracious Heart takes Directions

from the Law of God, in the Morning how he should Manage himself all the following parts of the Day.

Secondly, Another Season for Meditation, is the Evening. For this we have the example of Isaac Recorded in Scripture, that he went out to Meditate at the Eventide.

Thirdly, In the Night Season, when our Bodies are Reposed in the Bed, then our Souls should be Reposed in the Bosom of God by sweet Meditation. We have the Command of the Lord for this, "Commune with your own Hearts upon your Beds and be Still."[10] And there is a double argument which may move you to this Night-Meditation.

1. Because then our Souls are sequester'd from the Business of the World; they are Retired from all the Noise and Tumult of things here below, they are not distracted with the Incursions of sensible Objects; and at such a time as that is, we are best fitted for Meditation. Secrecy, silence and Rest, Dispose the Soul for meditation; and all these we enjoy in the Night Season; then we are excluded from Company, Motion, and Business.

2. Because when the Curtain of Darkness is drawn over the World, our Hearts are apt to be filled with a Religious Fear of God, our Souls are more Composed in the Night, and we have more Awful apprehensions of God. And therefore observe the Connexion, "stand in Awe and sin not, Commune with your own Hearts upon your Beds." The Bed is an Image and a Representation of the Grave, and at such a time as that is a Man may be more serious and Composed in this Work. David says, "My Reins[11] also instruct me in the Night Sea-

---

[9]Prov. 6:22.

[10]Ps. 4:4; Bates changed the singular "heart" and "bed" of the King James Version to the plural.

[11]reins: literally, kidneys; but here it has the connotation of being the seat of the feelings, or affections.

son[s]."[12] The meaning is David's inward Thoughts did then Read a Lecture of Divinity to him.

4. The Sabbath-Day, is a Season for Meditation. This should be the Temper of Every Christian to be in the Spirit on the Lord's Day. On that Day when our Saviour did arise from the Earth, our Souls should Ascend to Heaven.

Consider with yourselves, the Lord's Day is a Type of Heaven, and Contemplation is the Work of Heaven. The Rest of the Sabbath is but an Abridgement of that long Eternity which the Saints shall enjoy with God; and the Imployment of Heaven is Contemplation. The Glorified Spirits above are always exercised in a Steady view and Consideration of God's Infinite Glory. Now the Sabbath Being A Type of Heaven,

and Meditation being the work of Heaven, certainly this Day is the most fit Season for Meditation. As for you who disrelish this Duty, and are unacquainted with it, do you expect Heaven? Your Indisposition to this Duty will be a Bar to keep you from Blessedness, and hinder you from entring into that Rest. A Gracious Soul upon the Lord's Day by his Meditation may converse with God; he may discourse with the Inhabitants of another World, he may enjoy as much of God as this Interposing vaile of Flesh and Blood will admit; the only difference between a Saint in Heaven, and a Saint upon Earth who Meditates upon God, is in respect of the Degrees and the manner of their Fruition. For otherwise a Saint upon Earth enjoyes Heaven especially on the Lord's Day, when every Duty receives a Special Blessing, and therefore the Duty of Meditation.

---

[12]Ps. 16:7.

Introduction to Benjamin Keach, Poems from *The Glorious Lover* and *War with the Devil*

Benjamin Keach (1640-1704) came from Buckinghamshire and was a tailor by trade. Before the Restoration he joined the Baptists. In 1664 he suffered brief imprisonment, a fine, and the pillory because of the supposedly seditious nature of a catechism for children he had written. In 1668 he moved to London and became an elder of the General Baptist congregation in Southwark. But shortly thereafter he adopted the Calvinistic views of the Particular Baptists and formed a second Southwark Baptist congregation of which he was the pastor. He quickly rose to prominence as a Baptist leader, writing extensively on their behalf as well as in defense of strict Calvinist orthodoxy. He was a strong proponent of congregational hymn-singing among the Baptists, introducing the use of many hymns he had himself composed.

Keach was the author of several works of devotion written in allegorical and poetic form. His long poem The Glorious Lover: A Divine Poem, Upon the Adorable Mystery of Sinners' Redemption *was first published in 1679. It described the coming, life, and atonement of Christ as well as Christ's summons to sinners.* War with the Devil *was a poetic dialogue about the conflict of a young believer with Satan. First published in 1673, it went through twenty-two reprintings within a century.* The Progress of Sin; or the Travels of Ungodliness *and* The Travels of True Godliness *were prose allegories published in 1684.*

What follows consists of a portion of The Glorious Lover *(London, 1679; Wing K64) 252-56, and two poems appended to* War with the Devil: or The Young Man's Conflict with the Powers of Darkness, In A Dialogue . . . *(London, 1684; Wing K 106), 116-17, 121-24. The passage from* The Glorious Lover *presents a dialogue between Christ and the soul concerning their mystical union. The other two poems illustrate Keach's interest in the meditative praise of God. For more about Keach see the entry on his life by Richard L. Greaves in* Biographical Dictionary of British Radicals in the Seventeenth Century, *edited by Richard L. Greaves and Robert Zaller (Brighton: Harvester Press, 1982-1984) 2: 150-51.*

The Glorious Lover.

A Divine Poem, . . .

Chapter VIII.

The mutual and blessed Contract
between Christ and the Sinner.

Jesus:

Give me thy heart then, Soul, I do betroth
Thee unto me, that no approaching Wrath
May any ways be hurtful unto thee,
In Righteousness I thee betroth to me.
In Judgment also thou betrothed art,
And all I have to thee I do impart
In faithfulness and tender mercy, so
That thou thy Lord, thy Friend, & God
　　shalt know
I do betroth thee unto me for ever,
And neither Death, Nor Earth, nor Hell
　　shall sever
Thy Soul from me. If thou wilt pay thy vows,
I will be thine, and thou shalt be my Spouse.
I take thee now for better, and for worse:
Give me thy hand, let's jointly both of us
With mutual love tie the conjugal Knot,
Which on my part shall never be forgot.
My Covenant with thee is seal'd by bloud,
'Tis firmer than the Oath at Noah's Flood.[1]
Into my folded Arms I now do take thee,
And promise that I never will forsake thee.
Thy sins are cast behind my back, and I
Will cover each future infirmitie.

The Sinner's closing with Christ.

Soul:

Upon my bended knees I do this day
Accept of thee, my Lord, my Life, my Way,
By whom alone poor Sinners have access
Unto the Father; nay, and do confess,
Declare, pronounce i' th' sight of God, that I
Do enter now with all simplicity
Into a Contract with thee, make my Vows
That I will be to thee a faithful Spouse.
O blessed Jesus, I'm as one undone,
A naked, vile, loathsom[e] and guilty one,
Unworthy far to wash the very feet
Of th' Servants of my Lord; O how is it
That thou, the glorious Prince,
　　shouldst ever chuse
Such an unworthy Worm to be thy Spouse:
O what's thy Love!
　　O Grace, beyond expression,
Doth the great God on me place his affection?
But sith 'tis so, this I engage to do,
I'le leave all for thy sake, and with thee go.
And in all things own thee alone as Head,
And Husband dear, by whom I will be led,
And in all states and times will thee obey,
What ever comes, unto my dying-day.
I take thee as my Prophet, Priest, and King:[2]
And my own worthiness in every thing
I do renounce, and further vow that I
Upon thy Bloud and Righteousness will lie;
On that, and that alone, will I depend
By Faith always until my life shall end.
I covenant with thee, and so I take thee,
And whatsoe'r falls out, I'le ne'r forsake thee,
But run all hazards in this dolesom day,
And never from thy holy ways will stray.
All this and more I promise shall be done,
But in thy strength, Lord, in thy strength alone.
　　Th' Solemnity thus ended, presently
The glorious Prince, the Bridegroom,
　　casts his Eye
Upon the Soul, and bound up all her sores,

---

[1] God's promise not to destroy the world again by a flood, Gen. 9:8-17.

[2] Calvinist theologians divided the "offices" of Christ into prophet, priest, and king.

Nay healed them, and cancelld all her scores:
But be'ng her self defil'd, she soon espy'd
A precious Fountain flowing from his side,
A Fountain for uncleanness to wash in
In which she bath'd, and wash'd away her sin.
Then gloriously by him she was array'd
With Robes imbroid'red, very richly laid
With Gold and Diamonds, that she did seem
Like an adorned Heav'nly Seraphim.
One Vesture was especially most rare,
Without a seam, much like what he did wear;
It is the Wedding Robe, both clean and white,
Whose lustre far exceeds the Morning-light;
And other garments also, which she wore,
Curiously wrought with Silk, and spangl'd o're
With stars of Gold, of Pearl, of precious Stone,
Enough to dazle all to look upon:
Which be'ng made up of every precious Grace,
Did cause a splendent Beauty in her Face,
That whilst he did behold her, could discry
His Father's Image clearly in her Eye,
Which did so please him, that he now admires,
And after this her Beauty much desires.
O see the change, she which was once so foul,
Is now become a sweet and lovely Soul.
Her beauty far excels what it had been
In ancient days, no mortal Eye hath seen
So sweet a Creature, no such Virgin Queen.
Yet all her Beauty now's but spots and stains,
To what it will be when her Saviour raigns.
O hear the melody! Angels rejoice,

Whilst she triumphs in this most happy choice.
Who would not then all Earthly Glories slight,
To gain a minute's taste of such delight?
No sooner did Apollyon[3] cast his Eyes
On what was done, but furiously did 'rise
To damp her joy, or cause her mirth to cease,
And by some stratagems to spoil her peace.
He first stirs up the Old-man's broken force
For to estrange her: if he can't divorce
Her from her Friend, yet raises inward strife,
How to deprive her of those joys of life,
Which do abound in Lover's every way,
Betwixt th' espousal and the Marriage-day.
A thousand tricks contriv'd before had he
How to delay or spoil th' Affinite.[4]
But if he can't rob us of inward joy,
Our name, or goods, or life he will destroy.
For failing in the first, he stirs up Foes
To lay upon her persecuting blows.
He that will follow Christ, must look each day
To have his worldly comforts took away.
Besides, the Old-man being not yet slain,
Great troubles in her mind there rose again.
But her dear Friend so faithful is, that he
Will never leave her in Adversitie. . . .

---

[3]Apollyon: the angel of the abyss in Rev. 9:11; the name means "destroyer."

[4]Affinitie: a reference to the joining together of Christ and the soul.

War with the Devil:

Or, The Young Mans Conflict
with the Powers of Darkness, . . .

A Mystical Hymn of Thanksgiving.

My Soul mounts up with Eagle's wings,
*   And unto thee, dear God, she sings;*
Since thou art on my side
My enemies are forc'd to fly,
As soon as they do thee espy;
*   Thy name be glorify'd.*
Thou makest Rich by making Poor:
By Poverty add'st to my Store;
*   Such Grace dost thou provide*
Thou wound'st as well as thou mak'st whole.
And Heal'st by wounding of the Soul;
*   Thy name be glorify'd.*
Thou mak'st men blind by giving sight,
And turn'st their darkness into light:
*   These things can't be deny'd.*
Thou cloath'st the Soul by making bare,
And give'st food when none is there;
*   Thy Name be glorify'd.*
Thou killest by making alive,
By dying dost the Soul revive,
*   Which none can do besides;*
Thou dost raise up by pulling down,
And by abasing, thou dost Crown,
*   Thy Name be glorify'd.*
By making bitter thou mak'st sweet,
Amd mak'st each crooked thing to meet,
*   I'th' Soul which thou hast try'd:*
The fruitless tree thou mak'st to grow,

And the green tree dost overthrow;
*   Thy name be glorify'd.*
The conquered the conquest gains;
By being beat, the field obtains,
*   Which makes me therefore cry,*
Lord while I live upon the Earth,
Since thou hast wrought the second birth
*   Thy nature I'le magnifie.*
Thou mak'st men wise, by coming⁵ fools,
By emptying thou fill'st their Souls,
*   Such Grace dost thou provide:*
By making weary thou giv'st Rest;
That which seem'd worst, proves for the best;
*   Thy name be glorify'd.*
Thou art far off, and also neer,
And not confin'd, but ev'ry where,
*   And on the clouds dost ride.*
O thou art Love, and also Light;
Ther's none can go out of thy sight;
*   Thy name be magnify'd.*
Lord, thou art great and also good,
And sit'st upon thy mighty flood,
*   By whom all hearts are try'd:*
Though thou art Three, yet art but One,
And comprehended art of none;
*   Thy name be glorify'd.*

---

⁵coming: becoming.

A Spiritual Hymn.

The Sun doth now begin to shine,
    And breaketh forth yet more and more,
Meer darkness was that Light of mine,
    Which I commended heretofore.
        I was involved in my sin;
        Had day without but night within.
My former days I did compare,
    Unto the sweet and lovely Spring,
    I thought that time it was as rare,
    As when the chirping Birds do sing:
        But I was blind, I now do see
        There was no Spring nor Light in me.
My Spring it was the Winter-time,
    Yet, like the midst of cold December;
The Sun was gone out of my Clime,
    And also I do now remember
        My heart was cold as any stone,
        My leaves were off, and sap was gone.
God is a Sun, a Shield also,
    The glory of the World is He;
True Light alone from him doth flow,
    And he has now enlightned me:
        The Sun doth his sweet beams display,
        Like to the dawning of the day.
How precious is't to see the Sun,
    When in the morning it doth rise,
And shineth in our Horizon,
    To th' clearing of the cloudy Skies!
        The misty Fogs by his strong Light
        Are vanish'd quite out of our sight.
Thus doth the Lord in my poor heart,
    By his strong beams and glorious rays,
The light from darkness clearly part,
    And makes in me rare shining days.
        Though Fogs appear and Clouds do rise,
        He doth expel them from mine eyes.
Were there no glorious Lamp above,
    What dark confusion would be here!

If God should quite the Sun remove,
    How would the Seamen do to steer!
My Soul's the World, and Christ's the Sun
    If he shines not I am undone.
In Winter things hang down their head,
    Until Sol's beams do them revive;
So I in sin lay buried,
    Till Jesus Christ made me alive:
        Alas my heart was Ice and Snow,
        Till Sun did shine, and Winds did blow.
Until warm Gales of Heav'nly Wind
    Did sweetly blow, and Sun did dart
its Light on me, I could not find
    No heat within my inward part;
        Then blow thou Wind, and shine thou Sun,
        To make my Soul a lively one.
In nat'ral men there is a light,
    Which for their sins doth them reprove;
And yet are they but in the night,
    And not renewed from above:
        The Moon is given (it is clear)
        To guide men who in darkness are,
The Sun for brightness doth exceed
    The Stars of Heaven, or the Moon;
Of them there is but little need,
    When Sun doth shine towards high noon.
        Just so the Gospel doth excel
        The Law God gave to Israel,
All those who do the Gospel slight,
    And rather have a Legal guide;
The Sun's not risen in their sight,
    And therefore 'tis that they deride
        Those who commend the Gospel-Sun
Above the Light in ev'ry one.
Degrees of Light I do perceive
    Some of them weak, and others strong;
That which is saving none receive
    But those who unto Christ belong:
        Yet doth each Light serve for the end,
        For which to man God did it send.

Introduction to Ralph Venning,
A Spiritual Garden
of Sweet-smelling Flowers

Ralph Venning was born in Devonshire, probably in 1621. He was educated at Emmanuel College, Cambridge (an important center of Puritan influence), receiving the B.A. in 1646 and the M.A. in 1650. Thereafter he was lecturer at St. Olave's Church, Southwark, until his ejection by the Act of Uniformity in 1662. From then until his death in 1674 he was a colleague of Robert Bragge as pastor to a Congregational church that met in Pewterers' Hall, London. He died in 1674.

Venning was highly reputed for works of spirituality written in an aphoristic style. His Mysteries and Revelations Or the Explication and Application of severall Extra-essentiall and borrowed Names, Allusions, and Metaphors in the Scripture *went through five editions between 1647 and 1657. His* Canaans Flowings—*discussed in the introduction—was reprinted three times. After his death the "substance" of many of his sermons was pulled together in a volume entitled* Venning's Remains, or Christ's School *(London, 1675). The aphorisms of Venning printed here are selected from* A Spiritual Garden of Sweet-smelling Flowers, or Mr. Ralph Vanning's Divine Sentences, *113-63, 165-71, 173-75, which was published at London in 1674 as one part of* Saints' Memorials: or Words fitly spoken, Like Apples of Gold in Pictures of Silver. Being, A Collection of Divine Sentences Written and Delivered by those late Reverend and Eminent Ministers of the Gospel, Mr. Edmund Calamy, Jr., Joseph Caryl, Mr. Ralph Venning, Mr. James Janeway *(Wing C 263). Inexpensive reprints of a selection from Ralph Venning still circulated in the nineteenth century. There is a brief biographical notice by Irvonwy Morgan in the* Biographical Dictionary of British Radicals in the Seventeenth Century, *ed. Richard L. Greaves and Robert Zaller (Brighton: Harvester Press, 1982-1984) 3:270.*

"A Spiritual Garden of Sweet-smelling Flowers,

or Mr. Ralph Venning's Divine Sentences."

That Soul that is settled in the love of God, is blessed in the peace of Christ.

When such a Soul suffereth an outward War, she looseth not her inward peace.

No troubles whatsoever which do outwardly make a noise, do violently enter into the silence of her inward repose.

She coveteth nothing abroad, and therefore resteth wholly within by love,

Such a Soul the Angels do visit and honour; she being the Temple of the Lord, and the Habitation of the Holy Ghost.

Happy is that Conscience in which Mercie and Truth are met together, for there Justice and Peace have kissed each other.

God is a God of Mercie, and will take pity on him that is truly sorrowful for his sins.

The Kiss of Justice, is to love our Enemies, to forsake Parents and Possessions for the love of God; to endure with Patience injuries inflicted, and in all places to flie from honours that are offered.

The Kiss of Peace, is to invite Foes to friendship, peaceably to sustain Adversaries, lovingly to instruct such as do amiss, meekly to comfort those that mourn, and to be at amity with all men.

Is any man rich? let him not put his trust in them: for riches make themselves wings, and flie away.[1]

Lazarus was poor, but was received into Heaven: Dives was rich, but however was carried into Hell.

To hear Sermons, to commend them, or admire them, and not to practice what we hear and understand, is to make Sodom and Gommorha's case at the day of Judgment better than our's.

Those that are now so idly busie in heaping up their Treasures of an Ant-Hillock, and building up the tottering Fabricks of a child, remember not that the foot of death is coming to spurn it all abroad, and to trample down both you and it.

Let us search our hearts, that God may finde them in a condition to receive him.

Make not sale of Heaven for the false pleasure of a few sins, for a little delight and ease that vanisheth in a moment.

Repent before thou becomest Old, lest thy Repentance should come too late; for thou leftest not thy sin, but thy sin left thee.

To acknowledge God to be just is good, and it is just we likewise acknowledge him to be good.

When thou Prayest, rather let thy heart be without words, than thy words without an heart.

Prayer will make a man to cease from sin, or sin will intice a man to cease from Prayer.

It is good to have a good Name, but it is better to have a good Conscience.

It is good to be great, but it is better to be good.

Teach thy heart to walk wholly with thy God, as well as holily.

Your words and works may satisfie the judgments of men; but God is the great Judge of our hearts.

---

[1] Allusion to Prov. 23:5.

Vain sinner, thy Saviour is willing to save thee; but it is thy sin, and Satan, that studieth to destroy thee.

The Son of man had sinned against God, and the Son of God satisfies for the sin of man.

Let admiration produce amazement, that God should send his Son to suffer death for sinners that rebelled agaist him.

But man must dye unto Eternity, unless the Son of Eternity would dye for him.

He that was the God of Glory, becomes the Son of shame.

He that is the Righteous Redeemer, was counted an Unjust Usurper.

He that is the Lord of Life, was condemned to Death.

He was accounted sinful, to purchase thy Salvation.

Christ's Cross is thy Comfort, his dishonour is thy honour.

It was a sweet saying of an Ancient Father; The name of Jesus is *Mel in Ore, Melos in Aure, Jubilus in Corde:* Honey in the Mouth, Melody in the Ear, and a Jubily, or Joy in the Heart.[2]

It is great misery to see man so proud, and greater mercie to see God so humble.

God was the Creditor, man was the Debtor; but he that was both God and man, the Pay-Master.

There is no sinner so great, but after conversion he makes as great a Saint.

There is more pleasure in suffering, than in sinning; for a Saint of God may suffer and not sin, but he cannot sin and not suffer.

God never made a good promise, but he made good that promise.

We should[3] prize mercie, if we knew its price.

A rich man is poor without God, but with him a poor man is rich.

If a man would be ever good, he should believe he was never good.

A grain of Grace is of more value, than many pounds of Gold.

God Created us, and left us to our selves; afterwards he Redeemed us, and left himself to us.

To commit sin, is the part of an humane nature; to lament for sins committed, is Christian-like; but to continue in sin, bidding defiance to the Divine powers, is Diabolical.

If the heart of man be hard and stony, it makes the softer cushion for the Devil to sit on.

If we are among our friends without God, we are in continual danger; but with God a man is safe though in the midst of enemies.

Let young Women put on Piety instead of Paints, Sanctity instead of Sattin, Modesty for their Morning and dayly dress; so shall God and every good man love them more and more.

The Christian hopeth for the world to come, but the sinner feareth it.

He that detaineth a penny from the poor, puts a Plague into his own purse.

Doth any man fear to dye? it's an easie thing to live: slaves and beasts do so; but it ought to be every man's study to live and dye well.

Man's life is more full of grief than glory; and it is a seasonable time to dye in, when to live is rather a burthen than a blessing.

Gathering of Riches is a pleasant tor-

---

[2]Venning's marginal note attributes this apothegm to St. Bernard of Clairvaux, a twelfth-century monastic leader and spiritual writer whom Calvin often quoted with approval.

[3]should: would.

ment: the trouble of getting, the charging of the conscience, the care of keeping, and the watching over them when gotten, takes away a great part of the expected enjoyment.

The work of a Christian while he lives in the body, is to crucifie the body of death.

God made man in his own likeness; man hath made sin in his likeness, and sin hath made misery in his own likeness.

What God gives us for our good, we ought to employ for his glory.

If we set our affections on what we have, when we have it not, it adds the more to our affliction.

That man that deserves nothing, ought to be content with any thing.

What is all this world, but a world of nothing at all?

Man is no sooner born, but he begins to dye; so uncertain is the life of man, that none knows whether he that is born to day, shall live till to morrow.

Christ is the Physitian of our Souls, his comforts are cordial; but miserable comforts are the Physitians of the Body.

It is at present heaven with us to enjoy God and Christ; What will it then be, when we worship him with his innumerable company of Angels?

A Christian hath but two things to fear, God and Sin.

When thou sinnest, repent betimes,[4] lest thou plunge into a custom of sinning; and always remember God hath a certain custom to punish sinners.

What deceitful pleasures are those that require either Repentance or Damnation!

We are all born to dye; let us so dye, that we may be born again.

If thou canst hear, and bear the Rod of affliction which God shall lay upon thee, remember this Lesson: Thou are beaten, that thou mayst be better.

There is no better defence against our own Infirmities and the scandalous reproaches of others, than the Sincerity of our own hearts.

Why is it that sinners so rarely confess their sins? it is because they are in them: we use not[5] to declare our dreams till we wake.

The Old Testament veils the New, the New Testament reveals the Old.

The Saint hath the motion of grace, whilst the Hypocrite hath but the notion; the Saint sees, tasts [sic] and feels it, whilst the Hypocrite only reads, hears, and speaks of it.

There is a time for all things; but no time when all things may be spoken.

What a vain thing is man, when the best of men are but vanity at best!

The wife of a man's bosom, is better than the portions of the purse.

Marry not where you love not, lest you are tempted to love where you marry not.

A Christian should like all God's commands, because they are all alike, Holy, Just, and Good.

Be sober in advice, and moderate in reproofs; some hearts are sooner humbled with stroaks than with stripes.

Though our good works will not carry us to heaven, yet they shall finde a reward in heaven.

Till we get Christ within us, we are without Christ.

The Lord's bottle and basket are never empty; he bountifully invites us with this free offer of grace.

The world cannot exalt a proud man so high, but God will bring him low; neither

---

[4]betimes: early, without delay.

[5]use not: are not accustomed.

can all the world so debase an humble man, but God will exalt him.

In the seed-time of your life, let your Holiness be sown, that so you may reap Blessedness in the Harvest of Eternity.

He that will put Piety in practice, must set his heart to practice Piety.

There is a kind of Divine husbandry; saving grace is a heavenly thirst, and doth so improve, that it makes us Burgesses of the Holy City.

The Righteous man hath grace beyond expression; the Hypocrite hath expression beyond grace.

Our Saviour had a Father and a Mother, and yet he was from the beginning.

The Saints have no greater joy than to enjoy God, and to rejoyce in him.

We are commanded to love Peace, and follow after Righteousness; and yet the Saints themselves are in continual War, fighting the good fight of Faith.

The Salvation of a Saint may be sure, yet may not he be sure of his Salvation.

The Righteous man makes godliness his gain; the Wicked man makes gain his godliness.

The Soul is above the reach of any weapon but sin, and that pierces like a sting.

Some men will pretend to abhor such a sin, yet hug it in their bosom; such sinners sting their Consciences to magnifie their Credits.

If by suffering for Christ we loose all that we have in this world, we are sufficient gainers when we save our own Souls.

The Devil is indifferent whether we go to Hell in the frequented road of Profaneness, or in the smooth way of Hypocrisie.

Beware of impenitence, and of late repentance: true repentance cannot be too late, but a late repentance is rarely true.

Wherefore the real Christian should say betimes with holy Job, ''I abhor my self, and repent in dust and ashes.''[6]

It is one thing to hold the truth, and another thing to hold it in sincerity: we must be just, as well as orthodox.

One of the blessings of the Old Testament was Prosperity, and one of the blessings of the new Testament is Affliction.

Act not against the light of Conscience, lest your Light be darkned, and your Conscience shipwrack't.

Study not to live long, but to live well; for an hour mis-spent, is not liv'd, but lost.

No man is perfect, for there is none so good but he may mend.

Troubles, or Sickness, when sanctified, is much better than unsanctified Prosperity.

It is not talking of God, but walking with God, that makes a Christian compleat.

Beware of superstition, for that will not teach a man to fear God, but to be afraid of him.

It is good to be Learned, but it is better to be Religious; for Learning is but an Ornament to Religion, but Religion is a Blessing to Learning.

To profess Religion is good, but to practice Religion is better; to profess, and not to practice, is to dissemble with God and Man; and a cunning course it is for man to destroy his own Soul.

If we would have God hear our Prayers, we must have the sense of feeling them our selves.

He that would not have Time pass swiftly away, should not use much Pastime.

The way to understand the sweetness

---

[6]Job 42:6.

of God's mercie, is to get a sense of the bitterness of our own misery.

The tongue is an evil member; for he that hath no reputation himself, is master of another man's.

The delight of a gracious Soul is, to long to be dissolved, and to go to his long'd-for home, that he may be with Christ.

By the Scriptures we learn what God hath done for us, and what we are to do for God.

When we have done for God all that we can, our all is so little, and our good deeds so ill, that we are at best but unprofitable servants.

He that will not deny himself and his own ends for Christ, will deny Christ for his own ends, and will to his sorrow be denied by Christ in the end.

If we can be of the number of Christ's little ones, the mercie will be great.

A Saint's heart is in the Law of God, and the Law of God is likewise in his heart.

Let the wicked laugh at the godly for being godly, rather than God should laugh at them for being wicked.

The reputation of a good man, is to be rich in goodness, not in goods.

He is the only wise and rich man, that can learn to be content.

We may be instructed by a Prophet; but it is the Spirit of God by which we profit.

Whether God give or take, it is our duty to be thankful.

When we draw neer to Christ, he is ready to receive us; nay, when we fly from him, he is ready to invite us.

Many men in their doings, purchase their undoings.

He that receiveth a mercie, and doth not use it, doth abuse it.

There is nothing among us more rife than the name Christian, or the Christian name; and nothing among us more rare, than the Christian man.

The godly man sets a greater value by far upon the motions, than the notions of grace.

All the blessings that a Saint receives, are the more dear and welcom[e] because they savour of a Saviour.

When God sends us an evil visitation, even then God is good to us, for he sends that evil for our good.

The wicked man mindeth not the God that made him, but sets his affections upon the God of his own making.

Introduction to John Flavel,
Husbandry Spiritualized and *Navigation Spiritualized*

John Flavel (1627-1691) was born at Bromsgrove, Worcestershire, where his father—also eventually an ejected minister—was rector of the parish. After an education at University College, Oxford, John Flavel served as curate at Diptford in Devon, and then as a lecturer at Dartmouth in Devon. Although ejected in 1662, Flavel continued to live and preach in Dartmouth; pressured by the Five Mile Act of 1665, he moved to nearby Slapton. Under the Indulgence of 1672 he licensed a meeting place in Dartmouth. In 1682 he removed to London but was back at Dartmouth in 1687. After the toleration he preached in a large meeting house at Dartmouth.

Most of Flavel's writings were of the spiritual and devotional kind and were done in a more felicitous style and moderate tone than those of many Puritan writers. Characteristic were his two works in which he sought to find spiritual meanings in everyday activities and observations—known to his time as "improving the creatures." What follows is taken from his two principal works of this sort, Husbandry Spiritualized: Or, the Heavenly Use of Earthly Things, *to which was appended* Occasional Meditations upon Birds, Beasts, Trees, Flowers, Rivers, and other Objects, fitted for the help of such as desire to walk with God in all their Solitudes, and Recesses from the World *(London, 1669; Wing F1165, 1st ed.), sigs. A2ʳ-a4ʳ, 180-85, 232-35[33], 239-43, 246-50, 251-54, and* Navigation Spiritualized: Or, a New Compass for Seamen *(London, 1698; Wing F1173.2), 19-21, 34-37, 87-90. This was the fourth edition of* Navigation Spiritualized, *and the last printed before Flavel's death; the first edition had been published in 1677. The first selection from Flavel is an introduction in which he describes his method in these writings; the remainder of the selections illustrate that method. For more about Flavel, I have written a brief sketch in* Biographical Dictionary of British Radicals in the Seventeenth Century, *ed. Richard L. Greaves and Robert Zaller (Brighton: Harvester Press, 1982-1984) 1:287.*

Husbandry Spiritualized:
Or, The Heavenly Use of Earthly Things

by John Flavel

The Epistle Dedicatory
To the Worshipful Robert Savery, and William Savery, of Slade, Esquires.[1]

---

[1]Robert and William Savery of Slade were members of a family of Devonshire gentry.

Honoured Friends,

It hath been long since observ'd, that the world below is a Glass to discover the World above; *Seculum est speculum:*[2] And although I am not of their opinion, that say, The Heathens may spell Christ out of the Sun, Moon, and Stars; yet this I know, That the irrational and inanimate, as well as rational creatures, have a Language; and though not by Articulate speech, yet, in a Metaphorical sense, they preach unto man the wisdom, Power, and goodness of God, Rom. 1:20. There is (saith the Psalmist, Psalm 19:3) "No speech nor Language, where their voice is not heard." Or (as Junius[3] renders) there is no Speech, nor Words, yet without these their voice is understood; and their Line (i.e. saith Deodate)[4] their writing in gross and plain draughts, is gone out through all the earth.

As man is compounded of a fleshly and spiritual substance, so God hath endowed the creatures with a spiritual, as well as fleshly usefulness; they have not only a natural use in Alimental, and Physical respects, but also a spiritual use, as they bear the figures and similitudes of many sublime and heavenly mysteries. Believe me (saith contemplative Bernard)[5] thou shalt find more in the Woods, than in a corner; Stones and Trees will teach thee what thou shalt not hear from learned Doctors. By a skilful and industrious improvement of the creatures (saith Mr. Baxter[6] excellently) we might have a fuller taste of Christ and Heaven, in every bit of Bread that we eat, and in every draught of Beer that we drink, than most men have in the use of the Sacrament.

And as the Creatures teach divine and excellent things, so they teach them in a perspicuous and taking manner: *Duo illa nos maxime movent, similitudo et exemplum,* saith the Orator, these two things, similitude and example, do especially move us.[7] Notions are more easily con-

---

[2]Latin for "the world is a mirror."

[3]Franciscus Junius (1545-1602) was a Calvinist theologian who taught at several important continental universities, including Leyden and Heidelberg. His *Parallela Sacra* (1588), probably the work alluded to here, was an important source of exegetical notes.

[4]Giovanni Diodati (1576-1649) was an Italian exile who was a theological professor at Geneva. He translated the Bible into Italian. His *Pious Annotations upon the Holy Bible* (London, 1643) was influential in England.

[5]St. Bernard of Clairvaux (d. 1153) was an important medieval churchman and spiritual writer.

[6]Richard Baxter (1615-1691) was the leader of the English Presbyterians and an important Puritan author.

[7]The "orator" is the ancient Roman Cicero.

veyed to the understanding, by being first cloathed in some apt Similitude, and so represented to the sense. And therefore Jesus Christ, the great Prophet, delighted much in teaching by Parables; and the prophets were much in this way also, Hos. 12:10: I have "used Similitudes by the Ministry of the Prophets." Those that can retain little of a Sermon, yet ordinarily retain an apt Similitude.

I confess it is an humbling consideration, That man, who at first was led by the knowledge of God to the knowledge of the Creature, must now by the Creatures learn to know God, That the Creatures, (as one saith) like Balaam's ass, should teach their Master.[8] But though this be the unhappiness of poor man in his collapsed state, yet it is now his wisdom to improve such helps; and whilst others, by the abuse of the Creatures, are furthering their Perdition, to be, by the spiritual improvement of them, promoting our own Salvation.

It is an excellent Art to discourse with Birds, Beasts and Fishes, about sublime and spiritual Subjects, and make them answer to your questions; and this may be done, Job 12:7, 8: "Ask now the beasts, and they shall teach thee, and the Fowls of the Air, and they shall tell thee; or speak to the Earth, and it shall teach thee, and the Fishes of the Sea shall declare unto thee." That is (saith neat and accurate Caryl)[9] the creatures teach us when we think of them: "They teach us, though not formally, yet virtually; they answer and resolve the question put to them, though not explicitely to the ear, yet convincingly to the conscience. So then, we ask the creatures, when we diligently consider them, when we search out the perfections and virtues

that God hath put into, or stampt upon them. To set our mind thus upon the creature, is to discourse with the creature; the questions which man asks of a beast, are only his own Meditations. Again, the creatures teach us; when we in Meditation make our collections, and draw down a demonstration of the Power, Wisdom, and Goodness of God in making them, or the fraility of man in needing them; such Conclusions and Inferences are the teachings of the creatures."

Common objects (saith another)[10] may be improved two wayes: *viz.* In an argumentative, and in a Representative way; by reasoning from them, and by viewing the resemblance that is betwixt them and spiritual matters.

First, In Meditation argue thus, as in the present case and Similitude of the Apostle. If an Husbandman upon the ordinary principles of reason can wait for the Harvest, shall not I wait for the Coming of the Lord? The day of Refreshing; the Corn is precious to him, and so is the coming of Christ to me. Shall he be so patient, and endure so much for a little Corn? And not I for the Kingdom of Heaven? He is willing to stay till all causes have had their operations, till he hath received the former and the latter rain; and shall not I, till the Divine decrees be accomplished?

Secondly, In Meditation, make the resemblance, and discourse thus within yourselves: This is my Seed-time, Heaven is my Harvest; here I must labour and toyl, and there rest. I see the Husbandman's life is a great toyl: no excellent thing can be obtained without labour, and an obstinate patience. I see the Seed must be hidden in the furrows, rotten and corrupted, ere it can spring forth with any increase. Our hopes are hidden, light is sown for the righteous; all our comforts are buried under the clods,

---

[8]The story of Balaam is in Num. 22:24.

[9]Joseph Caryl (1602-1673) was an English Congregationalist who was among the ejected ministers of 1662. The work cited is his commentary on Job.

[10]Thomas Manton, for whom see above, 7.

and after all this there must be long wait-ing, we cannot sow and reap in a day; ef-fects cannot follow, till all necessary causes have first wrought. Tis not in the power of Husbandmen to ripen fruits at pleasure, our times are in the hands of God, therefore 'tis good to wait; a long-suffering patience will reap the desired fruit. Thus you have some hints of this heavenly Art of improving the Creatures.

The Motives inducing me to this un-dertakement, were the Lord's owning, with some success, my labours of a like nature, together with the desire and inclination (stirr'd up in me, I hope, by the Spirit of the Lord) to devote my vacant hours to his service in this kind. I considered, that if the Pharisees in a blind zeal to a faction, could compass Sea and Land to Proselyte men to their party, though thereby they made them sevenfold more the children of the Devil than before: how much more was I obliged by true love to God, and zeal to the ever-lasting happiness of souls, to use my utter-most endeavours, both with Seamen and Husbandmen, to win them to Christ, and thereby make them more than seventy-seven fold happier than before? Not to mention other incouragements to this work, which I received from the earnest desires of some Reverend and worthy Brethren in-viting thereunto; all which I hope the event will manifest to be a call from God to this work.

I confess I met with some discourage-ment in my first attempt, from my unac-quaintedness with rural affairs; and because I was to travel in a path (to me) untrodden; but having once engaged in it, those dis-couragements were soon overcome; and being now brought to what you here see, I offer to your hands these first fruits of my spare hours.

I presume you will account it no dis-paragement, that I dedicate a Book of Hus-bandry to Gentlemen of your quality. This is Spiritual Husbandry, which is here taught you; and yet I must tell you, that great per-sons have accounted that civil employ-ment (which is much inferior to this) no disparagement to them. "The king himself is served by the field," Eccles. 5:9. Or, as Montanus[11] renders the Hebrew text, *Rex agro fit servus;* The king himself is a ser-vant to the field. And of king Uzziah it is written, (2 Chron. 26:10) "That he loved Husbandry." And Amos 7:1, we read of the King's mowings. Yea, Pliny[12] hath ob-served, That Corn was never so plentiful at Rome, as when the same men tilled the Land that rul'd the Commonwealth. *Quasi gauderet terra laureato vomere, scilicet & aratore triumphali;* as though the earth it-self rejoiced in the laurelled Plow-share, and the triumphant Plowman.

What pleasure you will find in reading it, I know not; but to me it hath been a pleasant path, from first to last; who yet have been at far greater expence of time and pains in compiling it, than you can be in reading it. The Husbandman's work, you know, is no easie work, and the Spiritual-izing of it hath greater difficulties attend-ing it; but yet the pleasure hath abundantly recompensed the pains. I have found Erasmus[13] his Observation experimentally true; *Qui litteris addiciti sumus, animi las-situdinem a studiis gravioribus contrac-tam; ab iisdem studiis, sed amaenioribus recreamus:* "Those that are addicted to study," (saith he) "when they have wea-ried their spirits with study, can recreate

---

[11]Montanus—whose real name was Benedictus Arias—was a sixteenth-century Spanish Catholic biblical scholar who was attacked by the Jesuits for preferring the Hebrew, rather than the Vulgate, text of the Old Testament.

[12]Pliny was a Roman author of the early second century A.D.

[13]Erasmus (1466-1536) was a leading biblical scholar and humanist reformer who greatly influ-enced the Protestant Reformation.

them again with study, by making a diversion from that which is severe and knotty, to some more facile and pleasant Subject.''

But to hear that God hath used and honoured these papers to the good of any soul, will yield me the highest content and satisfaction imaginable.

May you but learn that Lesson, which is the general Scope and Design of this Book, *viz.* How to walk with God from day to day, and make the several Objects you behold, *Scalae & alae,* Wings and Ladders to mount your souls neerer to Him, who is the Center of all blessed Spirits. How much will it comfort me, and confirm my hope, that it was the Call of God indeed, which put me upon these endeavours!

O Sirs! What an excellent thing would it be for you, to make such holy improvements of all these earthly Objects which daily occur to your senses, and cause them to proclaim and preach to you Divine and heavenly Mysteries whilst others make them groan, by abusing them to sin, and subjecting them to their lusts. A man may be cast into such a condition, wherein he cannot enjoy the blessing and benefit of a pious and powerful Ministry; but you cannot (ordinarily) fall into such a condition, wherein any thing (except a bad heart) can deprive you of the benefits and comforts of those excellent Sermons, and Divinity Lectures, which the creatures here offer to preach and read to you.

Content not your selves, I beseech you, with that natural sweetness the creatures afford; for thereof the beasts are capable, as much, if not more, than you; but use them to those spiritual ends you are here directed, and they will yield you a sweetness far transcending that natural sweetness you ever relished in them; and indeed, you never use the creatures as their Lord's, till you come to see your Lord, in and by

them. I confess the discoveries of God in the Word are far more excellent, clear and powerful; he hath magnified his word above all his Name. And therein are the unsearchable riches of Christ, or rich discoveries of that grace that hath no footsteps in nature, as the Apostle's expression signifies, Eph. 3:8.

And if that which might be known of God by the Creatures, leave men without excuse; as it is manifest, Rom. 1:20, How inexcusable then will those be, who have received not only the teachings of the creature, but also the grace of the Gospel in vain! "How shall we escape, if we neglect so great salvation?"[14] They that are careless in the day of grace, shall be speechless in the day of judgment.

I am sensible of many defects in these Papers (as well as in myself); they have doubtless a taste of the distractions of the times wherein they were written; nor was I willing to keep them so long under-hand, as the accurateness and exactness with which such a subject ought to be handled did require. Had I designed my own credit, I should have observed that counsel, *Nonumque prematur in annum,* (i.e.) "To have kept it much longer under the file," before I had exposed it to publick view; but I rather inclined to Solomon's counsel, Whatever thy hand finds out to do, do it with all thy might; for there is no wisdom, nor knowledge, nor device in the grave, whither thou art going, Eccles. 9:10.

I apprehend a necessity of some such means to be used, for the instruction and conviction of countrey people; who either are not capable of understanding truth in another Dialect, or at least are less affected with it. The Proposition in every Chapter consists of an Observation in Husbandry; Wherein, if I have failed in using any improper expression, your candour will cover

---

[14]Heb. 2:3.

it, and impute it to my unacquaintedness in rural affairs—*In magnis voluisse sat est.*[15]

The Reddition or Application, you will find (I hope) both pertinent and close. The Reflections serious, and such (as I hope) your Consciences will faithfully improve. I have shut up[16] every chapter with a Poem, an innocent Bait to catch the Reader's Soul.

That of Herbert[17] is experimentally true:

> A verse may find him that a Sermon flies,
> And turn delight into a Sacrifice.

I should never have been perswaded (especially in this scribling Age, wherein we may complain with the Poet: *Scribimus indocti, doctique; poemata passim*)[18] to have set my dull fancy upon the Rack to extort a Poem to entertain my Reader; for I cannot say with Ovid, *Sponte sua carmen,*[19] &c. but that I have been informed, that many Seamen, induced by the pleasure of a Verse, have taken much pains to learn the Poems in their Compass by heart; and I hope both the Children at home, and the Servants in the fields, will learn to exercise themselves this way also. O, how much better will it be so to do, than to stuff their memories with obscene Ballads and filthy Songs, which corrupt their minds, and dispose them to much wickedness, by irritating their natural corruption! But these are purer flames, you will find nothing here of such a tendency.

> 'Tis guilt, not Poetry, to be like those,
> Whose wit in Verse is downright sin in Prose.
> Whose studies are prophaneness, as if then
> They only were good Poets, when bad men.[20]

I shall add no more, but to beg that God who instructeth the Husbandman in his civil Calling, to teach him wisdom spiritually to improve it; and particularly, that you may reap a crop of much spiritual benefit, from that seed which is here sown by the hand of the Lord's unprofitable servant, and in him,

Your very affectionate
Friend and Servant,
JOHN FLAVEL

---

[15]The Latin means "in great things it is enough to have wished."

[16]shut up: concluded.

[17]George Herbert (1593-1633) was an Anglican clergyman and poet. This line is from his "The Church Porch."

[18]The Latin means "we all, both learned and unlearned, write poems at random." It is from the Roman poet Horace, Epistles II. 1, line 117.

[19]Ovid was a Roman poet who died in A.D. 18. The phrase means "the poem comes of its own accord."

[20]Sir Dudley Digges—an English statesman and diplomat of the early seventeenth century—is credited with the authorship of these lines.

Chapter II. {of Part II}

Upon the Union of the Graff with the Stock.[21]

> When ere you bud or graft, therein you see;
> How Christ, and souls must here united be.

Observation.

When the Husbandman hath prepared his graffs in the season of the year, he carries them, with the tools that are necessary for that work, to the tree or stock he intends to ingraft, and having cut off the top of the limb in some strait smooth part, he

---

[21]Stock: the stem or trunk of a plant. This heading was marginal in the first edition.

cleaves it with his knife or chissel, a little beside the pith; knocks in his wedge to keep it open, then (having prepared the graff) he carefully sets it into the cleft, joyning the inner side of the barks of graff and stock together (there being the main current of the sap) then pulls out his wedge, binds both together (as in barking) and clayes it up, to defend the tender graff and wounded stock from the injuries of the Sun and rain.

These tender cyences[22] quickly take hold of the stock, and having immediate coalition with it, drink in its sap, concoct in into their own nourishment, thrive better, and bear more and better fruits than ever they would have done upon their natural root; yea, the smallest bud, being carefully inocculated and bound close to the stock, will in short time, become a flourishing and fruitful limb.

Application.

This carries a most sweet and lively resemblance of the soul's union with Christ by faith; and indeed there is nothing in nature that shadows forth this great Gospel-mystery like it: 'Tis a thousand pities, that any who are imployed about, or are but spectators of such an action, should terminate their thoughts (as too many do) in that natural object, and not raise up their hearts to these heavenly meditations, which it so fairly offers them.

When a twig is to be ingraffed, or a bud inocculated, it is first cut off by a keen knife from the Tree on which it naturally grew.

And when the Lord intends to graft a soul into Christ, the first work about it, is cutting work, Acts 2:37, their hearts were cut by conviction, and deep compunction; no cyence is ingraffed without cutting, no soul united with Christ, without a cutting sense of sin and misery, John 16:8,9.

When the tender shoot is cut off from the Tree, there are (ordinarily) many more left behind upon the same Tree, as promising and vigorous as that which is taken; but it pleaseth the Husbandman to chuse this, and leave them.

Even so it is in the removing or transplanting of a soul by conversion; it leaves many behind it in the state of nature, as likely and promising as it self; but so it pleaseth God to take this soul, and leave many others; yea, often such as grew upon the same root; I mean, the immediate parent, Mal. 1:2. ''Was not Esau Jacob's brother?'' (saith the Lord) ''yet I loved Jacob, and I hated Esau.''

When the graffs are cut off, in order to this work, 'tis a critical season with them: if they lye too long before they are ingraffed, or take not with the stock, they dye, and are never more to be recovered; they may stand in the stock a while, but are no part of the Tree.

So when souls are under a work of conviction, it is a critical time with them; many a one have I known then to miscarry, and never recovered again: they have indeed for a time stood like dead graffs in the stock, by an external dead hearted profession, but never came to any thing; and as such dead graffs, either fall off from the stock, or moulder away upon it; so do these, 1 John 2:19.

The Husbandman when he hath cut off graffs, or tender buds, makes all the convenient speed he can to close them with the stock; the sooner that's done, the better; they get no good by remaining as they are. And truly it concerns the servants of the Lord, who are imployed in this work of ingraffing souls into Christ, to make all the haste they can, to bring the convicted sinner to a closure with Christ. As soon as ever the trembling Jaylor cryed out, ''What shall I do to be saved?'' Paul and Silas immediately direct him to Christ, Acts 16:30, 31.

---

[22]cyences: cions or scions, shoots or twigs cut for grafting or planting.

They do not say, it is too soon for thee to act faith on Christ, thou are not yet humbled enough, but "believe in the Lord Jesus Christ, and thou shalt be saved."

There must be an incision made in the stock before any bud can be inocculated; or the stock must be cut and cleaved, before the cyence can be ingraffed; according to that in the Poet,[23]

Venerit insitio, fac ramum ramus adoptet; (i.e.)
> To graffs no living sap the stocks impart;
> Unless you wound, and cut them neer the heart.

Such an incision, or wound, was made upon Christ, in order to our ingrafting into him, John 19:34; the opening of that deadly wound gives life to the souls of believers.

The graff is intimately united, and closely conjoyned with the stock; the conjunction is so close, that they become one Tree.

There is also a most close and intimate union betwixt Christ and the soul that believeth in him. It is emphatically expressed by the Apostle, 1 Cor. 6:17: "He that is joined [un]to the Lord, is one spirit." The word imports the nearest, closest and strictest union. Christ and the soul cleave together in a blessed oneness, as those things do that are glewed one to another; so that, look as the graff is really in the stock, and the spirit or sap of the stock is really in the graff; so a believer is really (though mystically) in Christ, and the Spirit of Christ is really communicated to a believer. "I live," (saith Paul) "yet not I, but Christ liveth in me," Gal. 2:20. "He that dwelleth in love, dwelleth in God, and God in him," 1 John 4:16.

Graffs are bound to the stock by bonds made of hay or flags;[24] these keep it steddy, else the wind would loose it out of the stock.

The believing soul is also fastened to Christ, by bands which will secure it from all danger of being loosed off from him any more. There are two bonds of this union; the Spirit on God's part, this is the firm bond of union, without which he could never be made one with Christ, Rom 8:9: "If any man have not the Spirit of Christ, he is none of his;" and faith on our part, Eph. 3:17: "That Christ may dwell in your hearts by faith." These hold strongly.

Though the stock be one and the same, yet all graffs do not thrive and flourish alike in it; some outgrow the rest; and those that grow not so well as the others do, the fault is in them, and not in the stock: so it is with souls really united to Christ; all do not flourish alike in him, the faith of some grows exceedingly, 2 Thes. 1:3; the things that be in others, are ready to dye, Rev. 3:2, and such souls must charge the fault upon themselves. Christ sends up living sap enough, not only to make all that are in him living, but fruitful branches.

Reflections.

Is it so indeed betwixt Christ and my soul, as it is betwixt the ingraffed cyence and the stock? What honour and glory then hath Christ conferred upon me, a poor unworthy creature? What! to be made one with him, to be a living branch of him, to be joyned thus to the Lord! Oh! what a preferment is this! It is but a little while since I was a wild and cursed plant, growing in the wilderness amongst them that shall shortly be cut down and faggotted up for hell; for me to be taken from amongst them, and planted into Christ, O my soul! fall down and kiss the feet of free grace, that moved so freely towards so vile a creature! The dignities and honours of the Kings and Nobles of the earth, are nothing to mine; 'twas truly confessed by one of them, that

---

[23]The poet is Ovid, the line from "Remedium Amores" (1.195).

[24]flags: reeds or long slender leaves.

it is a greater honour to be a member of Christ, than the head of an Empire. Do I say, a greater honour than is put upon the Kings of the Earth? I might have said, it is a greater honour than is put upon the Angels of heaven: For to which of them said Christ, at any time, thou art bone of my bone, and flesh of my flesh? "Behold! what manner of love is this!" 1 John 3:1.

Look again upon the ingraffed cyences, O my soul! and thou shalt find, that when once they have taken hold of the stock, they live as long as there is any sap in the root; and because he liveth, I shall live also, for my life is hid with Christ in God, Col. 3:3. The graff is preserved in the stock, and my soul is even so "preserved in Christ Jesus!" Jude 1:1.

Am I joyned to the Lord as a mystical part or branch of him? How dear art thou then, O my soul, to the God and Father of my Lord Jesus Christ! What! a branch of his dear Son! What can God with-hold from one so ingratiated? Eph. 1:6. All is yours, (saith my God) for "ye are Christ's, and Christ is God's," 1 Cor. 3:23.

Once more, draw matter of instruction, as well as comfort, from this sweet observation. Seeing God hath put all this honour upon thee, by this most intimate union with his Christ, look to it (my soul) that thou live and walk as becomes a soul thus one with the Lord; be thou tender over his glory: doth not that which strikes at the root, strike at the very life of the graff? And shall not that which strikes at the very glory of Christ, tenderly touch and affect thee? Yea, be thou tenderly affected with all the reproaches that fall upon him from abroad, but especially with those that redound to him from thine own unfruitfulness. O, dis-

grace not the root that bears thee; let it never be said, that any evil fruit is found upon a branch that lives and fed is by such a root.

The Poem.

Oh what considering serious man can see
    The close conjunction of the graff and tree;
And whilst he contemplates, he doth not find
    This meditation graffed on his mind?
I am the branch, and Christ the vine;
    Thy gracious hand did pluck
Me from that native stock of mine,
    That I his sap might suck.
The bloudy spear did in his heart
    A deep incission make,
That grace to me he might impart,
    And I thereof partake.
The Spirit and faith is that firm band
    Which binds us fast together;
Thus we are clasped hand in hand,
    And nothing us can sever.
Bless'd be that hand which did remove
    Me from my native place!
This was the wonder of thy love,
    The triumph of thy grace!
That I, a wild and cursed plant,
    Should thus preferrèd be,
Who all those ornaments do want,
    Thou may'st in others see.
As long as e're the root doth live,
    The branches are not dry;
Whilst Christ hath grace and life to give,
    My soul can never dye.
O blessed Saviour! never could
    A graff cleave to the tree
More close than thy poor creature would
    United be with thee.
My soul, dishonour not the root,
    'Twill be a shame for thee
To want the choicest sorts of fruit,
    And yet thus graffed be.

Thus you may shake from graffs, before they blow,
More precious fruit than e'er on trees did grow.

Occasional Meditations
upon Birds, Beasts, Trees, Flowers, Rivers, and other Objects.

Meditations on Birds.

Meditation I.

Upon the singing of a Nightingale.

Who that hears such various, ravishing, and exquisite melody, would imagine the bird that makes it, to be of so small and contemptible a body and feather? her charming voice engaged not only mine attentive ear, but my feet also, to make a nearer approach to that shady bush, in which that excellent Musician sat vailed; and the nearer I came, the sweeter the melody still seemed to be; but when I had descried the bird herself, and found her to be little bigger, and no better feather'd than a sparrow, it gave my thoughts the occasion of this following application.

This Bird seems to me the lively emblem of the formal hypocrite: (1) In that she is more in sound than substance, a loud and excellent voice, but a little despicable body; and it recall'd to my thoughts the story of Plutarch,[25] who hearing a Nightingale, desired to have one killed to feed upon, not questioning but she would please the palate as well as the ear; but when the Nightingale was brought him, and he saw what a poor little creature it was, Truly, said he, thou art *vox et preterea nihil,* a meer voice, and nothing else; So is the hypocrite: did a man hear him sometimes in more public duties and discourses, O thinks he, what an excellent man is this! what a choice and rare spirit is he of! but follow him home, observe him in his private conversation and retirements, and then you will judge Plutarch's note as applicable to him as the Nightingale. (2) This Bird is observed to charm most sweetly, and set her spirits all on work, when she perceives she hath ingaged attention; so doth the hypocrite, who lives and feeds upon the applause and commendation of his admirers, and cares little for any of those duties which bring in no returns of praise from men; he is little pleased with a silent melody and private pleasure betwixt God and his own soul.

Scire tuum nihil est nisi te scire hoc sciat alter.
Alas! his knowledge is not worth a pin,
If he proclaim not what he hath within.

He is more for the Theatre than the Closet, and of such Christ saith, Verily "they have their reward."[26] . . .

Meditation III.

Upon the sight of a blackbird taking sanctuary in a bush from a pursuing Hawk.

When I saw how hardly the poor bird was put to it to save herself from her enemy, who hover'd just over the bush in which she was fluttering and squeeking, I could not but hasten to relieve her (pity and succour being a due debt to the distressed), which when I had done, the bird would not depart from the bush, though her enemy were gone; this act of kindness was abundantly repaid by this Meditation, with which I returned to my walk; my soul, like

---

[25]Plutarch (A.D. 46-120) was a Hellenistic Greek writer famous for his biographical studies, "Plutarch's Lives."

[26]Matt. 6:2, 5, 16.

this bird, was once distressed, pursued, yea, seized by Satan, who had certainly made a prey of it, had not Jesus Christ been a sanctuary to it in that hour of danger. How ready did I find him to receive my poor soul into his protection? Then did he make good that sweet promise to my experience, "Those that come unto me, I will in no wise cast out."[27] It call'd to mind that pretty and pertinent story of the Philosopher, who walking in the fields, a Bird, pursued by a Hawk, flew into is bosom; he took her out, and said, "Poor bird, I will neither wrong thee, nor expose thee to thine enemy, since thou camest to me for refuge." So tender, and more than so, is the Lord Jesus to distressed souls that come unto him. Blessed Jesus! how should I love and praise the, glorifie and admire thee, for that great salvation thou hast wrought for me? If this Bird had fallen into the claws of her enemy, she had been torn to pieces indeed, and devoured; but then a few minutes had dispatched her, and ended all her pain and misery: but had my soul fallen into the hand of Satan, there had been no end of its misery.

Would not this scared bird be flusht out of the bush that secured her, though I had chased away her enemy? And wilt thou (O my soul) ever be inticed or scared from Christ thy refuge? O let this for ever ingage thee to keep close to Christ, and make me say, with Ezra, "And now, O Lord, since thou hast given me such a deliverance as this, should I again break thy commandments!"[28]

Meditation IV.

Upon the sight of divers Lennets[29] intermingling with a flock of sparrows.

Methinks these birds do fitly resemble the gaudy Gallants, and the plain peasants;

how spruce and richly adorned with shining and various coloured feathers, (like scarlet, richly laid with gold and silver lace) are those? How plainly clad, in a homespun Countrey russet are these? Fine feathers (saith our Proverb) make proud birds; and yet the feathers of the Sparrow are as useful and beneficial, both for warmth and flight, though not so gay and ornamental, as the others; and if both were stript out of their feathers, the Sparrow would prove the better Bird of the two: by which I see, that the greatest worth doth not always lye under the finest cloaths. And besides, God can make mean and homely garments as useful and beneficial to poor despised Christians, as the ruffling and shining garments of wanton Gallants are to them, and when God shall strip men out of all external excellencies, these will be found to excel their glittering neighbours in true worth and excellency.

Little would a man think such rich treasures of grace, wisdom, humility, &c. lay under some russet Coats.

Saepe sub attrita latitat sapientia veste.
Under poor garments more true worth may be
Than under silks that whistle, who but he?

Whilst on the other side, the heart of the wicked (as Solomon hath observed) is little worth, how much soever his cloaths be worth. Alas! it falls out too frequently among us, as it doth with men in the Indies, who walk over the rich veins of gold and silver Oar[30] which lyes hid under a ragged and barren surface, and know it not. For my own part, I desire not to value any man by what is extrinsecal and worldly, but by that true internal excellency of grace, which makes the face to shine in the eyes of God and good men: I would contemn a vile person, though never so glorious in the eye of the world; but honour such as fear the Lord, how sordid and despicable soever to appearance.

---

[27]John 6:37.

[28]Ezra 9:13-14.

[29]Goldfinches in later editions.

[30]Oar: ore.

Meditation V.

Upon the sight of a robin-red-breast picking up a worm from a Mole-hill then raising.

Observing the Mole working industriously beneath, and the Bird watching so intently above, I made a stand to observe the issue; when in a little time the bird descends and seizes upon a worm, which I perceived was crawling apace from the enemy below that hunted her, but fell to the share of another which from above waited for her. My thoughts presently suggested these Meditations from that occasion: methought this poor worm seem'd to be the Emblem of my poor soul, which is more endangered by its own lusts of pride and covetousness, than this worm was by the Mole and Bird; my pride, like the aspiring bird, watches for it above; my covetousness, like this subterranean Mole, digging for it beneath. Poor soul! What a sad Dilemma art thou brought to! If thou go down into the caverns of the earth, there thou art a prey to thy covetousness that hunts thee; and if thou aspire, or but creep upward, there thy pride waits to ensnare thee. Distressed soul! whither wilt thou go? ascend thou mayest, not by vain elation, but by a heavenly conversation, beside which there is no way for thy preservation; the way of life is above to the wise, &c.

Again, I could not but observe the accidental benefit this poor harmless Bird obtained by the labour of the Mole, who hunting intentionally for her self, unburroughed and ferrited out this worm for the Bird, who possibly, was hungry enough, and could not have been relieved for this time, but by the Mole, the fruit of whose labours she now fed upon. Even thus the Lord oft-times makes good his word to his people: "The wealth of the wicked is laid up for the just." And again, "The earth shall help the woman."[31] This was fully exemplified in David, to whom Nabal, that churlish muck-worm, speaks all in possessives. "Shall I take my bread," &c. "and give it to one I know not whom?" And yet David reaps the fruit of all the pains and toyl of Nabal at last.[32] Let it never incourage me to idleness, that God sometimes gives his people the fruit of others' sweat; but if providence reduce me to necessity, and disable me from helping my self, I doubt not then but it will provide instruments to do it. The Bird was an hungry, and could not dig.

Meditation VI.

Upon the shooting of two Finches fighting in the Air.

How soon hath death ended the quarrel betwixt these two little Combatants! had they agreed better, they might have lived longer; 'twas their own contention that gave both the opportunity and provocation of their death; and though living they could not, yet, being dead, they can lye quietly together in my hand.

Foolish Birds, was it not enough that Birds of prey watched to devour them, but they must peck and scratch one another? Thus have I seen the Birds of Paradise (Saints I mean) tearing and wounding each other, like so many birds of prey, and by their unchristian contests giving the occasion of their common ruin; yea, and that not only when at liberty, as these were, but when incaged also; and yet, as one well observes, if ever Christians will agree, 'twill either be in a prison, or in heaven; for in a prison their quarrelsom lusts lye low, and in heaven they shall be utterly done away.

---

[31]Proverbs 13:22, "The wealth of the sinner is laid up for the just; Revelation 12:16, "the earth helped the woman."

[32]The story of David and Nabal is in 1 Samuel, chap. 25.

But O! what pity is it, that those who shall agree so perfectly in heaven, should bite and devour each other upon earth! That it should be said of them, as one ingeniously observed, who saw their carcasses lye together, as if they had lovingly embraced each other, who fell together by a Duel; *Quanta amicitia se invicem amplectuntur; qui mutua et implacabili inimicitia perierunt!*

Imbracing one another, now they lye
Who by each other's bloudy hands did dye.

Or, as he said, who observed how quietly and peaceably the dust and bones, even of enemies, did lye together in the grave; *Non tanta vivi pace conjuncti essetis;* "you did not live together so peaceably." If conscience of Christ's command will not, yet the consideration of common safety should powerfully perswade to unity and amity.

Meditation IX.

Upon the early singing of Birds.

How am I reproved of sluggishness by these watchful Birds! which cheerfully entertain the very dawning of the morning with their cheerful and delighted warblings! they set their little spirits all a-work betimes, whilst my nobler spirits are bound with the bonds of soft and downy slumbers. For shame, my soul! suffer not that Publican sleep to seize so much of thy time, yea, thy best and freshest time; reprove and chide thy sluggish body, as a good Bishop once did, when, upon the same occasion, he said, *Surrexerunt passeres, et sterunt pontifices.*

The early chirping Sparrows may reprove
Such lazy Bishops as their beds do love.[33]

Of many sluggards it may be said, as Tully said of Verres,[34] the deputy of Sicily, *Quod nunquam solemn nec orientem, nec occidentem viderat;* that he never saw the Sun rising, being in bed after, nor setting, being in bed before.

'Tis pity, that Christians of all men should suffer sleep to cut such large thongs out of so narrow a hide, as their time on earth is. But, alas! it is not so much early rising, as a wise improving those fresh and free hours with God, that will inrich the soul; else, as our Proverb saith, A man may be early up, and never the near; yea, far better it is to be found in bed sleeping, than to be up doing nothing, or that which is worse than nothing. O my soul! learn to prepossess thy self every morning with the thoughts of God, and suffer not those fresh and sweet operations of thy mind, to be prostituted to earthly things; for that is experimentally true which one in this case hath pertinently observed, That if the world get the start of Religion in the morning, it will be hard for Religion to overtake it all the day after.[35]

Meditation X.

Upon the haltering of Birds with a grain of hair.

Observing, in a snowy season, how the poor hungry Birds were haltered and drawn in by a grain of hair cunningly cast over their heads, whilst, poor creatures, they were busily feeding, and suspected no danger; and even whilst their conpanions were drawn away from them, one after another, all the interruption it gave the rest, was only for a minute or two, whilst they stood peeping into that hole through which

---

[33]Flavel's translations from the Latin are more poetic than literal; the Latin phrase means "sparrows get up, pontiffs lay down."

[34]Tully is in the Roman orator Cicero.

[35]Thomas Case (1598-1682) was a prominent Puritan who sat in the Westminster Assembly and preached a popular "morning exercise" at St. Mary Magdalene, London, until his ejection in 1662. Flavel cites the epistle to Case's *Morning Exercise Methodized* (London, 1660).

their companions were drawn, and then fell to their meat again as busily as before. I could not chuse but say, Even thus surprizingly doth death steal upon the children of men, whilst they are wholly intent upon the cares and pleasures of this life, not at all suspecting its so near approach. These birds saw not the hand that insnared them, nor do they see the hand of death plucking them one after another into the grave.

Omnibus obscuras injecit illa manus
Death's steps are swift, and yet no noise it make[s];
Its hand unseen, but yet most surely takes.[36]

And even as the surviving Birds for a little time seemed to stand affrighted, peeping after their companions, and then

---

[36]This line is from the Roman poet Ovid.

as busie as ever to their meat again: Just so it fares with the careless inconsiderate world, who see others daily dropping into eternity round about them, and for the present are a little startled, and will look into the grave after their neighbours, and then fall as busily to their earthly imployments and pleasures again, as ever, till their own turn comes.

I know, my God! that I must die as well as others; but, O let me not die as do others, let me see death before I feel it, and conquer it before it kill me; let it not come as an enemy upon my back, but rather let me meet it as a friend half way. Die I must, but let me lay up that good treasure before I go, Matt 6:19, carry with me a good conscience when I go, 2 Tim. 4:6,7, leave behind me a good example when I am gone, and then let death come, and welcom!

Meditations upon Beasts.

Meditation I.

Upon the clogging of a straying Beast.

Had this Bullock contented himself, and remained quietly within his own bounds, his Owner had never put such an heavy clog[37] upon his neck; but I see the prudent Husbandman chuses rather to keep him with this clog, than lose him for want of one. What [th]is clog is to him, that is affliction and trouble to me; had my soul kept close with God in liberty and prosperity, he would never thus have clogged me with adversity; yea, and happy were it for me, if I might stray from God no more, who hath thus clogged me with preventive afflictions. If with David, I might say, "Before I was afflicted I went astray, but now I have kept thy word," Psalm 119:67. O my soul! 'tis better for thee to have thy pride clogged with poverty, thy ambition

---

[37]clog: a heavy block fastened to an animal to impede movement.

with reproach, thy carnal expectancies with constant disapointments, than to be at liberty to run from God and duty.

'Tis true, I am sometimes as weary of these troubles, as this poor Beast is of the clog he draws after him, and often wish my self rid of them; but yet, if God should take them off, for ought I know I might have cause to wish them on again, to prevent a greater mischief. 'Tis storied of Basil,[38] that for many years he was sorely afflicted with an inveterate head-ach (that was his clog), he often prayed for the removal of it; at last God removed it; but instead thereof he was sorely exercised with the motions and temptations of lust, which when he perceived, he earnestly desired his head-ach again, to prevent a greater evil. Lord! if my corruptions may be prevented by my affliction, I refuse not to be clogged with them; but my soul rather desires thou

---

[38]St. Basil, one of the Greek church fathers of the fourth century.

wouldst hasten the time when I shall be for ever freed from them both.

Meditation II.

Upon the love of a Dog to his Master.

How many weary steps through mire and dirt, hath this poor Dog followed my horse's heels to day? and all this for a very poor reward, for all he gets by it at night, is but bones and blows, yet will he not leave my company, but is content upon such hard terms, to travel with me from day to day.

O my soul! what conviction and shame may this leave upon thee? who art often-times even weary of following thy Master Christ, whose rewards and incourage-ments of obedience are so imcomparably sweet and sure. I cannot beat back this Dog from following me, but every inconsider-able trouble is enough to discourage me in the way of my duty. Ready I am to resolve as that scribe did, Mat 8:19, "Master, I will follow thee whithersoever thou goest"; but how doth my heart faulter, when I must encounter with the difficulties of the way? O! let me make a whole heart-choice of Christ for my portion and happiness! and then I shall never leave him, nor turn back from following him, though the present difficulties were much more, and the present incouragements much less.

Meditation III.

Upon the fighting of two Rams.

Taking notice how furiously these Sheep, which by nature are mild and gentle, did yet, like Bulls, push each other, taking their advantage by going back to meet with greater rage and fury: me-thought I saw in this a plain Emblem of the unchristian contests and animosities which fall out amongst them that call themselves the people of God, who are in Scripture also stiled Sheep, for their meekness and in-nocency; and yet, through the remaining corruptions that are in them, thus do they push each other . . .

Shall Christians one another wound and push,
Like furious Bulls, when they together rush?

The fighting of these Sheep doth in two respects, notably comport with the sinful practices of contending Christians, (1) That in this fight they ingage with their heads one against another; and what are they but those head-notions, or opposition of Sci-ences,[39] falsly so called, that have made so many broyls and uproars in the Christian world? O! what clashings have these heady opinions caused in the Churches! first heads, and then hearts have clashed. Christians have not distinguished betwixt *adversarius litis, et personae;* an adver-sary to the opinion, and to the person; but dipt their tongues and pens in vinegar and gall, shamefully aspersing and reproach-ing one another, because their understand-ings were not cast into one mould, and their heads all of a bigness. But (2) That which Countrey-men observe from the fighting of Sheep, That it presages foul and stormy weather, is much more certainly conse-quent upon the fighting of Christ's sheep. Do these clash and push? Surely it is an in-fallible prognostic of an ensuing storm, Mal. 4:6.

Meditation IV.

Upon the catching of an Horse in a fat Pas-ture.

When this Horse was kept in poor short leas,[40] where he had much scope, but little grass, how gentle and tractable was he then? he would not only stand quiet to be taken, but come to hand of his own accord, and follow me up and down the field for a crust of bread, or handful of Oats; but since I turned him into this fat pasture, he comes

---

[39]Sciences: knowledge.

[40]leas, or leaze: pasture or meadowland.

no more to me, nor will suffer me to come neer him; but throws up his heels wantonly against me, and flies from me, as if I were rather his enemy than Benefactor. In this I behold the carriage of my own heart towards God, who the more he hath done for me, the seldomer doth he hear from me; in a low and afflicted state, how tractable is my heart to duty? Then it comes to the foot of God voluntarily; but in an exalted condition, how wildly doth my heart run from God and duty? With this ungrateful requital God faulted his own people, Jer. 2:31: teachable and tractable in the wilderness, but when fatted in that rich pasture of Canaan, Then "we are lords, we will come no more [un]to thee." How soon are all God's former benefits forgotten? And how often is that ancient observation verified, even in his own people?

μετὰ τὴν ὁλόσιν πάχις γερασνει χαρις.
Post munera cito consenescit gratia.
No sooner do we gifts on some bestow,
But presently our gifts gray headed grow.

But that's a bad Tenant, that will maintain a Suit at Law against his Landlord, with his own rent; and a bad heart, that will fight against God with his own mercies. I wish it may be with my heart, as it is reported to be with the waters in the Kingdom of Congo, that are never so sweet to the taste, as when the tide is at the highest.

Meditations upon Trees.

Meditation I.

Upon the fall of blossoms, nipt by a frosty morning.

Beholding in an early Spring, fruit Trees embossed with beautiful blossoms of various colours, which breathed forth the delicious odours into the circumambient air, and adorned the branches on which they grew, like so many rich jewels, or glittering pendents; and further observing, how these perfumed blossoms dropt off, being bitten with the frost, and discoloured all the ground, as if a shower of snow had fallen; I said, within myself, these sweet and early blossoms are not unlike my sweet and early affections to the Lord, in the dayes of my first acquaintance with him. O! what fervent love, panting desires, and heavenly delights beautified my soul in those dayes! The odoriferous scent of the sweetest blossoms, the morning breath of the most fragrant flowers, hath not half that sweetness with which those my first affections were inriched. O! happy time, thrice pleasant Spring! My soul hath it still in remembrance, and is humbled within me, for these also were but blossoms which now are nipt and faded, that first flourish is gone; my heart is like the Winter's earth, because thy face, Lord, is to me like a Winter Sun. "Awake, O North wind! and come, South wind, blow upon my garden, that the spices thereof may flow out, then let my beloved come into his garden, and eat his pleasant fruit!"[41]

Meditation II.

Upon the knitting or setting of fruit.

I Have often observed, that when the blossoms of a tree set and knit, though the flourish thereof be gone, and nothing but the bare rudiment of the expected fruit be left; yet then the fruit is much better secured from the danger of frosts and winds, than whilst it remained in the flower or blossom; for now it hath past one of those critical periods, in which so many trees miscarry and lose their fruit. And methought, this natural Observation fairly led me to this Theological Proposition, That good motions and holy purposes in the soul, are never secured and past their most

---

[41]Paraphrase of Song of Solomon 4:16.

dangerous Crisis, till they be turned into fixed resolutions, and answerable executions, which is as the knitting and setting of them.

Upon this Proposition my melting thoughts thus dilated: Happy had it been for thee, my soul! had all the blessed motions of the Spirit been thus knit and fixed in thee. O, how have mine affections blown and budded under the warm beams of the Gospel! But a chill blast from the cares, troubles and delights of the world without, and the vanity and deadness of the heart within, have blasted all; my goodness hath been but as a morning dew, or early cloud that vanisheth away: And even of divine Ordinances, I may say what is said of humane Ordinances, "They have perished in the using." A blossom is but *frutus imperfectus, et ordinabilis,* an imperfect thing in itself, and something in order to fruit; a good motion and holy purpose, is but *opus imperfectum, et ordinabile,* an imperfect work, in order to a compleat work of the Spirit; When that *primus impetus,* those first motions were strong upon my heart, had I then pursued them in the force and vigour of them, how many difficulties might I have overcome? Revive thy work, O Lord, and give not to my soul a miscarrying womb, or dry breasts.

Meditation III.

Upon the sight of a fair spreading Oak.

What a lofty flourishing Tree is here? It seems rather to be a little Wood, than a single Tree, every limb thereof having the dimensions and branches of a Tree in it; and yet as great as it is, it was once but a little slip, which one might pull up with two fingers; this vast body was contained virtually, and potentially in a small Acorn. Well then, I will never despise the day of small things, nor despair of arriving to an eminency of grace, though at present it be but as a bruised reed, and the things that are in me be ready to dye. As things in nature, so the things of the Spirit grow up to their fulness and perfection by slow and insensible degrees. The famous and heroical acts of the most renowned believers, were such as themselves could not once perform, or it may be think they ever should. Great things both in nature and grace, come from small and contemptible beginnings.

Navigation Spiritualized:
Or, A New Compass For Seamen,

by John Flavel

Chapter V.

Sea-men fore-see a Danger, and prepare;
Yet few of greater Dangers are aware.

Observation.

How watchful and quick sighted are Sea-men, to prevent Dangers! if the Wind die away, and then fresh up Southerly; or if they see the sky hazy, they provide for a Storm: if by the Prospective-Glass they ken a Pirate at the greatest distance, they clear the Gun-room, prepare for fight, and bear up, if able to deal with him; if not, they keep close by the Wind, make all the Sail they can, and bear away. If they suppose themselves by their reckoning, near Land, how often do they sound? And if upon a Coast with which they are unacquainted, how careful are they to get a Pilot that knows, and is acquainted with it?

Application.

Thus watchful and suspicious ought we to be in Spiritual Concernments. We should study, and be acquainted with Satan's Wiles and Policy: The Apostle takes it for granted, that Christians are not ignorant of his devices, 2 Cor. 2:11. The Serpent's eye (as one saith) would do well in the Dove's head: The Devil is a cunning Pirate, he puts out false Colours, and ordinarily comes up to the Christian in the disguise of a friend.

O the manifold depths and stratagems of Satan, to destroy Souls! Though he have no Wisdom to do himself good, yet [he hath] policy enough to do us mischiefe. He lies in ambush behind our lawful comforts and imployments; Yet, for the most of men, how supine and careless are they, suspecting no danger; Their souls, like Laish,[42] dwell carelessly; their Senses ungarded: O what an easie prize and conquest doth the Devil make of them!

Indeed, if it were with us, as with Adam in innocency, or as it was with Christ in the days of his flesh (who by reason of that overflowing fullness of Grace that dwelt in him, the purity of his Person, and the Hypostatical Union,[43] was secured from the danger of all temptations) the case then were otherwise; but we have a Traytor within, Jam. 1:14,15, as well as a Tempter without, 1 Pet. 5:8: "Our adversary the Devil goes about as a roaring lion, seeking whom he may devour." And, like the Beasts of the Forest, poor Souls lie down before him, and become his prey. All the

---

[42]Laish: a Canaanite city that was easily captured by the Israelites because of its inhabitants' carelessness, Judg. 18:7-19.

[43]The hypostatical union is the union of both divinity and humanity in the one person of Jesus Christ. The doctrine was developed in relation to the Creed of Chalcedon, A.D. 451.

sagacity, wit, policy and foresight of some Men, is summoned in to serve their Bodies, and secure their fleshly enjoyments.

Reflection.

Lord! how doth the care, wisdom, and vigilance of Men in temporal and external things, condemn my carelessness in the deep and dear concernments of my precious Soul! what care and labour is there to secure a perishing life, liberty, or treasure! When was I thus sollicitous for my Soul, though its value be inestimable, and its dangers far greater? Self-preservation is one of the deepest Principles in Nature. There is not the poorest Worm, or Flie, but will shun danger if it can: Yet I am so far from shunning those dangers to which my Soul lies continually exposed, that I often run it upon temptations, and voluntarily expose it to its enemies. I see, Lord, how watchful, Jealous, and laborious thy People are, what Prayers, Tears, and Groans, searching of Heart, Mortification of Lusts, guarding of Senses: and all accounted too little by them. Have not I a Soul to save or lose eternally, as well as they? Yet I cannot deny one fleshly lust, nor withstand one temptation. O how am I convinced, and condemned; not only by others' care and vigilancy, but my own too, in lesser and lower matters!

The Poem.

I am the Ship, whose Bills of Lading come
To more than Man's or Angel's art can sum,
Rich fraught with Mercies, on the Ocean, now
I float, the dangerous Ocean I do plow.
Storms rise, Rocks threaten, and in ev'ry Creek
Pirates and Pickeroons[44] their Prizes seek.
My soul should watch, look out, and use its Glass,
Prevent Surprizals timely; but, alas!
Temptations give it chase, it's grappled sure,

---

[44]Pickeroons: thieves.

And boarded whilst it thinks itself secure.
It sleeps like Jonah, in the dreadful'st storm,
Although it's case be dangerous, and forlorn.
Lord, rouze my drowsie Soul, lest it should knock,
And split it self upon some dangerous Rock.
If it of Faith and Conscience shipwrack make,
I am undone for ever; Soul, awake!
Till thou arrive in Heaven, watch, and fear;
Thou may'st not say, till then, the Coast is clear.

Chapter IX.

If Sea-men lose a gale, there they may lie;
The Soul, when once becalm'd, in sin may die.

Observation.

Sea-men are very watchful to take their opportunity of Wind and Tide, and it much concerns them so to be: the neglect of a few hours, sometimes loses them their passage, and proves a great detriment to them. They know the Wind is an uncertain variable thing; they must take it when they may; they are unwilling to lose one flow, or breath, that may be serviceable to them. If a prosperous Gale offer, and they not ready, it repents them to lose it, as much as it would repent us to see a vessel of good wine or beer tapt and run waste.

Application.

There are also seasons and gales of Grace for our Souls; golden opportunities of Salvation afforded to men, the neglect of which proves the loss and ruine of Souls. God hath given unto man a day of Visitation, which he hath limited, Heb. 4:7, and keeps an exact account of every Year, Month, and Day, that we have enjoyed it, Luke 13:7, Jer. 25:3, Luke 19:42. The longest date of it can be but the time of this Life: This is our day to work in, Job 9:4, and upon this small wyre, the weight of Eternity hangs. But sometimes the season of Grace is ended, before the night of Death comes; the accepted time is gone, men frequently out-live it, Luke 19:44, 2 Cor. 6:2. Or, if the outward means of Salvation be continued, yet the Spirit many times withdraws from those means, and ceases any more to strive with Men; and then the Blessing, Power, and Efficacy is gone from them, and instead thereof a Curse seizeth the Soul, Heb. 6:7,8, and Jer. 6:29.

Therefore it is a matter of high importance to our Souls, to apprehend these seasons. How pathetically doth Christ bewail Jerusalem, upon this account! Luke 19:42: "O that thou hadst known, at least in this thy day, the things of thy peace! but now they are hid from thine eyes."[45] If a company of Sea-men be set a-shore upon some remote, uninhabited Island, with this advice, to be a-board again exactly at such an hour, else they must left behind; how doth it concern them to be punctual in their time? The lives of those men depend upon a quarter of an hour. Many a Soul hath perished eternally (the Gospel leaving them behind in their sins) because they knew not the time of their Visitation.

Reflection.

What golden Seasons for Salvation hast thou enjoyed, O my Soul? what Halcyon days of Gospel-light and Grace hast thou had? How have the precious Gales of Grace blown to no purpose upon thee! and the Spirit waited and striven with thee in vain? "The kingdom of heaven," (being opened in the gospel dispensation) "hath suffered violence."[46] Multitudes have been pressing into it in my days, and I my self have sometimes been almost perswaded, and not far from the Kingdom of God: I have gone as far as conviction of sin and misery; yea,

I have been carried by the power of the Gospel, to resolve and purpose to turn to God, and become a new Creature; but sin hath been too subtil and deceitful for me: I see, my resolutions were but as an early Cloud, or Morning-Dew; and now my heart is cold and dead again, settled upon its Lees. Ah! I have cause to fear and tremble, lest God hath left me under that Curse, Rev. 22:11, Let him that is filthy, "be filthy still." I fear I am become as that myrie[47] place, Ezek. 47:11, that shall not be healed by the streams of the Gospel, but given to salt, and cursed into perpetual barrenness. Ah Lord, wilt thou leave me so? and shall thy Spirit strive no more with me? Then it had been good for me that I had never been born. Ah, if I have trifled out this Season, and irrecoverably lost it, then I may take up that lamentation, Jer. 8:20, and say, "My harvest is past, my summer is ended, and I am not saved."

Every Creature knows its time, even the Turtle,[48] Crane, and Swallow, know the time of their coming, Jer. 8:7. How brutish am I, that have not known the time of my Visitation! O thou that art the Lord of Life and Time, command one gracious Season more for me, and make it effectual to me, before I go hence, and be seen no more!

The Poem.

A fresh and whisking Gale presents to day,
But now the Ship's not ready; Winds must stay,
And wait the Sea-men's leisure. Well, to morrow
They will put out; but then, unto their sorrow,
That Wind is spent, and by that means they gain
Perchance a Month's repentance, if not twain.
At last another offers, now they're gone;
But e're they gain their Port, the Market's done.
For every work and purpose under Heaven,
A proper time and season God hath given.

---

[45]This is an inexact paraphrase of the biblical text.
[46]Matt. 11:12.

[47]myrie: miry.
[48]turtle: turtle-dove.

The Fowls of Heaven, Swallow, Turtle, Crane,
Do apprehend it, and put us to shame.
Man hath his season too: but that mis-spent,
There's time enough his folly to repent.
Eternity's before him, but therein
No more such golden hours as these have been.
When these are past away, then you shall find
That Proverb true, Occasion's bald behind.
Delays are dangerous; see that you discern
Your proper seasons. O that you would learn
This Wisdom from those Fools that come too
*   late*
With fruitless cries, when Christ has shut the
*   gate.*

Chapter XXIV.

In Seas the greater Fish the less devour:
So some Men crush all those within their
power.

Observation.

There are Fishes of Prey in the Sea, as
well as Birds and Beasts of Prey on the
Land. Our Sea-men tell us, how the devouring Whales, Sharks, Dolphins, and
other Fishes follow the Caplein, and other
smaller Fish, and devour multitudes of
them. It is frequent with us, in our own
Seas, to find several smaller Fishes in the
Bellies of the greater ones; yea, I have often
heard Sea-men say, That the poor little Fry,
when pursued, are so sensible of the danger, that they have sometimes seen multitudes of them cast themselves upon the
Shoar, and perish there, to avoid the danger of being devoured by them.

Application.

Thus cruel, merciless, and oppressive
are wicked Men, whose "tender mercies
are cruelty," Prov. 22:10. We see the like
cruelty in our Extortioners, and over-
reaching Sharks ashore, who grind the
faces of the Poor, and regard not the Cries
of the Fatherless and Widows, but fill their
houses with the gain of Oppression. These

are, by the Holy Ghost, compared to the
fishes of the Sea, Hab. 1:13, 14. This is a
crying sin, yea, it sends up a loud cry to
Heaven for Vengeance, Exod. 22:23: If
thou afflict the widow and the fatherless,
"and they cry unto me, I will surely hear
their cry." And Verse 27, I will hear his
cry, "for I am gracious." Nay, God will
not only hear their Cry, but avenge their
Quarrel. That is a remarkable text, 1 Thes.
4:6: "That no man go beyond and defraud
his brother in any matter, because that the
Lord is the Avenger of all such." This word
Avenger, is but once more used in the New
Testament, Rom. 13:4. And there it is applyed to the Civil Magistrate, who is to see
Execution done upon Offenders. But now
this is a Sin that sometimes may be out of
the reach of man's Justice, and therefore
God himself will be their Avenger. You
may overpower the Poor in this World, and
it may be they cannot contend with you at
man's Barr, therefore God will bring it before his Barr.

Believe it, Sirs, it is a sin so provoking
to God, that he will not let it 'scape without severe punishment, sooner or later. The
prophet Habbakuk, chap. 1, verse 13,
wondred how the holy God could forbear
such till the general day of reckoning, and
that he did not take exemplary Vengeance
on them in this Life. "Thou art of purer
eyes than to behold evil, and canst not look
upon Iniquity: Wherefore then lookest thou
upon them that deal treacherously, and
holdest thy tongue when the wicked de-
voureth the man that is more righteous than
he?" And Prov. 23:10, 11: "Enter not into
th Fields of the Fatherless," (i.e.) of the
poor and helpless. But why is it more dangerous violently to invade their right, than
another's? The reason is added, "for their
Redeemer is mighty, and he shall plead
their cause with thee." It may be they are
not able to retain a Counsel to plead their

cause there; therefore God will plead their cause for them.

Reflection.

Turn in upon thyself (O my Soul) and consider, Hast thou not been guilty of this crying sin? Have I not (when a Servant) over-reached and defrauded others, and filled my Master's house with Violence and Deceit? and so brought myself under that dreadful threatning, Zeph. 1:9. Or since I came to trade and deal upon mine own account, have not the Ballances of Deceit been in my hand? I have (it may be) kept many in my service and employment; have not I used their labours without reward, and so am under that woe, Jer. 22:13, or not given them Wages proportionable to their work, Isa. 58:3, Or by bad Payment and unjust Deductions and Allowances, defrauded them of a part of their due, Mal. 3:5, Or at least delayed payment, out of a covetous disposition to gain by it; whilst their necessities in the mean time cryed aloud for it; and so sinned against God's express commands, Deut. 24:14, 15, Lev. 19:30. Or have I not persecuted such as God hath smitten, Psalm 70:26, and rigorously exacted the uttermost of my due, though the hand of God hath gone out against them, breaking their estates? O my soul, examine thyself upon these particulars; rest not quiet, until this guilt be removed by the application of the Blood of Sprinkling. Hath not the Lord said, Jam. 2:13, That they "shall have judgment without mercy, that have shewed no mercy?" And is it not a fearful thing to fall into the hands of the living God, who hath said, he will take vengeance for these things?

The Poem

Devouring Whales, and ravenous Sharks, do follow
The lesser Fry, and at one gulp do swallow
Some hundreds of them, as our Sea-men say:
But we can tell far stranger things than they.
For we have Sharks ashore in every Creek,
That to devour poor Men do hunt and seek.
No Pity, Sense, or Bowels, in them be,
Nay, have they not put off Humanity?
Extortioners and Cheaters, whom God hates,
Have dreadful open Mouths, and through those Gates
Brave Persons with their Heritages pass
In Funeral-state, friends crying out, Alas!
O give me Agur's[49] wish, that I may never
Be such my self, or feel the hands of either.
And as for those that in their paws are grip'd,
Pity and rescue, Lord, from that sad plight.
When I behold the squeaking Lark, that's borne
In falcon's talons, crying, bleeding, torn;
I pity its sad case, and would relieve
The Prisoner, if I could, as well as grieve.
Fountain of Pity! hear the piteous Moans
Of all thy Captive and Oppressed Ones.

---

[49]Agur: the putative author of the maxims in Prov. 30. This wish is Prov. 30:7-9.

Introduction to Thomas Vincent,
God's Terrible Voice in the City

Thomas Vincent was educated at Oxford, receiving the M.A. in 1654. In 1657 he became rector of St. Mary Magdalene, Milk Street, London, from which position he was ejected in 1662 for refusal to accept the terms of the Act of Uniformity. He continued to preach at Hoxton, in Middlesex, and he was fined for preaching there illegally in 1670. During the plague year of 1665 he preached publicly in several London churches that had been deserted by their Anglican incumbents. After his death in 1678 a broadsheet collection of his Holy and Profitable Sayings *was published and distributed.*

Vincent was best known for his "improvements" upon divine providence in God's Terrible Voice in the City, Wherein you have I. The sound of the voice, in the Narration of the two late Dreadfull Judgments of Plague and Fire, inflicted by the Lord upon the City of London, the former in the year, 1665, the latter in the year 1666. II. The interpretation of the voice. . . . *(Wing V 440; n.p., 1667). This was one of the works that Daniel Defoe drew upon for his* Journal of the Plague Year. *Vincent argued at the beginning of his treatise that "God doth sometimes speak unto a People by terrible things," and after narration of the events he listed twenty-five sins for which London was punished, including "pride of apparel," "obscene and scurrilous jesting," cheating by tradesmen and "unmercifulness" towards the poor. The last part of the book consists of twenty lessons or exhortations to be drawn from meditation on the fire and plague which Vincent considered things that God is calling upon London to ponder. What follows are lessons twelve through eighteen, taken from pages 252-60 of the 1667 printing. There is a brief entry on Vincent by Alexander Gordon in the* Dictionary of National Biography.

God's Terrible Voice in the City

by Thomas Vincent

12. God doth expect that London should trust no more in arms of flesh, but in himself alone. By these Judgements God hath shown to London the weakness and insufficiency of arms of flesh, what broken reeds they are. Some put their trust in men, and their great expectation of relief and comfort hath been from their friends; by the Plague God hath shown, how frail and weak man is, how like grass or a flower that quickly withereth, or is cut down; how like glass or a bubble which is easily broken and vanisheth; many have lost by the Plague their chief friends upon whom they have had all their dependance, and the Lord hath shown how insufficient a foundation man is for any one's trust and confidence; therefore he calleth aloud to London to "cease [ye] from man, whose breath is in his nostrils, for wherein is he to be ac-

counted of?'' (Isa. 2:22) not to trust in any of the sons of men, ''in whom there is no help'' and the reason is, because their breath goeth forth, they return to their dust, ''in that very day all their thoughts perish,'' Psalm 146:3,4. Some put their trust in their wealth and riches. Proverbs 18:11: ''The rich man's wealth is his [strong] City, and as an high wall in his own conceit.'' God hath by the Fire, which hath consumed so much of the wealth of the City, shown how insufficient a foundation wealth is for any man's confidence; he hath made it evident that riches are uncertain, and that they fly away with Eagles' wings sometimes whilest the owners are looking on; may not that which is threatned, Psalm 52:5-7, be spoken of many in London, that God hath rooted some of them by the Plague out of the Land of the living, plucked and forced others out of their habitations by the Fire, and taken away their stay and prop from them, of whom it may be said, Lo these are they that made not God their strength, but trusted in the abundance of their riches, and strengthned themselves in their wickedness.

London, trust no more in arms of flesh, but trust in God alone: ''It is better to trust in the Lord, than to put confidence in men; it is better to trust in the Lord, than to put confidence in Princes,'' Psalm 118:8,9. God is knocking off your fingers from all things here below, his will is that you should put your trust in him; which is one promised effect of great desolations and afflictions, that you should labour after, Zephaniah 3:12: ''I will also leave in the midst of thee an afflicted, and poor people, and they shall trust in the Name of the Lord.'' You were not so forward to trust in the Lord when you had greater abundance; endeavour to trust in him, now you are brought into greater poverty and affliction: his Infinite Power, Wisdom, loving kindness, his promise, truth and faithfulness are a strong bottome[1] for your trust and confidence in God. Trust in him at all times, in the worst of times; when your danger is greatest, he will be your help and shield, Psalm 115:11; he will be your refuge under oppression, and present help in time of trouble, Psalm 46:1; he will be your rock and fortress, your high tower to defend you, or your deliverer to redeem you out of all your troubles: trust in God alone for all things: if you make use of creatures, do not lean and stay upon them, for they will slip from under you; but stay your selves on God. O the peace and quiet which this will yield in shaking troublesome dayes! When others' hearts tremble within them, and are moved like leaves upon the approach of danger, you shall not be afraid of evil tydings, but have your hearts fixed trusting in the Lord, Psalm 112:7.

13. God doth expect that London should have Death in continual remembrance: This God expects from the Judgement of the Plague; the Death of so many thousands a week in London, gave such a spectacle of Mortality, and Preached such a Sermon in the City, as should bring the remembrance of Death into their minds every day of their lives; the death, if it were but of one or two should put you in mind of your later end; but when you have seen so many go down into the pit before you, it should inscribe the remembrance of death more deeply upon your mindes, the record of which you should look daily into: the gates of the City in the year of the Plague seem'd to have this inscription upon them, ''All Flesh is Grass;''[2] Let that word sound every day in your ears, and remember your bodies are exposed to the stroke of death every day; and though you have outlived the Plague, that yet Death hath you in the chase, and will ere long (you know not how

---

[1]bottome: foundation, basis.
[2]Isa. 40:6.

soon) overtake you; remember your glass is running, and will quickly be run out;[3] and therefore all the dayes of your appointed time, as you should remember; so you should prepare for your great change.[4]

God expects that the remaining inhabitants of London should be prepared well for death now, when they have had death so much in their view: some of you have been sick of the Plague and brought to the very brink of the Grave; all of you have been in danger of the Plague, when the disease was so sore and raging: I fear most of you were unprepared for death at that time, and had you dyed then, that it would have been with horrour; and I believe that there are few of you, but did in the time of your fears and danger, make vows and promises, if the Lord would shelter you from the arrows, which flew about you, and spare your lives then; that you would lead new lives, and be more carefull to prepare for your change; so that Death should not take you so unprovided any more: God expects the fulfilling of your promises; and that you should live up to the vowes, which you made in the time of your distress; and so provide your selves whilest you are well, that the messenger of Death may have a welcome reception, when ever he summoneth you to leave this world.

14. God expects that London should retain great impressions of Eternity. You have had the door of Eternity set wide open in your view, when so many were thronging in at the door, and I believe you had deeper apprehensions of Eternity in those dayes, than ever you had in your lives; take heed that those impressions do not wear off, and that you lose not those apprehensions, especially when you are drawing every day nearer and nearer thereunto. Think often of the vast Ocean of Eternity without bottome or bank on the other side, into which the whole steam of time will empty it self; and how quickly the small rivulet of your appointed dayes may fall into it: Think often of the unalterable state of Joy or Misery, which you must enter into at the end of your course: think how thin and short the pleasures of sin are in this life, in comparison of the horrible and endless torments of hell; and how light and momentaneous[5] the afflictions of God's people are here, in comparison with the exceeding and eternal weight of glory prepared for them in Heaven, 2 Corinthians 4:17.

15. God doth call upon London by the Fire which burnt down the City to secure themselves against the Fire of Hell. London's Fire was Dreadful, but the Fire of Hell will be a thousand-fold more Dreadfull. The Fire of London was kindled by man; be sure some second cause was made use of herein; but the Fire of Hell will be kindled by God himself, Isaiah 30:33: "Tophet is ordained of old, [yea] for the King it is prepared, he hath made it deep and large: the pile thereof is Fire and much Wood, and the breath of the Lord like a stream of brimstone doth kindle it." The Fire of London burnt the houses of the City, and consumed much of the goods; but the Fire of Hell will burn the persons of the wicked, Matthew 15:41: "Depart ye cursed into everlasting Fire." The Fire of London did burn most, but not all the houses in the City, some are yet remaining, but the Fire of Hell will burn all the persons of the wicked, not one of them shall escape and remain. The Fire of London was extinguished, and did last but four dayes; but the Fire of Hell will be unextinguishable, it will burn for ever, it is called everlasting Fire, in which the damned must lye and burn eternally, without any possibility of ever getting forth. If you had known before of

---

[3]The image is that of an hour-glass with the sand running out.

[4]change: passage from this life to the next.

[5]momentaneous: momentary.

London's Fire, where it would begin, and how it would spread, and seize upon your houses, surely you would have taken some course for the prevention of it: you know before of the Fire of Hell, the Word of God hath revealed it; O take some course for prevention of it, at least for securing of your selves against it: when the Fire was burning in London, you did fly from it, least it should have consumed your persons as well as houses; O fly from the Fire of hell, into which your persons will be thrown if you go on in sin; fly from the wrath which is to come; fly unto Jesus Christ who alone can deliver you.

16. God doth call upon Londoners by the Fire to be like Strangers and Pilgrims in the world. God hath burned you out of your habitations, that he might loosen your affections from houses, and riches, and all things here below; that he might unsettle you, unhinge, unfix you, that you might never think of Rest and Settlement in the Creatures, as long as you live: God calls upon you by this Judgement, to take off your hearts from this world, which is so very uncertain, and to be like Strangers and Pilgrims upon the earth, who are to take up your lodging here but a few dayes and nights in your passage to the other world; God expects you should live as those who have here no certain dwelling place, and therefore that you should not lavish away too much of your thoughts, and affections, and time about these uncertain things, which are of so short a continuance, and with which you cannot have a long abode; God hath by his Judgements crucified the World very much before you, and he expects that the world should be crucified in you; God hath poured contempt upon the world, and set a mark of disgrace thereon; he hath cast dirt upon the face where you fancied before so much beauty to lye; and

he expects that you should fall in esteem, and grow out of love with the world, and never go a whoring from him to the creatures any more.

17. God calls upon London to make him their habitation. Psalm 90:1: "Lord thou hast been our dwelling place in all generations." God is the hiding-place, and he is the dwelling-place of his people; you have lost your dwellings by the Fire, make God your habitation, and dwell in him, to whom you may have constant resort, and in whom you may have a sure abode. Get possession of this house by your union to God through his Son: and when you are in, keep possession, abide in this house, do not wander from him, and turn your selves out of doors by breaking of his houshold laws; make God your home, and labour to be much acquainted at home; spend your time with God, and give your hearts to him: Rest and repose your selves in God daily; look for all your provisions in him, and from him; walk in him and with him. Make God your habitation.

18. God calleth upon London to seek after an abiding City. Hebrews 13:14: "We have here no continuing City, but we seek one to come." London hath reason to say the former, therefore let London do the latter: you have seen the City fall by the Fire, seek after a City which hath more lasting foundations, and is of such strong building, that neither time can wear and weaken, nor flames of Fire reach and consume. I mean the New Jerusalem, which is above, the Heavenly City, whose builder and maker is God; there are Mansions, abiding places for the Saints, John 14:12. There the wicked will cease from troubling, and the weary will be at rest; seek after this City, labour for a title to it, lay up your Treasure in it, get your affections set upon it; above all Trades drive a Trade for Heaven, which in the issue will yield you the best returns.

Introduction to Thomas Doolittle,
A Treatise Concerning the Lord's Supper

Thomas Doolittle (1631-1707) came from Kidderminster, where as a boy he had been converted by the preaching of Richard Baxter. Educated at Cambridge, in 1653 he received Presbyterian ordination and began preaching in London, quickly becoming popular. He refused to conform to the Act of Uniformity and thereafter kept a school, though preaching occasionally—notably in London, in 1666, after the fire. After the Toleration Act he was pastor to a Dissenting congregation in London.

Doolittle is best known as the author of works of practical divinity. Among these are such titles as The Young Man's Instructer, and the Old Man's Remembrancer: or Controversies and Practical Truths, fitted to the capacity of Children, and the more Ignorant sort of People; Captives Bound in Chains, Made Free by Christ their Surety; The Mourner's Directory; *and a work improving a remarkable providence,* Earthquakes Explained and Practically Improved: Occasioned by the Late Earthquake on September 8, 1692. *In these works Doolittle consistently exhibited a compassionate and commensensical attitude. In* The Young Man's Instructer *(London, 1673) 32, there appears an early example of the "watchmaker" argument for God's existence when Doolittle says that "a good going watch" leads to the conclusion that "some workman" was its "artificer."*

Doolittle's most popular work was A Treatise Concerning the Lord's Supper: with Three Dialogues, for the more full Information of the Weak, in the Nature and Use of this Sacrament. *This was first published in 1667, and it was reprinted many times before 1700. It was one of the most popular religious books in English for several generations. What follows is almost the entirety of chapter nine. It is taken from the first edition (Wing D1899), 112-133, 137-150. Alexander Gordon wrote a brief biography of Doolittle for the* Dictionary of National Biography.

A Treatise Concerning the Lord's Supper

by Thomas Doolittle

Chapter IX

*Containing some Direction to get our hearts rightly
disposed for the receiving of the Lord's Supper.*

Having thus far proceeded in proving it your important duty, to prepare your hearts for this Ordinance, and laying down some serious Questions for quickening you thereunto: I next come to give you some Directions, what you must do, that your receiving may be acceptable unto God, and profitable unto you; and they are these four.

First, Search your own heart, enquiring narrowly into the state of your soul, how it is betwixt God and you.

Secondly, Solemnly consider such things as have a tendency in them to dispose your heart thereto.

Thirdly, Fervently pray to God before you go, that you may receive worthily when you are there.

Fourthly, Seriously discourse with some (if you have opportunity) about such things that may conduce to raise your affections and quicken your graces before you go.

First, Strictly search thine own heart, 1 Cor. 11:28. "But let a man examine himself, and so let him eat of that bread, and drink of that cup." The word signifieth a diligent and narrow search into the nature, [and] properties of the thing, that is the object thereof, as a Goldsmith proves the goodness of his Metal. Now Christian Reader, for thine help herein, I would advise thee to put such questions as these unto thy self, and after due deliberation with thy self, and prayer unto God, that he would discover the state of thy Soul unto thee,

give in a true and serious answer, as one that knows thou must again be called to an account, and be examined by God himself at the last day.

Question 1. Have I a principle of spiritual life, or am I yet dead in trespasses and sins? Oh my soul! the work thou art intending at a Sacrament, it is lively work, and if thou art dead thou canst not to it; thou art to go to feed upon the bread of life; and if thou art dead thou canst not do it. Thou art to feast not only with, but upon the Lord, but if thou art dead, thou canst not do it. I finde it recorded in Numbers 9:10-11, If any man was defiled by reason of a dead body, he was not to eat the Lord's Passeover till the second month. How much more unfit am I to eat the Lord's Supper, if yet my heart be dead, not only dull but dead; there is no converse between the living and the dead; dead men do not converse with living men; and a dead heart, altogether void of spiritual life, cannot converse with a living God.

In order therefore to the discovering of thy spiritual life I will propound these following Enquiries, to which give in thy answer seriously, as in the fear of God; and solemnly, as in the presence of that God, that doth search thy heart, and know thy state, and let thy conscience make reply, as thou wouldest do, if thou wast now to dye.

First, Hast thou ever had any spiritual sense of things good and evil? Didst thou ever see the excellency and the beauty of Christ, and the vileness and deformity of sin? Is Christ most lovely, and sin most loathsome in thine eyes? didst thou ever taste such sweetness that there is in Christ, in a promise, or in communion with God, that it makes thee chuse Christ, embrace a promise, prefer communion with God above all things in this world? or didst thou ever taste such bitterness in sin, that makes thee loathe it, and unfeignedly willing to leave and to forsake it? once thou hadst no relish in spiritual things, but hast thou now? time was when thou didst taste sweetness in thy sin, when thou didst delight therein, but is it as bitter to thee now, as then it was pleasant and delightful? Thou hast had an ear to hearken to the temptations of the Devil, the flatteries of the world, to sinners enticing thee to sin, to the corruptions of thine own heart, calling thee to yield to all these: but thou hadst not an ear to listen to the motions of the Spirit of God, nor to the voice of the Ministers of God, nor to the voice of the mercies, nor the judgements of God, nor to the voice and cry of thy own conscience; but now thou art deaf unto the former, the Devil calls, but thou wilt not hear, and sinners call, but thou wilt not hearken: and thine ears are open to the latter, if God calls, thou sayest, speak Lord, thy servant heareth; if the Spirit whispereth to thy heart, thou perceivest his meaning, and obeyest, etc. Thou once didst feel Ordinances and duties to be a burden to thee, and groanedst under them as a load too heavy for thee to bear; and this was when thou didst make light of sin: Christ's easie yoak thou thoughtest to be intollerable, but sin's intollerable yoak thou judgest to be easie; because sin was in thine heart, as (an element) in its proper place: but tell me, dost thou not now groan under the weight of sin? dost thou not really think there is no evil of affliction so heavy as the evil of transgression? doth it not make thee to cry out, O wretched man that I am, who shall deliver me from this body of death![1] that now thou couldest, at least, sometimes desire that thou mightest be loosed from thy body of flesh, that thou mayest be freed from this body of sin; if so, thou art alive.

Secondly, Hast thou mortified sin, or hast thou not? Is sin dead or alive? if thy sin do live and reign, then thou art dead; if thy sin be dead, then thou dost live; the life and reign of sin, and the life and power of grace cannot consist in the same soul at the same time; though sin be in thine heart, yet thine heart is not for, nor in thy sin; though sin be in thy affections, yet indeed sin hath lost thine affections, as there is sin in thy love, but thou dost not love thy sin; there is sin in thy joy, but thou dost not rejoyce in thy sin; thou dost not find those flaming desires of thine heart after forbidden things, as sometime thou didst; neither hath sin that universal, acknowledged authority in thy soul, as once it had; nor that peaceable possession in thy heart, which once thou wast contented to give and yield unto it; but it is even death to thee to feel these lusts so much as crawling in thy heart, though they do not rule; if so, then sin is dead, and thou dost live; if not so, then sin doth live, and thou art dead.

Thirdly, Canst thou groan and cry unto the Lord, and will nothing still thee but a Christ? then surely dost thou live; though thou canst not word thy desires at the throne of grace (as new-born babes cannot ask, but yet can cry for the breast) nor in such language (as others) ask for Christ and grace; Yet thou canst cry for Christ, and weep for grace, and all the creatures cannot quiet thee till thou hast hopes that Christ is formed in thee: surely they have spiritual life, that in this sense do thus cry after Christ.

---

[1]Allusion to Rom. 7:24.

Fourthly, Dost thou grow in the graces of the Spirit? it may be thou darest not say, thou hast more grace, but this thou findest, thou hast more desires after grace; that is more grace. Art thou indeed thankful for a little grace, but yet art reaching after more? Thou prizest one dram of grace above thousands of gold and silver; yet it is not a little will serve thy turn; dost thou grow more weary of thy sin? dost thou grow more earnest after Christ, and God, and Heaven? surely growth is a proof of life.

Fifthly, Dost thou work for God, and Christ, and Heaven, and for thy soul in a spiritual manner? Spiritual operations do discover[2] spiritual life. Many live a natural life, that will not work; but those that be spiritually alive, be at work, though some more, and some less.[3] Dost thou pray, and labour in thy prayers? dost thou hear, and take pains with thy heart in hearing? dost thou do thy work according to those spiritual Rules which God hath given thee in his word, or wherein thou failest, thou art grieved for it? dost thou work from a spiritual principle of love to God and holy fear of him? dost thou pray unto him because thou lovest him? and dost thou abstain from sin, and watch and pray against it, because thou wouldest neither offend nor grieve him? Hast thou a spiritual end in working while thou livest? that thou mayest glorifie and honour God; though all thy working in this manner deserve nothing from the Lord, neither dost thou thus labour in all thy duties, to rely upon them, and to take thee off from resting upon Christ; yet are they evidences that thou art raised from the death of sin, to a life of grace; and having life, thou must have food, and God hath prepared it for thee upon his Table, and thou mayest go and feed thereon. This is the first

thing that you should enquire after, as to your state, whether you be spiritually alive.

Question 2. Do I hunger and thirst after Christ? This also will be an evidence of your spiritual life: For dead men do not hunger, they do not thirst: say then to thy self, Lo, oh my soul! thou art invited to a feast, to a banquet of Gospel-dainties, to "a feast of fat things, a feast of wines on the Lees, of fat things full of marrow, of wines on the Lees well refined," Isaiah 25:6. Lo, oh my soul! Wisdome "hath killed her beasts, she hath mingled her wines, she hath also furnished her Table, she hath sent forth her Maidens, she cryeth upon the high[est] places of the City; who-so is simple, let him turn in hither: as for him that wanteth understanding, she saith unto him, come, eat of my bread, and drink of the wine which I have mingled," Proverbs 9:2-5. Thus the Lord doth call thee, Oh my Soul, to rich and costly provisions, but where is thy hunger? where is thy appetite? If I could finde I hunger, I could find an Invitation to go; for I read my Lord hath said, Isa. 55:1, "Ho! every one that thirsteth come ye to the waters, and he that hath no money, come ye, buy and eat, yea come, buy wine and milk without money, and without price." And John 7:37, "In the last day, the great day of the feast, Jesus stood and cryed, saying, If any man thirst, let him come unto me and drink." If I could finde I hunger, I can finde a promise that I shall be satisfied, Matthew 5:6: "Blessed are they which hunger and thirst after righteousness, for they shall be filled." Come then, tell me, oh my soul! dost thou feel an emptiness in thy self, and a want of those things which alone can satisfie spiritual hungerings? Art thou pinched?[4] Art thou pained with the sense of the want of Christ? Art thou impatient till he come unto thee? Dost thou think time is long till he doth fill

---

[2]discover: reveal.

[3]The work of the spiritual life is meant.

[4]pinched: under stress.

thee? Canst thou take any pains that thou mightest enjoy him? Must thou have a Christ, or nothing will content thee? Then thou art one whom God doth call; be encouraged, arise and go to the Table of thy Lord. This is another thing that thou must enquire after, because it is not only thy duty to have life, but to have spiritual hungerings after Christ, when thou goest unto the Table of the Lord.

Question 3. Do I love God and Christ? or do I not? If I do not love him, what have I to do to go unto his Table? If God be an enemy to me, and I yet an enemy to God, wherefore should I go and bring down wrath upon my self? but if I love him, why should I be so dismayed because I am a sinner, since the Lord is willing freely to bestow all things that are here provided, upon them that love him? The more sin I find I have, if I love him, I see the greater need I have to go unto him: put then the question to thy self, as Christ did unto Peter, John 21:15: "So when they had dined Jesus said unto Simon Peter, Simon, Son of Jonas, lovest thou me more than these? He saith unto him, yea, Lord, thou knowest that I love thee." And this question Christ put to him the second and the third time: So do thou before thou goest to this Supper; ask thy soul, oh my soul! Lovest thou the Lord Jesus? Canst thou say, the Lord knoweth that I love him? Yet ask again the second time, oh my soul! Lovest thou the Lord Jesus? Canst thou again with Peter answer, Yea, Lord, thou knowest that I love thee: but that thou mayest be sure, enquire again the third time; Tell me, oh my soul! Lovest thou indeed the Lord Jesus? For there are many that be mistaken, and think they love him, but they do not: canst thou therefore appeal to God and say, Lord, thou that knowest all things, thou knowest that I love thee. I do not indeed love thee, as thou hast loved me, yet I love thee: I do not love thee, as much as others do, nor as

much as I my self desire to do, and that is my grief and sorrow: but yet I love thee, and that is my peace and comfort; And I have these evidences of my love, that make me say, Lord, I love thee; for I hate that which is a grief unto thee, and that because it grieves thee. Lord, I love thee, for I am grieved at thy absence, and am rejoyced at thy presence: Lord, I love thee, for I love any that are like thee, that bear thy image and thy stamp upon their hearts; O my Lord, I love thee, for I love the place and duties where thou wert wont to warm thy people's hearts; but if thou beest not there, I cannot take up contentedly with them, except I see thee. Lord, I do humbly say, I love thee, for I dare not deny but that I am grieved, when thou art dishonoured by my self or others; though I grieve for this less than I should, because I love thee less than I ought. Lord, I love thee, for I desire to have an heart that should be willing to part with all for thee; things sinful in themselves at all times, and things lawful when thou callest me to it. Once more, I humbly say, I love thee, for I would have an heart to love, and long, and look for thy coming and appearance in thy glory; come away then, O my Love (saith Christ unto thee) and commemorate the death of thy Lord whom thou dost love. O my soul! thy Lord doth call thee, arise and go unto his Table, where thou shalt see how he hath loved thee, and where thou mightest have thy love to him more increased and inflamed. Thus thou shouldest enquire concerning thy love to Christ, when thou art to go unto this feast of Love.

Question 4. Do I believe on Jesus Christ? or do I not? Have I the faith of God's Elect? or have I not? If I should not eat in faith, and drink in faith, I should not receive aright; but if I do believe, though my faith be weak, I have a right to him, and to his privileges which he hath purchased by his death, unto me in the Sacrament.

Then turn thy speech to God, and say, Lord, If I do prize thy Son above all things in the world, may I then conclude I do believe? God tells thee, that thou mayest, 1 Peter 2:7: "Unto you therefore that believe, he is precious." If I make it my business to purifie my heart, do I then believe? God tells thee that thou dost, Acts 15:9, "Purifying their hearts by faith." If I take thy Son for my Lord and Saviour, and receive him upon Gospel terms into my heart, might I then conclude that I have faith? God tells thee thou mayest, John 1:12: "But as many as received him, to them gave he power to become the Sons of God, even to them that believe on his name." If so, then Lord I will, in obedience to thy command, do this in remembrance of thee.

Question 5. Once more enquire of thy self, and say, Have I repented of my sins that I have committed against the Lord, and am I truly humbled for the same? For how shall I behold my Saviour broken for my sins, if my heart was never broken for my sins? Though I do come short of that degree of brokenness of heart for sin, as some of God's people have attained unto, yet have I that repentance which will prove repentance unto life? Though my tears are not so many as my sins, nor my sorrows as great as my transgressions, yet have I so much sight and sense of sin, as makes me loathe my self, and abhor my sin, and willing to forsake them; and separates me from the love of them, and delight in them? Oh my conscience, canst thou not bear me witness, that it is the breaking of my heart, that I have broken God's commands? That my mourning proceeds from love, and sense of God's kindness and his goodness to me? That it is my unfeigned desire to be washed from the filth, as well as delivered from the guilt of sin; to be freed from the power and dominion, as well as from the punishment and damnation that is due unto

me for my sin; that though I did not know but Hell might be my portion, yet I would not sin against the Lord. Canst thou not bear me witness, that I do indeavour (though I come short in my indeavours) to keep my self unspotted from the world, and that I hate the garments spotted with the flesh? That sin in the temptation to it, is grievous to me, as well as after the Commission of it; that I do groan (though not so much as I should) under this body of sin, longing for the time when I shall be delivered from it: crying out in the bitterness of my soul, Lord, when shall it be? Lord, when shall it be that I shall be perfectly freed from the loathsome body of sin which (through thy grace) is so offensive to my soul? If so, then I will arise, and approach unto this Ordinance, where I may be assured of my pardon, and be furnished with further strength and power against my sin. Thus thou shouldest enquire, whether thou hast repented of thy sin, when thou art to go and see, what hath been done unto thy Lord by reason of thy sins. Thus far for Tryal.

Secondly, When thou hast thus proceeded to finde out the truth of thy grace, then next go on to solemn meditation, to consider of those things which might excite and stir up thy graces, the truth of which thou findest already to be wrought in thy heart: that so thou mightest go unto this Ordinance with lively exercise of grace, that all thy graces might be ready to act according to thy duty in this work: for it will be thy sin to go unto the Table of the Lord with dull affections, and deadness upon thy heart; and it is an aggravation of thy sin, if it be through want of diligent endeavour to get thy Soul affected and inflamed with love before thou goest. Now for thy help herein, I shall instance in some of those things whch will be fit and suitable objects for thy thoughts before thou goest, and not unseasonable to meditate upon while thou art there.

First, Meditate and dwell in thy thoughts upon the love of God in the great work of man's Redemption. Consider that thou wast in a fallen and miserable estate; under the curse of the Law, liable to the wrath of God, the torments of Hell; under the Power of thy lusts, and the bondage of the Devil; and couldst not help thy self, nor recover thy self to the happiness from which thou didst fall; then get thy heart affected with the love of God, who in the eternal project of his counsel, hath contrived a way for thy salvation; and here if thy heart be not yet affected,

Urge it with the freeness of this love: Consider, oh my soul! it was free love, that God would send his Son to dye for fallen man, and not for fallen Angels; to take upon him not the nature of Angels, but the seed of Abraham. But yet consider, O my soul! the freeness of this love to thee, who hath ordained thee to salvation by the death of Christ, when thousands of others are passed by, and suffered to perish in their sins! God might have passed thee by, and applyed it unto others, . . .

Secondly, Meditate and dwell in thy thoughts upon the sufferings of thy Lord Redeemer when he came into the world. It will be profitable before thou goest to the Sacrament, to view over the history of his sufferings, from his birth to his Cross. Oh what love was this, that God should give his Son, and the Son should give himself to dye for thee! never love like this! John 15:13, "Greater love hath no man than this, that a man lay down his life for his friends." But greater love than this had the Son of God, when he laid down his life for his enemies. But if thine heart be not yet affected, Consider,

1. The dignity of the Sufferer; He that had the Heavens for his Throne, was laid in a Manger; the ancient of daies became a Babe: He that was above all, was abased more than all; He that was richer then any, being Lord of all, was made so exceeding poor, that he had not where to lay his head; He that was the wisest in the world, that never man spake like him, was derided and laughed to scorn, and was reproached in all his offices: The King of Kings, the great and only Potentate is crowned with thorns: The Prophet of Prophets hath his face covered, and then smitten, and then they reproached him, saying "Prophesie who it was that smote thee;" To the great High Priest it was said in Scorn, "he saved others himself he cannot save:" the most mighty is bound; the most innocent is scourged and condemned; the most lovely is despised; the Physician is wounded, that the sick Patient may be healed; the Lord dyeth for his servants. Oh think of this, till thou feel thine heart to work in love, and to reach forth in burning desires after him.

2. The variety of his sufferings; he that was more precious then Rubies, and all things that can be desired are not to be compared to him; yet was sold for thirty pieces of Silver, a goodly price that he was prised at by the Sons of Sinners, Zachariah 11:13. He was sold by one, denyed by another, forsaken of all: He was buffeted and spit upon: a murderer preferred before him: while he lived he was accounted a blasphemer, and when he dyed, he was reckoned among transgressours. I cannot tell, what it was he did endure, but I can tell it was his love that moved him to it. Oh with what heart, inflamed with love shouldst thou go unto that Ordinance, wherein all this is represented to thy faith! O Love, Love, Love! art thou banished from my soul, that I do not feel thee more working in my heart, while I ponder these things within my thoughts? O my Lord thou lovedst me in my blood, and when I see thee in thy blood (if my heart were not so very bad) I could not but exceedingly love

thee! When thou sawest me in my blood, it was polluted blood; but when I see thee in thy blood, I see, I find, I feel it is love-inflaming blood.

Thirdly, Meditate and dwell in thy thoughts upon the priviledges and benefits that were purchased by the death of Christ; And surely if we may judge by the price that was paid for them, they must be very great. Some believing thoughts upon this subject would affect and warm thy heart before thou goest to this Table, and when thou art there. Oh what a priviledge is it to be united unto Christ, to be justified by his blood, to be sanctified by his Spirit, to have sin pardoned and subdued, to be reconciled unto God, to be adopted now, and saved hereafter! All these be blessed fruits that thou wilt finde to grow upon the tree on which thy Saviour dyed; and there is much in these, in every one of these, to inflame thy Love to God and Christ, and to stir up thy heart to go unto that Ordinance, where thou mightest be assured of them, by having them sealed to thy soul.

Fourthly, Meditate and dwell in thy thoughts upon thy sin, that thou mayest be humbled, because thy sins were the procuring cause of all the sufferings of thy Lord: It was not for himself, but for thee; there was not guile in his mouth, nor wickedness in his heart; but the just suffered for the unjust. Thy sins were the Judas that betrayed him, the thorns that crowned him, the spears that pierced him, the nails that fastened him upon the tree; to see an ordinary man dying for thy faults would it not affect thy heart? Yonder is one that is groaning, bleeding, dying for the evil I have done; oh then, how should thy affections work, when thou seest the Son of God bleeding (having his side opened that thou mightest look into his heart), when thou seest him wounded, his hands and his feet pierced; when thou hearest him cry out with a loud voice, and seest him give up the

Ghost, and all this for thy pride and unbelief, for thy worldliness and passion, for thy disobedience and rebellion, how will this fill thy Soul with sorrow and joy! thy eyes with tears, and thy mouth with praises; the one, because thou hast sinned; the other, because thy Lord would dye to save thee from thy sins.

And here it would not be unuseful nor unseasonable, to produce the catalogue of thy sins, that thou mayest see how far thou hast acted, to bring all these sorrows and sufferings upon thy Loving Lord: for if thou shalt be saved by his death, surely then thy sins were causes of his death: for it was the pardon of thy sin, the sanctifying of thy heart, and the saving of thy soul, with the rest of God's Elect, that he intended effectually to procure when he was lifted up upon the Cross; but did not intend or purpose the certain application of his death and sufferings unto Reprobates: so that had it not been for the sakes of God's Elect and chosen people, he never had exposed himself to so great sufferings, nor come down from Heaven, nor gone up upon the Cross; and will not this yet affect thine heart? Consider then what thy sins have been before and since conversion, in their nature, in their numbers, and in all their aggravations; every one of which deserved the heavy and eternal wrath of God: Oh then what loads and heaps of wrath they did all deserve! How much more all the sins of all the Elect of God! Oh what a burden did thy Saviour bear, when all these were laid upon him! What didst thou do against thy Lord, all those years thou livdst in an unconverted state? How many sins didst thou commit every day, every week, and every month? When thou wast in that estate in which thou didst nothing else but sin, when all thy thoughts were sin, and all thy words and actions, all were sin, all which thy Lord was to make satisfaction for when he was dying on the Cross. Dear Jesus! how unkinde and cruel was I then to thee, who was so kind and merciful unto me!

But yet consider what thy sins have been, since thy Lord hath applied his death to thee; which should have engaged thee to be more holy, and to walk more closely with him: but since, thy sins in some respects have been worse then all thou didst before thou wast converted: for thou hast sinned against dearer love, and clearer light; thou hast sinned against the Lord that dyed for thee, and after, by his Spirit he hath applied his death unto thy soul: thou hast sinned after thou hast had a pardon of thy sin, and after he did assure thee of thy pardon; thou hast sinned against the Father, who did ordain thee unto life; against the Son, that did redeem thy soul from death, and purchase for thee eternal life; against the holy Spirit, that hath been fitting and preparing thee to be partaker of the inheritance of the Saints in light; thou hast sinned after rich and large experiences of God's goodness and mercy to thy soul; after thou hadst tasted the bitterness of sin, and sweetness of the love of God; after thou hadst resolved against thy sin, and promised unto God upon thy knees, that if he would pardon thee, and tell thee, he had pardoned thee, thou wouldest be more watchful for the time to come: God did what thou didst desire, but thou hast not done that which thou didst promise. Let all this then awaken thee to sorrow and repentance, before thou goest to the Table of the Lord.

Thirdly, Then next proceed to solemn, serious fervent prayer, and make thine addresses to thy God: For all that thou canst think upon, and all the course that thou canst take, will not affect thine heart, except the God of Heaven shall work them on thy heart, and cause them to make some impression on thy soul: then go to God and say, O Lord, I am ashamed to think how dully I do think of these great affecting things: with what an hard and stupid heart I roll over in my mind the death and sufferings of thy Son: O Lord, it is time that I should come to thee, that I might have some warmth from thee, that I might be inflamed with love; and, were it possible, might be turned into love, that I might be made up all of love: O Lord, I have been trying to get my heart affected with the death of Christ, and with thy love and his, manifested to my soul therein, but Lord, my heart is dull: And sometime when the coale begins to glow, it is covered with ashes before I am aware; it is too great a work for me to raise my heart to him who condescended to come down for me: If I could, I would, Lord, I would but cannot: but this I know, that if thou wilt, thou canst: Yea Lord, I do believe thou canst, and wilt; and therefore it is that I come to thee. O Lord, the time draws near, in which I am to go unto thy Table; but shall the time of receiving come, before thou comest into my heart, to stir up thy graces in me, that I may be fitted to receive: True, Lord, I am unworthy, altogether unworthy of what I do desire; but what thou dost to any, it is not because they be worthy, but because it pleaseth thee to do for thine, what they ask of thee according to thy will: I am vile, I am vile, O Lord, I am exceeding vile; but if thou wilt cloathe me with the righteousness of thy Son, and look upon me through his wounds, then thou wilt love me. Remember not my sins against thee, but remember what thy Son hath done and suffered for me: thou commandest me in the Sacrament to remember what thy Son hath suffered, that I may be thankful unto thee; do thou remember what thy Son hath suffered, and be thou gracious unto me; that I might see thy smiles, and perceive thy love when I am there; that I might come from thence with my pardon sealed, my sins subdued, my soul strengthened to run the waies of thy commandments, till thou shalt come and take me to thy self, where I shall see my Saviour in his glory, and behold my Lord that dyed for me on the Cross.

Fourthly, Next I would advise thee (if thou hast opportunity) to discourse with others of such things that tend to raise, and not to damp thy heart. When thou hast been taking pains with thy self in secret; when thou comest from thy chamber take heed with whom thou dost converse, and what thou sayest: for if in secret thou didst finde thy love excited, thy desires enlarged, thy faith fastening upon Christ; frothy and unseasonable discourse before thou goest might damp all again: or if in secret thy heart were dull, yet God might bless a word or two in holy discourse for the quickening of thy heart, and raising of thy affections towards him. When thou sittest at thy table, or by the fire, the night before the Sacrament, be speaking of the wonderful grace of God, the death of Christ, of the benefits thereby, of hope of Heaven, of the coming of the Lord, of the glory there is above, of the Sabbath the Redeemed of the Lord shall keep above in the Kingdom of their Father. When the two Disciples were discoursing of Christ's death and sufferings, Christ came and joyned himself unto them, Luke 24:13-15. If you be two discoursing together, Christ might come and make the third, and then your hearts will burn within you.

Having thus endeavoured to get thine heart prepared, as thou passest from thine house to the House of God, from thine house unto this Ordinance, watch over thy thoughts as thou walkest along, and let thine heart be working towards God and Christ. Oh that I might feel the power of Christ's death this day! Oh that I might have my pardon sealed to me this day! that I might be made conformable to Christ's death, see his smiles, taste his love, and be strengthened with strength in my soul: and when thou comest to joyn in the publick solemn worship with others of God's people, then minde the work that is before thee, and labour so to behave thy self in the duty, that thou mightest not lose thy pains that hast taken in preparing for the duty. . . .

Holy Comforts
for the Afflicted and Uncertain

Much of Puritan pastoral care and spiritual advice centered on providing comfort to those who found themselves afflicted in this life, and to those who lacked assurance that they were in a state of grace. In the first selection that follows, Edmund Calamy the elder wrestles with the problem of why God afflicts his saints. In the next selection, Benjamin Keach depicts the kind of opposition from the worldly that the people of God must expect in this life. In the comforting letters of spiritual advice from Joseph Alleine that follow, Alleine concerns himself particularly with the persecutions that God's children must face from those who are enemies to true religion. The brief selection from Bates suggests that prosperity, too, has its perils. The last two selections—from Thomas Brooks and Walter Marshall—deal with the pressing matter of how persons may receive assurance that they are among the elect of God. Both labor to formulate specific guidelines for such a determination and reveal themselves to be eager to give comfort to those of God's children who are struggling to achieve such comfort.

Introduction to Edmund Calamy,
The Godly Man's Ark

Edmund Calamy the elder (1600-1666) is so designated because he had both a son and grandson of the same name who were also clergymen. The grandson was a noted historian of Puritan Nonconformity. Edmund Calamy the elder was the son of a London merchant and was educated at Cambridge University, from which he received both the B.A. and M.A. He was later awarded a Bachelor of Divinity by Cambridge. In 1626 Calamy was ordained to the priesthood of the Church of England, and for a while he was both chaplain to the Bishop of Ely and vicar of a Cambridgeshire parish. From 1627 to 1637 he was lecturer at Bury St. Edmunds, Suffolk. After 1639 he was lecturer and minister of St. Mary Alder-manbury in London. During the turmoil leading up to the civil wars, Calamy be-came one of the foremost Puritan advocates of reforming the Church of England, and a leader of the English Presbyterians. He often preached before Parliament, and he was a member of the Westminster Assembly. He opposed the execution of King Charles I and the Protectorate of Oliver Cromwell; and he favored the res-toration of the monarchy in 1660. After 1660 he worked with Richard Baxter for a more inclusive Church of England and was offered the bishopric of Lichfield; but he finally refused, unable to accept all the terms of the proposed religious set-tlement. He was ejected from his London parish in 1662 and was briefly impris-oned for illegal preaching. He died in 1666.

Most of Calamy's writings consisted of published sermons. Most popular of these was The Godly Man's Ark, *which first appeared in 1657 and went through seventeen editions by 1693. It consisted of five sermons, the first of which was preached at the funeral of Elizabeth Moore, a godly woman who had been under his spiritual direction. Appended to the volume were Mrs. Moore's spiritual mus-ings, under the title of "Evidence for Heaven." They consisted of consoling and assuring thoughts.*

The text of Calamy's funeral sermon for Mrs. Moore follows. It deals with the pressing problem that had troubled Job—the affliction of the godly. Calamy lays to rest many of the clichès that have been uttered about the Puritan equation of godliness and prosperity. His emphasis is on spiritual comfort. Calamy's sermon is also a good illustration of the Puritan plain style, with its aphorisms and homely illustrations. But Calamy also draws on his considerable learning, citing many biblical commentators, often in Latin (though he almost always provides a trans-lation). Like many Puritan sermons, this one features practical applications or "uses."

The text is taken from the first edition, The Godly Mans Ark or, City of Ref-uge, in the day of his Distresse. Discovered in divers Sermons, the first of which was Preached at the Funerall of Mistresse Elizabeth Moore. The other four were afterwards preached, and are all of them now made publick, for the supportation and consolation of the Saints of God in the hour of Tribulation *(London, 1657;*

Wing C 247) 1-55. There is an extensive new biography of Calamy by Richard Greaves, in that author's Saints and Rebels: Seven Nonconformists in Stuart England *(Macon GA: Mercer University Press, 1985) 9-62.*

The Godly Man's Ark,

by Edmund Calamy

Sermon I.
Psalm 119:92.

"Unless thy Law had been my delights, I should then have perished in mine affliction."

This Psalm (out of which my Text is taken) exceeds all the other Psalms, not onely in length, but in excellency, so far (in the judgement of Ambrose)[1] as the light of the Sun excels the light of the Moon. As the Book of Psalms is stiled by Luther, An Epitome of the Bible, or a little Bible: So may this Psalm fitly bee called, An Epitome of the Book of Psalms. It was written (as is thought) by David in the dayes of his banishment under Saul, but so penned, that the words thereof suit the condition of all Saints. It is *penu doctrinae publicum unicuique apta & convenientia distribuens,* a publick store-house of heavenly doctrines, distributing fit, and convenient instructions to all the people of God; and therefore should bee in no less account with those who are spiritually alive, than is the use of the Sun, Air, and Fire, with those who are naturally alive: It is divided into two and twenty Sections, according to the Hebrew Alphabet, and therefore fitly called A Holy Alphabet for Sion's Scholars. The A, B, C of godliness, Sixtus Senensis[2] calls

it, an Alphabetical Poem. The Jews are said to teach it their little children the first thing they learn, and therein they take a very right course, both in regard of the heavenly matter, and plain stile fitted for all capacities. The chief scope of it, is to set out the glorious excellencies and perfections of the Law of God. There is not a verse (except one onely, say some Learned men in Print, but are therein deceived; but I may truly say, Except the 122. and the 90. verses) in this long Psalm, wherein there is not mention made of the Law of God, under the name of Law, or Statutes, or Precepts, or Testimonies, or Commandements, or Ordinances, or Word, or Promises, or Wayes, or Judgements, or Name, or Righteousness, or Truth, &c.

This Text that I have chosen, sets out the great benefit and comfort, which David found in the Law of God in the time of his affliction—It kept him from perishing. Had not "thy Law been my delights, I had perished in my affliction."

The word Law is taken diversly in Scripture, sometimes for the Moral Law,

---

[1]St. Ambrose (339-397) was a bishop of Milan who was instrumental in the conversion of St. Augustine and in the shaping of the imperial state church.

[2]Sixtus of Siena (1520-1569) was an Italian

preacher and theologian. He narrowly escaped execution for heresy as a result of his protection by Pope Pius V. He was the author of *Biblioteca Sancta,* exegetical notes mainly on the Old Testament. It is this work to which Calamy refers.

James 2:10; Sometimes for the whole Oeconomy, Polity, and Regiment of Moses, for the whole Mosaical dispensation by Laws, partly moral, partly Judicial, partly Ceremonial, Gal. 3:23; Sometimes for the five Books of Moses, Luke 24:44; Sometimes for the whole Doctrine of God, contained in the Scriptures of the Old Testament, John 7:49. By Law in this place is meant, all those Books of the Scripture which were written when this Psalm was penned. But I shall handle it in a larger sense, as it comprehends all the Books both of the Old and New Testament. For the word Law is sometimes also taken for the Gospel, as it is Micah 4:2, Isa. 2:3. The meaning then is, Unless thy Law, that is, Thy Word, had been my delights, I should have perished in mine affliction.

David speaks this (saith Musculus)[3] of the distressed condition hee was in when persecuted by Saul, forced to flye to the Philistins, and sometimes to hide himself in the rocks and caves of the earth. *Hic vero simile est, fuisse illi ad manum codicem divinae legis,* &c. It is very likely (saith hee) that hee had the Book of God's Laws with him, by the reading of which, hee mitigated and allayed his sorrows, and kept himself pure from communicating with the Heathen in their superstitions. The Greek Scholiasts[4] say, That David uttered these words, *A Saule pulsus, & apud Philistaos & impios homines agere coactus,* when driven from Saul, and compelled to live amongst the wicked Philistins, &c. for he would have been allured to have communicated with them in their impieties, had

hee not carried about him the meditation of the word of God. "Unless thy Law had been my delights," &c.

In the words themselves, wee have two Truths supposed, and one Truth clearly proposed.
Two Truths supposed:
> That the dearest of God's Saints, are subject to many great and tedious afflictions.
That the word of God is the Saints' darling, and delights.
One Truth clearly proposed:
> That the Law of God delighted in, is the afflicted Saints' Antidote against ruine, and destruction.
Two Truths supposed:
> The first is this:
> Doctrine. I. That the best of God's Saints are in this life subject to many great and tedious afflictions.

David was a man after God's own heart, and yet hee was a man made up of troubles of all sorts and sizes, insomuch as hee professeth of himself, Psal. 69:1, 2, 3: "Save mee, O God, for the waters are come in unto my soul, I sink in deep mire where there is no standing, I am come into deep waters, where the flouds over-flow mee; I am weary of my crying, my throat is dryed, mine eyes fail while I wait for my God." And in this Text he professeth that his afflictions were so great, that hee must necessarily have perished under them, had hee not been sustained by the powerful comforts he fetched out of the word. There is an emphasis in the word *Then,* I should then have perished; that is, long before this time; then, when I was afflicted, then I should have perished. Junius and Tremelius[5] translate it, *Jam diu periissem,*

---

[3]Wolfgang Musculus (1497-1563) was the reformer of Augsburg, Germany, and a leading Protestant theologian and biblical commentator.

[4]The Greek Scholiasts were Byzantine biblical scholars who produced "scholia" or annotations to the Bible. These were first marginal notes and later were compiled as a full commentary.

[5]Franciscus Junius (1545-1602) was a Reformed theologian who spent his final years as a theological professor at Leiden, in the Netherlands. Emanuel Tremellius (1510-1580) was an Italian Jew who

&c. "I should long ago have perished." Job was a man eminent for godliness; and yet as eminent for afflictions. Nay Jesus Christ himself was a man of sorrows, Isa. 53:3. Insomuch as that it is truly said, God had one Son without sin, but no Son without sorrow.

This our Dear Sister at whose Funeral wee are met, was a woman full of many and great afflictions, which (no doubt) would have quite drowned, and swallowed her up, had not the word of God supported her; therefore it was that shee desired that this Text might bee the subject of her Funeral Sermon.

Question: But why doth God afflict his own children with such variety of long and great afflictions?

Answer. I. God doth not do this, because hee hates them, but because hee loves them, "For whom the Lord loveth hee chastiseth," &c. Heb. 12:6. Did the Lord hate them, hee would suffer them to go merrily to hel. There is no surer sign of God's reprobating anger, than to suffer a man to prosper in wicked courses. God threatneth this as the greatest punishment, not to punish them, Hos. 4:14. And therefore because God loveth his children, hee chastiseth them in this world, that they many not bee condemned in the world to come, 1 Cor. 11:33.

2. God doth not do this, because hee would hurt them, but for their good, Jer: 24:5: The good figs were sent into captivity for their good. Heb. 12:10, "Hee for our profit," &c. God hath very gracious and merciful ends and aims in afflicting his people. Give mee leave here to inlarge my discourse, and to give you an account of some of these divine aims.

1. God's design is to teach us to know him, and trust in him, and to know our selves. It is a true saying of Luther, *Schola crucis, est Schola lucis,* the School of Affliction, is a School of Instruction. God's παθήματα are μαθήματα,[6] His rods (when sanctified) are powerful Sermons to teach us,

1. To know God: "And this is life Eternal to know him," Joh. 17:3. It is said of Manasseh, 2 Chron. 33.13, "Then Manasseh knew that the Lord hee was God." Then, when hee was caught among the thorns, bound with fetters, and carried to Babylon; before that time hee knew not the Lord: Afflictions teach us to know God, not only in his power and greatnesse, in his anger, and hatred against sin, but also in his goodnesse and mercy: For God doth so sweeten the bitter cup of affliction, that a child of God doth many times taste more of God's love in one month's affliction, than in many years of prosperity, 2 Cor. 1:4, 5, 2 Cor: 7.4. Adde to this, Afflictions teach us to know God Experimentally[7] and affectionatively, not cerebraliter (as Calvin saith) but cordialiter,[8] so to know him, as to love and fear him, and to flye unto him as our rock and hiding-place in the day of our distress. It is said, Cant. 3:1: "By night [. . .] I sought him whom my soul loveth," &c. Some by the word Night, understand the night of divine desertion, and from the words Gilbertus[9] hath this saying, *Qui quaerit in nocte, non quaerit ut videat, sed ut amplectatur;* Hee that seeks after God in the night of adversity, doth not seek to see him, and know him formally and superficially, but to imbrace

---

converted to Christianity and eventually joined the Reformation. He taught Hebrew at Cambridge but fled at the accession of Mary Tudor. He and Junius produced a five-volume translation of the Old Testament into Latin. It is this that Calamy cites.

[6]The Greek means literally "sufferings" and "instructions."

[7]experimentally: by experience.

[8]literally, not by the mind but by the heart.

[9]Gilbert de la Porrée (d. 1154), a medieval bishop and theologian.

him, and to love him really and cordially: And therefore the Church never left till shee had found Christ, and when shee had found him, she held him and would not let him go, Cant. 3:2, 3, 4.[10]

2. Not only to know God, but also to trust in him, 2 Cor. 1:9: "Wee had the sentence of death in our selves, that wee should not trust in our selves, but in God, which raiseth the dead." Note here, 1. That an Apostle is apt in time of prosperity to trust in himself. 2. That God brings his children to the gates of death, that they might learn not to trust in themselves, but in God, which raiseth the dead, that is, from a dead and desperate condition.

3. Not only to know God, but to know our selves, which two are the chief parts of Christian Religion: It is said of the Prodigal, that when hee was in adversity, then hee came to himself, Luke 15:17: "And when hee came to himself." He was spiritually distracted, when hee was in prosperity: Afflictions teach us to know that wee are but men, according to that of David, Psalm 9:20: Put them in fear, O Lord, that they may know themselves to bee but men. Caligula and Domitian, Emperors of Rome, who in prosperity would bee called Gods, when it thundred from Heaven, were so terrified, that then they knew they were but men. In prosperity wee forget our mortality. Adversity causeth us to know, not only that wee are men, but frail men, that God hath us between his hands (as it is Ezek. 21:17), and can as easily crush us, as wee do moths: That wee are in God's hands, as the Clay in the hands of the Potter: That hee hath an absolute soveraignty over us, and that wee depend upon him for our being, well-being, and eternal-being.

These things wee know feelingly and practically in the day of affliction. And it much concerns us to know these things, and to know them powerfully. For this will make us stand in awe of God, and study to serve and please him. Hee that depends upon a man for his livelihood, knowing that hee hath him at an advantage, and can easily undo him, will certainly endeavor to comply with him, and to obtain his favour. The ground of all service and obedience is dependence. And did wee really and experimentally know our dependence upon God, and the advantages hee hath us at, wee could not, wee would not but comply with him, and labour above all things to gain his love and favour.

2. God's aim in afflicting his children, is either to keep them from sin, or when they have sinned, to bring them to repentance for it, and from it.

1. To keep them from sin: This made him send an Angel of Satan to buffet Paul, lest hee should bee lifted up in pride, and exalted above measure, 2 Cor. 12:7.

2. When they have sinned, to bring them to repentance for it, and from it. God brings his children low, not to trample upon them, but to make them low in their own eyes, and to humble them for sin, Deut. 8:2. God brings them into the deep waters, not to drown them, but to wash and cleanse them, Isa. 27:9. "By this [therefore] shall the iniquity of Jacob bee purged, and this is all the fruit, to take away [his] sin," &c. Afflictions (when Sanctified) are divine hammers, to break, and as Moses his rod, to cleave our rocky hearts in peeces.

1. They open the eyes to see sin, *Oculos quos culpa claudit, paena aperit*. When the Brethren of Joseph were in adversity then they saw (and not before) the greatnesse of their sin in selling their Brother, Gen. 42:21.

They open the ear to Discipline. In prosperity wee turn a deaf ear to the voice

---

[10]This discussion depends upon the interpretation of the biblical Canticles, or Song of Solomon, as an allegory of the love of Christ and the church for each other.

of the charmer, though he charm never so wisely. But adversity openeth the ear, and causeth us to attend; When God spake upon Mount Sinai in a terrible manner, then the people said unto Moses, "Speak thou unto us, all that the Lord our God shall speak unto thee, and wee will hear it, and do it," Deut. 5:27. Memorable is that Text, Jer. 2:24: "A wilde Ass used to the Wilderness, that snuffeth up the wind at her pleasure, on [in] her occasion who can turn her away? all they that seek her, will not weary themselves, in her month they shall finde her;" in her month, that is, when she is great with young, and near her time. A wicked man in the day of his prosperity, is like a wilde Ass used to the wilderness, hee snuffeth at any that shall reprove him, hee is of an uncircumcised ear,[11] and a rebellious heart, but in his month, that is, when hee is bigge with Afflictions, then hee will be easily found; this will open his ear to discipline.

3. They will open the mouth to confess sin, Judg. 10:15.

4. They will command us to depart from iniquity, Job. 36:8, 9, 10.

Afflictions are God's furnaces, to purge out the dross of our sins, God's files to pare off our spiritual rust, God's fannes to winnow out our chaffe. In prosperity wee gather much soil, but adversity purgeth and purifieth us. This is its proper work, to work out unrighteousness, Dan. 11:35, Dan. 12:10.

3. God's end is not only to keep us from sin, but to make us holy and righteous; therefore it is said, Isa. 26:9, "When thy judgements are in the earth, the inhabitants of the world will learn righteousness." And Heb. 12:10.—"Hee for our profit, that wee may bee partakers of his holiness." As the waters that drowned the old world, did not hurt the Ark of Noah, but bare it up above the earth, and as they increased, so the Ark was lifted up nearer and nearer to Heaven: So afflictions (when sanctified) do not prejudice the Saints of God, but lift them up nearer unto God in Holiness, and heavenly-mindednesse.

4. God's design in afflicting his children, is to make the world bitter unto them, and Christ sweet. 1. To imbitter the world: There are two lame leggs upon which all worldly things stand, uncertainty and insufficiency. All earthly things are like the earth, founded upon nothing.[12] They are like houses made of wax, that quickly melt away. Riches, and honours, wife, and children, have wings, and flye away; they are like unto Absolom's mule, they will fail us, when wee have most need of them;[13] They may puffe up the soul, but they cannot satisfie it, *inflare possunt, satiare animam non possunt:* They are all vanity and vexation of spirit, so saith the Preacher;[14] but most people in time of health, will not beleeve these things; but when some great sickness betides them, this is as a real Sermon, to make out the truth of them; then they see, that a Velvet slipper cannot cure the Gout, nor a golden cap the head ache, Prov. 10:4, That riches avail not in the day of wrath, and this imbitters the world.

2. To make Christ sweet and precious. When Christ and his Disciples were in a ship together, Mat. 8:25, it is said, That Christ was asleep, and as long as the Sea was calm, his Disciples suffered him to sleep, but when they were ready to bee drowned, then they awoke Christ, and said, Master, save us, wee perish. Even the best of Saints, when fatted with outward plenty

---

[11]Allusion to Jeremiah 6:10.

[12]i.e., the world does not stand on a base.

[13]When Absalom, King David's rebellious son, caught his hair in a branch, his mule rode on, leaving him hanging there. 2 Sam. 18:9.

[14]The Preacher is the spokesman in the Old Testament book of Ecclesiastes.

and abundance, are prone to suffer Christ to lye asleep within them, and so neglect the lively actings of Faith upon Christ: But when the storms of affliction, and outward calamity begin to arise, and they are ready to bee overwhelmed with distresses, then none but Christ, none but Christ.

5. God's design in afflicting his children, is to prove, and improve, their graces.

1. To prove their graces, Rev. 2:10, Deut. 8:2, to prove the truth, and the strength of them. 1. The truth and sincerity of their graces; For this cause hee loaded Job with afflictions, to try whether hee served God for his Cammels and Oxen, or for love to God. As Solomon's sword tried the true Mother from the false,[15] So the sword of affliction discovers the sincere Christian from the Hypocrite. Distresses are divine touchstones, to try whether wee bee true or counterfeit Saints; That grace is true, which upon tryal is found true. 2. To try the strength of our graces: For it requires a strong faith to endure great afflictions. That Faith which will suffice for a little affliction, will not suffice for a great one. Peter had faith enough to come to Christ upon the Sea, but as soon as the storm began to arise, his Faith began to fail, and Christ said, "Why art thou afraid, O thou of little Faith?" Mat. 14:30, 31. It must bee a strong Faith that must keep us from sinking in the day of great Distress.

2. To improve our graces. It is reported of the Lionesse, that she leaves her young ones, till they have almost killed themselves with roaring and howling, and then at last gasp, shee relieves them, and by this means they become more couragious.[16] So

God brings his children into the deeps, and suffers Jonah to bee three daies and three nights in the belly of the Whale, and David to cry till his throat was dry, Psalm 69:3, and suffers his Apostles to bee all the night in a great storm till the fourth watch, and then hee comes and rebukes the winds, and by this means hee mightily increaseth their patience and dependence upon God, and their Faith in Christ. As the Palm-tree, the more it is depressed,[17] the higher, stronger, and fruitfuller, it growes; So doth the graces of God's people.

Lastly, God's aim in afflicting his people, is to put an edge upon their prayers, and all their other holy services.

1. Upon Prayer: What a famous Prayer did Manasseh make, when hee was under his iron fetters. It is thrice mentioned, 2 Chron. 33:13, 18, 19. When Paul was struck off his horse, and struck with blindness, then hee prayed to purpose. Therefore it is said, Act. 9:11, "Behold hee prayeth!" In prosperity wee pray heavily and drowsily, but adversity adds wings to our prayers, Isa. 26:16. The very heathen Marriners cryed aloud to God in a storm. It is an ordinary saying, *Qui nescit orare discat navigare,* There are no Saylors so wicked, but they will pray when in a great storm.

2. Upon Preaching: Prosperity glutteth the spiritual appetite, adversity whetteth it.

3. Upon a Sacrament: How sweet is a Sacrament to a true Saint after a long and great sickness.

1. It makes God, and the word of God precious. If God sets our Corn-fields on fire (as Absalom did Joab's)[18] then hee shall bee sure to cause us to come running to him: And how sweet is a Text of Scripture to a childe of God in the hour of his distress?

By all this it appears that God afflicts

---

[15]King Solomon threatened to cut a child in half in order to determine who was its true mother, 1 Kings 3:16-28.

[16]This is the kind of lore found in the medieval bestiaries, which combined pseudoscience with a moral.

[17]depressed: pressed down.

[18]To get Joab's attention, 2 Sam. 14:28-31.

his children not to hurt them, but to help them, and that God hath many glorious and gracious ends and aimes in afflicting of them. Therefore it is that David saith of himself in the 71. verse of this Psalm, "It is good for me that I have been afflicted, that I might learn thy statutes;" Hee never said, It is good for mee that I have been in prosperity; but hee rather saith the contrary in the 67. verse, "Before I was afflicted, I went astray, but now I have kept thy word." God's people will bless God as much (if not more) in Heaven, for their adversity, than for their prosperity.

Use 1. Let us not pass rash censures upon persons under great afflictions. Say not, such a woman is a greater sinner than others, because more afflicted. This was the fault of Job's friends, and God expresseth his anger against them for it, Job 42:7: "My wrath is kindled against thee, and [against] thy two friends, for you have not spoken the thing that is right," &c. This was the fault of the Barbarians, Act 28:4: When they saw the venimous beast hang upon the hand of Paul, "they said among themselves, no doubt this man is a murderer," &c. But remember they were Barbarians. It is a sign of a Barbarian, not of a Christian, to pass a rash censure upon persons in affliction. Think you (saith Christ) that "those eighteen upon whom the Tower in Siloam fell and slew them, that they were sinners above all men that dwelt in Jerusalem. I tell you, nay, but except you repent, ye shall all likewise perish," Luke 13:4, 5. Think you that they which have the stone and gout in extremity, that have cancers in their faces and breasts, are greater sinners than others? I tell you nay, &c. For my part, if I would censure any, it should bee such as live wickedly, and meet with no affliction; These have the black brand of reprobation upon them. These are men

designed to damnation. Ambrose[19] would not tarry a night in the house of a Gentleman that had never in all his life been afflicted, for fear (as hee said) lest some great and sudden judgement should betide it. But when I see a godly woman afflicted, then I say, this is not so much for her sin, as for her tryal; this is not to hurt her, but to teach her to know God, and to know her self, to break her heart for Sin, and from sin, to make the world bitter, and Christ sweet. God hath put her into the fire of affliction, to refine her, and make her a vessel fit for his use. God is striking her with the hammer of affliction, that shee may bee squared, and made ready to bee laid in the heavenly Jerusalem.

Use 2. Here is rich comfort to the children of God, under the greatest afflictions. For the best of Saints are subject to the worst afflictions: This is the lot of all God's children, Christ himself not excepted. Afflictions (indeed) considered in their own nature, are evil things, and so are called, Amos 5:13. They are part of the curse due to sin, the fruit of God's revenging wrath; they are as a biting and stinging Serpent. And to a wicked man, remaining wicked, they are the beginning of Hell: Unsanctified afflictions parboil[20] a wicked man for hell and damnation. But now to a child of God, they have lost both their name and nature, they are not punishments properly, but chastisements, not τιμωείαι, but παιδείαι. They are not satisfactory, but castigatory.[21] Jesus Christ hath taken away the sting of these Serpents; they are not fiery, but brazen Serpents, they have a healing, not a hurting power.[22] Christ hath

---

[19]See n. 1.

[20]parboil: precook.

[21]The Greek means literally, "not punishments but corrections."

[22]Like the brazen serpent used by Moses to heal the Israelites, Num. 21:9.

removed the curse, and bitterness of them; as the wood sweetned the waters of Marah, Exod. 15:25. So Christ's Cross hath sweetened the bitterness of Afflictions.

These are eight comfortable considerations to chear the heart of a childe of God in the day of his distress.

1. God never afflicts his people, but out of pure necessity, 1 Pet. 1:6, "Though now for a season, if need bee, yee are in heavinesse." As a most loving Father, never corrects his childe, but when hee is forced to it. Hee willingly provides for his childe, but punisheth him unwillingly. So God freely loadeth with his blessings, but hee never chastiseth his children, but when forced to it, therefore hee saith expressly, Lam. 3:33, "Hee doth not afflict willingly," Isa. 27:1, "Fury is not in mee." It is wee that put Thunderbolts in God's hand. If the Sun did not first draw up the vapours from the earth, there would never bee any thundering, or lightening. God would never thunder from Heaven with his judgements, if our sins did not first cry to Heaven for punishment. As Christ whipt the sellers of Oxen and Sheep out of the Temple with a whip made (in all probability) of their own cords; So God never scourgeth us, but it is with a whip made of our own sins, Prov. 5:22. Rom 2:5—"Thou treasurest up to thy self," &c. God hath a double treasure, a treasure of mercy, and a treasure of wrath; his treasure of mercy is alwaies full, but his treasure of wrath is empty, till wee fill it by our sins. And therefore when God punisheth his children, hee calls it a strange work, and a strange act,[23] Isa. 28:21. It is observed of the Bee, that it never stings, but when provoked: Sure I am, that God never afflicts his children, but out of pure necessity.

2. Not only out of pure necessity, but out of true and real love; as I have shewed, Heb. 12:6, 7, 8.

Objection: Do not divine afflictions proceed out of anger? Was not God angry with Moses for speaking unadvisedly with his lips? And angry with David for his Adultery, and thereupon afflicted both of them?

Answer. This anger was a Fatherly anger, rooted in love; It was not *ira quae reprobat,* but *ira quae purgat:* It was not *ira hostilis & exterminativa,* but *ira paterna & medicinalis.*[24] As it is a great punishment, for God sometimes not to punish, Isaiah 1:5, Hos. 4:14, So it is a great mercy, sometimes for God to withdraw his mercy.

3. Afflictions are a part of Divine predestination. That God which hath elected us to salvation, hath also elected us unto afflictions, 1 Thes. 3:3, "That no man should bee moved by these afflictions; for you your selves know that wee are appointed thereunto." The same love with which God elects us, and bestoweth Christ, and his Spirit upon us, with the very same love hee afflicts us.

4. They are part of the gracious Covenant which God hath made with his people, Psalm 89:31, 32, 33. In which words we have three things considerable:[25]

[a.] A supposition of sin; "If his children forsake my Law," &c. For sin is alwayes *causa sine qua non,* the cause without which God would never chastise us, and for the most part it is the cause for which.

[b.] Wee have a gracious promise, "Then I will visit their transgression with the rod, and their iniquity with stripes."

[c.] Wee have a merciful qualification: "Nevertheless my loving kindnesse will I

---

[23]Strange: alien to God's nature; also, a hidden mystery of God.

[24]The Latin means "not anger that condemns, but anger that purges;" not hostile and exterminating anger, but paternal and medicinal anger.

[25]considerable: to be considered.

not utterly take from him, nor suffer my faithfulness to fail, my Covenant will I not break,'' &c.[26] Afflictions are not only mercies, but Covenant-mercies. Therefore David saith, Psalm 119:75—''and that thou in faithfulness hast afflicted mee.'' God would bee unfaithful, if hee did not afflict his children.

5. Consider that afflictions are part of the Saint's blessednesse, Job 5:17: ''Behold! happy is the man whom God correcteth,'' &c. Behold (saith Eliphaz)[27] and wee had need behold, and consider it, for there are few that beleeve it, and yet it is most true, That afflictions (when sanctified) when they are not only corrections, but instructions, then they are evidences that wee are in a blessed condition. Eliphaz his saying must bee interpreted by what David saith, Psalm 94:12: ''Blessed is the man whom thou chastenest, O Lord, and teachest out of thy Law;'' It is not correction simply, but correction joyned with instruction, which intitles us to happiness. Job even while hee was upon the dung-hill, wonders that God should set his heart so much upon him, as to visit him every morning, and trye him every moment, Job 7:17, 18. Job upon the dung-hill was happier than Adam in Paradise. Adam in Paradise was conquered by the Devil; but Job upon the dung-hill overcame the Devil. Lazarus in his Rags was happier than Dives in his Robes; Philpot in his Cole-house, than Bonner in his Palace;[28] and godly Mr. Whitaker upon his bed of pain, than a wicked man upon his bed of Down. There

were many in Christ's time who would never have known him, or come to him, had it not been for their bodily diseases.

6. Consider the gracious and merciful ends, aims and designes, that God hath in afflicting his people; what these are, ye have heard already.

7. The sweet and precious promises, which hee hath made to his children in the day of their adversity, to comfort them, and support them; what these are, you shall hear afterwards.

8. Consider that all afflictions shall work at last for the good of God's children, Rom. 8:28. Though they are not *bonae,* yet they shall bee *in bonum;* Though they are not good in themselves, yet they shall turn to their good. God beats his children, as wee do our cloaths in the Sun, onely to beat out the Moths; God puts them into the fiery furnace, not to hurt them, but onely to untie the bonds of their sins, as hee dealt with the three children, Dan. 3:25.[29] God will either deliver them out of their afflictions, or send them to Heaven by them; Wherefore comfort one another with these words.

Use 3: If the best of Saints are subject in this life unto many, great, and tedious afflictions, then let us.

1. Expect	
2. Prepare for	Afflictions
3. Improve	

1. Let us expect Afflictions; for Christ hath said expresly, John 16:33, ''In the world yee shall have tribulation.'' There is in every child of God,

a. *Sufficiens Fundamentum,* a sufficient Foundation for God to build a house of correction upon: There is sin enough to deserve affliction.

b. There is *sufficiens Motivum,* Mo-

---

[26]Ps. 89:32-33.

[27]One of Job's friends.

[28]John Philpot was the Protestant archdeacon of Winchester who was burned at the stake in 1555 during the reign of Queen Mary; Edmund Bonner was a Henrician bishop who joined the persecutors during the reign of Mary and was accordingly a target of Protestant opprobrium. This story of Philpot in the coal bin comes from John Foxe's ''Book of Martyrs.''

[29]Daniel's friends who were miraculously preserved in the midst of the fiery furnace, Dan. 3:1-30.

tives sufficient to prevail with God, to chastize them when they sin against him; some of these you have heard already, let mee adde one more: Because hee is more dishonoured by the sins of his own children, than by the sins of wicked men: As it is a greater discredit to an earthly Father, when his own children, than when other men's children, live wickedly; so it is a greater disparagement to our heavenly Father when his own Sons and Daughters, than when the Devil's children, transgresse his Law: And therefore God will chastize them sooner, surer, and more than others. 1. Sooner, Rom. 2:9: "Tribulation and anguish upon every soul of man that doth evil, of the Jew first, and also of the Gentile." First, the Jew, and then the Gentile. 2. Surer than others, Amos 3:2 "You only have I known of all the families of the earth, therefore I will punish you for all your iniquities." 3. More than others, Lam. 4:6: "The punishment of the iniquity of the Daughter of my people, is greater than the punishment of the sin of Sodom," &c. Dan. 9:12: "under the whole heaven hath not been done, as hath been done upon Jerusalem."

c. There is *sufficiens necessitas,* sufficient necessity to provoke God to afflict them. It is needful that the Wheat bee winnowed, that so the chaffe may bee separated from it. It is needful that the Wind blow upon the Wheat, to cleanse it, and that Gold bee put into the furnace, to purge and purifie it. When the Sheep of Christ are divided one from the other in judgement, and affections, when separated in Doctrine, Worship, and Discipline, It is very needful that God should send afflictions and distresses, which may bee (as the Shepherd's Dog) very serviceable and instrumental, to unite them together, and to gather them into one Sheepfold. And therefore let the Saints of God expect afflictions.

2. Let us prepare and provide against the day of tribulation. Let us provide,

[a.] A stock of graces. For sickness is a time to spend grace, but not to get grace. A Christian in sickness without grace, is like a souldier in war without armour, like a house in stormy weather without a foundation, and like the men of the old world, when ready to bee drowned without an Ark. Woe bee to that person that hath his graces to get when hee should use them! And therefore if wee would bee comforted in the day of tribulation, wee must provide aforehand a furniture of graces.

1. A true Faith (for a painted Faith will avail no more than a painted helmet, or a painted ship) and not only a True, but also a strong Faith. A little faith will faint under great afflictions; when the winds began to blow fiercely, Peter's little Faith began to fail, Matth. 14:30.

2. A great measure of patience to inable us to wait quietly and contentedly, till God come in with help, for many times hee tarrieth till the fourth watch of the night, as hee did, Matth. 14:25. And therefore wee have need of patience to keep us from murmuring or repining.

3. A great stock of Self-denial, humility, repentance, contempt of the world, and heavenly-mindednesse. Hee that is furnished with grace in an evil hour, will bee as safe and secure, as Noah was in the Ark, in the time of the deluge, or as those were who had sufficiency of corn in the time of the seven years dearth in Aegypt.

[b.] A stock of assurance of salvation: For though a man hath never so much grace, yet if hee wants the assurance of it, hee cannot receive any comfort by it in the day of his distresse. Jacob was not at all quieted in his spirit, for Joseph's being alive, till hee came to know of it. And therefore wee must not only provide grace, but the assurance of grace, that wee may be able to say with confidence, as Job did upon the dung-hill, Job 19:25, "I know that my Redeemer liveth," and with the holy Apostle, Rom. 8:38, "I am perswaded, that neither death, nor life, nor Angels, nor principalities, nor powers, nor things present, nor things to come, nor height, nor depth, nor any other creature shall bee able to separate us from the love of God, which is in Christ Jesus our Lord." That man who hath got a Scripture assurance of his salvation, will bee more than a conqueror in the day of his distresse.

[c.] A stock of divine experiences. Happy is that man that lodgeth up in his heart all the former Experiences hee hath had of God's love and mercy towards him, and knoweth how to argue from them in the day of calamity; Thus did Moses in his prayer to God, Numb. 14:19: "Pardon I beseech thee, the iniquity of this people, according unto the greatness of thy mercy, and as thou hast forgiven this people from Egypt, even until now." Because God had forgiven them, therefore Moses intreats him to forgive them; this argument is drawn from former experience. And thus David incourageth himself, 1 Sam. 17:37, "The Lord hath delivered mee out of the paw of the Lion, and out of the paw of the Bear, and hee will deliver mee out of the hand of the Philistine." Thus also Paul reasoneth, 2 Cor. 1:10, "Who delivered us from so great a death, and doth deliver, and in whom wee trust that hee will yet deliver us!" Divine experiences are the Saint's great incouragements in the day of Affliction. Blessed is the man that hath his quiver full of these arrows.

[d.] A stock of Sermons. Wee must do with Sermons, as the Trades-men do with the mony they get; some of it they lay out for their present use, and some of it they lay up against the time of sicknesse. That man is an ill husband, and an unthrifty tradesman that makes no provision for old age, or for an evil day; and that man is an un-profitable hearer of the word, who doth not stock and store himself with Sermons, whereby hee may be comforted in the hour of affliction. And therefore the Prophet Isaiah adviseth us, Isa. 42:23, "to hear for the time to come," or (as it is in the Hebrew) for the after-time. Sermons are not only to bee heard for our present use, but to bee laid up for after-times, that when wee lye upon our sick-beds, and cannot hear Sermons, wee may then live upon the Sermons wee have heard.

[e.] And lastly, Wee must prepare and provide a stock of Scripture-promises, which will bee as so many reviving Cordials, to chear us, and as so many spiritual Anchors, to uphold us from perishing in the day of our tribulation. What these promises are, you shall hear afterwards: These upheld David in the hour of his distresse, and therefore hee saith in the Text, "Unless thy Law had been my delight, I had perished in mine affliction." If this our dear Sister had not had this stock, shee had been quite overwhelmed under the grievousnesse of her tormenting pains. Bee wise therefore, O yee Saints of God, and prepare these five provisions in the time of health, that so you may live joyfully in the time of sicknesse.

3. As wee must expect and provide for afflictions, so also wee must labour (when afflicted) to improve them for our spiritual benefit and advantage. Wee must pray more for the sanctification of them, than for their removal: It was not the staffe of Elisha that revived the dead childe, but Elisha himself. It was not the troubling of the waters of the Pool of Bethesda, that made them healing, but the comming down of the Angel. It was not the Clay and spittle that cured the blinde eyes, but Christ's anointing them with it. It was not the cloak of Elijah that divided the waters, but the God

of Elijah:[30] Troubles, stroaks, blows, afflictions, and distresses will do us no good, unless the Lord bee pleased to make them effectual; And therefore let us pray unto God that hee would give us grace together with our affliction, That hee would adde instruction to his correction, that hee would make us good schollars in the school of afflictions, and inable us to take out all those excellent lessons, which hee would have us to learn in it, that thereby wee may come to know God more powerfully, and experimentally, and to know our selves, and our own frailty, and our absolute dependence upon God more effectually, that thereby wee may bee more purified and refined, that the wind of temptation may cleanse us from the chaffe of our corruption, that wee may learn righteousness by God's judgements, and bee made partakers of his holinesse. Such a good Scholar was Manasses, hee got more good by his Iron chain, than by his Golden chain: Such another was the Prodigal child, who was happier amongst the Swine, than when in his Father's house; Such was Paul, his being strucken down to the ground, raised him up to Heaven; by the blindness of his body, his soul received sight; and hee was turned from a persecuting Saul, to a persecuted Paul. Such another was David, who professeth of himself, that it was good for him that hee was afflicted; and such Scholars ought wee to bee.

There are some that are arrant dunces in this School, that are like unto the bush which Moses saw, which burned with fire, but was not consumed; the fire did not consume the thorny bush. Many such thorny sinners are burnt up with the fire of divine afflictions, but their sins are not consumed. Of these the Prophets complain, Amos 4:6-12—"Yet they have not returned," &c. Jer. 5:3: "Thou hast stricken them, but they have not grieved; thou hast consumed them, but they have refused to receive correction; they have made their faces harder than a rock, they have refused to return." Rocks and stones by hewing and polishing may bee made fit for a building: But there are some men who by no afflictions will be amended. The Mountains melt at the presence of the Lord, and the rocks rend asunder, when hee is angry: But there are some that have made their faces harder than the Rocks, and the Mountains, and are not at all affected with God's anger. Of such as these Bernard complains, *Multi humiliati, pauci humiles, corripimur, sed non corrigimur, plectimur, fed non flectimur; Multo facilius fregeris, quam flexeris. Non cessant vitia civium usque ad excidia civitatum; Prius est interire quam corrigi. Prius ipsos, quam in ipsis vitia non esse.*[31]

There are others that are the worse for their afflictions, like the Smith's Anvil, the more they are strucken, the harder they are: Such a one was King Ahaz, 2 Chron. 28:22: "In the time of his distress hee did trespass yet more against the Lord:" There is a brand put upon him—This is that King Ahaz, that wicked King Ahaz, that repro-

---

[30]Elisha's staff could not raise a dead child, but the prophet in person could, 2 Kings 4:26-27; John 5:4, a verse omitted in recent translations because of poor manuscript attestation, says: "For an angel went down at a certain season into the pool, and had troubled the water: whosoever then first after the troubling of the water stepped in was made whole of whatsoever disease he had;" Elijah parted the waters by striking them with his mantle, 2 Kings 2:8.

[31]St. Bernard of Clairvaux was a twelfth-century mystic and monastic leader. Calvin had often quoted him, and so did the Puritans. The Latin may be translated "many are lowly, few humble; many are reproached, but not corrected; punished, but not changed; many are more easily broken than turned about (converted); the vices of the city do not pass away even up to the disappearance of the city; rather to perish than to be corrected; rather to be what one is, than not to be vicious."

bate King Ahaz. As Pearls put in Vinegar lose their colour and beauty, so many, when under God's hand, lose all their glory and excellency, and begin to distrust God's providence, to call his justice into question, to murmure and repine against God's dealings, and to use unlawful means for their deliverance. Of these the Prophet Isaiah complains, Isa. 1:5, "Why should you bee stricken any more? Yee will revolt more and more;" Such was Ahaziah, 2 King. 1:2, that sought for help from Baalzebub the god of Ekron; and such was Saul, who sought to the Witch of Endor for health in the day of his distress.

Both of these sorts are in a sad and miserable condition; For God hath two furnaces, the furnace of affliction, and the furnace of hell-fire. If the first Furnace will not purge us, the second will everlastingly consume us. As the Roman Consuls had a man appointed to go before them, carrying a Rod, and an Axe; a Rod for the punishing of corrigible offenders, an Axe for the destruction of incorrigible; So God hath his Rod, and his Axe, his Pruning-knife, and his Chopping-knife, his Warning-peeces, and his Murdering-peeces. Afflictions are his Rods to correct us for our sin, his Pruning-knife to pare off our luxuriant branches; his Warning-peeces to call upon us to repent.

But if his Warning-peeces will do us no good, wee must expect his Murdering-peeces. If his Pruning-knife will not amend us, his Chopping-knife will confound us. If his Rods will not reclaim us, then his Axe will hew us down, and cast us into everlasting fire. God hath three houses, the house of Instruction, of Correction, and of Destruction. The place where God's people meet to hear his word, is his house of Instruction. And if we profit in this house, he will never carry us unto the house of Correction. But if we bee stubborn and rebellious in the house of Instruction, then he will send us to the house of Correction. And if we profit in this house, he will never send us into the house of Destruction. But if wee continue incorrigible in the house of Correction, hee will inevitably send us to the house of Destruction, that is, unto hell fire.

And therefore whensoever God brings us into the School of Affliction, let us labour to bee good Schollars in it; and to answer all those ends, aimes, and designes which God hath in afflicting of us. Let us pray to God that our afflictions may bee Divine Hammers, to break our hearts for sin, and from sin, may make the world bitter, and Christ more precious, may prove, and improve our graces, and may put an edge upon all holy duties.

There are two things I would have you in an especial manner to labour after.

1. Labour when afflicted, to know the meaning of God's Rod.

2. That the good you get by afflictions, may abide upon you after your recovery from them.

1. You must labour to know the meaning of God's Rod, and what the particular arrant[32] is, which hee hath to you in the day of your distresses; you must do as David did, 2 Sam. 21:1: hee inquired of the Lord to know the reason why hee sent a Famine amongst them. So must you, you must pray as Job doth, Job 10:2. "Shew mee, O Lord, wherefore thou contendest with mee." When the cause of a disease is found out, it is half cured. Your great care therefore must bee to study to know the particular cause and reason, why God turns your prosperity into adversity. The Prophet Micah tells us, Micah 6:9, That the Rod hath a voyce, and that the man of wisdome shall see God's Name upon it. There is a great measure of spiritual Art and Wisdome required, to inable a man to hear this voice,

---

[32]arrant: older spelling of errand, with the obsolete meaning of a message sent.

and to understand the language of it. A spiritual Fool cannot do it.

Question. What must wee do, that wee may understand the voice of the Rod?

Answer. You must know, that the Rod of God ordinarily speaks three languages; it is sent for correction for sin, for the tryal and exercise of Grace and for instruction in holiness; Sometimes indeed it is sent only for tryal and instruction, and not at all for sin. Upon this account was Job afflicted, and the blinde man, John 9:3. But for the most part it hath a threefold voice; it is appointed for instruction, probation, and also for correction, Lam. 3:39, Isa. 42:24, Luke 1:20, 1 Cor. 11:30.

Question. How shall a man know whether his afflictions bee only for tryal and instruction, and not at all for sin?

Answer. The safest and best way for a Christian in this case, is to beleeve that all his afflictions are both for trial and instruction, and also for sin: Indeed when hee seeth another man, who is very godly, grievously diseased, hee may charitably beleeve, that this is for his tryal, and not for his sin; but when it is his own case, then (as D. Ames saith most excellently) *Aequissimum, tutissimum, & Deo gratissimum est, ut in afflictionibus omnibus peccata nostra intueamur, quae illas vel directe procurarunt, vel saltem promeruerunt. Quamvis enim omnes afflictiones non immittantur semper directe & precipue propter peccatum, peccatum tamen est omnium afflictionum fons & fundamentum,* Rom. 5:12. "It is most equal, most safe, and most acceptable to God, to have an eye upon our sins, which have either directly procured them, or at least deserved them. For though afflictions are not alwayes sent directly and especially for sin, yet sin is the original and foundation of all afflictions."[33]

Question. What course must wee take to finde out what that sin is in particular, for which God corrects us?

Answer: 1. Sometimes wee may read our sin in our punishment. Adonibezek, though a Heathen King, did this, Judg. 1:7: "Threescore and ten kings, having their Thumbs, and their great Toes cut off, gathered their meat under my table; as I have done, so God hath requited mee." I read of holy Ephrem, that hee was converted by the suitableness of his affliction, unto the sin hee had committed,[34] for hee saw clearly that his misery came not by chance, but from God immediately, and for sin. As a man may sometime gather the disease of the Patient by observing the Physitian's Bill, so hee may guess at his sin, by considering his punishment.

2. Consider what that sin is for which thy conscience doth most of all accuse thee. Conscience is God's Vicegerent, his bosome Preacher. And when wee sleight the voyce of conscience, God seconds it with the voyce of his rod, which speaks the very same language that conscience doth.

3. Consider what is the sin of thy Complexion,[35] and Constitution, what is thy *Dilectum delictum*, thy *peccatum in delitiis*, thy beloved sin, what is that sin to which thou art most of all inclined; and if that sin prevaile over thee, and thou canst not say with David, Psalm 18:23, "I have kept my self from mine iniquity," it is very probable that for the subduing of that sin, thou art corrected of God.

4. If ever thou hast been at the gates of death, despairing of life, consider what that sin was, which did then most of all trouble and perplexe thy conscience; or if ever thou hast been in a dream, supposing thy self to

---

[33]William Ames (1575-1633) was a Puritan theologian who taught theology at the University of Franeker in the Netherlands.

[34]i.e., he was converted by the appropriateness of his afflictions for his sins. Ephrem is probably Ephraem Syrus, a fourth-century Syrian church father.

[35]complexion: temperament, disposition.

bee dying, and breathing out thy last; what was that sinne which did then most of all affright thee. It is very likely that God by afflicting thee, intends to get that sin more conquered and mortified.

5. Consider what those sins are for which thy godly Minister (under whose care thou livest) doth reprove thee, and of which thy true and real friends do accuse thee; for, if thou hast sleighted the voice of thy faithful Minister and friends; surely God out of his love to thee, followeth their advice with the voice of his Rod, that thereby hee may open thine ear to discipline, and command thee to depart from those iniquities.

But if thou canst not finde out that particular sin, for which God afflicts thee, labour to repent of every sin, and then thou wilt bee sure to repent of that sin. If thou canst not finde out the Bee that stings thee, pull down the whole hive, or the thorn that pricks thee, pull down the whole hedge. Do that out of wisdome, which Herod did out of malice, who because hee could not finde out the Babe Jesus, killed all the children in Bethlehem from two years old, and under, that so hee might bee sure to kill Jesus. Let us seek the utter ruine and death of all our sins, and then wee shall bee sure to destroy that sin for which God afflicts us, and when the cause is removed, the disease will forth-with bee cured, and the Almighty pacified, and reconciled unto us.

2. Let us labour that the good wee reap by our afflictions, may abide upon us after our recovery from them. There are very many who while they are under the Rod, seem to bee very penitent, and do purpose and promise to amend their lives, but as soon as the Rod is removed, they returne like the Dog to the vomit, &c.[36] Such was Pharaoh, whilst he was plagued he confessed his sin, and prayed for pardon, but

as soon as ever the judgement was gone, hee hardened his heart. Such were the Israelites, Psalm 78:34, 35, 36, 37, "They were not stedfast, they turned back." Just like a truantly School-boy, who while his Master is whipping him, will promise any thing, but when it is done, forgets presently to doe what hee promised: Or like unto water, which while it is upon the fire is very hot, but as soon as ever it is taken off the fire, presently groweth cold. I knew a man who in the time of his sickness was so terrified in his conscience for his sins, that hee made the very bed to shake upon which hee lay, and cried out all night long, I am damned, I am damned, and made many and great Protestations of amendment of life if God would bee pleased to recover him. In a little while hee did recover, and being recovered, was as bad, and as wicked as ever before.

And therefore let us labour that the good wee get by our afflictions, may not vanish away with our afflictions, but may abide on us after wee are recovered, that wee may bee able to say with David, It is good for mee that I was afflicted, not onely that I am, but that I was. David praiseth God in health, for the good hee had got in sickness, and which still abode with him. Let us say with the same Prophet, Psalm 66:13, 14, "I will go into thy house with burnt offerings, I will pay thee my vows which my lips have uttered, and my mouth hath spoken, when I was in trouble." Let us pray unto God that his afflictions may not onely skin over our spiritual diseases, and coup up our sins, but mortifie them, and so change our natures, that wee may never return to folly.

I will conclude this point with a famous saying of Plinius Secondus,[37] wor-

---

[36]Prov. 26:11, 2 Pet. 2:22.

[37]Pliny the younger, a Roman provincial governor of the early second century, was known for his letters and an important early reference to persecution of Christians.

thy to bee written in letters of gold. A friend writes to him, and intreats him to give him advice how to frame his life, so as hee might live as becomes a good man. Hee returns him this answer: I will not prescribe many rules, there is this one only which I commend to thee above all other. *Ut tales esse perseveremus sani, quales nos futuros profitemur infirmi.* "Let us labour to continue and persevere to bee such, when wee are well, as wee purpose, and promise to our selves to bee, when wee are sick."

There is hardly any man so wicked, but hee will in sickness make many and great promises of a new life, and of universal reformation if God would restore him. Now then if we not onely bee such, but continue to bee such when restored, as wee promise to bee when sick, then wee shall bee excellent Schollars, in the School of Affliction, and God will either (as I have already said) deliver us out of afflicton, or send us to heaven by affliction. So much for the first Truth supposed.

Introduction to Benjamin Keach, *The Travels of True Godliness*

For a general introduction to Keach, see above, 107. What follows consists of a chapter taken from Keach's prose allegory, The Travels of True Godliness, From the Beginning of the World to this present Day; in an apt and Pleasant Allegory, Shewing the Troubles, Oppositions, Reproaches and Persecutions he hath met with in every Age *(London, 1684; Wing K98), 89-99. This third edition of a work first published in 1683 is the earliest edition of the work still extant.*

In the chapter reproduced here, the reader is presented with Godliness' appearance at the door of Mr. Formalist, who represents the outer forms of religion but is destitute of the inner spirit. Before this, Godliness had visited such characters as Legalist and Riches with similarly barren results. Keach had a strong sense of the worldly opposition with which the true Christian could expect to meet. Keach's allegory has much in common with those of John Bunyan in both form and ideas, but it lacks the literary skill of Bunyan.

The Travels of True Godliness

by Benjamin Keach

Chapter IX.

Shewing how Godliness came to one Mr. Formalist's Door, who bid him very welcome; but he suspecting his Integrity, and that he harboured divers grand Enemies of his, particularly one Hypocrisie; refused to go in: also How Hypocrisie came to be discovered; wherein you have his Character, or a clear and compendious Discription of him; shewing likewise, how Mr. Formalist at last refused to entertain True Godliness.

Godliness being (as I told you) informed that there was another great Professor[1] living in this Village or Town of Religion, he thought it was convenient for him to see whether he might not get a Lodging in his House, because he was a man whom all the Neighbourhood said had a great Love to True Godliness; nay, many verily thought he had for a long time taken up his Lodging with him, and wondered when they heard him ask for his House (for by that means they perceived he was a stranger to him) but it was a considerable time before he could find where he dwelt. For it appeared he was called by another Name, viz. Devotion; but at last coming by

---

[1]professor: one who professes religion.

one man's door and by another, he heard a man at Prayer, and he spoke so loud, that all who walked along the Street, with much ease might hear him; he then presently concluded it was very probable he might dwell there; and to his door he came, and knock'd as he us'd to do, and was soon heard.

Formal. Who's there?

Godli. My Name Sir, is True Godliness.

Formal. True Godliness, Pray Sir, come in; there is none in all the World I love more dearly; the best Room in all my house is at your Service; pray where have you been, and what News do you hear? Are the Imperialists[2] and Turks yet come to engage? how goes things in the World? How doth it fare with our poor Protestant Brethren in France?[3] What News from Scotland? when will the Times be better? I hear the Penal Laws are prosecuted severely against Dissenters:[4] Many such Questions he asked, and professed abundance of Respect to True Godliness (and as you heard) bid him come in, but never went about to open the door. Godliness was grieved to find him so full of words; but more especially because he took up his time, and troubled his head so much to enquire after News; nay and that too, when he should open to True Godliness; and just upon ending his Devotion; for it appears he had

---

[2]Imperialists: the Holy Roman Empire, often at war with the Turks in the sixteenth and seventeenth centuries.

[3]By the time of this publication, the situation of the French Protestants had grown very difficult. Later, in 1685, with the Revocation of the Edict of Nantes, they were forced either to flee the country or to adopt Roman Catholicism.

[4]The laws of the Clarendon Code, by which the Nonconformists were harassed. In 1683—the year of the publication of *The Travels of True Godliness*—the aftermath of the Rye House Plot had led to increased repression of Dissenters.

newly done Prayer; yet nevertheless Godliness very coolly answered him to this purpose.

Godli. Sir, As to your first Question, I answer (being willing to inform you where I have been) I have wandred about from place to place to seek entertainment, I mean a fit and convenient Lodging for a little time; for it will not be long e'er I have done travelling; but I am fallen into such an evil and perilous time, that scarcely any body will shew me the favour as to take me in, and make me welcome. Riches, Poverty, Youth and Old-age have all refused me, and shut their doors most basely upon me; and since I came into these parts, and particularly to your Town, where every one concluded I should be most kindly embraced, the very first man I came to hath denied me entertainment, nay, and not only so, but also called[5] me at his pleasure.

Formal. What man's that for God's sake?

Godli. Friend, don't take God's name in vain, I cannot bear it; but to answer your Question, the man is called Legalist.

Formal. O Sir, there is not a man in all this Town more haughty, proud and conceited than he; he concludes I warrant you, that he hath Godliness enough already; he makes in truth the whole of Religion to consist in Principles of Morality: I have heard him say, that if a man do lead or square his Life but as near as he can, according to the Law of the Ten Commandments, not being guilty of gross Sins, or wilfully breaks any Precepts of the Two Tables, he shall be saved: Now he never considers all the while the necessity of Faith and Regeneration, and although he trusteth thus to his own Righteousness, yet I could pick many holes in his Coat; for he is a very worldly, proud, and passionate[6]

---

[5]called: insulted, i.e., called me names.

[6]passionate: hot-tempered.

person; nay, and he himself confesseth he is a Sinner, and yet would be justified by the Law; whereas you know the least Sins, Lusts of the Heart, and evil Thoughts, are a breach of it, and the smallest breach is Death, and eternal Wrath, without a compensation made to offended Justice; and none was able to do this, but Jesus Christ, and none have the blessing of his undertaking, but such only who do believe.

Godli. You seem to have a good understanding, and can talk well, but how comes it about you let me stand all this time at your door? is this your kindness to me? what signifies your knowledg and parts,[7] except you entertain True Godliness.

Formal. I have opened (you may perceive) to you already, you are in my affections and I will further open to you; pray come in.

Godli. Nay do not mistake your self; you have opened to me in one respect, but not in another; you seem to like my form, but not my power; my external Rites, but not my internal Life. I am indeed received into your Head, but not into your Heart; I may be in your Judgment, worth embracing, but your will consents not to receive me; you like my Garb, but love not my Person; you are (I know) a Professor of me, but not a Possessor of me: The truth is, I Suspect you.

Formal. Suspect me Sir! for what?

Godli. That you have one or two implacable enemies of mine hid secretly in your House.

Formal. Who, I Sir! God forbid I should hide any cursed Enemies of True Godliness: Who are they? pray tell me their Names.

Godli. Old-Man, Carnal Affections, and Hypocrisie.

Formal. As touching the Old-Man,

there is no Christian (you know) can be quite rid of him; but God forbid I should shew him any countenance: And as to Carnal Affections, in this you do mistake; for my Affections are spiritual. But why should you think I harbour Hypocrisie in my House? I will assure you there is none in all the world I hate more than this base Fellow; for I know God abhors him; and shall I shew countenance to him? Lord, far be it from me!

Godli. Nay Formalist, be not too confident; 'tis not your bare denial of it which is sufficient to acquit you of the suspicion I have of you upon this account; but since you deny it, I will see if I cannot find him out, for you have a certain Officer in your House, whom I am sure can make a righteous decision, if he be not basely corrupted and blinded by your pretending so much Love and Zeal to seeming Holiness. I know he will not flatter any man, but speak according to his Light and Knowledg[e] impartially at all times. Sir, I appeal unto him.

Formal. What is his Name?

Godli. His Name is Conscience.

Upon this, Conscience was called, and enquired of, after this manner;

Godli. Conscience, I do require you in the fear of God, to answer me a question or two concerning your master; Doth he not secretly lodg[e] and hide one in his house called Hypocrisie? for I very much suspect him herein to be guilty; What do you say?

Conscience. Sir, if you please to give me his Character, or give me some certain signs of his behaviour and properties, whereby I may know him, I will faithfully discover all that I understand touching this matter.

Godli. Conscience, I thank you, you speak like an honest man; and indeed I have alwaies found you impartial according to your Light: I will then give you such a Description of this subtil and deceitful Enemy

---

[7]parts: abilities.

of mine, that you cannot well mistake, and this I shall do by propounding a few questions to you.

Sir, was he ever throughly wounded in the sense of sin as 'tis sin, being convinced of the ugly and abominable Nature thereof; there being nothing in all the world more hateful to God than that; not only convinced of the evil which does attend it, or is the limit of it, but also of that cursed evil there is in it, it being utterly contrary to the holy and pure Nature of God, a breach of his Law, and that which hath made a breach between God and Man, and basely defaced the Image of God in Him, and is the absolute cause of all that abominable enmity that is in his heart against God and Me his Blessed Offspring; and also makes man in love with the waies of the Devil, nay to be like the Devil, conformable to him, and to do his will?

Secondly, Is there no one Sin that secretly he loves and lives in (the evil habit never being broken) have you not found him now and then telling [a] Lie for his advantage sake; or in telling of tales or stories, adding to them, to please the company; or to excuse himself when accused of this or that, that so he may gain credit? Is he not sometimes overtaken by Drunkenness? Is he not proud, minding more the Honour, praise and applause of men in what he doth in Religion, than the praise of God? Is he not Covetous? Doth he give according to his ability to the poor? Doth he not rob God, to serve the World? I mean neglect hearing of God's Word, and other indispensable Duties, for worldly Profit sake, and so prefer the World above the Word? Doth he never in Trading offend you in speaking better of his Commodities than they deserve? Is not the World more in his love and affections than God and Jesus Christ? Does he alwaies give good and just weight and measure and not take unlawful profit? Doth he not make

gain of Godliness, and use Religion as a Cloak to cover his secret sins? Doth he concern himself for the interest of the Gospel, and by his open-heartedness, shew upon that account he loves Christ above Son or Daughter? Is he resolved to part with all rather than to sin against God, and to offend you his poor Conscience? Doth he see more evil in the least Sin, than in the greatest Suffering?

Thirdly, Doth he desire as much to have his Sins mortified as pardoned; to be made holy here, as well as happy hereafter? Is he as much in love with the work of holiness, as with the wages of holiness? Doth he love the word of God, because of the purity of it? Is he willing to bear the Cross, as well as wear the Crown, to be with Christ in his Temptations here, as well as with Christ in his Exaltations hereafter? to live to God on earth, as well as to live with God in heaven?

Fourthly, Is he the same in private as in publick? Doth he not rest satisfied upon the bare performance of Duty, not minding whether he hath met with God or not? Doth he pray in private, as if men saw him, and in publick, as knowing God sees him? Doth not his satisfaction more lie in his asking of God, than in his receiving from God? Does he not seek more for suitable words in Prayer, than for a suitable heart? Doth not he study more for acute expressions to affect the hearts of others, than to meet with powerful impressions upon his own? Doth he not lengthen his Prayers before others, and hurry them over in private? Doth he as much endeavour after what he needs from God, as that which he seeks of God?

Fifthly, Can he bear reproofs kindly for his faults, and take them patiently; nay, and esteem him his greatest friend who dealt most cordially[8] with him? is he ready to take shame to himself, and give glory to God? Can he be contented in the waies of

---

[8]cordially: from the heart.

God, though he meets with little sensible comfort from God, nor outward respect from Saints?

Sixthly, Doth he as much desire to have his heart filled with Grace, as his head with knowledge? Doth he take as much care to make the Glory of God his end in what he doth, as the Command of God his ground in what he doth.

Seventhly, Is he not more severe in pressing the lesser concerns of Religion, than in urging the greater? Doth he not require those Duties of others which he himself is loth to practice? Is he not more curious to know other men's conditions than his own?

Eighthly, Hath he received a whole Christ with a whole heart? First, A whole Christ comprehends all his Offices, and a whole heart comprehends all his Faculties. Hath he received Christ not only as Priest, to die for him, but also as a Prince to rule over him? Doth he obey all God's Precepts, as well as believe all God's Promises? As to his Faculties, his understanding may be somewhat enlightned, but his affections may be carnal, and his will oppose me, being averse to True Godliness. Is not his Heart divided? Come Conscience, I do now command you, in the presence of the great and dreadful God who searches all hearts, to make a righteous decision, tell me plainly; Is my Enemy Hypocrisie here or no? By these brief Hints you may easily know him.

Conscience, Sir, I must confess Hypocrisie is here; now I have found him out; nay Sir, and he hath hid him secretly in his House ever since he came to live in this Town Religion; he is seemingly holy, but really wicked; he loved the Face of Holiness, but is without the Grace of Holiness; his greatest care has been to wash the outside of the Platter; if he can but keep his name from being reproach'd by men, he cares not though his Heart be grievously defiled before God. Should I tell you of all those Lusts which he harbours in his heart, and what favour he shews to that Old-Man (you mentioned before) I should quite shame him; he is a Saint indeed abroad, but a Heathen (to say no worse) at home, he prayes, hears, and reads, but 'tis to keep up his Credit, Name, and Esteem amongst many Christian men of this Town; for I have often found him very weary of these Duties, God knows it as well as I: Nay Sir, he would seldom pray at all were it not to quiet me; for he doth not love my lashes; besides, he performs them with a sad, cold, dead, carnal and lifeless spirit; he is much for the lesser things of Religion (as you minded) he keeps a mighty stir about Mint, Anise, and Cummin,[9] but quite neglects the greater and more weighty things; nay there is one thing more I will tell you, as he does not love strict Godliness himself, so his heart is ready to rise against all such who outdo him. Sir, he is a meer Dissembler, yet he would be thought as religious a man as any in the Town. I find him also much abroad finding of faults in others, or spying the mote that is in his Brother's eye, but never minds the beam that is in his own; nay, and he is ready to fall out with many good Christians, because they will not follow him in Habit, Mode and Gesture, &c. In a word, most of all those black Marks of this deceitful Villain Hypocrisie, you hinted at, I find in him also.

Godli. Conscience, say no more, I see [I] was not mistaken; and now Formalist, are not you a wretch to pretend kindness to me, and secretly thus to entertain one of my worst Enemies? Sir, 'tis you who have brought so great a reproach upon this poor Town, and on all its Inhabitants; Nay, and 'tis through your means I am so basely villifi'd and condemned by that blind Fellow Ignorance; for he is ready to conclude, that

---

[9]Allusion to Matt. 23:23.

all my Friends and true Favourites are such as your self, *viz.* meer loose and Formal Hypocrites. Besides, you are like to be undone and perish for ever, unless you do the sooner turn this vile Enemy of mine out of doors; for I expect no other but that you will in a little time fall into Apostacy: but should you die first, yet assure yourself you will be damned; for Hell is indeed prepared for such as you are; you are, poor Creature! in the worst condition of all men; for the wicked hate you because you pretend so much love to Religion and Godliness; God also and all good men hate you, because you are not real, but only pretend love to them, being not sincere and upright in your Profession.

Formalist At this began to be very angry, being greatly offended at True Godliness; for he could not endure to see his State ript open, nor did he like to hear of his present nor future misery; being perswaded by Mr. Vain-hope, Unbelief, and Good-Opinion, to think his condition for all this might be safe enough; however Vain-hope told him, though at present his state might be doubtful, yet he should have many daies on earth, and that he might repent, and set all things at rights before he died; whose word and promise he adventur'd to take, and so bid True Godliness be gone; at this, great grief seem'd to seize upon True Godliness, and no man's state in all his Travels he did indeed more lament, and his Soul being almost overwhelmed with sorrow, he broke out to this purpose, and departed;

Passion o'reflows; why melt I thus with grief,
For him whose trayt'rous Heart denies relief?
But what could I expect, false wretch! from thee,
Who harbour'st in thy House Hypocrisie?
A feigned Friend's worse than an open Foe,
And unto me oft-times more wrong does do.
Of all to whom I am by Jesus sent,
O're thee O Formalist! I do lament.
I know there's cause, were things consider'd well;
Thou suffer'st here, and yet must go to hell.
Hated of God and man, what can be worse
Than th' wrath of man, and great Jehovah's Curse?
Farewel, poor Soul! is this thy love to me;
Must I begone? adieu, adieu to thee.

Introduction to Joseph Alleine,
Christian Letters

Joseph Alleine (1634-1668) was born in Devizes, Wiltshire, where his father had been mayor. In 1649 he entered Oxford. In 1653 he became chaplain to Corpus Christi college, Oxford. Two years later he went to Taunton, Somerset, where he assisted George Newton at the St. Mary Magdalene parish. Both he and Newton were ejected from the parish in 1662 because of their Nonconformity. Alleine remained at Taunton and preached to a gathering of people who still desired to hear him. He spent much of 1663-64 in prison at Ilchester for this illegal preaching; but, when released in May 1664, he continued to hold secret meetings. He was imprisoned again in 1665, and when released his health was broken. Seeking recovery he went to Dorchester and then to Bath "to take the waters." He died in November, 1668, only thirty-four years of age.

As an author he wrote a fiery tract defending illegal preaching (A Call To Archippus) and a devotional classic known by two titles, An Alarme to Unconverted Sinners *or* The Sure Guide to Heaven. *Usually under the first title, this went through a great many editions up to the present. Thus it ranks as one of the classics of Puritan devotional literature. The selections that follow are taken from a volume of Alleine's spiritual writings that came out after his death, entitled* Christian Letters, Full of Spiritual Instructions, Tending to the Promoting of the Power of Godliness, both in Persons, & Families *(London, 1672). This is presumably the same as Wing A966, although that is given a 1673 date. Thereafter it was several times reprinted as an addition to* The Life and Death of That Excellent Minister of Christ Mr. Joseph Alleine. *I have taken the text of the following letters from the 1672 edition, 10-11, 24-27, 37-39, 77-79, 107-110, 133-35, 153-56. I have written a brief biographical notice of Joseph Alleine for the* Biographical Dictionary of British Radicals in the Seventeenth Century, *ed. Richard L. Greaves and Robert Zaller (Brighton: Harvester Press, 1982-1984) 2:7-8.*

Letters two, six, ten, and twenty-two were written from prison and addressed to his Taunton congregation. Letter two exhorted his Taunton flock to be steadfast under persecution. Letter six meditates upon death. Number ten discusses God's love for his people; and the twenty-second is an exhortation to the spiritual life. Letter thirty was also written to his former congregation, but after he had been released from prison and was seeking the restoration of his health. The thirty-sixth letter is addressed to his wife and is undated; but since it makes reference to his being urged to accept preferment in the Church of England, it is probably from the period right after 1662. Its theme is the love of God; its style is rapturous. The last letter was written to an unnamed friend who was a clergyman of the Church of England, and instead of arguing the case for Nonconformity, it simply urges the friend to be diligent in his pastoral duties.

Christian Letters

by Joseph Alleine

Letter II.
(Prepare for Suffering.)

To my dearly beloved the Flock of Christ in Taunton,
Grace and Peace.

Most dear Christians:

My extream straights of time will now force me to bind my long loves[1] in a few short lines; yet I could not tell how to leave you unsaluted, nor chuse but write to you in a few words, that you should not be dismayed neither at our present sufferings, or at the evil tidings that by this time I doubt not are come unto you. Now, Brethren, is the time when the Lord is like to put you upon the trial; now is the hour of temptation come. Oh! be faithful to Christ to the death, and he shall give you a Crown of life: Faithful is he that hath called you, and he will not suffer you upon his faithfulness to be tempted above what you are able. Give up your selves and your All to the Lord, with resolution to follow him fully, and two things[2] be sure of, and lay up as sure grounds of everlasting consolation.

1. If you seek by prayer and study to know the mind of God, and do resolve to follow it in uprightness, you shall not fail either of direction or pardon; Either God will shew you what his pleasure is, or will certainly forgive you if you miss your way. Brethren, fix upon your Souls the deep and lively affecting apprehensions of the most gracious, loving, merciful, sweet, compassionate, tender nature of your Heavenly Father, which is so great that you may be sure he will with all readiness and love accept of his poor Children when they endeavour to approve themselves in sincerity to him, and would fain know his mind and do it, if they could but clearly see it, though they should unwillingly mistake.

2. That as sure as God is faithful, if he do see that such or such a temptation (with the forethought of which you may be apt to disquiet your selves, lest you should fall away when thus or thus tried) will be too hard for your Graces, he will never suffer it to come upon you. Let not, my dear Brethren, let not the present tribulations or those impending move you. This is the way of the Kingdom: persecution is one of your Land-marks: self-denial and taking up the Cross is your ABC of Religion; you have learnt nothing that have not begun at Christ's-Cross. Brethren, the Cross of Christ is your Crown; the reproach of Christ[3] is your riches; the shame of Christ is your glory; the damage attending strict and holy diligence, your greatest advantage: sensible you should be of what is coming, but not discouraged; humbled, but not dismayed; having your hearts broken,

---

[1] The shortness of his time is contrasted with the length of his love for the Taunton congregation in this obscure sentence.

[2] The two things are those that follow in the remainder of the letter.

---

[3] i.e., that you are reproached for Christ's sake.

and yet your spirits unbroken; humble your selves mightily under the mighty hand of God; but fear not the face of man: may you even be low in humility, but high in courage; little in your own apprehensions of your selves, but great in holy fortitude, resolution and holy magnanimity, lying in the dust before your God, yet triumphing in faith and hope, and boldness and confidence over all the power of the enemies. Approve your selves as good Souldiers of Jesus Christ, with No Armour, but that of righteousness; No Weapons, but strong crying and tears; looking for no Victory but that of Faith; nor hope to overcome, but by patience: now for the faith and patience of the Saints now for the harness of your suffering Graces: O gird up the loyns of your mind, and be sober, and hope to the end: Fight not but the good fight of Faith: here you must contend and that earnestly: Strive not but against sin, and here you may resist even unto blood: now see that you chuse life, and embrace affliction rather than sin. Strive together mightily and frequently by prayer: I know you do, but I would you should abound more and more: Share my loves among you, and continue your earnest prayers for me, and be you assured that I am and shall be through Grace, a willing thankful Servant of your Souls' concernments.

From the common Gaole
May 2, 1663   Joseph Aleine.

Letter VI.
(Look out of your Graves upon the World.)

To my most dearly Beloved Friends, the chosen of God in Taunton,
Grace and Peace.

Most endeared Christians:

My heart is with you, though I am Absent as to my Bodily presence from you, and therefore as I have often already, so I have now Written to you to stir up your pure minds by way of Remembrance, and to call upon you for your stedfast continuing, and vigorous proceeding in the ways of God. Dear Friends, and fellow Souldiers under Christ the Captain of our Salvation, consider your Calling and Station, and approve your selves as good Souldiers of Jesus Christ, as men of resolution and courage, be discouraged with no difficulties of your present Warfare. As for humane affairs, I would have you to be as you are, Men of Peace: I would have you Armed not for resisting, God forbid, but for Suffering only, as the Apostle hints: You should resist, even to the uttermost, striving against Sin. Here you must give no Quarter, for if you spare but one Agag,[4] the life of your Souls must go for the life of your Sins: you must make no Peace, for God will not smile on that Soul that smiles on Sin, nor have any Peace with him, that is at peace with his Enemy. Other Enemies you must forgive, and love, and pray for (which I again desire you to mind as one special duty of the times) but for these Spiritual Enemies, all your affections, and all your Prayers must be engaged against them; yea, you must admit no Parley: It's dangerous to dispute with Temptations. Remember what Eve lost by Parleying with Satan: you must flie from Temptations, and put them off at first with a Peremptory denial. If you will but hear the Devil's Arguments, and the Fleshe's Pleas, and fair Pretences, it is an hundred to one but you

---

[4] Saul was commanded by the Lord to Kill Agag, but did not, so that the prophet Samuel had to hew Agag in pieces, 1 Sam. 15:33.

are insnared by his Sophistry. And for this present evil World, the Lord deliver you from its Snares. Surely you had need watch and be sober, and use your spiritual Weapons dexterously and diligently, or else this World is like to undo you, and destroy you. I have often warned you not to build upon an External happiness, and that you should promise your selves nothing but hardship here: Oh still remember your Station; Souldiers must not count upon Rest, and Fulness, but Hunger, and Hardness. Labour to get right apprehensions of the World. Do not think these things necessary; one thing is needful: You may be happy in the want of all outward comforts. Do not think your selves undone, if brought to Want or Poverty: study Eternity, and you will see it to be little material to you, whether you are Poor or Rich; and that you may have never such an opportunity for your advantage in all your lives, as when you put all to hazard, and seem to run the Vessel upon the Rocks. Set your enemies one against the other: Death against the World; no such way to get above the World, as to put your selves into the possession of Death. Look often upon your Dust that you shall be Reduced to, and imagine you saw your Bones tumbled out of your Graves, as they are like shortly to be, and men handling your Skulls, and enquiring whose is this. Tell me of what account will the World be then, what good will it do you: put your selves often into your Graves, and look out from thence upon the World, and see what Judgement you have of it then. Must not you be shortly forgot among the Dead? your places will know you no more, and your Memory will be no more among men, and then what will it profit you to have lived in fashion and repute, and to have been Men of esteem? one serious walk over a Church-yard, as one speaks, might make a man mortified to the World. Think upon how many you Tread,

but you know them not: no doubt they had their Estates, their friends, their Trades, their businesses, and kept as much stir in the World as others do now. But alas, what are they the better for any, for all this? know you not that this must be your own case very shortly: oh the unhappiness of deceived man! how miserably is he bewitched, and befooled, that he should expend himself for that which he knows shall for ever leave him. Brethren, I beseech you lay no stress upon these perishing things, but labour to be at a Holy indifferencie about them: Is it for one that is in his wits to sell his God, his conscience, his soul, for things that he is not sure to keep a week, nor a day, and which he is sure after a few sleepings and wakings more, to leave behind him for ever? go and talk with dying men, and see what apprehensions they have of the World. If any should come to such as these, and tell them here is such and such preferments for you, you shall have such titles of Honour and delights, if you will now disown Religion, or subscribe to iniquity; do you think such a motion would be embraced? Brethren, why should we not be wise in time! why should we not now be of the mind of which we know we shall be all shortly! woe to them that will not be wise, till it be to no purpose! woe to them whose eyes nothing but Death and Judgment, will open! woe to them that though they have been warned by others, and have heard the World's greatest Darlings in Death to cry out of its vanity, worthlesness and deceitfulness, and have been told where and how it would leave them; yet would take no warning, but only must serve themselves to[o], for warnings to others.[5] Ah my Beloved, beware there be no worldly Professors[6] among you, that will

---

[5] i.e., the purpose of their carelessness will only be to warn others.

[6] professors: those who profess religion.

part rather with their part in Paradise, than their part in Paris; that will rather part with their Consciences, than with their Estates; that have secret reserves in [their] hearts to save themselves whole,[7] when it comes to the pinch; and not to be of the Religion that will undo them in the World. Beware that none of you have your hearts where your Feet should be, and love your Mammon before your Maker. It is time for you to learn with Paul, to be Crucified to the World.

But it is time for me to remember that 'tis a Letter, and contain my self within my Limits. The God of all Grace, stablish, strengthen, and settle you in these shaking times, and raise your hearts above the fears of the World's Threats, and above the Ambition of its favours. My dearest loves to you all, with my fervent desire of your Prayers. May the Lord of Hosts be with you, and the God of Jacob your refuge. Farewel my dear Brethren, Farewel and be strong in the Lord, I am

> Yours to serve you in the Gospel,
> whether by Doing or Suffering,

From the common Goale at Ilchester, June 31, 1663.

Joseph Alleine.

---

[7] i.e., that think in their hearts that they can be saved and yet also have the esteem of the world.

Letter X
By Joseph Alleine
(The Love of Christ)

To my beloved in the Lord, the flock of Christ in Taunton, Grace, and Peace:

Most Loving and best beloved,

My heart is with you, my affections are espoused to you. And methinks I could even say with the Apostle, ''You are in my heart, to live and die with you.''[8] And who can but love where they have received so much love (and continually do) as I have from you! The Lord requite your love, which is great, (and if compared with his, but little) with his, which is infinite; this is a love worthy of your ambition, worthy of your adoration and admiration. This is the Womb that bore you from eternity, and out of which have burst forth all the Mercies, Spiritual and Temporal, that you enjoy. This was the love that chose you, when less offenders, and those, that being converted, might have been a hundredfold more serviceable to their Maker's Glory, are left to perish in their sins: May your souls be filled with the sense of this love.

But it may be you will say, how shall I know if I am an object of Electing love? Lest an unbelieving thought should damp your joy, know in short, that if you have chosen God, he hath certainly chosen you. Have you taken Him for your blessedness? And do you more highly prize, and more diligently seek after conformity to him, and the fruition of him than all the goods of this World? If so, then away with doubts, for you could not have loved, and have chosen him, unless he had loved you first. Now may my Beloved[9] dwell continually in the thoughts, the views, the tastes of the [that] love. Get you down under its shadows, and taste its pleasant Fruits. Oh the Provisions that love hath made for you, before the Foundation of the World! Ah silly dust, that ever thou shouldest be thought upon so long before thou wast, that the contrivances of the infinite Wisdom, should be taken up

---

[8] A paraphrase of the apostle Paul, in 2 Cor. 7:3.

[9] beloved: his former parishoners.

about thee! That such a Crawling thing, such a Mite, a Flea, should have the consultations of the Eternal Deity exercised about thee! Verily His love to thee is wonderful. Lord, what is man! Thou tellest us he is Dust and Vanity, a Worm, nothing, less than nothing—how then dost thou love him? Oh wonderful! Be astonished ye Heavens at this; be moved ye strong foundations of the Earth! Fall down ye elders, strike up ye Heavenly Quires, and sing yet again, "Glory to God in the highest:" for all our strings would crack to reach the notes of love, praise, and admiration that this love doth call for. Oh that ever emptiness and vanity should be thus prized! That Jehovah should make account of so worthless, so useless a thing as man! That ever baseness should be thus preferred! That ever nothing should be thus dignified! That ever rottenness should be thus advanced, a Clod, a shaddow, a Potsheard, should be thus glorified! Oh Brethren, study I beseech you, not to requite or retaliate[10] (there's impossibility and blasphemy in such a thought), but to admire and imitate his love. Let love constrain you, let love put you upon doing, and prepare you for suffering; forget not a love so memorable, undervalue not a love so invaluable; I would have you all the captives of love; may the cords of love draw you towards, and knit you to your Redeemer; may the divided streams be united in him. Alas, that our souls are so narrow, that the Waters are so shallow with us! How little, how very little, would our love be, if He had it all— infinitely less than Glow-worm to the Sun, or the Atome to the Universe! And have we any of this little to spare for Him? Oh that we might love Him with our little All! That all our little powers were engaged for him! Brethren, here is no excess: oh love the Lord, ye his Saints! He is worthy for whom you shall do this. Do but think what love hath done for you, and think if you can, what it means to do for you. This is the love that yearned upon you, when in your Blood no eye pitying you. This is the love that took you up when you were Robbed, and wounded, and left for dead, and poured in Wine and Oyl into your wounds. This is that love that repreived, and spared, and pardoned, when the Law had condemned you,[11] and Justice would have had you delivered up, and your Self-condemning consciences gave up all for lost, concluding there was no hope. This is the love, the expensive love that bought you from the power of darkness, from the eternal burnings, the devouring fire in which you must otherwise have dwelt. Do you not remember how you were hungry, and it fed you, naked and it cloathed you, strangers and it took you in, sick and it visited you, in Prison and it came unto you?[12] You were dead and are alive, you were lost and are found. And methinks I see how love runs to meet you, and falls upon your necks, and kisseth the Lips that deserve to be loathed, and rejoyces over you, and makes a Festival, and as it were a Holiday in Heaven for you, inviting Angels to rejoyce. And if the friends do rejoyce, how much more doth the father? For, saith he, "these my Sons were dead and are alive, were lost and are found."[13] Oh melting love! Ah Brethren, how strange is this, that our recovery should be Heaven's triumph, the joy of God and Angels. That this love should feast us, and feast over us, and our Birthday should be kept in Heaven; that this should be the round[14] at heaven's table, and the burden

---

[10]retaliate: repay.

[11]i.e., the Mosiac law, in Paul's understanding of it.

[12]Allusion to Matt. 25:35-40.

[13]Allusion to the story of the prodigal son, Luke 15:11-32.

[14]round: as in music.

of the songs above, ''For this my Son was dead, and is alive.'' and well, what remains but that you should be another manner of People than ever yet you have been—more Holy, more humble, more even, more resolved, more lively, more active? Where is your zeal for the Lord of Hosts? Will slender returns suffice you in answer to such a love? God forbid. But necessity calls off from going any further. May the love that chose you, and redeemed you, forever dwell in you, and overshaddow you, and bear you safe to the kingdom. In the Holy Arms of Divine Love I desire to leave you. May you live under its daily Influences, and be melted and overcome with its warming Beams, with its quickning, piercing, powerful Rays. My most dear love to you all. See that you live not in a dull, fruitless, lifeless course. Be patient, be watchful, instant in Prayer, fervent in spirit, serving the Lord: I am very healthful and chearful through grace. See that none of these things move you that befal us.[15] Fare you well my dear Brethren, farewell in the Lord, I am Yours in the strongest Bonds of Affection and Affliction,

Joseph Alleine
From the prison at Ilchester,
October 25, 1663

---

[15]i.e., do not be distressed by what has happened to us.

Letter XXII.
(Christian Care, Faith, Self-denial.)

To the most Beloved People, the Servants of God in Taunton, Salvation:

Most endeared Christians,

The reason why my Letters have not of late come so thick as formerly to you, is not because I forget to love you, and to care for you; but because I have been busily taken up in other Labors of sundry kinds for you. I am yours, and love to be so, being ambitious not to have dominion over your faith, but to be a helper of your Joy. Christ's Officers are so your Rulers in the Lord, as yet to Preach not themselves, but the Lord Jesus Christ, and themselves your Servants for Jesus' sake. I have no greater felicity under God, than to serve the good of Souls. Brethren beloved, How fares it with your Souls? Are they in Health? Do they prosper? I wish your Temporal prosperity. It is a joy to me to hear when your Trade doth flourish: But these are but very little things if we look into Eternity. Brethren, my ambition for you is, that you should be Cedars among the Shrubs, that from you should sound out the Word of the Lord, and that in every place your Faith to God-ward should be spread abroad. That Taunton should be as a Field that the Lord hath blessed: That you should not onely have the Name, but the Spirit, Life, Power, Heat, Growth, Vigour of Christianity among you. Let not Taunton onely have the Name to live, and be noted for the Profession of Religion, but see to it my Brethren, that the Kingdom of God be with you: Oh that every one of your Souls might be a Temple of God! Oh that every one of your Families might be a Church of God! Beloved, look to it, that every one that nameth the Name of Christ among You do depart from Iniquity, secret as well as open, of the Heart as well as of the Life. Let no man think that to make an out-cry upon the Wickedness of the Times, and to be of the Professing Party, will serve his turn; many go to Hell in the company of the wise Virgins.[16] That

---

[16]Allusion to Matt. 25:1-13.

no man may be a Self-deceiver, let every man be a Self-Searcher. He that keeps no Day-Book in his Shop, and no Account, no Record in his Conscience, his Estate and his Soul will thrive both alike. Beloved, I would that You should remember whither You are going. If a man be after a few Months to be Transported into another Countrey, never to return more, he will send whatever he can, and make the best Provision that he may against[17] he comes into another Countrey. Dear Brethren, You are Strangers and Pilgrims here, and have but a few Months abode in this Countrey, see that you Traffique much with Heaven. Christ is our Common Factor,[18] O send over to him what possible you can. Give Alms plentifully, Pray continually, be much in Meditation and Consideration; Reckon with your selves daily: Walk with God in Your Callings: Do all the Duties of your Relations as unto God: Live not one day to your selves, but unto Christ: Set forth continually his Name, so shall you be continually Transporting into another World, and laying up Treasure in Heaven: And O the blessed Store that You shall find there after a few Years diligence in such a holy Course! Beloved, While you are here in this World, You are but like a Merchant's Ship in a strange Port, the day for your Return is set, and You are to stay no longer than till your Fraight[19] is ready. Be wise, know your season, improve your time, You are made or or mar'd for ever, as You speed in this one Voyage. There is no returning again to this Countrey to mend a bad Market, God will call in all his Talents,[20] Time shall be no longer. Oh come

in, come and buy now while the Market is open, that You that want[21] may have Grace, and You that have may have it more abundantly. Go and plead with the Lord Jesus, that he hath bid You come, buy and eat without Money, and without Price, that he hath counselled You to come buy of him Gold, Raiment, and Eye-salve; tell Him You are come according to his call, and wait upon him for Grace, for Righteousness, for Light and Instruction: Lay hold on his Word, plead it, live upon it; he is worthy to be Believed, worthy to be Trusted, go out of your selves to him, unlearn[22] your selves. There is a threefold foot that Carnal-self stands upon, our own Wisdome, our own Righteousness, our own Strength, these three Feet must be Cut off, and we must learn to have no subsistence in our selves but only in Christ, and to stand only on his bottom.[23] Study the excellent Lesson of Self-denial, Self-annihilation. A true Christian is like a Vine that cannot stand of it self, but is wholly supported by the Prop it leans on. It is no small thing to know our selves to be nothing, of no might, of no worth, of no understanding, nor reality; to look upon our selves as helpless, worthless, foolish, empty shadows. This holy Littleness is a great matter; when we find that all our Inventory amounts to nothing but Folly, Weakness, and Beggary; when we set down our Selves for Cyphers, our Gain for loss, our Excellencies for very Vanities, then we shall learn to live like Believers. A true Saint is like a Glass without a Foot,[24] that set him where you will, is ready to fall every way till you set him to a Prop: Let Christ be the only support you lean unto.

---

[17]against: until.

[18]factor: one who conducts business for another—middleman.

[19]fraight: freight.

[20]Talents: a weight of money, or coin; allusion to the parable in Matt. 25:14-30.

[21]want: lack.

[22]unlearn: put aside from knowledge or memory, discard.

[23]bottom: foundation.

[24]i.e., a mirror without a stand.

When you are throughly Emptied and Nullified,[25] and see all comeliness to be but as a withered flower, dead, dried, and past Recovery, then You will be put upon the happy necessity of going out to Christ for all.

The Messenger's haste forceth me

Abruptly to end here: I can add no more, but my Prayers to my Counsels, and so commending you to God, and the Word of his Grace, I rest

> The fervent Well-willer
> of your Souls
> Jos. Alleine

From the Prison at Ilchester,
April 16, 1663

---

[25]nullified: made nothing.

Letter XXX.
(An Admiration of the Love of God.)

To the loving and most Dearly Beloved, the Servants of God in Taunton, Salvation.

My most dear Friends,

I Love you, and long for you in the Lord, and I am weary with forbearing that good and blessed Work that the Lord hath committed to me, for the furtherance of your Salvation. How long Lord, how long shall I dwell in silence! How long shall my Tongue cleave to the Roof of my Mouth! When will God open my Lips, that I may stand up and praise him? But it is my Father's good pleasure yet to keep me in a total disability of publishing his Name among you; unto him my soul shall patiently subscribe. I may not, I cannot complain that he is hard to me, or useth me with Rigour: I am full of the Mercies of the Lord, yea, Brimful and running over, And shall I complain? Far be it from me.

But though I may not murmur, methinks I may mourn a little, and sit down and wish, O if I may not have a Tongue to speak, would I had but Hands to Write, that I might from my Pen drop some heavenly Councels to my Beloved People. Methinks my feeble Fingers do even Itch to Write unto you, but it cannot be, alas my Right-hand seems to have forgot her cunning,[26] and hath much ado with trembling to lift the Bread unto my Mouth. Do you think you

should have had so little to shew under my Hand, to bear witness of my Care for you, and Love to you if God had not shook my Pen as it were out of my Hand? But all that he doth do is done well, and wisely and therefore I submit. I have purposed to borrow Hands[27] wherewith to Write unto my Beloved rather than to be silent any longer.

But where shall I begin, or when should I end? If I think to speak of the Mercies of God towards me, or mine enlarged affections towards you, methinks I feel already how strait this Paper is like to be,[28] and how insignificant my Expressions will be found, and how insufficient all that I can say will prove at last to utter what I have to tell you; but shall I say nothing because I cannot utter all? this must not be neither.

Come then all ye that fear the Lord, come and I will tell you what he hath done for my Soul. O help me to love that precious Name of his, which is above all my Praises. O love the Lord all ye his Saints, and fear before him! magnifie the Lord with me, and let us exalt his Name together! he hath remembred my low estate, because his

---

[26]cunning: skill, ability. An allusion to Ps. 137:5.

[27]i.e., to write through an amanuensis. The reference is to the paralytic illness that struck him in his last years.

[28]i.e., how small the paper is for all that he wishes to write.

Mercy endureth for ever. O blessed be you of the Lord, my dearly Beloved, O thrice blessed may you be for all your Remembrances of me before the Lord, you have wrestled with the Lord for me, you have wrestled me out of the very Jaws of Death it self: O the strength of Prayer! Surely it is stronger than Death. See that You even honour the power and prevalency of Prayer: Oh be in Love with Prayer, and have high and venerable thoughts of it. What Distresses, Diseases, Deaths can stand before it? Surely I live by Prayer, Prayer hath given a Resurrection to this Body of mine, when Physicians, and Friends had given up their hopes.

Ah my dearly Beloved, methinks it delights me to tell the Story of your Love, how much more of the Love of God towards me. I have not forgotten, O my dearly Beloved, I have not forgotten your tender Love in all my Distresses. I remember your kindness to me in my Bonds, when once and again I was delivered up to a Prison for your sakes. I remember with much delight, how You refreshed and comforted me in my Tribulations, how open your hearts were, and your hands were not straightned[29] neither, for I was in want of nothing. I may not, I must not forget what painful Journies you took to visit me, when in places Remote the hand of the Lord had touched me, and though my long Sickness was almost incredible Expensive to me, yet your Supplies did not a little lighten my Burthen.

And though I put it last, yet I do not mind it[30] least, that You have been so ready in returning Praises to God in my behalf, your Thanksgiving to God, my dear Brethren, do administer abundant cause to me of my giving thanks unto You.

And now my Heart methinks is big to tell You a little of my Love to You, surely You are dear unto me; but though it be sweet to tell the story of Love, yet in this I will restrain myself. For I fear least[31] as the Wise man saith of the beginning of strife, so I should find of the beginning of Love, that it is like the letting forth of the Water;[32] and the rather I do forbear, because I hope you have better Testimonies than Words, to bear Witness herein unto you.

But if I sing the Song of Love, O let Divine Love overcarry the Praise;[33] I found myself in straights when I began to speak of the natural Love between my dear People, and an unworthy Minister of Christ to them; and it seemed that all that I have said was much too little, but now I have to speak of the Love [of] God,[34] it seems to be by far too much.

O infinite Love never to be Comprehended, but ever to be Admired, Magnified, and Adored by every Creature! O let my Heart be filled, let my Mouth be filled, let my Papers be filled, ever ever filled with the thankful Commemoration of this matchless Love. O turn your Eyes from other Objects! O Bury me in Forgetfulness, and let my Love be no more mentioned nor had in remembrance among You, so that You may be throughly possessed and inflamed with the Love of God. This, my Beloved, this is that Love which is ever to be Commended, and Extolled by you. See that You studie this Love, fill your Souls with wonder, and feast your Souls with joy, and be ravished with rich contentment in the Divine Love: Take your daily walk, and lose your selves in the Field of Love: Drink, O Friends, yea drink

---

[29]straightened: ungenerous.

[30]mind it: remember it.

[31]least: lest.

[32]Allusion to Prov. 17:14.

[33]i.e., receive more of the praise.

[34]I have emended the textual "love God" to "love of God," since as it stands it would be an unusual turn of phrase; however, as it stands it is striking.

abundantly, O Beloved, fear no excess. O that your Souls may be drencht and drowned in the Love of Christ, till You can every one say with the ravisht Spouse, I am sick of Love.[35] Marvel not that I wander here, and seem to forget the bounds of a Letter, this Love obligeth me, Yea, rather constraineth me. Who in all the Earth should admire and commend this Love if I should not? I feel it, I taste it, the sweet Savour thereof Reviveth my Soul, it is Light to mine Eyes, and Life to mine Heart; the warm beams of this blessed Sun, O how have they Comforted me, Ravished, and Refreshed me both in Body and Soul! My benumbed Limbs, my withered Hands, my feeble Knees, my Bones quite naked of Flesh do yet again Revive through the Quickning, Healing, and Raising influence of Divine Grace and Love. Now my own Hands can feed me, and my own feet can bear me, my Appetite is quick,[36] my

Sleep comfortable, and God is pleased to give some increase continually though by insensible Degrees; And shall not I praise that Love and Grace that hath done all this for me? Yea, what is this to all I have to tell you? My Heart is enlarged, but I told You Paper could not hold what I have to speak of the Goodness of the All-Gracious God, in which I live. I am forced to end, least you should not bear my length. My dearly Beloved, I send my Heart unto You, divide my Love amongst you all, and particularly tender it to your Reverend and Faithfull Pastour,[37] whose Presence with you, and Painfulness,[38] and Watchfulness over you, and Zeal and Courage for you in so dangerous a time, is matter of my great Joy and Thanksgivings unto God. The Grace of our Lord Jesus be with you all. Fare you well in the Lord, I remain

> Your unworthy Minister
> and fervent
> Well wisher in the Lord,
> Jos. Alleine.

[35]i.e., made ill by an excess of love, an allusion to Song of Sol. 2:5.

[36]quick: lively.

[37]A reference to his successor at Taunton.

[38]painfulness: painstakingness.

Letter XXXVI.
(To his Wife, Desires after Heaven.)

My dear Heart,

My heart is now a little at rest to write to thee. I have been these three days much disturbed, and so out of frame. Strong solicitations I have had from several hands, to accept very honourable preferment in several kinds, some friends making a Journey on purpose to propound it, but I have not found the invitations (though I confess very honourable, and such as are or will be suddenly embraced by men of far greater worth and eminency) to suit with the inclinations of my own heart, as I was confident they would not with thine. I have sent away my friends satisfied with the reasons of my refusal, and am now ready with joy

to say with David, Soul return unto thy rest: But alas, that such things should disturb me, I would live above this lower region, that no passages or providence whatsoever might put me out of frame, nor disquiet my soul, and unsettle me from my desired rest. I would have my heart fixed upon God, so as no occurrences might disturb my tranquility, but I might be still in the same quiet and even frame. Well, though I am apt to be unsettled, and quickly set off the hinges, yet methinks I am like a Bird out of the nest, I am never quiet till I am in my old way of Communion with God, like the needle in the Compass that is restless, till it be turned towards the Pole. I can say through grace with the Church, with my soul have I desired thee in the night, and with my Spirit within me have I sought thee early, my heart is early and late with God, and 'tis the business and delight of my life to seek him. But alas, how long shall I be a seeking? how long shall I spend my days in wishing and desiring, when my glorified Brethren spend theirs in rejoycing and enjoying? look as the poor imprisoned captive sighs under the burdensome clog of his Irons, and can only peer through the Grate, and think of, and long for the sweetness of that liberty which he sees others enjoy: such methinks is my condition: I can only look through the Grate of this Prison my flesh, I see Abraham, and Isaac, and Jacob, sitting down in the Kingdom of God, but alas, I my self must stand without, longing, striving, fighting, running, praying, waiting, for what they are enjoying. Oh happy, thrice happy souls! when shall these Fetters of mine be knocked off? when shall I be set at liberty from this Prison of my body? you are clothed with glory, when I am clothed with dust. I dwell in flesh, in a House of Clay, when you dwell with God in a House not made with hands, eternal in the Heavens. I must be continually clog'd with the cumbersome burden of this Dung-hill Body, that had it not a soul dwelling in it like Salt as it were to preserve, it would soon turn to putrefaction and corruption, and be as odious and loathsome as the filthiest Carrion, when you have put on incorruption and immortality. What continual molestation am I subject to by reason of this flesh? what pains doth it cost me to keep this earthen Vessel from breaking; it must be fed, it must be clothed, it must be exercised, re-created, and which is worst of all cherished with time-devouring sleep, so that I live but little of the short time I have allotted me here: but oh blessed souls, you are

swallowed up of[39] immortality and life, your race is run, and you have received your Crown. How cautious must I be to keep me from dangers, how apt am I to be troubled with the cares and fears of this life, molesting my self with the thoughts of what I shall eat, and what I shall put on, and wherewithal I shall provide for my self and mine; when your souls are taken with nothing but God, and Christ, and 'tis your work to be still contemplating, and admiring that love that redeemed you from all this. Alas, how am I encompast with infirmities, and still carry about me Death in my bosome, what pains and cost must I be at to repair the rotten and ruinous building of this earthly Tabernacle, which when I have done I am sure will shortly fall about my ears: when you are got far above mortality, and are made equal with the Angels. Oh I groan earnestly to be clothed upon with my house which is from Heaven, being willing rather to be absent from the Body, and present with the Lord! Oh, when shall I come and appear before him? When shall I receive the Purchase of my Saviour, the fruit of my prayers, the harvest of my labours, the end of my Faith, the Salvation of my soul? Alas, what do I here? this is not my resting place. My treasure is in Heaven, and my heart is in Heaven. Oh when shall I be where my heart is? woe is me that I sojourn in Mesech, and dwell in the Tents of Kedar.[40] Oh that I had wings like a Dove, that I might flie away and be at rest. Then would I hasten my escape from the windy storm and tempest, and be out of the reach of fears, disturbances, and distractions. How long shall I live at such a distance from my God, at such a distance

---

[39]of: by.

[40]Mesech, north of Assyria, represented remoteness. The tents of Kedar were dark (Song of Sol. 1:5), and here they represent the veil of flesh separating persons from the heavenly realm.

from my Countrey? Alas, how can I be merry, how can I sing the Lord's Song in a strange Land; no, I will hang my Harp upon the Willows, and sit down and weep when I remember Sion.[41] But yet my flesh shall rest in hope, and I will daily bathe my soul in the sweet thoughts of my blessed home. I will rejoyce in hopes of what I do not yet enjoy, and content my self with the taste of what I shall shortly have my fill of. But stay this Pen, run not beyond thy Commission. Alas, now I receive what I have gotten, I perceive I have set down what I would be rather than what I am, and

wrote more of my dears heart than my own penning, rather a Copy for my self, than a Copy of my self. Well, I thank God I have got some heat[42] by it for all, the Lord grant thou mayst get a thousand times more. The Lord grant the request I daily pour out before him, and make us helps and furtherances to each other's soul, that we may quicken and promote and forward one another in his ways. Help my by thy Prayers as thou dost always. The God of all peace and comfort be with thee my sweet love, Farewel,

> Thine beyond Expression,
> Joseph Alleine.

---

[41]Allusion to Ps. 137, traditionally considered a lament of the Israelites in captivity.

[42]heat: ardor, warmth of feeling.

Letter XXXVIII.

(Do all in reference to God and his glory.)

Dear Friend,

I have received yours of the 19th of September, but it came to me in the time of my sickness, in which I was much a stranger to writing; it continued upon me five Months, and to this day so much weakness remains in my arms, that I am not able to put off or on my own clothes. Your Letter was exceeding welcom to me, not only as reviving the remembrance of our old friendship; but also, as bringing me news of some spiritual good that you received by me, which is the best tidings that I can receive: for what do I live for, but to be useful to souls in my generation? I desire to know no other business than to please and honour my God, and serve my generation in that short allowance of time that I have here, before I go hence, and be seen no more. Shall I commend to you the Lesson that I am about to learn? But why should I doubt of your acceptance, who have so readily embraced me in all our converses?

The Lesson is, To be entirely devoted unto the Lord, that I may be able to say after

the Apostle, To me to live is Christ. I would not be serving God onely for a day in the week, or an hour or two in the day; but every day, and all the day: I am ambitious to come up towards that of our Lord and Master, To do always those things that please God. I plainly see, that self-seeking is self-undoing; and that then we do promote our selves best, when we please God most. I find, that when I have done all, if God be not pleased, I have done nothing; and if I can but approve my self to God, my work is done: I reckon I do not live that time I do not live unto God.

I am fain to cut off so many hours from my days, and so many years from my life (so short as it is) as I have lived unto my self. I find no enemy so dangerous as self; and O that others might take warning by my hurt! O that I had lived wholly unto God! then had every day and every hour that I have spent, been found upon my account at that great day of our appearing before God: then I had been rich indeed, in treasure laid up there, whither I am apace removing; then I had been every day and hour adding to the heap, and encreasing the reward which God of his meer grace hath promised, even to the meanest work that is done to him, Col. 4:24. I verily perceive I am an eternal loser by acting no more as for God; for what is done to my self, is lost; but what is done for God, is done for ever, and shall receive an everlasting reward. Verily, if there be another world to come, and an eternal state after this short life, it is our onely wisdom to be removing, and, as it were, transplanting and transporting what we can, from hence, into that Countrey to which we are shortly to be removed, that what we are now doing, we may be reaping the fruit of for ever more. The world think themselves wise; but I will pawn my soul upon it, that this is the true wisdom.

Well, let us be wholly swallowed up in the concerns of Religion, and know no other interest but Jesus Christ's. I cannot say, I have already attained; but this is that my heart is set to learn, That in all that I do, whether sacred or civil actions, still I may be doing but one work, and driving on one design, That God may be pleased by me, and be glorified in me; that not onely my praying, preaching, alms, &c. may be found upon my account; but even my eating, drinking, sleeping, visits, discourses, because they are all done as unto God. Too often do I take a wrong aim, and miss my mark; but I will tell you what be the Rules I set my self, and do strictly impose upon my self from day to day: Never to lie down, but in the Name of God, not barely for natural refreshment, but that a wearied servant of Christ may be recruited, and fitted to serve him better the next day. Never to rise up but with this resolution: Well, I will go forth this day in the Name of God, and will make Religion my business, and spend the day for Eternity. Never to enter upon my calling, but first thinking, I will do these things as unto God, because he requireth these things at my hands in the place and station he hath put me into. Never to sit down to the Table, but resolving, I will not eat meerly to please my appetite, but to strengthen my self for my Master's work. Never to make a Visit, but upon some holy design, resolving to leave something of God where I go; and in every company to leave some good savour behind. This is that which I have been for some time a learning, and am pressing hard after; and if I strive not to walk by these Rules, let this Paper be a witness against me.

I am not now in my former Publick Capacity, such things being required of me to say and subscribe, as I could by no means yield to, without open lying and dissembling with God and Men: Yet, that I am unuseful, I cannot say; but rather think, that possibly I may be of more use than heretofore. I thank the Lord, I have not known what it is to want a Tongue to speak, but in my sickness; nor a People to hear; but so, as that we both follow the things that make for peace.

I perceive you are otherwise perswaded in some things, than I am:[43] but however, I trust we meet in our end. Since you are in, may it be your whole study to gain souls, and to build them up in holiness, which is with too many the least of their cares. One duty (miserably neglected) I shall be bold to commend to you from my own experience, and that is, the visiting your whole Flock from house to house, and enquiring into their spiritual estates particularly,[44] and dealing plainly and truly with them about their conversion to God: to the usefulness of this great work, I can set my Probatum est.[45]

---

[43]His correspondent is not a Nonconformist but a clergyman of the Church of England.

[44]particularly: of each individually.

[45]Latin phrase meaning "it is approved," or excellent.

I hear you have two Parsonages:[46] O tremble to think how many precious souls you have to look to! And let it be seen, however others aim at the Fleece, you aim at the Flock;[47] and that you have indeed Curam animarum.[48]

You see how free I am with you; but I know your candor.

I rejoyce in your happy Yoke-fellow: salute her from your old Friend; and accept the unfeigned Respects of him who is,

> SIR:
> Your real and faithful Friend,
> Joseph Alleine.

---

[46]two parsonages: two parishes under his care.

[47]i.e., that you shepherd the flock rather than fleece them for profit.

[48]Curam animarum: Latin for "cure of souls," or pastoral care.

Introduction to William Bates,
The Danger of Prosperity

*For an introduction to Bates, see above, 99. Reproduced here is the intro-
duction to Bates's sermons on* The Danger of Prosperity. *In it he discusses the way
in which wealth jeopardizes the spiritual well-being of God's people, as a preface
to a longer discussion of the Christian's proper relationship to economic pursuits.
The text is taken from* The Danger of Prosperity: Discovered in several Sermons
Upon Prov. 1:27 *(London, 1685), sigs. A2ʳ-A4ᵛ.*

The Danger of Prosperity
by William Bates

The Preface

The Experience of all Ages has verified, that none are exposed to more dangerous Trials than the Prosperous in this
World. The great Tempter has found the
Temptations of Prosperity so insinuative
and prevailing with Men, that he attempted[1]
our blessed Saviour; expecting, by the
pleasant prospect of the Kingdoms of this
World, and their Glory, to have fastened
an impression upon his Spirit, and tainted
his inviolable Purity. But he found nothing
in our Saviour, not the least irregular inclination to his Allurements, and could
work nothing upon him. 'Tis otherwise
with Men born of the Flesh, in whom there
is a carnal Heart (the Centre of Apostacy
and Corruption) that is easily inticed and
overcome by charming Complacencies.[2]
Prosperity is a disguised Poison, pleasant
to the unwary sense, but deadly in the operation; and the more pernicious in the Effects, because less dangerous in the

Opinions of Men. The Temptations of
Prosperity are so frequent and favour'd by
us, that they give vigour to the inward enemy, the sensual Affections, and boldness
to the malicious Tempter. They foment the
carnal Appetites, that defile and debase the
Soul; and are the more rebellious and ex-
horbitant the more they are gratified.

Prosperity is the strongest obstacle
against the Conversion and Reformation of
Sinners. Whilst they are playing their various Pleasures, they have neither will nor
leisure to advert[3] to the Voice of Conscience, so reproachful and stinging to
them. And many times Prosperity stupifies
Conscience, that Men are fearless of Divine Judgments, involved in sensual Security. They will not reverence and obey
God's Authority, till they feel his Power;
they abuse his Blessings to Pride and Vanity, Idleness and Luxury, and are hardened
in their Impenitence, dyed with the deepest tincture of Ingratitude: they drive on

---

[1]attempted: tempted.
[2]Complacencies: civilities.

[3]advert: turn to.

through a course of Sin, till Death puts a period to their Lusts. How destructive, how penal is Prosperity to such graceless Souls? When God rains Snares upon the Wicked, when the affluence of this world is abused to satisfy their vicious Desires, it is a sad forerunner of the Shower of Fire and Brimstone, and the horrible Tempest that shall overwhelm them at last.

Others in Prosperity are not openly profane, and boldly vicious, yet are corrupted, and insensibly destroyed by it. They over-value and over-delight in the good things of this World, and please themselves in an opinionative Felicity in their present State. They enjoy the World with more appearance of Reason, and less Sensuality than the Riotous and Luxurious; but their conversation[4] with so many charming Objects, alienates them from God. They do not sanctify him in their hearts, placing their highest esteem upon his most amiable Excellencies, and their dearest delight in communion with him. They look upon Religion as a sour Severity, and count nothing delightful, but what is suitable to the fleshly Affections. A deceit like that of a sick Person, who feeling no pleasure but in the easy intervals between his Fits, and the remission of his Distemper, should imagine that if he were freed from his Disease, he should lose all Pleasure: whereas the Delights of Health are more full and durable. The Angels are incapable of sensual Pleasures; their Happiness arises from the perfection of Good, not the allays of Evil. The Beasts are only capable of sensual pleasures, the remedies of natural Evils, Hunger, Thirst, Weariness, or accidental Evils, Diseases and Pains: and many are so sottishly decieved,

as to prefer brutish Pleasures that affect the Senses, before Angelical Joys that arise from the fruition of God's Favour, and Obedience to his Laws. This is a sad Symptom of an unrenewed Heart, and an heavy Presage of future Misery; for God will not be our everlasting Joy in Heaven, if he be not our exceeding Joy upon the Earth.

Others surrounded with Riches and Honours, are neither thankful to their Divine Benefactor, nor careful to employ their Prosperity and Power for his Glory. The Law of Mercy requires a solemn affectionate recognition of God's Benefits: but the Current of Prosperity drowns their sense of the Divine Goodness; and incogitant[5] practical Atheism, is as destructive as Absolute and Speculative. And how many by the deceitfulness of Riches, are apt to imagine, that they possess with Dominion what they receive in trust: they might be rich in good Works, and if their Hearts were according to their Ability, be fruitful as Paradise, but are as barren as the Sands of Africa. They are in a mighty Debt for so many received Blessings, for which their Account will be heavy and undoing with the highest Lord. These and many other Considerations, make it evident how dangerous Prosperity is to the most that enjoy it here.

It is therefore a Point of high and holy Wisdom how to manage Prosperity so, as to avoid the impendant Evils that usually follow it, and to improve it for our eternal Advantage. This is the Design of the present Treatise, and humbly recommended to the Divine Blessing, from one who most unfeignedly desires the Salvation of Men's Souls.

---

[4]conversation: familiarity.

[5]incogitant: thoughtless.

Introduction to Thomas Brooks,
A Cabinet of Choice Jewels

Thomas Brooks (1608-1680) was educated at Emmanuel College, Cambridge, ordained in the Church of England, and after 1648 he was rector of St. Margaret's in London. Having adopted Congregationalist views, he reorganized his parish along those lines. He preached before parliament on several occasions. Brooks opposed the restoration of the king and was ejected in 1660. He remained in London and preached occasionally, but devoted himself mainly to writing. His Apples of Gold *went through seventeen editions from 1657 to 1693.*

A Cabinet of Choice Jewels, or A Box of precious Ointment. Being a plain Discovery of, or, [sic] what men are worth for Eternity, and how 'tis like to go with them in another World *was printed at London by John Hancock in 1669 (Wing B4937). It deals primarily with the problem of assurance of salvation and how a believer may detect the signs of grace in himself. What follows is from the first chapter, which offers eighteen maxims or ''considerations, rules, and directions'' for determining grace and finding assurance. The selection is a good illustration of this Puritan preoccupation and also illustrates the author's sense of working within an ongoing tradition of spiritual writing, as he quotes from many earlier authors. It consists of pages 1-7, 17-20, 57-58, 60-62, 79-83, 84-85, and 86-87, taken from the 1669 edition. There is a recent biographical notice of Brooks by J. Sears McGee in the* Biographical Dictionary of British Radicals in the Seventeenth Century, *ed. Richard Greaves and Robert Zaller (Brighton: Harvester Press, 1982-1984), 1:101-102.*

A Cabinet of Choice Jewels

The first Maxim or Consideration.

First, Some have made the witness of the Spirit to be the only mark or evidence of our interest in Christ, and deny all signs from the fruit of the Spirit; but this is to deny the fruit growing upon the Tree to be a sign that the Tree is alive, whereas our Saviour expressly tells us, that the tree is known by his fruit, Mat. 12:33. Certainly 'tis one thing to judge by our graces, and another thing to rest on our graces, or to put our trust in our graces, or to make a Saviour of our graces; there is a great deal of difference between declaring and deserving. Doubtless Christians may look to their graces as evidences of their interest in Christ, justification and salvation, though not as causes of their interest in Christ, justification, and salvation. O Sirs, we must always carefully distinguish 'twixt the root and ground of our comfort, and between the testimonies or evidences of our interest in the root of our comfort. Now it must be readily granted that Jesus Christ is the only root and ground of a Christian's comfort and triumph; and, therefore, saith

Paul, "God forbid that I should rejoyce in any thing, but in the cross of Christ."[1] And so in that, 2 Cor. 2.14, "Now thanks be unto God, which always causes us to triumph in Christ." So that, if at any time we behold this or that saving grace, or this or that part of holiness shining in our hearts or lives, we take comfort in it, not as the cause, or root, or ground of our comfort or triumph, but as in a testimony or evidence, because it doth manifest our interest in him, who is our comfort, our peace, our joy, our salvation, our all in all.[2] Look as the Rainbow is not a cause, why God will not drown the world, but a sign that God will not drown the world; and as it is a sign that God will not drown the world, we may and ought to rejoice in it, and to take comfort from it. So here, &c. 'Tis agreed on all hands, that sanctification is a precious benefit of the Covenant of grace, as well as justification; and what crime can it then be, to evidence one benefit of the Covenant of Grace, by another benefit of the same Covenant. That he that is justified, is also sanctified, and that he that is sanctified is also justified, is so clear, so bright, so sparkling, and so full a truth contained in the Covenant of grace, that no man or devil can deny. Now what evil or error can it be for a man to assert, that he that is certainly sanctified, is certainly justified; (it being the very language of the covenant of grace) and that therefore he that knows himself to be sanctified, may also know thereby that he is justified. Certainly, those persons that shall deny sanctification to be a most sure, sweet and comfortable evidence of man's justification, they must not only blot out and abolish the Epistles of James and John,

but must also race[3] out and abolish all those Evangelical promises of grace and mercy, of happiness and blessedness, that are made to such persons as are invested, enriched and bespangled with the several graces of the holy Spirit; this might be made evident by many hundred Scriptures: but take that one for all, Mat. 5, where our Saviour himself (who was the most evangelical preacher that ever was in the world) makes eight or nine promises of mercy and blessedness to those very persons that had the graces of the Spirit inherent in them, as poverty of spirit, mourning, meekness, hungering and thirsting after righteousness, &c. O sirs, why should we be so eloquently and earnestly call'd upon to try and examine our selves, whether we be in the faith or no, if we were not to come to the knowledge of our faith, in a discoursive way, arguing from the effect to the cause? Have not the Saints of old come to assurance and the knowledge of the goodness of their estates this way? Ponder seriously on that: 2 Cor 1:12, "For our rejoycing is this, the testimony of our conscience, that in simplicity and godly sincerity, . . . we have had our conversation in the world." Mark, their joy was founded on the testimony of their conscience, and their conscience gave in this testimony from the sincerity of their conversation[4] in this world. So Paul in that, 2 Tim. 4:7, 8, "I have fought a good fight, I have finished my course, I have kept the faith: henceforth is laid up for me a crown of righteousness." How plainly, how fully, how with open mouth (as I may say) does he conclude his right to the crown of Righteousness (so called, partly because 'tis purchased by the righteousness of Christ, and partly, because he is righteous that hath promised it, and partly because 'tis a just

---

[1]This paraphrase of Gal. 6:14 seems to conflate the translations of the King James Version and the Geneva Bible.

[2]Col. 3:11.

---

[3]race: erase.

[4]conversation: manner of life.

and righteous thing with God to crown them with glory at last, who have for the Gospel sake, and his glory sake, been crowned with shame and reproach in this world, and partly (if not mainly) because 'tis a crown that can only be had (or obtained) in a way of righteousness and holiness) from his graces and gracious actings in this world. "I have fought a good fight, I have finished my course, I have kept the faith;" yea, 'tis further observable, that in the blessed Scripture, we are strongly pressed to do good works, that by them we may make our calling, election and salvation sure, 2 Peter 1:10, "Wherefore the rather brethren, give diligence to make your calling and election sure. By good works;" so say all the Latine Copies, and so say some Greek Copies, though not those that our English Translators have been pleased to follow, and that is the reason why those words ("by good works") are not in our English Bibles; but he that shall seriously weigh the scope of the Apostle in this place, he must of necessity grant, that good works are to be understood, though they are not exprest in the Text; and that of the Apostle, in 1 Tim. 6:16, 17, 18, seems plainly and strongly to sound the same way.

The second Maxim or Consideration.

II. Secondly, consider, That true, sound, solid marks, signs, and evidences, are the best way to prevent delusions; there is no such deceit in sound and solid evidences, as there is in fleshly joyes, and in high and strange raptures, by which many glistering[5] Professors have been sadly deceived and deluded. Young Samuel being not acquainted with any extraordinary manifestations of the presence and power of God, took the voice of God from heaven to be the voice of old Ely.[6] Ah, how many

have there been in our dayes, that have taken the irregular motions of their own hearts, and the violent workings of their own distempered fancies, and imaginations, and Satanical delusions, to be the visions of God, celestial raptures, divine breathings, and the powerful impulses of the Spirit of God, and so have been stirred up to speak, write and act such things that have been, not only contrary to the holy Word of God, but also contrary to the very Laws of nature and Nations. Satan by transforming of himself into an Angel of light, hath seduced and ruined many Professors, against whom, as an Angel of darkness he could never prevail. Gerson[7] tells a remarkable story of Satan's appearing to a holy man, in a most glorious and beautiful manner, professing himself to be Christ; and because he for his exemplary holiness was worthy to be honoured above others, therefore he appeared unto him; but the good old man readily answered him, that he desired not to see his Saviour in this wilderness, it should suffice him to see him hereafter in heaven, and withal added this pithy prayer: "Oh let thy sight be my reward, Lord, in another life, and not in this;" and so he became victorious over Satan, though he had transformed himself into a glorious Angel of light; but such a victorious crown has not been set upon every one's head to whom Satan has appeared as an Angel of glory. Certainly, they that stand so much, so mightily for an immediate testimony, seem to open such a gap to Enthusiasm, as will not be easily shut; yea, how will they be ever able to secure to purpose, poor souls from sad delusions? for how easy a thing it is for Satan (who is the father of lyes, Joh. 8:44; who is an old deceiver, Gen. 3:13, 1 Tim. 2:14; who is

---

[5] glistering: glittering.
[6] 1 Sam. 3:5.

[7] Jean Gerson (1363-1429) was a Chancellor of the University of Paris, a leader in the conciliar movement, and a mystical writer.

the grand deceiver, Rev. 12:9, 13:14, 19:20, 20:10; who has his devices [2] Cor. 2:11; his wiles, Eph. 6:11; his snares, 1 Tim 3:7; his depths, Rev. 2:24) to find various artifices to counterfeit this immediate testimony, and bear witness in the Spirit's stead; so that, when poor souls think that they have the Spirit of grace and truth to assure them that all is well, and shall be for ever well with them; they have none but the father of lies to deceive them, they have none but the devil in Samuel's mantle, to put a soul-murdering cheat upon them. I am not fond of advising any poor souls to lay the stress of their hopes in heaven and salvation meerly upon immediate impressions, lest they should subject themselves to infinite delusions. O sirs, the way of immediate Revelation is more fleeting and inconstant, such actings of the Spirit are like those outward motions that came upon Sampson, Judges 13:25. The Spirit came upon him at times; and so upon every withdrawment, new doubts and scruples arise; but the trial of a man's estate by grace is more constant and durable, saving grace being a continual pledge of God's love to us; flashes of joy and comfort, are only sweet and delightsom whilst they are felt, but grace is that immortal seed that abideth for ever, 1 John 3.9 But, [*sic*]

The third Maxim or Consideration.

III. Thirdly, consider, In propounding of evidences for men to try their spiritual and eternal estates by, there are two special Rules for ever to be minded and remembred, and the first is this, That he that propounds evidences of grace, which are only proper to eminent Christians, as belonging to all true Christians, he will certainly grieve and sad those precious Lambs of Christ that He would not have grieved

and sadded.[8] Look, as there is a strong faith, and a weak faith, so there are evidences that are proper to a strong faith, and evidences that are proper to a weak faith: Now, he that cannot find in himself the evidences of a strong faith, he must not conclude that he has no faith; for he may have in him the evidences of a weak faith, when he has not the evidences of a strong faith in him; in Christ's School, House, Church, there are several sorts and ranks of Christians, as babes, children, young men, and old men; and accordingly, Ministers in their preaching and writing, should sort their evidences, that so babes and children may not be found bleeding, grieving and weeping, when they should be found joying and rejoycing. Secondly, no man must make such characters, marks or evidences of a child of God, which may be found in a hypocrite, a Formalist, &c. for this were to lay a stumbling block before the blind, this were to delude poor souls, and to make them glad whom God would not have made glad; yea, this is the highway, the ready way, to make them miserable in both worlds. The rule or evidence that every Christian is to measure himself by, must be neither too long nor too short, but adequate to the state of a Christian; that is, it must not be so long on the one hand, as that all Christians cannot reach it, not yet so short on the other hand, as that it will not reach a true Christian; but the rule or evidence must be such as will suit and fit every sincere believer, and none else: Some Christians are apt to judge of themselves, and to try themselves, by such rules or evidences as are competent only to those that are strong men in Christ, and that are grown to a high pitch of grace, of holiness, of communion with God, of spiritual enjoyments, and heavenly attainments, and

---

[8]sad . . . sadded: sadden . . . saddened or discourage . . . discouraged.

sweet and blessed ravishments of soul; and by this means they come to conclude against the works of the blessed spirit in them, and to perplex and disquiet their own souls with needless fears, doubts, and jealousies; others on the other hand, are apt to judge of themselves, and to try themselves, by such things, rules or evidences that are too short (and will certainly leave them short of heaven) as a fair, civil deportment among all sorts and ranks of men, a good nature, paying every man their due, charity to the poor, a good name or fame among men (yea, happily among good men) outward exercises of Religion, as hearing, praying, reading, fasting, or that they are good negative Christians, that is to say, that they are no drunkards, swearers, lyars, adulterers, extortioners, oppressors, Sabbath-breakers, persecutors, &c. Thus far Paul attained before his conversion, but if he had gone no further, he had been a lost man for ever; and by this means they flatter themselves into misery, and are still a dreaming of going to heaven, till they drop into hell, and awake with everlasting flames about their ears: And oh, that all that preach or print, read or write, would seriously lay this to heart, some in describing the state of a Christian, shew rather what of right it should be, than what indeed it is; they shew what Christians ought to be, rather than what they find themselves to be, and so they become a double edged sword to many Christians.

The sixth Maxim or Consideration.

VI. Sixthly, consider, That 'tis granted on all hands, that the least degree of grace, if true, is sufficient to salvation; for the promises of life and glory, or remission and salvation, of everlasting happiness and blessedness, are not made over to degrees of grace, but to the truth of grace, not to faith in triumph, but to faith in truth; and therefore the sense and evidence of the least

grace, yea of the least degree of the least grace, may afford some measure of assurance. Grace is the fruit of the Spirit, Gal. 5:22, and the tree is known by his fruit, Mat. 12:33. I don't say, that weak grace will afford a strong assurance, or a full assurance (for that rather arises from strength of grace, than from truth of grace) but I say, weak grace may afford some assurance: And oh, that all weak Christians would seriously lay this to heart, for it may serve to relieve them against many fears, doubts, discouragements and jealousies, which do much disturb the peace and comfort of their precious souls; though the least measures of grace can't satisfie a sincere Christian, yet they ought to quiet his conscience, and chear his heart, and confirm his judgement of his interest in Christ. The least measure of grace is like a Diamond, very little in bulk, but of high price and mighty value, and accordingly we are to improve it for our comfort and encouragement. A Goldsmith makes reckoning of the least filings of gold, and so should we of the least measures of grace. A man may read the King's Image upon a silver penny, as well as upon a larger piece of coyn. The least dram of grace bears the Image of God upon it; and why then should it not evidence the goodness and happiness of a Christian's estate? It's a true saying, That the assurance of an eternal life, is the life of this temporal life. I have read that Mr. Jordain, one of the Aldermen of the City of Exeter,[9] would use to ask grown Professors, whether they had any assurance; which if they denied, he would tell them, that he was even ashamed of them; "In good earnest," saith he, "I would study the promises, and go into my closet, and lock the door, and there plead them to God, and say, that I would not go

---

[9]Ferdinando Nicolls, *The Life and Death of Mr. Ignatius Jurdain*, (London, 1654), sig. a2ʳ, was the source for this story.

forth, till he gave me some sence [*sic*] of his love." He would often mention and try himself by these three Marks: First, a sincere desire to fear the name of God, which he grounded upon that, Neh. 1:11. Secondly, a sincere desire to do the will of God in all things required; which he grounded upon Psalm 119:6; Thirdly, a full purpose of heart to cleave to the Lord, which he grounded upon Acts 11:23. These he would often press upon others, and these he frequently tryed himself by, and from these he had much assurance and comfort. Mr. Stephen Marshal,[10] in a sermon of his on Isa. 9:2, saith, "Look and examine, whether thou dost not loath thyself as a base creature; and dost thou make this nothing? Secondly, Dost thou not in thy heart value and prize the meanest child of God, more than the greatest men in the world, that have not the image of God, the image of grace and holiness stamped upon them? I pray God," saith Mr. Marshal, "that many of God's people do not want[11] these evidences." "If our souls," saith another, "shall like of Christ for a suitor, when we find no other jointure but the cross, we may be sure we are Christians. A man may want the feeling of his faith, and cry and call again and again for it, and feel nothing all this while, and yet nevertheless have true and sound faith: For the feeling of, and mourning for the want of faith, and the earnest and constant desire of it, is an infallible sign of faith. For this is a sure Rule, that so long as one feeleth himself sick he is not dead; and the high estimation of faith, joined with a vehement desire of it, is a singular evidence that there is a sound and lively root of faith in our hearts."[12] "All the elect of God shall have the sanctification of the Spirit unto obedience, and the sprinkling of the bloud of Christ upon their hearts, sooner or later. I do not press the having of these things perfectly, but sincerely; an elect person may want many a degree of grace, but if he have them in sincerity, though in the least measure, it is a sufficient evidence of his election."[13] "An earnest is little in regard of the whole: perhaps we have but a shilling to secure us of many pounds; so then the point is this, That howsoever we may be assured of our estate in grace, and likewise that we shall hold out, yet the ground of this assurance is not from any great measure of grace; but though it be little in quantity, it may be great in assurance and security. As we value an earnest, not for the worth that is in itself, but because it assures us of a great bargain; we have an eye more to the consummation of the bargain, than to the quantity of the earnest; so it is here, grace is but an earnest: yet not withstanding, though it be little, as an earnest is, yet it is great in assurance and validity, answerable to the relation of that it hath to assure us. Though grace be little, yet as little as it is, seeing it is an earnest, and the first fruits (as the Apostle saith) which were but little in regard of the whole harvest, yet it is of the nature of the whole, and thereupon it comes to secure. A spark of fire is but little, yet it is fire as well as the whole element of fire; and a drop of water is but little, yet it is water as well as the whole Ocean.

---

[10]Stephen Marshall (d. 1655) was a leader of the Presbyterians during the unsettled 1640s. He was a member of the Westminster Assembly and a frequent preacher to Parliament.

[11]want: lack.

[12]Brooks's marginal notation attributes this quotation to John Dod and Robert Cleaver, *A Plaine and Familiar Exposition of the Ten Commandments,* a popular work among Puritans. But I cannot find it on the page cited or elsewhere.

[13]Christopher Love, *The Zealous Christian Taking Heaven by Holy Violence* (London, 1654), 134, 136. Love was executed in 1651 for complicity in a royalist plot against the government.

When a man is in a dark place, put the case it be in a dungeon, if he have but a little light shining in to him from a little crevice, that little light discovers that the day is broke, that the Sun is risen. Put the case there be but one grape on a Vine, it shews that it is a Vine, and that the vine is not dead: so put the case that there be but the appearance of a little grace in a Christian, perhaps the Spirit of God appears but in one grace in him at that time, yet that one grace sheweth that we are Vines, and not thistles, or thorns or base plants, and it shews that there is life in the root.'' Thus you see how fully this Reverend Doctor speaks to the case.[14] That friend that writes the life and death of Mr. John Murcot, once Preacher of the Gospel at Dublin, saith, ''That in preparation for the Supper Ordinance, he would bring himself unto the Test, and to say the truth, was very clear in the discovering and making out of his own condition, being well acquainted with the way of God's dealing with the soul, and with the way of the soul's closing with Christ. Instance, April 3, 1653. Upon search I find, 1. Myself an undone creature. 2. That the Lord Jesus sufficiently satisfied as Mediator the Law for sin. 3. That he is freely offered in the Gospel. 4. So far as I know my own heart, I do through mercy heartily consent, that he only shall be my Saviour, not my works or duties, which I do only in obedience to him. 5. If I know my heart, I would be ruled by his Word and Spirit. Behold, in a few words,'' saith he that writes his life and death, ''the sum and substance of the Gospel.''[15] By these instances we may see, that some of the precious servants of God have found a great deal of comfort, support, rest, content, and some measure of assurance, from a lower rank of evidences, than those that many strong Christians do reach unto, &c.

The Ninth Maxim or Consideration.

IX. Ninthly, consider this, That in divers men there are divers degrees of Assurance, and in one and the same gracious Soul, there are different degrees of Assurance at divers times, but there is in no man at any time in this life, perfection of degrees, for our understandings and knowledg in this life is imperfect both as to the faculty and its acts, 1 Cor. 13:12, ''For now we see through a glass darkly (Greek in a Riddle) but then face to face: Now I know in part, but then shall I know even as also I am known.'' A clear distinct, immediate, full and perfect knowledg of God is desirable on earth, but we shall never attain to it till we come to Heaven; this Well is deep, and for the most part we want a bucket to draw withal, the best of men can better tell what God is not, than what he is; the most acute and judicious in divine knowledg, have and must acknowledg their ignorance, witness that great Apostle Paul, who learned his Divinity among the Angels, and had the Holy Ghost for his immediate Tutor, yet he confesses that he knew but in part; certainly there is no man under heaven that hath such a perfect, compleat and full assurance of his Salvation (in an ordinary way) as that one degree cannot be added to the former; Neither is there any repugnancy in asserting an infallible assurance, and denying a perfect assurance, for I infallibly know that there is a God, and that this God is holy, just and true, and yet I have no perfect knowledg of a Deity, nor of the holiness, justice and truth of God, for in this life the most knowing man knows but in part: Dear friends, in the Church of Christ there are Believers of several

---

[14]Richard Sibbes, *A Learned Commentary upon the first chapter of the second epistle of Saint Paul to the Corinthians* (London, 1655), 491-92.

[15]*Several Works of Mr. John Murcot* (London, 1657), 36-37. John Murcot was a Puritan who went to Ireland to preach in 1651.

growths: there are Fathers, young men, Children, and Babes, 1 John 1:13, 14; 1 Peter 2:2. And as in most families there are commonly more children and babes than grown men; so in the Church of Christ there are commonly more weak, staggering, doubting Christians than there are strong ones, grown up to a full assurance. Some think, that as soon as they be assured, they must needs be void of all fears, and filled with all joy in believing; but this is a real mistake, for glorious and ravishing joy is a separable accident from Assurance, nor yet doth Assurance exclude all doubts and fears, but only such doubts and fears as ariseth from infidelity and reigning hypocrisy. But,

The Tenth Maxim or Consideration.

X. Tenthly, Consider, We have no ground from Scripture to expect that God should either be a Voice from Heaven, or by sending an Angel from about his Throne, or by any glorious apparitions or strong impressions, or by any extraordinary way of Revelations, assure us that we do believe, or that our Grace is true, or that our interest in God and Christ is certain, or that our pardon is sealed in Heaven, or that we are in a justified state, and that we shall be at last undoubtedly saved, O no! But we are to use all those blessed helps and means that are appointed by God, and common to all Believers, for the obtaining of a particular Assurance that we are Believers, and that our state is good, and that we have a special propriety[16] in Christ, and in all the fundamental good that comes by him. Mark, he that will receive no establishment, no comfort, no peace, no assurance, except it be administered by the hand of an Angel, and witnesed to by some Voice from Heaven, &c., will certainly live and

dye without establishment, comfort, peace, or assurance. . . .

The eleventh Maxim or Consideration.

XI. Eleventhly, consider that probablities of Grace, of sincerity, of an interest in Christ, and of Salvation, may be a very great stay, and singular support, and a special cordial and comfort to abundance of precious Christians that want that sweet and blessed Assurance that poor Souls do earnestly breathe and long after. There are doubtless many thousands of the precious sons and daughters of Zion comparable to fine Gold,[17] that have not a clear and full Assurance of their interest in Christ, nor of the saving work of God upon their souls, who yet are able to plead many probabilities of grace and of an interest in Christ. Now doubtless probabilities of Grace and of an interest in Christ may serve to keep off fears and doubts, and darkness, and sadness, and all rash and peremptory conclusions against a man's own Soul, and his everlasting welfare, and may contribute very much to the keeping up of a great deal of peace, comfort, and quietness in his Soul. The probable grounds that thou hast Grace, and that God has begun to work powerfully, and savingly upon thee, are mercies more worth than ten thousand Worlds. Will you please seriously and frequently to dwell upon these ten particulars.

First, That though many weak gracious souls don't enjoy communion with God in joy and delight, yet they do enjoy communion with God in sorrow and tears. A man may have communion with God in a heart humbling, a heart melting, and a heart abasing way, when he hath not communion with God in a heart reviving, a heart cheering, and a heart comforting way.

---

[16]Propriety: interest.

[17]Allusion to Lam. 4:2.

Tis a very great mistake among many weak tender spirited Christians, to think that they have no communion with God in duties, except they meet with God embracing and kissing, cheering and comforting up their Souls: And O that all Christians would remember this once for all, *viz.* That a Christian may have as real communion with God in a heart-humbling way, as he can have in a heart comforting way; A Christian may have as choice communion with God when his eyes are full of tears, as he can have when his heart is full of joy; when a godly man upon his dying bed was askt which were his most joyful dayes (either those before his Conversion, or those since his Conversion) upon which he cryed out, "O give me mourning dayes again, Give me my mourning dayes again, for they were my joyfullest dayes." Many times a poor Christian has never more joy in his heart than when his eyes are full of tears. But,

Secondly, Though many poor weak doubting trembling Christians dare not say that they do love the Lord Jesus Christ, yet they dare say that they would love the Lord Jesus Christ with all their hearts, and with all their Souls, and they dare say, that if it were in their power, they would even shed tears of blood because they cannot love Christ, both as they would and as they should. Blessed Bradford[18] would sit and weep at Dinner till the tears fell on his Trencher,[19] because he could love God no more. So the poor doubting trembling Christian mourns and laments because he can love Christ no more. "A man may love Gold, and yet not have it, but no man loveth God but he is sure to have God," saith

Augustine.[20] A good man once cried out, "I had rather have one Christ, than a thousand Worlds."

Thirdly, Though many poor weak doubting trembling Christians dare not say that they have Grace, yet they dare say that they prize the least dram of Grace above all the gold and silver of the Indies; were all the world a lump of gold, and in their hands to dispose of it, they would give it for Grace, yea for a little Grace. Now certainly no man can thus highly prize Grace but he that has Grace. No man sees the worth and lustre of Grace; no man sees a beauty and excellency in Grace, nor no man can value Grace above the gold of Ophir,[21] but he whose heart has been changed, and whose eyes have been opened by the Spirit of Grace. . . .

The Fifteenth Maxim or Consideration.

XV. Fifteenthly, Consider in judging of your selves and your spiritual estates and conditions, you must always have an eye to your natural tempers, complexions, constitutions, and inclinations, and the sins and temptations that these do lay you most open to, and remember that as in some tempers a little grace makes a very great shew; so in other tempers a great deal of grace makes but a very little shew. A little water in a long narrow mouth'd glass seems to be a great deal, when ten times, yea, twenty times as much in a large Cistern is hardly discernible; the application is easie. A little sugar will serve well enough for sweet wines, but much more is requisite to sweeten that wine that is sharp and harsh. A little grace will make a very glorious

---

[18]John Bradford (1510-1555) was one of the Protestant martyrs burned at the stake for heresy during the reign of Queen Mary. He wrote moving letters of spiritual consolation that made him an early exponent of many themes later important to the Puritans.

[19]trencher: a square or rectangular wooden plate for meat.

[20]This quotation from St. Augustine illustrates the kind of apt expression the Puritans loved to glean from that church father.

[21]gold of Ophir: an ancient region famous for gold that is frequently mentioned in the Old Testament. Solomon sent ships there for gold (1 Kings 10:11).

shew in such men and women whose very natural tempers are sweet, soft, gentle, meek, affable, courteous; when a great deal of Grace is hardly discernible in those whose very natural tempers are cross, crooked, cholerick, fierce, passionate, ruff, and unhewen. As a good man said of an eminent light now in Heaven, ''That he had Grace enough for ten men, but scarce enough for himself,'' his natural temper was so bad, which he would himself often lament and bewail, saying to his friends, ''That he had such a cross crooked nature, that if God had not given him grace, none would have been able to have lived one day quietly with him.'' A sincere Christian may have more roughness of nature, and more sturdiness[22] of passions, than is in many a moral man; he that hath more Christianity, may have less Morality, as there is more perfection of animal and sensitive faculties in some bruits than in some men. Tis an old experienced truth, that those sins are with the greatest pains, labour, travel, and difficulty subdued and mortified, which our natural tempers, complexions, and constitutions do most strongly incline and dispose us to, and were but those lusts subdued and brought under, it would be no difficult thing to bring all other sins to an under;[23] when Goliath was slain, the Philistines fled; when a General in an Army falls, the common Souldiers are quickly routed. So tis here; get but the sins of your natural tempers, complexions, and constitutions under your feet, and you will quickly ride in a holy triumph over the rest. When justice is effectually done upon your constitution sins,[24] other sins will not be long lived; thrust but a dart through the heart of Ab-

salom,[25] and a complete conquest will follow. Now before I close up this particular, let me advise you frequently to consider, that you can never make a true, a right, a serious judgment of your selves, or of your spiritual estates and conditions, without a prudent eye upon your natural tempers, complexions, and constitutions, granting to yourselves such indulgence and grains of allowance upon the account of your natural tempers, as will stand with sincerity and the Covenant of Grace. But,

The Sixteenth Maxim or Consideration.

XVI. Sixteenthly, Consider, if you cannot, if you dare not say that you have grace, yet do not say that you have no Grace, for the being of Grace in the soul is one thing, and the seeing of Grace in the Soul is another thing. A man may have Grace, and yet not know that he has Grace; he may have a seed of God in him, and yet not see it; He may believe, and yet not believe that he does believe; the child lives before it knows that it lives. If you cannot say that your Graces are true, yet do not say that they are counterfeit, lest you bear false witness against the real work of the Spirit in you. There are none so apt to question the truth of their Grace as those are that are truly gracious; though Satan cannot hinder the holy Spirit from working true grace in the Soul, yet he will do all he can to fill the Soul with fears and doubts and jealousies about the truth of that grace that the holy Spirit has wrought in it. When did you ever know the Devil to tempt an Hypocrite to believe that his Graces were not true, and that certainly he had not the root of the matter in him? If you cannot say that you have an interest in Christ, yet do not say that you have no interest in Christ; for a man may have an interest in Christ, and yet

---

[22]sturdiness: harshness, rebelliousness.

[23]to an under: under control.

[24]constitution sins: sins attributable to one's disposition.

---

[25]Absalom, David's son, was killed by darts thrown by Joab, 2 Sam. 8:14.

not see his interest in Christ, not know his interest in Christ; there are many precious Christians that walk in darkness, who yet have an interest in that Jesus that is all Light, Life, and love; if you cannot say that your pardon is sealed in the Court of your own Conscience, yet do not say that tis not sealed in the Court of Heaven, for many a Christian has his pardon sealed in the Court of Heaven, before it is sealed in the Court of his own Conscience. A pardon sealed in the Court of Conscience, is that new name and white stone[26] which God does not give to every one at first Conversion; God will take his own time to seal up every Christian's Pardon in his bosome. If you cannot say that your name is written in the Book of life, yet do not say that tis not written in the Book of life; the Disciples' names were first written in Heaven before Christ bid them rejoyce, because their names were written in Heaven.[27] A man may have his name written in Heaven, and yet it may be a long while before God may tell him his name is written in Heaven. I,[28] you cannot say that the precious Promises are yours, yet do not say that they are children's Bread, and such dainties that your Soul shall never tast[e] of; tis not every precious Christian that has an interest in the Promises, that can run and read his interest in the Promises. If you cannot say that the heavenly inheritance is yours, yet do not say that tis not yours, do not say that it shall never be yours. A Christian may have a good title to the heavenly inheritance, and yet not be able to make good his title, to clear up his title; as a child in the arms or in the Cradle, may be heir to a Crown, a Kingdom, and yet he is not able to make good his title. If you cannot say that you have Assurance, yet do not say that you shall never

---

[26]Rev. 2:17.

[27]Luke 10:20.

[28]I: aye.

have Assurance, for a man may want Assurance one year, and have it the next; one Moneth, and have it another; one week, and have it another; one day, and have it another; yea, one hour, and have it another. If you cannot say that you shall certainly go to Heaven, yet do not say that you shall undoubtedly go to Hell, for who made you one of the Privy Councellors of Heaven, who acquainted you with the secret decrees of God, &c! Now were this rule but thoroughly minded, and conscientiously practiced, O how well would it go with many tempted, troubled, bewildered, and clouded Christians! O how would Satan be disappointed, and poor souls quieted, composed, and refreshed. But,

The seventeenth Maxim or Consideration.

XVII. Seventeenthly, When ever you cast your eye upon your gracious evidences, it highly concerns you seriously to remember that you have to deal with God in a Covenant of Grace, and not in a Covenant of Works. Every breach of peace with God, is not a breach of Covenant with God. Though the Wife hath many weaknesses and infirmities hanging upon her, and though she may often grieve, provoke, and displease her Husband, yet as long as she remains faithful, and truly loving, and in the main obedient to him, though he may alter his carriage toward her, yet he will not withdraw his love from her, or deny his relation to her. No more will God towards his weak miscarrying ones, . . .

. . . Seriously consider that many weak Christians are much mistaken about the terms and condition of the Covenant of Grace, they think that the condition of the Covenant is perfect and unsinning obedience, whereas tis only sincere obedience. Mark, that man sincerely obeyes and sincerely walks in Covenant with God, who sincerely, who heartily, who ordinarily desires, labours, and endeavors to obey the

Law of God, the will of God, and to walk in Covenant with God. Mark, particular actions do not denominate any estate, it is the course of actions which denominate a man's walking in Covenant with God, or his not walking in Covenant with God; if his course of actions be sinful, he walks not in Covenant with God; but if his course of actions be holy and gracious, he walks in Covenant with God. Though the needle of the Seaman's Compass may jog this way, and that way, yet the bent of the needle will still be Northward; so though a Christian in Covenant with God may have his particular sinful joggings, this way or that way, yet the bent of his heart will still be to walk in Covenant with God. . . .

Doubtless many precious Christians have charged and condemned themselves for those things that the great God will never charge them with, nor condemn them for. Blessed Bradford[29] wrote himself an Hypocrite, a painted Sepulcher, but doubtless God will never bring such a charge against him. O Sirs, the stirrings of sin, and the workings of sin, and the prevalency of sin, for particular acts will stand with the Covenant of Grace, though not with the Covenant of Works. You may not by any means conclude that you are not in a Covenant of Grace, because such and such corruptions stir in you, or because such or such weaknesses now and then break forth and discover themselves, either in your lips or lives: Did Christians but study the Covenant of grace more, and understand better than they do the difference between the Covenant of grace and the Covenant of works, how would their fears and doubts about their spiritual and eternal estates vanish, as the clouds before the Sun when it shines in its greatest strength and glory, &c.

'Twas the saying of an eminent Minister on his death-bed, That he had much peace and quietness, not so much from a greater measure of grace than other Christians had, or from any immediate witness of the spirit, but because he had a more clear understanding of the Covenant of grace than many others, having studied it, and Preached it so many years as he had done. Doubtless had Christians a more clear and a more full understanding of the Covenant of grace, they would live more holily, serviceably, humbly, fruitfully, comfortably and sweetly than they do, and they would dye more willingly, readily, and cheerfully than many (may I not say than most) Christians use to do.

---

[29]see above, n. 18.

Introduction to Walter Marshall,
The Gospel-Mystery of Sanctification

Walter Marshall (1628-1680) was the son of a Durham clergyman. He was educated at Oxford, where he remained as a fellow until 1661, in which year he became the parish minister at Hursley, near Winchester. The next year he was ejected because of his refusal to accept the terms of the Act of Uniformity. Thereafter he settled down to a relatively undisturbed life as pastor to a Dissenting congregation at Gosport, Hampshire.

He is well-known through a posthumous publication, The Gospel-Mystery of Sanctification Opened in Sundry Practical Directions, Suited especially to the Case of those who labour under the guilt and power of Indwelling Sin, To which is added a Sermon of Justification, *first printed in 1692, at London, by T. Parkhurst and frequently reprinted thereafter, sometimes in abbreviated editions. The preface by James Hervey in the 1761 printing praised it as the next book after the Bible that it would be good to have if one were lost on a desert island. The English poet William Cowper called Marshall ''one of the best writers and the most spiritual expositor of scriptures I have ever read.''* [1]

The following selections, which consist of the first parts of directions three and four, (of fourteen), are taken from the original 1692 edition (Wing M809), Sigs. Aa2ʳ-Aa4ʳ, 40-47, 59-70. The anonymous preface fills out the picture of Marshall's reputation. The third direction develops the important theme of the believer's union with Christ, and the fourth direction stresses the importance of a faith that includes trust and commitment. Whether the sanctification of the third direction or the justification of the fourth, Marshall insists on the preeminence of grace. The argumentative element expresses Marshall's concern over the growth of a liberalism that would reduce Christianity to little more than morality, abandoning its more mystical themes. There is a brief life of Marshall by Charlotte Fell-Smith in the Dictionary of National Biography.

---

[1]Gordon Wakefield, *Puritan Devotion* (London: Epworth Press, 1957) 4.

The Gospel-Mystery
of Sanctification Opened
in Sundry Practical Directions

by Walter Marshall

The Preface

Reader,

Mr. Walter Marshal, Composer of these Directions how to attain to that practice and manner of Life which we call Holiness, Righteousness, or Godliness, was Educated in New Colledge in Oxford, and was a Fellow of the said Colledge, and afterwards he was chosen a Fellow of the Colledge at Winchester, but was put under the Bartholomew Bushel,[2] with nigh two Thousand more Lights, (a Sin not yet repented of) whose illuminations made the Land a Goshen. He was esteemed a Presbyterian, and was called to be Pastor to a People at Gospert in Hampshire, where he shined though he had not the Publick Oile;[3] the substance of these Meditations were there Spun out of his own Experiences, he having been much exercised with troubled Thoughts, and that for many Years, and had by many Mortifying Methods sought Peace of Conscience; but notwithstanding all, his Troubles still increased. Whereupon he consulted others, particularly Mr. Baxter,[4] (whose Writings he had been much conversant with,) who thereupon told Mr. Marshal he took them too Legally: He afterwards consulted an Eminent Divine, (giving him an Account of the State of his Soul, and particularizing his Sins that lay heavy on his Conscience;) who in his Reply told him, He had forgot to mention the greatest Sin of all, the Sin of Unbelief, in not believing on the Lord Jesus for the Remission of his Sins, and [for] Sanctifying his Nature. Hereupon he set himself to the studying and preaching of Christ, and attained to eminent Holiness, great peace of Conscience, and joy in the Holy Ghost. Mr. Marshal's dying Words were these, ''The wages of sin is death, but the gift of God is eternal life through Jesus Christ our Lord,''[5] having but just before said to those about him, that he now dyed in the full perswasion of the Truth, and in the comfort of that Doctrine which he had Preached; the sum whereof is contained in the ensuing Discourse.

Some time since he was translated by Death, Elijah-like, dropping these sheets, as his Mantle, for succeeding Elisha's to go forth with for the Conversion of Sinners, and Comfort of drooping Souls.

These Papers are the profound Experiences of a studious Holy Soul, Learned of the Father, coming from his very Heart, and smell of no Party or Design but for Ho-

---

[2]i.e., ejected on St. Bartholomew's Day, August 24, 1662, along with other ministers of Puritan views who could not subscribe to the liturgy and government of the Restoration Church of England.

[3]i.e., was not the regular Church of England parish minister.

[4]Richard Baxter (1615-1691), a leader of the English Presbyterians, was an expert on spiritual counsel and assurance, as his extensive writings testify.

[5]Rom. 6:23.

liness and Happiness; yet it is to be feared they will scarcely go down with the heady Notionalists[6] of this Age, who are of the Tribe of Reuben, wavering with every Wind of Modish Doctrine, but in Judah it will be praised, and we may hope that many Shrubs and Cedars hereby may advance in knowledge and comfort. But not to detain thee longer, read over all these Directions (that you may fully understand the Author) or read none; if you do it with the serious humble spirit in which they were wrote, it may be hop'd (the matter being so weighty, and from so able an Hand) through the Grace of God they will sink into thy Conscience, and make theee a solid Christian, full of Faith, Holiness and Consolation.

[6]notionalists: those with special ideas of their own, or "axes to grind."

Direction. III.

The way to get holy Endowments and Qualifications necessary to frame and enable us for the immediate Practice of the Law, is to receive them out of the fulness of Christ, by Fellowship with him; and that we may have this Fellowship, we must be in Christ, and have Christ himself in us, by a Mystical Union with him.

Explication.

Here, as much as any where, we have great cause to acknowledge with the Apostle, that without Controversie great is the Mystery of of Godliness, even so great that it could not have entred into the Heart of Man to conceive it, if God had not made it known in the Gospel by supernatural Revelation. Yea, tho' it be revealed clearly in the holy Scriptures, yet the Natural Man hath not Eyes to see it there, for it is foolishness to him; and if God express it never so plainly and properly, he will think that God is speaking Riddles and Parables. And I doubt not but it is still a Riddle and Parable even to many truly Godly, that have received an holy Nature in this way: For the Apostles themselves had the saving benefit of it before the Comforter discovered it clearly to them, John 14:20. And they walked in Christ, as the way to the Father, before they clearly knew him to be the way, John 14:5. And the best of us know it but in part, and must wait for the perfect knowledge of it in another World. One great Mystery is, that the holy frame and disposition whereby our Souls are furnished and enabled for immediate Practice of the Law, must be gotten by receiving it out of Christ's fulness, as a thing already prepared and brought to an existance for us in Christ, and treasured up in him; and that as we are justified by a righteousness wrought out in Christ, and imputed to us, so we are sanctified by such an holy frame and qualifications, as are first wrought out, and compleated in Christ for us, and then imparted to us: and as our natural corruption was produced originally in the first Adam, and propagated from him to us; so our new nature and holiness is first produced in Christ, and derived from him to us, or as it were propagated. So that we are not at all to work together with Christ, in making or producing that holy frame in us, but only to take it to ourselves, and use it in our holy Practice, as made ready to our hands. Thus we have fellowship with Christ in recovering that holy frame of Spirit that was originally in him: for fellowship is when several Persons have the same things in common, 1 John 1. This Mystery is so great, that notwithstanding all the Light of the Gospel, we commonly think that we must get an holy frame by producing it a new in ourselves, and by forming and working it out of our own Hearts. Therefore many that are seriously devout, take a great deal of pains to mortifie their corrupted Nature, and beget an holy frame of Heart in themselves, by striving earnestly to master their sinful lusts, and by pressing vehemently upon their Hearts many motives to Godliness, labouring importunately to squeeze good qualifications out of them, as Oyl out of a Flint. They account that tho' they be justified by a righteousness wrought out by Christ, yet they must be sanctifi'd by a holiness wrought out by themselves. And tho' out of humility they are willing to call it infused Grace, yet they think they must get the infusion of it by the same manner of working, as if it were wholly acquired by their endeavours. On this account they acknowledge the entrance into a Godly Life to be harsh and unpleasing, because it costs so much struling with their own Hearts and Affections to new frame them; if they knew that this way of entrance is not only harsh and unpleasant, but altogether impossible, and that the true way of mortifying sin, and quickning themselves to holiness, is by receiving a new nature out of the fulness of Christ, and that we do no more to the production of a new nature, than of original sin, tho' we we do more to the reception of it. If they knew this, they might save themselves many a bitter agony, and a great deal of mispent burdensome labour, and employ their endeavours to enter in at the strait Gate, in such a way as would be more pleasant and successful.

Another greater mystery in the way of Sanctification, is the glorious manner of our Fellowship with Christ in receiving an holy frame of heart from him. It is by our being in Christ, and having Christ himself in us, and that not meerly by his universal presence, as he is God, but by such a close union as that we are one spirit, and one flesh with him, which is a priviledge peculiar to those that are truly santified. I may well call this a mystical union, because the Apostle calleth it a great mystery, in an Epistle full of Mysteries, Eph. 5:20, intimating, that it is great, eminently above many other Mysteries; it is one of the three Mystical Unions that are the chief Mysteries in Religion: the other two are the Union of the Trinity of Persons in One Godhead, and the Union of the Divine and Human Nature in One Person, Jesus Christ, God and Man. Though we cannot frame an exact Idea of the manner of any of these Three Unions in our Imaginations, because the depth of these Mysteries is beyond our Comprehension, yet we have cause to believe them all, because they are clearly revealed in Scripture, and are a necessary Foundation for other Points of Christian Doctrine, particularly this Union betwixt Christ and Believers, is plainly [revealed] in several places of Scripture, affirming that Christ is, and dwelleth in believers, and they in him, John 6:56, and 14:20. And that they are so joyned together as to become one Spirit, 1 Cor. 6:17. And that Believers are Members of Christ's Body, of his Flesh, and of his Bones; and they two, Christ and the Church, are one flesh, Eph. 5:30, 31. Furthermore, this Union is illustrated in Scripture by various resemblances, which would be very much unlike the things which they are made use of to resemble, and would rather seem to beguile us by obscuring the Truth, than instruct us by illustrating it, if there were no true proper Union betwixt Christ and Believers. It is resembled by the Union betwixt God the Father and Christ, John 14:20. and 17:21, 22, 23, betwixt the Vine and its Branches, John 15:4, 5, betwixt the Head and Body, Ephes. 1:22, 23, betwixt Bread and the Eater, John 6:51, 53, 54. It is not only resembled but sealed in the Lord's Supper, where neither the Popish Transubstantiation, nor the Lutheran's Consubstantiation, nor the Protestants'[7] spiritual Presence of Christ's Body and Blood to the true Receivers can stand without it, and if we can imagine that Christ's Body and Blood are not truely eaten and drunk by Believers either spiritually or corporally, we shall make the Bread and Wine joyned with the Words of Institution, not only naked Signs, but such Signs as are much more apt to breed false Notions in us, than to establish us in the Truth. And there is nothing in this Union so impossible or repugnant to Reason, as may force us to depart from the plain and familiar sence of those Scriptures that express and illustrate it. Though Christ be in Heaven and we on Earth, yet he can joyn our Souls and Bodies to his at such a distance, without any substantial Change of either, by the same infinite Spirit dwelling in him and us, and so our Flesh will become his, when it is quickned by his Spirit, and his Flesh ours as truly as if we did eat his Flesh, and drink his Blood, and he will be in us himself by his Spirit who is one with him, and who can unite more closely to Christ than any material Substance can do, or who can make a more close and intimate Union betwixt Christ and us. And it will not follow from hence that a Believer is one Person with Christ, any more than that Christ is one Person with the Father by that greater mystical Union. Neither will a Believer be hereby made God's, but only the Temple of God, as Christ's Body and Soul is, and the Spirit's lively Instrument, rather than the principal Cause. Neither will a Believer be necessarily perfect in Holiness hereby, or Christ made a Sinner, for Christ knoweth how to dwell in a Believer by certain measures and degrees, and to make

them holy so far only as he dwelleth in them. And though this Union seem too high a Preferment for such unworthy Creatures as we are, yet considering the preciousness of the Blood of God whereby we are redeemed, we should dishonour God if we should not expect a miraculous Advancement to the highest Dignity that Creatures are capable of through the Merits of that Blood. Neither is there any thing in this Union contrary to the Judgment of Sense, because the Bond of the Union being Spiritual, falleth not at all under the Judgment of Sense.

Several learned Men[8] of late acknowledge no other Union betwixt Christ and Believers, than such as persons or things wholly separated, may have by their mutual relations each to other, and accordingly they interpret the places of Scripture that speak of this Union. When Christ is called the Head of the Church, they account that a Political Head or Governour is the thing meant when Christ is said to be in his People, and they in him, they think that the proper meaning is, that Christ's Law, Doctrine, Grace, Salvation, or that Godliness is in them, and embraced by them; so that Christ here must not be taken for Christ himself, but for some other thing wrought in them by Christ. When Christ and Believers are said to be one Spirit and one Flesh, they understand it of the Agreement of their Minds and Affections, as if the greatness of the Mystery of this Union mentioned, Ephes. 5:32, consisted rather in a harsh Hope, or a dark improper Expression, than in the depth and abstruceness [sic] of the thing it self, and as if

---

[7]Protestants: Reformed or Calvinist.

[8]Some seventeenth-century English theologians, such as the Anglican conformists Edward Fowler, Samuel Parker, and William Sherlock—all active during the Restoration period—denied the doctrine of the imputation of Christ's righteousness to the believer and consequently the doctrine of the mystical union of the believer with Christ.

Christ and his Apostles had affected obscure intricate Expressions, when they speak to this Church of things very plain and easie to be understood. Thus that great Mystery the Union of Believers with Christ himself, which is the Glory of the Church, and hath been highly owned formerly both by the ancient Fathers, and many eminent Protestant Divines, particular Writers concerning the Doctrine of the Lord's Supper, and by a very general Consent of the Church in many Ages, is now exploded out of the new Model of Divinity. The reason of exploding it, as I judge in Charity, is not because our late learned Refiners of Divinity think themselves less able to defend it than the other two mysterious Unions, and to silence the Objections of those proud Sophisters that will not believe what they cannot comprehend; but rather because they account it to be one of the Sinnews of Antinomianism[9] that lay unobserved in the former usual Doctrine; that it tendeth to puff up Men with a Perswasion that they are justified, and have eternal Life in them already, and that they need not depend any longer upon their uncertain Performances of the Condition of sincere Obedience for Salvation, whereby they account the very Foundation of a holy Practice to be subverted. But the Wisdom of God hath laid another manner of Foundation for an holy Practice than they imagine, of which this Union, (which the Builders refuse) is a principal stone next to the head of the corner. And in opposition to their corrupt Glosses upon the Scriptures that prove it, I assert that our Union with Christ is the cause of our Subjection to Christ as a Political head in all things, and of the abiding of his Law, Doctrine, Grace, Salvation, and all Godliness in us, and of our Agreement with him in our Minds and Affections, and therefore it cannot be altogether the same thing with them. And this Assertion is useful for a better Understanding of the Excellency of this Union. It is not a Priviledge procured by our sincere Obedience and Holiness, as some may imagine, or a reward of good works reserved for us in another World; but it is a Priviledge bestowed upon Believers in their very first entrance into an holy state, on which all ability to do good works doth depend, and all sincere Obedience to the Law doth follow after it as Fruit produced by it. . . .

---

[9]Antinomianism was generally taken as the doctrine that the redeemed cannot sin after regeneration; Marshall is sensitive to the charge made against Calvinists that they undercut an emphasis on morality by their belief in the imputation of Christ's righteousness to the believer.

Direction IV.

The Means or Instruments whereby the Spirit of God accomplisheth our Union with Christ and our Fellowship with him in all Holiness, are, the Gospel whereby Christ entereth into our Hearts to work Faith in us, and Faith whereby we actually receive Christ himself, with all his Fulness, into our Hearts. And this Faith is a Grace of the Spirit, whereby we heartily believe the Gospel, and also believe on Christ, as he is revealed and freely promised to us therein, for all his Salvation.

Explication.

That which I asserted in the foregoing Direction, concerning the necessity of our being in Christ, and having Christ in us, by a mystical Union, to enable us for an holy Practice, might put us to a stand[10] in our Endeavours for Holiness, because we cannot imagine how we should be able to raise our selves about our natural Sphere, to his glorious Union and Fellowship, until God be pleased to make known to us, by supernatural revelation, the means whereby his spirit maketh us Partakers of so high a Privilege. But God is pleased to help us at a stand to go on forward, by revealing two Means or Instruments, whereby his Spirit accomplisheth the mystical Union and Fellowship betwixt Christ and us, and whereby rational Creatures are capable of attaining thereunto, by his Spirit working in them. One of these Means is the Gospel of the Grace of God, wherein God doth make known to us "the unsearchable Riches of Christ," and Christ in us "the hope of Glory," Eph. 3:8, Col. 1:27, and doth also invite us, and command us to believe on Christ for his Salvation, and doth encourage us by a free Promise of that Salvation, to all that believe on him, Acts 16:31, Rom. 10:9,11. This is God's own Instrument of Conveyance, wherein he sendeth Christ to us, to bless us with his Salvation, Acts 3:26. It is the ministration

of the spirit, and of righteousness, 2 Cor. 3:6, 8, 9. Faith cometh by the hearing of it, and therefore it is a great instrument whereby we are begotten in Christ, and Christ is formed in us, Rom. 10:16, 17, 1 Cor. 4:15, Gal. 4:19. There is no need for us to say in our Hearts, "Who shall ascend into Heaven, [that is,] to bring Christ down from above? Or, who shall descend into the deep, [that is,] to bring up Christ [again] from the dead," that we may be united, and have fellowship with him in his death and resurrection? For the word is nigh to us, the Gospel, the word of Faith, in which Christ himself graciously condescendeth to be nigh to us; so that we may come at him there, without going any further, if we desire to be joyned to him, Rom. 10:6, 7, 8.

The other of these means is Faith, that is wrought in us by the Gospel: This is our Instrument of Reception, whereby the Union betwixt Christ and us is accomplished on our part by our actual receiving of Christ himself, with all his Fulness, into our Hearts; which is the principal Subject of the present Explanation.

The Faith which Philosophers commonly treat of, is only an Habit of the Understanding, whereby we assent to a Testimony upon the Authority of the Testifier: Accordingly some would have Faith in Christ to be no more than a believing the truth of things in Religion, upon the authority of Christ testifying them; but the

---

[10]stand: pause, delay.

Apostle sheweth, that the Faith whereby we are justified, is Faith in Christ's Blood, Rom. 3:24, 25, not only in his Authority as a Testifier. And tho' a meer assent to a Testimony were sufficient Faith for knowledge of things, which the Philosophers aimed at, yet we are to consider, that the Design of Saving Faith is not only to know the Truth of Christ and his Salvation, testified and promised in the Gospel, but also to apprehend and receive Christ and his Salvation, as given by and with the Promise. Therefore Saving Faith must necessarily contain two Acts, believing the Truth of the Gospel, and believing on Christ, as promised freely to us in the Gospel for all Salvation. By the one it receiveth the Means wherein Christ is conveyed to us; by the other it receiveth Christ himself and his Salvation in the Means. As it's one act to receive the Breast or Cup wherein Milk or Wine are conveyed, and another act to suck the Milk in the Breast, and to drink the Wine in the Cup, and both these acts must be perform'd heartily with an unfeigned love to the Truth, and a desire of Christ and his Salvation above all things; this is our spiritual Appetite, which is necessary for our eating and drinking Christ, the Food of Life, as a natural Appetite is for Bodily Nourishment. Our assenting unto, or believing the Gospel, must not be forced by meer conviction of the Truth, such as wicked Men and Devils may be brought to, when they had rather it were false: Neither must our believing on Christ be only constrained for fear of Damnation without any hearty Love and Desire towards the enjoyment of him, but we must receive the Love of the Truth, by relishing the Goodness and Excellency of it; and we must account "all things [but] loss for the excellency of the knowledge of Christ Jesus our Lord," and "count them but dung, that we [I] may win Christ, and be found in him," 2 Thess. 2:10, Phil. 3:8, 9, es-

teeming Christ to be all our Salvation and Happiness, Col. 3:11, in whom all fulness doth dwell, Col. 1:19. And this Love must be to every part of Christ's Salvation, to Holiness as well as Forgiveness of Sins. We must desire earnestly, that God would create in us a clean Heart, and right Spirit, as well as hide his face from our sins, Psalm 51:9, 10, not like many, that care for nothing in Christ but only Deliverance from Hell. "Blessed are they that hunger and thirst after righteousness, for they shall be filled," Mat. 5:6. The former of these Acts doth not immediately unite us to Christ, because it is terminated only on the means of Conveyance, the Gospel, yet it is a saving Act, if it be rightly performed, because it enclineth and disposeth the Soul to the latter Act, whereby Christ himself is immediately received into the Heart. He that believeth the Gospel with hearty love and liking, as the most Excellent Truth, will certainly with the like heartiness believe on Christ for his Salvation. They that know the name of the Lord, will certainly put their trust in him, Psalm 9:10. Therefore in Scripture, Saving Faith is sometimes described by the former of these Acts, as if it were a meer believing the Gospel; sometimes by the latter, as a believing on Christ or in Christ. Rom. 10:9, If thou "believe in thine heart that God raised him from the dead, thou shalt be saved." [Rom. 10:11,] the Scripture saith, "Whosoever believeth on him shall not be ashamed." 1 John 5:1. "Whosoever believeth that Jesus is the Christ is born of God." 5:13, "These things I have written unto you that believe on the name of the Son of God, that you may know ye have eternal life, and that ye may believe on the name of the Son of God."

For the better understanding of the nature of Faith, let it be further observed, that the Second and Principal of it, believing on Christ, includeth believing on God the Father, Son, and Holy Ghost, because they are one and the same infinite God, and they all concurr in our Salvation by Christ, as the only Mediator betwixt God and us, ''in whom all the promises of God are yea and amen,'' 2 Cor. 1:20. By him, as mediator, we believe on God that raised him from the dead, and gave him glory, that our faith and hope might be in God, 1 Pet. 1:21. And it is the same thing with trusting on God or on the Lord, which is so highly commended in the whole Scripture, especially in the Old Testament, as may easily appear by considering that it hath the same Causes, Effects, Objects, Adjuncts, Opposites, and all the same Circumstances, excepting only that it had a respect to Christ, as promised before his Coming, and now it respecteth him, as already come in the Flesh. Believing in the Lord, and trusting on his Salvation, are equivalent terms, that explain one another, Psalm 78:22. I confess, that trusting on things seen or known by the meer Light of Reason, as on our own Wisdom, Power, Riches, on Princes, or any Arm of Flesh, may not so properly be called believing on them, but trusting on a Saviour, as discovered by a Testimony is properly believing on him. It is also the same thing that is expressed by the terms of resting, relying, leaning, staying our selves on the Lord, because it is the Ground of that Expectation that is the proper Act of Hope, though our Believing and Trusting be for the present as well as future benefit of this Salvation. The reason why it is so commonly expressed in the Scriptures of the New Testament, by the terms of believing on Christ, might be probably because when that part of Scripture was written, there was cause in a special manner to urge believing the Testimony that was then newly revealed by the Gospel.

Having thus explained the nature of Faith, I come now to assert its proper Use and Office in our Salvation, That it is the Means and Instrument whereby we receive Christ, and all his Fulness, actually into our Hearts. This excellent Use and Office of Faith is encountered by a multitude of Errors; men naturally esteem, that it is too small and slight a thing to produce so great effects; as Naaman thought washing in Jordan too small a matter for the cure of his Leprosie.[11] They contemn the true meaning of entering in at the streight Gate, because they seem too easie for such purpose, and thereby they make the Entrance not only difficult, but impossible to themselves. Some will allow, that Faith is the sole condition of our Justification, and the Instrument to receive it, according to the Doctrine maintained formerly by the Protestants against the Papists, but they account, that it is not sufficient or effectual to Sanctification, but it rather tendeth to Licentiousness, if it be not joyned with some other means, that may be powerful and effectual to procure an holy Practice. They commend this great Doctrine of Protestants as a comforable Cordial for Persons upon their Deathbeds, or in Agonies under Terrors of Conscience, but they account, that it is not good for ordinary Food, and that it is Wisdom in Ministers to preach it seldom and sparingly, and not without some Antidote or Corrective to prevent the licentiousness to which it tendeth. Their common Antidote or Corrective is, That Sanctification is necessary to Salvation as well as Justification, and that though we be justified by Faith, yet we are sanctified by our own performance of the Law; and so they set up Salvation by works, and make the Grace of Justification to be of none effect, and not at all comfortable. If it had indeed such a malignant influence upon Practice, it could not be owned as a Doctrine proceeding from the most holy God, and all the Comfort that it affords must

---

[11] 2 Kings 5:1-14.

needs be ungrounded and deceitful. This Consequence is well understood by some late Refiners of the Protestant Religion, and therefore they have thought fit to new-model this Doctrine, and to make Saving-Faith to be only a Condition to procure a Right and Title to our Justification by the Righteousness of Christ, which must be performed before we can lay any good claim to the enjoyment of it, and before we have any right to the actual receiving of it; and this they call an accepting of, or receiving Christ. And that they may the better secure the practice of Holiness by their Conditional Faith, they will not have trusting on God or Christ for Salvation to be accounted the principal Saving-act of it, because as it seemeth to them, many loose wicked People trust on God and Christ for their Salvation, as much as others, and are by their Confidence hardened the more in their Wickedness: But they had rather it should be Obedience to all Christ's Laws, at least, in their Resolution, or a Consent that Christ should be their Lord, accepting of his terms of Salvation, and a resignation of themselves to his Government in all things. It is a sign that the Scripture form of Teaching is grown into disesteem with our great Masters of Reason, when trusting in the Lord, so much commended in Scripture, is accounted a mean and ordinary thing. They endeavour to affright us from owning Faith to be an Instrument of Justification, by telling us, that thereby we that use the Instrument are made our own principle Justifiers to the dishonour of God; though it might be easily answered, that we are made thereby only the principle receivers of our own Justification from God, the Giver of it, to whom all the Glory doth belong.

All these Errors will fall, if it can be proved, that such a Faith as I have described is an Instument whereby we actually receive Christ himself into our Hearts, and Holiness of Heart and Life, as well as Justification by Union and Fellowship with him. For the proof of it, I shall offer the following Arguments.

First, By Faith we have the actual enjoyment and possession of Christ himself, and not only of Remission of Sins, but of Life, and so of Holiness: Christ dwelleth in our hearts by faith, Ephes. 3:17. We live to God, and yet not we, but Christ liveth in us by the Faith of the Son of God, Gal. 2:19, 20. He that believeth on the Son of God, hath the Son and everlasting life that is in him, 1 John 5:12, 13. John 3:36: He that heareth Christ's word, and believeth on him that sent Christ, hath everlasting life, and is passed from death into life. These Texts express clearly such a Faith as I have described; therefore the efficiency or operation of Faith, in order to the enjoyment of Christ and his Fulness, cannot be the procurement of a bare Right or Title to this Enjoyment, but rather it must be an entrance into it, and taking possession of it. We have our access and entrance by faith into the Grace of Christ wherein we stand, Rom. 5:2.

Secondly, The Scripture plainly ascribeth this effect to Faith, that by it we receive Christ, put him on, are rooted and grounded in him, and also receive the Spirit, remission of sins, and an inheritance among them which are sanctified, John 1:2, Gal. 3:26, 27, Col. 2:6, 7, Gal. 3:14, Acts 26:18. And the Scripture illustrateth this Receiving by the Similitude of Eating and Drinking; He that believeth on Christ, drinketh the living water of his spirit, John 7:37, 38, 39. Christ is the bread of life, his flesh is meat indeed, and his blood drink indeed; and the way to eat and drink it, is to believe in Christ, and by so doing we dwell in Christ, and Christ in us, and have everlasting life, John 6:35, 47, 48, 54, 55, 56. How can it be taught more clearly, that we receive Christ himself properly into our Souls by Faith, as we do receive Food into our Bodies by eating and drinking, and that Christ is as truly united to us thereby as our Food when we eat or drink it? So that Faith cannot be a Condition to procure a meer Right or Title to Christ, no more than Eating or Drinking procureth a meer Right or Title to our Food, but it is rather an Instrument to receive it, as the Mouth that eateth and drinketh the Food.

Thirdly, Christ with all his Salvation is freely given by the Grace of God, to all that believe on him; for we are saved by Grace through Faith, and that not of our selves, it is the Gift of God, Eph. 2:8, 9. We are justified freely by his Grace, through Faith in his blood, Rom. 3:25. The Holy Ghost, who is the Bond of Union betwixt Christ and us, is a Gift, Acts 2:38. Now that which is a Gift of Grace must not be at all earned, purchased, or procured by any Work or Works performed as a Condition to get a right Title to it; and therefore Faith it self must not be accounted such a Condition. If it be by Grace, it is no more of Works, otherwise Grace is no more Grace, Rom. 11:1. The Condition of a free Gift is only take and have; and in this sense we will readily acknowledge Faith to be a Condition, allowing a Liberty in Terms where we agree in the thing; but if you give a Peppercorn to purchase a Title to it, then you spoil the freeness of the Gift. The free Offer of Christ to you is sufficient to conferr upon you a Right, yea, to make it your Duty to receive Christ and his Salvation as yours; and because we receive Christ by Faith as a free Gift, therefore we may account Faith

to be the Instrument, and as it were the Hand whereby we receive him.

Fourthly, It hath been already proved, that all spiritual Life and Holiness is treasured up in the Fulness of Christ, and communicated to us by Union with him; therefore the accomplishing of Union with Christ is the first work of Saving Grace in our Hearts, and Faith itself, being an holy Grace, and part of spiritual Life, cannot be in us before the beginning of it, but rather it is given to us, and wrought in the very working of the Union. And the way wherein it conduceth to the Union, cannot be by procuring a meer Title to Christ as a Condition, because then it should be performed before the uniting Work beginneth; but rather by being an Instrument, whereby we may actively receive and embrace Christ, who is already come into the Soul to take possession of it [as] his own Habitation.

True Saving-Faith, such as I have described, hath in its nature and manner of Operation a peculiar aptitude or fitness to receive Christ and his Salvation, and to unite our Souls unto him, and to furnish the Soul with a new holy Nature, and to bring forth an holy Practice by Union and Fellowship with him. God hath fitted natural Instruments for their Office, as the Hands, Feet, etc. so that we may know by their nature and natural manner of operation, for what use they are designed. In like manner we may know, that Faith is an Instrument formed on purpose for our Union with Christ, and Sanctification, if we consider what a peculiar fitness it hath for the Work. The discovery of this is of great use for the understanding of the mysterious manner of our receiving and practising all Holiness by Union and Fellowship with Christ. . . .

Holy Expectations

Puritanism was a profoundly eschatological religious outlook. Not only was individual piety to be focused on heavenly-mindedness, but Puritan piety often envisioned an imminent millennial age in which Christ would rule directly over his saints. Nevertheless, Puritan devotional writers also dealt with the traditional Christian topics where piety and eschatological doctrine intersected—death, judgment, heaven, and hell. In the following selections, the excerpt from Edward Pearse's devotional classic The Great Concern *presents a Puritan warning to be prepared for death; that from Theophilus Gale takes up one aspect of impending judgment, the second coming of Christ. And the final selection from William Bates exemplifies the devotional discourse on the heavenly rest, a popular genre for Restoration Dissenters.*

Introduction to Edward Pearse,
The Great Concern

Edward Pearse (1633?-1674?) received the B.A. from Oxford in 1654 and in 1657 was appointed preacher at St. Margaret's, Westminster. Of Puritan outlook, he was ejected by the Act of Uniformity in 1662 and lived thereafter in London. Out of his retirement came three works of a practical and devotional sort: The Great Concern; or a Serious Warning to a Timely and Thorough Preparation for Death: With Helps and Directions in order thereunto *(London, 1671),* The Best Match, or the Soul's Espousal to Christ *(London, 1673), and* A Beam of Divine Glory *(London, 1674).*

The Great Concern *immediately became one of the most popular devotional books of its time, with twenty-five editions by 1715. It is a prime example of the Puritan use of the hoary Christian theme of remembering death. What follows is taken from the third edition printed at London in 1674 (Wing P983A), 1-3, 8-18, 26-31, 84-98, 211-18. This was presumably the last edition printed during his lifetime. There is a brief entry for Pearse in the* Dictionary of National Biography *by A. F. Pollard.*

Edward Pearse, *The Great Concern*

To walk with God here on earth, while we live; and to be ready to live with God for ever in Heaven, when we come to die, is the Great Work we have to do, the Great Concern we have in mind, in our present Pilgrimage. To grow great and high in the World, to build our Names and Families, to live a Life of sensual pleasures and delights, spending our dayes in mirth; these are low, mean, poor things; things infinitely beneath the dignity of a soul, and altogether unworthy of the least of its care and solicitude: but to know God, to love God, to obey God, to delight in God, to contemplate the glorious excellencies and perfections of God, to live upon God, and to live to God; upon him as our chief good and happiness, and to him as our last end; and withall to be found ready at last to live with him for ever, to enter upon the beatif-

ical Vision, and to pass into that Life of love and holiness, which the Saints and Angels live above, being made perfect in the Vision and Fruition of the God of Glory; this is truly noble, this is worthy of the care and solicitude of Souls. To promote these things, and more especially the latter, is my design in fixing my Meditations on this Scripture,[1] which I am the rather induced to do, because I am apprehensive, that the time of my going hence, when I shall be seen no more, is drawing very nigh. . . .

Dying Work, my Beloved, is great Work, and a dying hour is a difficult hour, and therefore we had need have all things well ordered, and ready in the matters of

---

[1] The text upon which the entire book is based, Ps. 39:13: "O spare me, that I may recover strength, before I go hence, and be no more."

our Souls, against[2] that time, that Work, that hour comes. I will lay the Weight of dying work, and the difficulty of a dying Hour before you in four Propositions.

First Proposition is this: that Death in it self, and in its own nature (if we look no further) is a very terrible thing; and we had need have all things set right in our souls, all things in order, when we come to encounter with it: The Philosopher who lookt not beyond the natural notion of death, called it, "πάντων τόν φοβερῶν φοβερώτατον," (Aristotle) "the most terrible of all terrible things." And in Job 18:14 the Holy Ghost himself calls it, the King of Terrors: His confidence (speaking of a wicked man) shall bring him to the King of Terrors, i.e., to death, which is most formidable; Indeed 'tis therefore called the King of Terrors, because it is the greatest and strongest Terror, and Death must needs be terrible in it self.

1. Because it deprives us of all our sweet comforts and enjoyments here in this World, and puts an eternal Period to our fruition of them; here we enjoy much good, many streams which run pleasantly on each hand of us, (it may be) but when Death comes, that deprives us of all. Naked came I into the World, "and naked shall I return," Job 1:21. So the Apostle, "We brought nothing into this World, and it is certain we shall [can] carry nothing out," speaking as to outward comforts here, 1 Timothy 6:7. The Psalmist to the same effect, Psalm 49:17, speaks of a rich man: "He shall carry nothing away, His Glory" (saith he) "shall not descend after him." Death, as one observes, is the greatest Leveller in the World, it levels Scepters and Plow-shares, it makes the Prince as poor as the Peasant.

2. Because it dissolves the Union between the Soul and the Body: Death is indeed the rending of Body and Soul (those old and loving Companions) asunder. Now all disunions, (as a worthy Divine observes) are uncomfortable, and some disunions are terrible: And, as some disunions are terrible, so those are of all others most terrible, that do rend them from us which are most dear to us: Now what Union so near, as that between the soul and body? and therefore what disunion so terrible, as the dissolution of this Union? The dissolving the Union between a man and his Wife is terrible, because they are nearly[3] united each to other; but the dissolving the Union between the Soul and Body is more terrible, because the Union is more near and close. A man and his Wife are one flesh; but the Soul and Body make but one Person: Now Death dissolves this Union: while we live, the Soul dwells in the Body, informs[4] the Body, acts in and by the Body: But when Death comes, then the Soul and Body part, till the Resurrection; one returning to the dust, whence it came, the other to God who gave it, Ecclesiastes 12:7.

3. It is the destroying and demolishing of the body of man, that famous and curious Fabrick, and a bringing it into dust and putrefaction, Psalm 90:3. It turns a living body into a dead carcass, a lifeless lump of clay, and causeth it to become meat for Worms to feed on, Job 19:26. The body of man is a very curious piece of Workmanship, such as wherein the infinite power and wisdom of God is much seen and manifested, Psalm 139:14-15. But when Death comes, it marrs and demolishes all, stains all its beauty, and draws a Veil upon all its Glory. Sickness often makes a man's beauty to consume away like a moth, as you have it, Psalm 39:11. But Death utterly defaces it, and draws a Veil upon it,

---

[2]against: in preparation for.

[3]nearly: closely.
[4]informs: gives form to.

that turns his beauty into blackness and deformity. One of the Ancients, standing by Caesar's Tomb, wept, saying, Where is now the beauty of Caesar? What now is become of all his Magnificence? In a word, as life is the sweetest of all outward mercies, so death is the sharpest of all outward Afflictions: The pains of it are pains to a Proverb:[5] "The Sorrows of Death compass me about," Psalm 116:3. Now if Death be thus terrible in it self; then judge ye, whether we had need to have all things ready, and in order when it comes.

Second Proposition is, That in a dying hour the Devil is most fierce and terrible in his assaults and temptations upon the Soul. The Devil is in the Scripture called a Roaring Lyon; And is usually most so against the poor people of God, when they come to die: Then he hath wrath, because he knows his time is short: To allude to that, Revelation 12:12. When a man or woman comes to die, the Devil knows he has but a short time to tempt, to vex, to terrifie that Soul in; and therefore, then usually he exercises great wrath; then he stirs up all his wrath, all his malice, all his cruelty against him; he sees this is the last cast[6] he is like to have for it, the last on-set he is ever like to make upon the Soul's Faith and Comfort, and that now the Battle is to be won or lost for ever; therefore now he roars and rages terribly indeed, now he discharges all his Murdering Pieces[7] against the Soul, to make batteries,[8] if possible, upon the Soul's Fort of Salvation, and to shake its foundation of life and happiness. The Devil is the Enemy of Souls, Malachi 13:25, and his Enmity works especially one of these two ways: Either first to keep them from life and happiness; and here he acts rather like an Angel of Light, than a Roaring Lyon: He works rather in a way of Flattery, than in a way of Terror. Hence we read of his Wiles, Methods, Devices, and the like; his cunning and fallacious workings, thereby to destroy Souls. Or, secondly, to trouble and torment Souls in their way to life and happiness; and here he is indeed like a Roaring Lyon, and nevermore, than when we come to die. There are among others two seasons, wherein the Devil is most fierce and terrible in his assaults upon the Soul. The first is, when a man is going from Sin to Grace, when he is fully resolved to close with Christ, to shake off the yoke of sin, and to take upon him the yoke of Jesus. The second is, When a man is going from Grace to Glory: when he is going off the Stage of Time to Eternity; when a man begins to live the spiritual life, and when a man comes to die the natural death. I know, first, That as for his own children, he usually lets them alone, when they come to die: he is afraid to have them disturbed; though sometimes he cannot forbear, but torments them before their time. Secondly, God can, and sometimes does chain him up, so that he shall not be able to trouble and torment the Saints in their passage out of this World: yet still I say, for the most part he does fiercely assault them then; and doubtless, there are but very few of the Children of God, but do meet with very sore Assaults from Sathan, when they come to die; then he turns Accuser; then he charges the soul with all its sins; then he tells him he is an hypocrite, that all his profession hath been nothing but a delusion, and the like: Now is Sathan thus fierce and terrible in his assaults upon the soul in a dying hour. Surely then we had need have all ready against that hour comes.

The third Proposition is this: that in a dying hour Conscience is most awakened; and so most quick and smart in its threats

---

[5]To a Proverb: proverbially.

[6]cast: i.e., of the dice.

[7]Pieces: pistols.

[8]batteries: assaults.

and charges against the Soul, if all be not right within; and therefore we had need have all so, in that hour. . . . Oh you little think, how strict Conscience will be in its search, how sharpe in its charge, and how severe in its censure in a dying hour. . . .

The fourth Proposition is this, That in a dying hour we shall have to do with God in a very stupendious and amazing way, in such a way as may well startle and affright us to think of it: we are said to have to do with God here, Hebrews 4:13, we have here to do with God in Duties, in Ordinances, in Mercies, in Afflictions: indeed we had as good never have to do with these, unless we have to do with God in these: But though we have to do with God here, while we live; yet know, we shall have to do with God in another-guess[9] way, when we come to die; in such a way as may well overwhelm us to think of it. I shall give it you in three steps: then we have to do with God immediately; with God immediately, as our Judge; with God immediately, as our Judge for Eternity: And O how loud do these things call upon us to get all in order in the matters of our soul, against a dying hour comes! . . .

As dying work is weighty work, and a dying hour is a difficult hour; so to have all things set right, all well ordered and composed, in the matters of our souls, against such an hour comes, is an high, sweet, and blessed attainment, an attainment which carries infinite sweetness and desireableness in it: a taste of which I shall give you in two things only. (1) Hereby we come to be glorious Conquerours over Death and the Grave. (2) Hereby we come to have abundant entrance ministered to us into Heaven and Glory: And, my Beloved, what more sweet and desirable than this? Surely this speaks it to be a very sweet and blessed attainment.

---

[9]another-guess: another kind of.

1. Hereby we come to be glorious Conquerours over Death and the Grave. Death is an Enemy, 'tis the last enemy the Children of God have to grapple and conflict with: "The last enemy that is to [shall] be destroyed is Death," 1 Cor. 15:26. And being the last Enemy, in conquering this they conquer all; conquering this, they are compleat and eternal Conquerours: Now, by having all things set right in the matters of our souls, all things ready, and in order for a dying hour, we come to conquer this last Enemy; yea, to get a glorious Conquest over it; Hereby Death comes to be swallowed up of Victory, as you have the Expression, 1 Cor. 15:54. Hereby "we are more than Conquerours over it," Romans 8:37. Take the Conquest which this gives us over Death, in these three things.

1. Hereby the soul is carried above the fear of Death: In Heb. 2:15 we read of some, who all their life-time were subject to bondage through Fear of Death: And, if in their life-time, much more when they come to a dying Hour; Then Conscience (as you have heard) is more awake: O the fears, the terrors, the Hell upon Earth, that the sight of Death's approach fills many a poor Soul withall! But now take a soul that has all things right, and in order in his spiritual concerns, and he is carried above the fear of this King of Terrours; and that when made as terrible as the wit and malice of men can possibly make it: He can converse with his last enemy as one that hath lost his sting and power, and so without the least fear or dismayedness of spirit: None of these things move me, says Paul, neither count I my Life dear unto my self, that I may finish my course with joy. His Afflictions did not move him, did not terrifie him; but if death should come, what then? Why, that shall be welcome too, saith he, Acts 20:24. Who is afraid of a conquered enemy, an enemy which a man seeth dead and slain in the field? One that has all things

ready for a dying hour, he sees death to be a conquered enemy, an enemy conquered by the death of Christ; and so is carried above the fear of it.

2. Hereby the soul is inabled in a holy manner to triumph over death, and even to scorn and contemn it; which is an higher Conquest still. A Man that has all things set right, and well ordered in the matters of his soul, he is not only carried above the fear of death, but be rides in triumph over it, as one that divideth the spoil: he can with Boldness and comfort challenge this last Enemy of his, and even dare it to do its worst to him: "O Death where is thy Sting? O Grave where is thy Victory?" (saith the Apostle) "The sting of death is sin, [and] the strength of sin is the Law: but thanks be to God, who giveth us the Victory through our Lord Jesus Christ," 1 Cor. 15:55-57. As if he should say, Death, you talk of a Sting; but where is it? Grave, you would threaten me with Victory and overthrow, but do your worst, conquer us if you can. As a man that has disarmed his Enemy, thrown him upon his back, sayes to him; O Sir, where is your Sword? Where is your Pistol? Where is the execution you threatened? Do your worst!

3. Hereby the Soul comes to be able, solemnly to choose and desire Death; yea, to exult, and rejoyce in Death; as that which of an Enemy is become a Friend, and an inlet into all happiness to him. . . .

Would you indeed set all things right in your souls, make all ready for a dying hour? Then in your most prosperous and flourishing State here, maintain a frequent and serious remembrance of death and the grave upon your spirits. "If a man live many years" (saith Solomon) "and rejoyce in them all, yet let him remember the days of darkness; for they are [shall be] many," Ecclesiastes 11:8. By the days of darkness here we are to understand death, and the state of death; the abode of our bodies in the grave, which is "a Land of darkness," "and where the light is as darkness," Job 10:22. Now, saith he, though a man live many years, and rejoyce in them all; that is, though a man live long and prosperously, long and joyfully; yet let him remember death and the grave, the future state. 'Tis true, there are other days of darkness, which we are subject to in this world, and should be remembred by us, days of outward darkness, the darkness of outward trouble and affliction; and days of inward darkness, the darkness of spiritual distress and direlection; and indeed 'tis of marvellous use to us in our prosperity, to remember these days of darkness; but especially we should remember death and the Grave: we should carry a lively remembrance of these days of darkness daily upon us; and indeed our not remembering these days of darkness, is one great cause why we are so unready for Death, and the Grave, as we are. When we are in the midst of our enjoyments, and the streams run pleasantly about us, we are too apt to forget these days of darkness; we are so taken with our earthly comforts, that we are loth to think of Death and Eternity, putting far from us the evil day; as those in their enjoyments did, Amos 6:3. And therefore, when these days come, they find us so unready, and our spiritual concernments so discomposed as usually they do. But (my beloved) as ever you would have all right, and in order in your souls, against a dying hour comes, let me recommend this to you as one special help, maintain a deep and frequent remembrance of Death and the Grave upon your Spirits, remember the days of Darkness; and that especially these two ways.

1. Remember them so, as to have them much in your meditation: Be much and frequent in the contemplation of Death and the Grave. This the Holy Ghost calls a considering our latter end; and withal, mentions

it as a business of great importance to us, Deut. 32:39. To consider, is to revolve a thing in our minds, and to keep it much in our thoughts and meditations. And thus we should consider our latter end, and remember the days of darkness: This is that the Saints of old have been much conversant in; they were much and frequent in the thoughts and meditations of death: as I might instance in the good old Patriarchs, Job, David, and others: And 'tis what does marvellously conduce to our preparation for it. The meditation of death (saith one) is life; it is that which greatly promotes our spiritual life; therefore walk much among the Tombs, and converse much and frequently with the thoughts of the dying hour.

2. Remember them so, as to have them daily in your expectation. In the midst of all your enjoyments, expect Death's approach daily: This is called a waiting for our change. "All the days of my appointed time, will I wait, till my change comes," Job 14:14. And we are commanded to wait for the coming of our Lord, as that which lies in the directest tendency to the exactest readiness and preparation for his coming, Luke 12:36. "Expect death every hour" (saith one) "for 'tis every hour approaching thee: in the morning when thou risest, think with thy self, This may be the last day: in the evening, when thou liest down, think with thy self, this may be the last night I may ever have in this world: I know not when my Lord will come, whether in the morning or in the evening, at midnight, or at the Cock-crowing: therefore I will be always expecting his coming." Woe, and alas for us! We are apt to talk of many years to come, as he did, Luke 12:9, whereas we should live in the expectation of death every moment. Thus let us consider the days of darkness, it will marvelously conduce to the Preparation of the Soul for them: The meditation and expectation of

death will conduce much (among others) to these four things:

1. It will conduce much to our humbling and self-debasing: "Let a Man own himself to be a mortal (saith Austin)[10] and pride will, it must, down." And, "think frequently of death, (saith another) and thou wilt easily bring down thy proud heart." Hence also the consideration of Death is often in Scripture mentioned by the Holy Ghost, as an argument to make us humble; "Dust thou art, and unto Dust thou shalt return," Gen. 3:19 as elsewhere.

2. It will conduce much to the Weaning of our Hearts from this World, and the loosening of them from the things here below: "The time is short:" (saith the Apostle) what then? Why "it remaineth, that [both] they that have Wives, be as though they had none; and those that weep, as though they wept not; and those that rejoyce, as though they rejoyced not; [and] those [they] that buy, as though they possessed not; and they that use this world, as not abusing it; for the fashion of this world passeth away," 1 Cor. 7:29, 30, 31. He mentions the shortness of time, as that the meditation and expectation whereof, has the directest tendency in it, to wean and loosen the heart from all things here below. And indeed (as St. Bernard[11] hath it) "he easily contemns all things here, who looks upon himself as dying daily."

3. It will conduce much to the engaging the heart to Heaven, and the things of Heaven, to a serious Pursuit of a blessed Eternity. So we find, Heb. 11:13, etc. Those all dyed in the Faith (saith the Apostle) "not having received the Promises, but having seen them afar off, and were perswaded of them, and confessed, that they

---

[10]Austin: St. Augustine.

[11]St. Bernard of Clairvaux, a twelfth-century mystic and monastic leader, whom Calvin and the Puritans often quoted.

were Strangers and Pilgrims on the Earth;'' that is, they were apprehensive they had but a little time to stay here; And what then? They desire a better Countrey, that is, an Heavenly: the apprehension they had of their departure hence, quickned them unto earnest desires and pursuits after the better Countrey, the Heavenly Land; and indeed one great reason why we breath[e] no more, and press no more after Heaven, and a blessed Eternity, is, because we so seldom remember these days of darkness.

4. It will conduce much to the quickning of the Heart to Duty, and to diligence, and faithfulness therein. Christ himself made use of it for this end: ''I must work the works of him that sent me, while it is day; the night cometh when no man can work,'' John 9:4. Peter also, that holy Apostle, made use of it to that end. I will not be negligent (saith he) to do so and so in the way of my Duty, as ''knowing that shortly I shall put off this [my] Tabernacle,'' 2 Pet. 1:12, 13, 14. The consideration of the near approach of his death quickned him to his Work and Duty. And the Scripture propounds it, as that which has a tendency to this thing: ''Whatsoever thy hand findeth to do, do it with all thy might,'' (saith Solomon) for there is no work nor counsel in the grave, whither thou art going, Eccles. 9:10. He propounds the consideration of our going to the Grave, as a means to quicken us to our present Work. By all which we see, how much the serious remembrance of the dayes of darkness must needs contribute to our readiness and preparedness for these days: Therefore be much in this work. For my own part, I have hardly found any one thing more quickning and engaging upon my Spirit than this: And Souls, I would beg you, as you would live for ever, think often of death.

2. Would you indeed set all things right in your souls, and make all ready for a dying hour? Then be not fond of long Life here in this World, but rather covet to live, as much as possibe, in a little time: I would speak of each distinctly.

1. Be not fond of long life here in this World. A fond hope and desire of long life here, is one of the greatest Enemies to a true preparation of Soul for our departure hence. For pray observe, take a man that is fond of long Life here, and all this Thoughts and Projects are for this World: He is wholly taken up about, and carried out after the concerns of Time, scarce allowing himself one serious Thought for Death and Eternity: A sad instance you have hereof in the rich man, Luke 12:19. He reckoned upon many years, upon a long life here; and what are the things he is taken up about? Verily the things of this world only, the increase of his Goods, and where to store his Treasures: Fond hopes, and desires of long life here, will certainly produce great delays, if not utter neglects, in the great work and concern of your Souls and Eternity: As ever therefore you would have all right and well in the concerns of your souls, when you come to die, be not fond of long life here; but sit as loose in your thoughts, hopes, and desires, both of this life, and all the enjoyments of it, as possibly you can. And indeed (my Beloved) to reason it a little with you, why should you be fond of long life here? why should you covet a long stay in this world? I would only plead with you in two things as to this.

1. What is this world, and what have we here, that we should here covet a long stay? is this world such a sweet, such an amiable, such a desirable thing? it is an angry world, a frowning world, a dirty world, a bewitching, ensnaring world: 'Tis a waste howling Wilderness, a strange Land, an house of Bondage, a troublesome, tempestuous Sea, an Aceldama, a Field of Blood:[12]

---

[12]Aceldama: a place for the burial of strangers, where Judas hanged himself, Matt. 27:7, Acts 1:18-19.

such I am sure 'tis oftentimes to the poor Saints and people of God: And what have we here? Why here we have fears within, and fightings without, troubles on every side, and from all hands; from friends, from enemies, from men, from devils: here we have sorrows, snares, losses, wounds, deaths, dangers, temptations, seductions, disappointments, vexation of spirit; and truly little else is to be expected by us here, except that which is worse than all this, viz. dayly risings and ebolitions[13] of lust, violent eruptions of corruption, great aboundings of sin and iniquity, both in our selves and others; continual breakings with God and departings from him, renewing and increasing sin and guilt dayly. Indeed this world is full of sin, and temptation to sin: 'Tis (as Augustin speaks of it) *tota tentatio,* all temptation, and as it is all temptation, so 'tis little else but sin: and why should we covet a long stay here? Why (saith one of the Ancients) ''should we so much desire that life, in which by how much the longer we live, by so much the more we sin; and the more numerous our days are, the more numerous will our sins be?'' Who would desire to stay long in a Prison, or a Dungeon, in a state and place of sin and sorrow? And such is this world.

2. Is there not a better life, a better place, a better state for our souls to long and aspire after? what do you think of the Life above, a whole Eternity spent in the Divine Presence, in the Bosom of Divine Love, a life of love, a life of pleasure, a life of joy, a life of admiration,[14] a Life of holiness, perfect and unspotted holiness, a life every way correspondent to the Divine Life, and the Divine Will? Is not this a better life? to be with Christ is best of all, Phil. 1:23. To possess a mansion in our Father's House, prepared by our Lord and Head,

Jesus Christ, for us; to live for ever in the vision and fruition of Father, Son, and Spirit; to dwell in the Heavenly City, where no unclean thing can enter; to joyn in with the glorious Host of Saints, and Angels above, and with them to spend a whole Eternity in Songs of Praise and Hallelujahs to God, and the Lamb; to take up all our waters of the Fountain head; and indeed to dive and bathe unchangeably in the Fountain of all delights at the Father's right hand: O how sweet is this life, and how much to be desired by us! In a word (my beloved) the Saints, when in the best frame, have many of them been so far from being fond of long life here, that indeed they have thought it long till the time came, when they should go hence and be no more, crying out with an holy impatiency, Why is his Chariot so long a coming? Why tarry the wheels of his Chariot?

Covet to live much in a little time: 'Tis said of that Reverend and worthy Divine, Dr. Preston,[15] that he desired to, and accordingly did, live much in a little time. And our Lord himself (you know) did not live long in this world; but he lived much in a little time; he did much Work in a few Days for God and souls. And indeed (my beloved) 'tis not a long life, but a fruitful life, that is most amiable, most desirable, and most like his life, who is life it self. 'Tis not he that lives many years, but he that lives much in a few years, that is the most happy soul. I know those, whose ambition is not to live long, but to live fruitfully, and to do as much, as possibly they can, in a little time: and might they have their opinion or choice, it would be this, to live much in a little time, and then have their dimission to rest. And (my Beloved) let this be

---

[13]ebolitions: ebulitions.
[14]admiration: wonder.

[15]John Preston (1587-1628), a Puritan leader who was in his last years master of Emmanuel, Cambridge, and a chaplain to the prince who became Charles I.

your choice, and your ambition; be casting about in your selves, how you may live much in a little time; how you may compass much spiritual work and business in a few days: Labour to treasure up much grace, much experience of God, and his love; to bring a large revenue of glory to him, and the like: And for this end possess your souls with a deep sense of the exceeding worth and preciousness of time; and accordingly set your selves to redeem it, looking upon the loss thereof to be the greatest loss in the world, Ephesians 5:16, we are commanded to redeem the time; and what is it to redeem the time, but to esteem time as precious, as a thing of incomparable worth and value; and accordingly to make the best and highest improvement of it for the honour of God, and good of our souls, that possibly we can? It is to fill up our time with duty and our duties with grace: to make use of time for those ends, for which time is given us; not to eat, and drink, and solace our selves in the Creature, but to serve and honour the Creator; "to work out our Salvation;"[16] to get acquaintance with God and Christ; to make sure of Heaven and a blessed Eternity. O Sirs! look upon time as precious; so indeed it is: Time is the most weighty and momentous thing in the World, 'Tis that which our eternal all depends upon: According as we do, or do not manage to improve our time well, so will it go with us for ever. 'Tis a sweet Meditation which I have read in a Discourse of an holy Man: "This Life" (saith he) "of ours is most swift; and yet in it Eternal Life is either gotten or lost for ever. This life of ours is most miserable; and yet in it Eternal Happiness is either gotten or lost for ever." No less than a whole Eternity of Happiness or Misery, Salvation or Damnation, depends upon our Use and Management of our little time here

in this world. As the tree falls so it lies, Eccles. 11:3. As it is with us when we go out of time, so it will be with us to all Eternity; and this we should be much in the thoughts of, accounting therefore the loss of time to be the greatest loss. 'Tis a weighty saying, which I have read in one of the Ancients, "It is a great and heavy loss indeed" (saith he) "when we neither do good nor think good" (and let me add, nor get good) "but we suffer our hearts to wander abroad about vain and unprofitable things; and yet it is too difficult to restrain or keep them back from these things;" Truly, no loss like the loss of time; the loss of estate, the loss of Trade, the loss of this or the other outward comfort is nothing to the loss of time. These being lost may be recovered again; but time being lost can never be recovered more: accordingly set your selves to redeem it, and do it as much as possibly you can; accounting that day lost, wherein you have not done something for God, and your souls: the truth is, we live no more than we are conversant in the work of God and our souls: For, as for that which we call life, that [which] is not spent in this work, it is not indeed to be accounted Life . . .

Death, when ever it comes, will set thee above all afflictive Distances, between God, Christ, the Comforter, and thee, and will set down thy soul in the full, constant, and immediate vision and fruition of all for ever; and is not this sweet? Poor Saint, here thou complainest, that God is as a Stranger to thee, "and as a wayfaring man, that turnest aside to tarry" but for a night: Thou hast only now and then a short visit from him, Jer. 14:8. Thou complainest that thy Beloved withdraws himself, and is gone, Cant. 5:6. Thou complainest, that the Comforter that should relieve thy Soul, is far from thee, Lam. 1:18[16]. Thou complainest of many sad and woful distances from God, and of the lowness of thy communion, and well thou maiest; for indeed,

---

[16]Allusion to Phil. 2:12.

how little a portion is there here seen, or enjoyed of him by thee? Well, but when death comes, that will lift thee above all those distances between God and thee, Christ and thee, and set thee down in the full, constant, and immediate vision and fruition of him for ever: The thoughts of which made Paul, and others, to desire to be gone, and to chuse death rather than life, 2 Cor. 5:6-8. We are confident, (says he) "knowing that whilst we are at home in the body, we are absent from the Lord; for we walk by faith, not by sight; we are confident, I say, and willing rather to be absent from the body, and to be present with the Lord." Pray observe, Paul enjoyed as much of God and Christ here, as most did, and yet all that communion he enjoyed here, he accounted as no communion, to that which he should enjoy after death; while we are present in the body, says he; that is, while we live in this World, we are absent from the Lord, absent from God and Christ, our communion here is but distance and estrangement, so low and unconstant is it, in comparison of what we know we shall enjoy after death: And therefore, says he, we had rather be absent from the body, we had rather be gone hence, and be present with the Lord: Death will bring us to another-guess presence and enjoyment of God and Christ, than here we shall ever be able to reach unto. Alas! All we enjoy of God and Christ here, is but an earnest; so the Apostle speaks in the verse forgoing: "He that hath wrought us for this self-same thing is God, who also hath given us the earnest of the spirit:"[17] But when Death come, we shall enjoy the full inheritance: all we enjoy here, is but as the first-fruits; "we that have the first-fruits of the spirit," saith the Apostle, Rom. 8:23. But when death comes, we shall have the full vintage, full incomes of love, full mani-

festations of light, and life, and glory, fulness of joy and pleasure in the Divine Presence, Psalm 16:11, full embraces in Christ's bosom, full views of his face, full visions of his glory. Death, when it comes, will bring us to the Beatifical Vision, which is all good and happiness in one; "Blessed are the pure in heart, for they shall see God," Mat. 5:8. They do see God now, they see him by Faith, and those sights of him are sweet, glorious, soul-ravishing and transforming sights: but after death they shall have other sights of him, such sights of him as will even infintely surpass all that ever they had, or were capable of here. Here "they see him but through a Glass darkly;"[18] that is, they have but low, obscure, mediate sights of him; they see and enjoy but little of him; but when death comes then "they shall see him face to face;" that is, fully, clearly, immediately, 1 Cor. 12:12. The sum is, as a learned man gives it us, that "in this Life we have but slow and slender sights and enjoyments of God, in comparison of what we shall see, know, and enjoy of him in eternal life."[19] Here they see but his back parts, as God said to Moses; but When death comes, they shall see his face, that is, his glory: here they see him but negatively, as it were, what he is not; but then they shall see him as he is, 1 John 3:2, "We shall see him as he is," in all his glorious excellencies and perfections. In short, they shall then have such sights and enjoyments of God and Christ, as shall eternally fill, delight, solace, satisfie, and set at rest their souls for ever; such sights, and enjoyments, as shall so solace and satisfie them, as that there shall be no room for the least tittle or iota

---

[17]2 Cor. 5:15.

[18]1 Cor. 13:12.

[19]The text gives *Glas. Rhet.* for this reference, probably a citation of the fifth book, *Rhetorica Sacra,* of a noted exegetical work of the German Lutheran Salomon Glass, (1593-1656) entitled *Philologia Sacra.*

of a desire for ever; yea, such sights and enjoyments, as shall so satisfie them, as to leave them under an utter impossibility of ever turning aside from them to any thing else, and so an eternal impossibility of sinning. O how sweet must this be! And indeed the School-men,[20] I find, and others from them, give this as one reason, why the Saints in Heaven are impeccable, because the sight and enjoyment they have of God there, is so full and satisfying, as they cannot turn aside to any thing else. O welcom Death, that brings us to those sights, those enjoyments of God, the Chief Good. Once more:

Death, when ever it comes, will bring you to, and set you down in the enjoyment of an eternal Sabbath: And, oh how sweet is this! There remaineth a Rest (the Word is, a Sabbath, or Sabbatism) "to the People of God," Heb. 4:9. Ay, but when shall they enjoy it? Why truly, when death comes, that will enter them upon it: immediately, upon the night of death, dawns the eternal Sabbath. True, the Saints enjoy a Sabbath here, and the Sabbath to them is the sweetest and amiablest day in all the week, 'tis a day of joy and holy feasting to their souls; and oh how how many times do your souls long for it? But alas these Sabbaths have an end; but the Sabbath death will set them down in, will be an eternal Sabbath, and an eternal Sabbath wherein they shall be employed in the highest acts of worship and adoration; even Love, Praise, Admiration, and Halleluja's for ever; wherein there will be no weariness, no faintness; wherein there shall be no intermission; no going to duties, and break off again, as here we do; but a whole Eternity shall be imployed in acts of Divine Worship and Adoration; wherein there shall be no deadness, no dulness, no spiritual indispositions, no unsuitableness in us to those high and holy Exercises which this Sabbath will be fill'd with; but our souls shall be perfectly suited to, and fitted for those glorious employs; wherein not a few only, and those, some Saints, and some sinners, some good, and some bad, shall join together in acts of worship; but an innumerable company both of Saints and Angels, and these all perfect holy, Heb. 12:22-24. Oh, how sweet and glorious will this be! 'Tis a great saying which I have read in a worthy Divine, "Sabbaths here are comfortable," says he, "and we have tasted some sweet, some comfort in some Sabbaths; but take all the comfort that ever you had in all the Sabbaths you have enjoyed here, and all will be nothing to the comforts and sweetness of the Eternal Sabbath." Alas! the perpetual Sabbath that shall be hereafter, that will be the accomplishment of all these Sabbaths; how sweet then must that be! O ye Saints of God, lift up your heads, death will set you down in this Sabbath. How have some of us longed sometimes for the coming of the Sabbath! And how have we grieved when it has been gone! Well, but when death comes, that will bring you to a Sabbath that shall never end. 'Tis a sweet saying of Austin, There (says he, speaking of Heaven) "is the great Sabbath, a Sabbath that hath no evening, no end, on which we shall rest and behold, behold and love, love and praise for ever." Oh blessed be God for this Sabbath: and blessed be God that death, when it comes, shall bring us to this Sabbath. Well then, fear not death, dread not death, but be found diligent and faithful in the use of the helps prescrib'd for the preparing of your souls for it; and then 'twill greatly befriend you, when ever it comes, and you may exult and rejoyce in it.

---

[20]School-men: the medieval theologians such as Thomas Aquinas who were active at the universities, and hence known as school men or scholastics.

Introduction to Theophilus Gale,
A Discourse of Christ's Coming

Theophilus Gale (1628-1678) was the son of a Church of England clergyman and was educated at Oxford. He became a fellow of Magdalen College but lost his Oxford posts at the Restoration in 1660. He lived for a while in France as a tutor to the sons of Lord Wharton. After 1666 he conducted an academy for the education of the children of Dissenters at Newington Green and was also pastor of a Congregational Church in London. He had a reputation for extensive if somewhat eccentric learning, as evidenced by his enormous work The Court of the Gentiles, *which traced all learning back to the ancient Hebrews. Gale was also the author of a book on the Jansenist Roman Catholics in France, whom he regarded favorably because he thought them close to Calvinism, of which he was a vigorous defender.*

A Discourse of Christ's Coming: And the Influence, which the Expectation thereof hath on al manner of Holy Conversation and Godlinesse *(Wing G147) was published at London in 1673. The selection that follows is the last part of this treatise, 194-211, in which he draws out the practical meaning of the second advent of Christ. His treatment emphasizes the relation of the expectation of Christ's coming to the piety of the individual believer rather than to the millennium or to reformation of the English nation—themes that appeared often in earlier Puritan eschatological speculation. For more about Gale's life, see J. W. Ashley Smith,* The Birth of Modern Education: The Contribution of the Dissenting Academies, 1600-1800 *(London: Independent Press, 1954), 41-46.*

A Discourse
of Christ's Coming:

*And the Influence, which the Expectation thereof hath
on all manner of Holy Conversation and Godlinesse.*

By Theophilus Gale

Section 2.

Practic[1] Uses.

The practic[1] Uses, which this subject as before explicated,[2] are of great moment, and therefore deserve serious Attention.

I. Here is matter of doleful Lamentation, and Humiliation, to consider, what strangers the most of Professors[3] are to the coming of our Lord. It is the observation of a late great Divine, now with God: At this day the world is coming to the last fit of madnesse against Christ. And wherein lies this last fit of the world's madnesse against Christ, but in men's endeavors to banish out of the World, al thoughts of the coming of the Day of God, as 2 Peter 3:3,4? And oh! what sad matter of Lamentation is it to thinke, how far many Professors fal under this condemnation? Alas! how few understand what this means, to look for and hasten to the coming of the day of God? Where is the awakened soul, that stands on his watch tower, looking forth towards the coming of his Lord? when was it, that you had any lively heart-affecting views of that great day? Doth it not give us a dreadful prognostic, that some astonishing Jugement is at the dore, because men so little

expect the great day of Jugement, at the coming of our Lord? Has it not ever been a sad presage of some impendent[4] Jugements, if not ruine to a professing people, when they have banisht from their hearts al serious thoughts of future Jugement, as Lam. 1:9? O that professors would daily be humbled for, and lament over this sin, their not daily looking for, and hastening to the coming of the day of God!

2. Our subject affords us also matter of Caution, Advice, and Counsel to professors, and that chiefly in four particulars. (1.) That they beware of a carnally secure, sleepy, and loitering spirit in their Christian Race. O! what a contradiction is a sleepy Christian to the Religion he professeth! How near akin is a sleepy Christian to a dead hypocrite! It's true, the Hypocrite's spiritual death is a total privation of al principles of life: but doth not carnal securitie[5] bring a suspension of the Acts of life, even in a real Christian? O! beware of carnal securitie after great peace and comforts, whether inward or outward. How doth carnal securitie creep insensibly on most professors, first or last! And what a danger are such in of losing their peace, exercices of Grace, and Communion with

---

[1]practic: practical.

[2]"of this subject previously explicated" is perhaps Gale's meaning.

[3]professors: those who profess religion.

---

[4]impendent: impending.

[5]carnal securitie: trusting in the flesh.

Christ! Remember, carnal securitie comes not alone: and when it comes, it exposeth you to the violent incursion of every Tentation:[6] and, that which is worst of al, it binds up al your spiritual senses and Faculties; so that you can neither look for, nor hasten unto the coming of the day of God. O! fear the terrors of the Lord at that great day. How are the Consciences of most men bound up with chains of securitie, so that they cannot see or fear their miserie, before they feel it!

(2.) Be advised also not to expect or desire much Rest in this Life. Remember it is inconsistent with your present state, to have your Rest here, because you are now in your Motion and Race towards your approaching Lord. The Saint's triumph here lies in conflicts against sin and tentation; his Rest, in a life of faith under troubles. He that expects other Rest here, wil find the greater troubles and disappointment. And this also know, that the Hopes which a believer has, under al his troubles, of a Rest, at the coming of his Lord, are much better than al the present enjoyments of others. Expectation of Rest here is a great bar to our looking for the coming of our Lord.

(3.) Beware of secret heart-backslidings from Christ: For these are most opposite to our looking for, and hastening to the coming of the Day of God. It was the saying of an holy eminent Divine now in Glorie; ''Thinke on this speech, when you see me dead, that of al Churches in the World, the Lord Jesus carries a most Jealous eye, over these for whom he hath done such great things; and I know it, he taketh exceeding il[l] your secret wantonnesses, and whoredomes of heart.''

(4.) Take heed of a formal, remisse, sleight spirit in private duties, or public Ordinances: For hereby you lose your communion with Christ; and so, by consequence, your looking for, and hastening to the coming of the Day of God.

3. Here is also matter of Heart-examination.

(1.) Whether we look for the coming of our Lord. Are our hearts taken off from gazing on the fading Glorie of this lower world? Do we value althings [*sic*] as they refer unto the coming of the Day of God? Are our souls drawen by the Glorie of that day, as the Iron is by the Load-stone?[7] Do we by faith feed on the good things of that day? What influence hath the expectation of this day on our Hearts and lives? Are we made more holy and heavenly-minded hereby? If it be thus with us, then al is wel. But if, after al our awakened thoughts, we are again grown secure, carnal, earthly-minded, formal in duties, proud, and confident in our selves, it is a black marque we look not for the coming of our Lord.

(2.) Examine whether you are prepared to meet the Lord, when he comes. Suppose you should this night hear the crie, Behold, the Bridegroom cometh![8] are you ready to enter into the wedding chamber? Have you the Wedding garment of Faith and Holinesse? Do you stand with your loins girt, and your lamps burning, ever ready to entertain your Lord? How stands it with you in point of Assurance, and wel-grounded evidences, as to your eternal state? Can you look Christ in the face with confidence, when he comes? Are you sure your sins are pardoned, and your persons accepted? Dare you look death in the face without change of countenance, when ever it comes? Remember, the Lord hath taken al other cares on himself, that so we might care for nothing, but to prepare for our Lords approche. Examine whether this be your care.

(3.) Examine wel both your Notions

---

[6] tentation: temptation.

[7] loadstone: magnet.

[8] Matt. 25:6.

and Practice of Godlinesse. Count nothing Godlinesse, but what wil bear the fiery trial, at the coming of our Lord: let there not be a loose pin in the main parts of your Christianitie. Thinke oft, whither you are going, and where you shal loge at night: and this wil make you exceding accurate and curious, both in your notions, and practice of Godlinesse.

4. Here is mater of conviction, rebuke, and shame, both to secure sinners, and Saints, who mind not the coming of the day of God.

(1.) Here is mater of conviction and confusion to carnal secure sinners, such as Peter prophesieth of, 2 Peter 3:3, 4: Who walk after their own lusts: saying, where is that promisse of his coming? I fear there are too many, who pretend much friendship to Christ, and yet seldome or never think of his returne. I shal therefore take libertie, to reason the case with such. Thou thinkest, per-adventure, it may be long enough ere Christ come, if he come at al: Mean while thou art resolved to take thy fil of thy lusts. Very good: Ay, but what grounds hast thou to thinke, it wil be long ere Christ come? Doth not the Scripture tel thee in expresse terms, the Judge standeth at the dore, James 5:9? and darest thou contemne plain Scripture? doest thou consider whose word it is thou doest contemne? whose threats thou thinkest scorne of? Canst thou not believe he is so near at hand? Why, yet believe that he wil surely come, first or last, and then cal thee to an account for al thine evil deeds! I say, do but believe this, and I question not but it wil make thine heart to ake. Ay but possibly thou mayst presume to find favor with him in that day: Why not? What sinner! canst thou expect to find favor in his eyes at [the] last day, and yet despise, and reject al proffers of his Grace in this day of salvation; spit in his face; and prefer a few sensual delights before him? Oh! what a foolish soul-deluding presum-

tion is this? It's true, our great Lord is exceding merciful, pure Grace, al love: But is he not also as just and righteous? Is it not a righteous thing with him to recompense tribulation to carnal secure sinners? and, what! wouldst thou have him unrighteous that he may shew mercie to thee? Ah! what a sad contemplation is this for awakened sinners, to thinke, that God must either be unrighteous, or al their foolish hopes of mercie must perish! And let me tel thee, sinner, the mercie and Free-grace of God wil be so far from favorising[9] of thee, in that great day, if thou continuest in thy sin, as that it wil prove a stinging aggravation of thy miserie. Oh! what a dreadful worme wil this breed in thy Conscience, to be spurned into hel by a foot of Mercie and Grace![10] Do not thy hopes yet fail thee? Is not thine heart yet pained, and rent at the thoughts of thy Lord's coming to Jugement? Doest thou not, as it were, see the Lord of Glorie coming in Chariots of flaming fire, to take vengeance on carnal secure sinners? Methinkes, that voice should be ever ringing in thine ears, Lo! Yonder, yonder comes the Judge of the whole Earth! What meanest thou, sinner, by plodding,[11] how thou mayst keep thy lusts, and yet escape future wrath? How long wilt thou procede to harden thy wicked heart to thine own destruction, by putting far off the evil day? Assure thy self the day of the Lord is never the farther off, for thy thinking it is so: but this advantage it wil have by the putting of it far off, it wil surprise thee unawares. And what wil become of al thy fond hopes and groundlesse presumtions? how wil al thy cruel self-flatteries end in everlasting horror, confusion, disappointment and despair?

---

[9]favorising: making a favorite of.

[10]i.e., though God is a God of mercy and grace, his foot will spurn you into hell.

[11]plodding: plotting.

(2.) Here is matter of conviction and shame even to Believers, to thinke how little the most of them have their thoughts fixed on the second coming of their Lord. Alas! how little are your expectations of that great day raised! How coldly and faintly do your Affections worke towards that good time! Ah Sirs! are there such glorious things to be reveled then? and hath the forethoughts hereof so much influence, upon al manner of holy Conversation and Godlinesse? How comes it to passe then, that Believers have their hearts no more bent towards this great day? How comes it to passe, that their Affections are not carried out more to meet their approching Lord? Is it not strange, that Christians should be so seldome, and so low in the thoughts of this glorious day? Alas! where can we spend our meditations better than to meet our Lord? where can the Spouse better employ her thoughts and affections, than with her absent Husband? Who should look towards the coming of their friend, their Savior, if not Believers? As for the secure world no wonder, if they endeavor to stifle al thoughts of their Lord's approche, sithat[12] it wil be a black day to them: But as for believers, O! what a joyful time wil it be to them! Wil it not be the time of their complete redemtion, their marriage-day? Should not their thoughts therefore be always musing on this day? How should their hearts leap for joy, at the very reports of it? But is it thus with them? Are not all too much strangers to this day? And oh! what an hainous sin is it for believers, not to look for this great day!

How much do such sin against the many intimate relations they bear to Christ. Is it possible that the member should forget its Head? Was it ever known, that the affectionate faithful Spouse forgat her absent husband? Is it not then strange

unkindnesse, that the members of Christ should put far from them the coming of their Head, and Lord?

What a strange violence do such offer to al the principles of the New Creature! Is there any thing more injurious to the divine nature, than not to mind the approche of Christ? Doth not this greatly provoke and grieve the Spirit of Adoption? How is faith opprest, and kept under hereby! What a check and contradiction is this to al Divine Affections!

For Believers not to mind the coming of their Lord, is a sin against the strongest and deepest obligations. Doth not this oppose al our Covenants, Resolutions, Experiences, Ordinances; yea, the blood and heart of our dying and exalted Savior? Was not this one main end of the death and exaltation of Christ, that believers might live always in the expectation of him?

What a World of other sins are maintained by our not looking for our Lord's approche! What more prevalent to feed Idol lusts? How is Conscience cast into fits of spiritual slumber hereby, as Mat. 25:5? What a world of sloath, deadnesse, and formalitie is nourished hereby! How much Instabilitie, confusion, and distraction of spirit is caused hereby!

Yea, how cruel and injurious are such to their own souls! What a sting and poison doth this put into every affliction! How doth it embitter the sweetest mercies! Yea, doth it not open a dore to al tentations, and leave men shiftlesse under the greatest difficulties?

5. Let us then al be exhorted henceforth daily to look for, and hasten unto the coming of our Lord. And to provoke our hearts hereto, let these following motives be duely considered by us.

(1.) Is not that great day our time of Rest? and do not al mind their Rest, specially after hard labor, and a tiresome journey? would not al fain be at home, when

---

[12]sithat: so that.

night comes? What is this world, but our Wildernesse?

(2.) Consider the nearnesse of your Relation, and the manifold engagements you stand in unto Christ. Are you not maried unto Christ? and doth not the law of mariage require, that you daily expect the coming of your absent husband? Remember you are not maried to the clay-Gods of time, but to Christ, who has laid infinite obligations on you, daily to expect his returne.

(3.) Consider also Christ's Regard, and Affection towards you. Though his Bodie be in the supreme Heaven, yet is not his eye of pitie and care; yea, and his heart with you? Doth he not long for you? and wil you not also long for him?

(4.) Remember also what Influence this looking for your approching Lord hath on your heart and ways. Oh! What Vigor and Strength doth it infuse into al that you do or suffer! How much is the heart hereby fortified against al tentations and difficulties! This wil be wings and spurs to the soul in every dutie: The more you eye your home, the more active wil you be in your way.

(5.) Is not this likewise your Glorie and triumphe, to turne your back on althings of time, and daily to look for, and hasten to the coming of your Lord? Are you not hereby advanced into the highest forme of Christians; yea, taken up into the very spirit and life of Heaven? Have you not hereby a beginning of Heaven, a stampe of Glorie on your hearts and lives?

(6.) Remember, that al you do for your souls, without a regard to the coming of the day of God, is nothing. You neither mind, nor affect, nor act any thing to purpose, longer than you mind your Lord's approche. What is al your Religion without this, but a dreaming, sleepy, loitering formalitie? Al your Actions and passions for God, which refer not to this day, are lost.

(7.) To look for and hasten unto the coming of your Lord, puts you into a state of Libertie and freedome: it makes you freeborne Citizens of Heaven, as Phil. 3:20, Whereas al others are chained to the Idols of time, prisoners to their lusts, of servile ignoble spirits. Nothing brings so much Amplitude and Libertie of heart and ways, as daily looking for that great Day.

(8.) Remember the judge standeth at the dore; you are on the brink of Eternitie; and dare you sleep or loiter, when the judge is so near? Is it not prodigious folie,[13] to lie dreaming on the precipice of Eternitie? If you look not for the coming of your Lord, is it not a black marque, that wrath and jugement look for you? Have you not sufficient cause to question your Interest in Christ, if you altogether neglect and disregard his second coming?

(9.) Know that your choisest comforts, peace, hopes, Graces, with the whole of the Divine Life depend greatly on your looking for, and hastening unto the coming of your Lord. Christ wil never honor you with peace, joy, and Grace, if you wil not honor him, with looking for and hastening unto his second coming.

(10.) Future Blessednesse is entailed on our present looking for and hastening unto the coming of our Lord. Thus Heb. 9:28. ''And [un]to them that look for him, shal he appear the second time without sin, unto salvation.'' So that you see Christ wil appear to none in a way of salvation but such as look for him.

(11.) Doth not the whole Creation, excepting the secure sleepy world, look for the coming of our Lord, as Rom. 8:19, 20, 21, and wil you not do the same?

(12.) Lastly, To be altogether unmindful of your Lord's approche, argues a lifelesse, senselesse heart. Is not the expectation of your Lord's approche, your safest, sweetest, richest, noblest life? Oh! then what a sad death is it, to be deprived,

---

[13]folie: folly.

either in part or in whole, of that which is your highest life! To be dead to Christ and his second coming, which brings eternal life, what a miserable death is this? Is not al life dead and gone, if your looking for your Lord's returne be dead and gone?

To give a few Directions for our better looking for, and hastening unto the coming of our Lord:

1. Make the promisse the mesure of thine expectations; and let thy spirit be unsatisfied, til thou hast got some assurance of an interest in the good things promissed, at the coming of thy Lord. As the promisse alone can give being to thy faith and hopes; so the Assurance of an interest in the things promissed, gives life and vigor to thy looking for, and hastening unto the coming of thy Lord. Thou canst not hope for the coming of thy Lord, without a promisse; neither wilt thou hasten towards it, without some persuasion of an Interest in the things promissed. Leave not soul-concerns under any hazards, or peradventures: Rest not satisfied in any condition, 'til you are sure, you can look Christ in the face, when he comes, without fear or shame. In order hereto cast up your accounts daily; and never be satisfied without some assurance your sins are pardoned.

(2.) Be ever parting with the Idols of time: Let no false God, or Image of Jealousie loge in your heart. Remember the Lord usually conveigheth his most deadly poison, through the sweet wine of prosperitie. O! how many, by having their eyes dazled with the glorie of this world, have lost the sight of their Lord's approche! How soon are our eyes misted, and hearts bewitched with the golden pleasures of that heart-inveigling Idol, the World? Oh! at what a distance ought we to keep from the wals of this Pest-house,[14] what have we to

---

[14]The pest house was the hospital for those ill with the plague.

do with this dirty Idol, which the degenerate Sons of Adam Worship and adore?

(3.) Let your Thoughts and Affections ever worke according to the Dignitie of those objects you expect, at the coming of your Lord, and your Relation to them. Hast thou a clear apprehension of thy Lord's approche, and some Assurance of an Interest in him? O! then how should thy Love, by al manner of vehement exercices both of desire, hope, Joy and satisfaction, move towards thy Lord! Or, doest thou behold the coming of thy Lord, but want a prevalent assurance of an Interest in him? what an holy awe and filial fear of thy Lord; what hatred and Indignation against sin oughtest thou to have!

(4.) Make frequent suppositions of thy Lord's Approche; and thinke what thoughts thou wilt then have of things. Remember, with what swift wings time posteth away, and Eternitie, hastens towards thee. Make such suppositions as these: What if this night I should hear the midnight-crie, Behold, the bridegroom cometh? how am I prepared to meet my Lord? Can I look him with confidence in the face? Wil my soul then be able to passe the fiery trial, without being consumed?

(5.) Do nothing, but what thou wouldst do, if the Lord were come. This wil give thee much confidence in looking for the coming of thy Lord. They, who mesure al their Actions by that day, wil not care how soon it come. Such as keep their spirits in an absolute submission to the Divine wil, both as to doing and suffering, are in the fittest posture to entertain their Lord. The reason why the most of men are so averse from looking for, and hastening unto the coming of the day of God, is the Irregularitie of their Actions, which they know wil not bear the trial of that day.

(6.) Contend daily with invincible Resolution, and violent efforts towards the coming of the Day of God. Go forward, in the strength of the Lord, with invincible courage and vigorous activitie to meet your Lord: and remember, what difficulties you meet with in your way, wil be made up in the enjoyments that follow. Alas! what is it that keeps our souls at such a distance from the coming of the Day of God, but the Formalitie and Deadnesse of our Spirits in our race? Is there much deadnesse in thine heart, whereby thou art hindred in thy race? And is there not much life in Christ to quicken thee? then adhere to him, draw from him of his fulnesse Grace for Grace, that thou mayst run with speed, the race set before thee. Dread a loitering formal spirit as much as Hel.

(7.) Muse and consider much on the glorious effects, which follow the coming of the day of God. Remember that thy present thirsty desires, wil then be turned into a love of Fruition and complacence. How soon wil the Saints present tears be changed into eternal joys! O! what an excellent thing is Heaven! Doth it not as much (or much more) excede our present apprehensions, as our present apprehensions excede our present enjoyments? What are al present enjoyments, whether spiritual or temporal, but shadows, in comparison of those celestial enjoyments? Yea, al we here enjoy is scarce a picture of that glorious state. O! what a blessed day wil that be, when the Saints shal leave, though not their Natures, yet al their imperfections both natural and sinful! When al their Spiritual Darknesses, Errors, and Doubts, shal end in the beatific Vision of God, as he is, face to face: When al their Rebellions of heart, shal end in a perfect conformitie and subjection to the Divine Wil: When al their unlawful passions and exorbitant Affections shal end in a regular harmonie and motion: when al their Deadnesses in Duties, shal end in the most vigorous and lively exercices of al manner of Graces: When al their convulsions and terrors of Conscience shal end in complete assurance of God's Love: when al their Distances and Estrangements from God shal end in perfect Union and communion with God: When al their troubles, disgusts, and dissatisfactions in this world shal end in perfect Rest and Satisfaction: O! what a glorious blessed Day wil this be! How would the serious and lively views hereof by faith fixe the heart, in looking for and hastening to the coming of the Day of God!

(8.) Familiarise thoughts of death unto thy soul; and never rest satisfied, 'til thou hast brought thine heart to a wel-grounded, chearful willingnesse to be dissolved. None look for and hasten to the coming of their Lord, so much as they who daily wait for their change. O! how welcome is death, when it comes, to those, who daily look for it! Who live better lives, than they, who continually thinke of death? What more effectually engageth men to die unto althings of time, than daily expectations of Death? They who look for the dreadful hour of Death and Jugement, how much do they despise al the dreadful things of this life? Remember, that death comes not, the sooner for your expectation of it: But the more you look for it, the better prepared you wil be to entertain it, when it comes: You wil die out of choice, not merely from necessitie. I shal conclude with a great saying, of that holy man, Mr. John Rowe (p. 124. of his life), when he drew near to death; why, said he, "should we not be willing to die: Christ came from Heaven to Earth, to free us from sin and miserie, and why should not we be willing, to go from Earth to Heaven, to be freed from sin and miserie?"[15]

Finis

---

[15]Gale wrote the preface to Rowe's biography, *The Life and Death of Mr. John Rowe of Credition in Devon* (London, 1673). The quotation is on 124-25.

Introduction to William Bates,
The Four Last Things

For the introduction to Bates, see above, 99. In this treatise Bates discussed death, judgment, heaven, and hell. The title page noted that the book was "recommended as proper to be given at funerals." The excerpt that follows is a portion of his treatment of the heavenly rest and the heavenly vision of the saints in eternity. Bates's work first appeared as The Four Last Things: Viz. Death, Judgement, Heaven, Hell, Practically considered and applied in Several Discourses *(London, 1691) and was dedicated to Rachel Lady Russell, the widow of Lord William Russell who had been executed for his complicity in Monmouth's Rebellion. The following text is taken from 297-301, 302-306, and 315-19.*

The Four Last Things

by William Bates

I will consider the blessed Effects of the Vision of God in Heaven upon the Saints. Our Saviour tells us, "This is Life eternal, to know thee the only true God, and Jesus Christ whom thou hast sent."[1] The beginning and introduction of our Felicity, is by a lively Faith here, the consummation of it is by present sight in Heaven. From the Vision of his Glory there will be a resultance of his Likeness imprest on us. "We shall be like him, for we shall see him as he is."[2] All the Perfection and Happiness of the Saints is comprised in that Promise. The Sun, when the Sky is clear and serene, forms its image on a Cloud tempered to receive it, with that orient brightness, that the Eye cannot distinguish between the Copy and the Original. Thus the uncreated Sun by powerful emanations transforms the Soul into its likeness, in that divine Degree of Holiness and Felicity, as gloriously resembles God. Moses by conversing with God in the Mount, and seeing his backparts, return'd to the Israelites with such a radiancy in his Face, that they could not look on it without a Vail.[3] What an impression of Glory is in the Saints, who see his perfections in their infinite lustre? 'Tis the priviledge of Christians in this life, above the Church under the Law,[4] "they behold in the Gospel as in a Glass, the Glory of the Lord, and are chang'd into the same Image, from Glory to Glory: they become more Holy and Heavenly, more purified and adorn'd with his Vertues and Graces. Now if the Vision of Christ here in a Glass, an eclipsing Medium, be so influxive[5] upon Believers, what an illustrious and infalli-

[1]John 17:3.

[2]1 John 3:2.

[3]Exod. 33:23, 34:33-35.

[4]Church under the Law: ancient Israel under the old covenant; the quotation is from 2 Cor. 3:18.

[5]influxive: influential.

ble efficacy has the immediate, clear, and permanent view of his Glory upon the Saints in Heaven? That sight is productive and conversative of his Image in its purity and perfection for ever.

The Divine Presence affects the Saints with the most humble reverence and solemn veneration of God. This is an eternal respect due from the intellectual Creature to the Creatour, upon the account of his infinite and incommunicable Excellencies. He is distinguish'd not only from Idols, but from creatures of the highest Order, by his essential supreme and singular name ''I AM.'' Every kind of Being, every spark of Life, every degree of Perfection is from his Efficiency, and depends entirely upon his supporting Power. The most eminent qualities of the Creatures are but in show and appearance, compar'd with the reality and stability of his glorious Nature. In the Scripture, Wisdom, Holiness, Goodness, Power, Truth, Immortality, are attributed to God, with the exclusion of all Creatures from those prerogatives; they being his essential, infinite and incomparable Perfections. They are separable Qualities in the Creatures, like the gilding and enameling of baser Metal: but in the Deity, they are like substantial massy Gold. There is a vast distance between created Beings; but the Distance between a Fly, or a Worm, and an Angel, is nothing to the distance between an Arch-angel and God: there being no comparison between finite and infinite. All Creatures equally vanish, and disappear as nothing, compar'd to the glorious Creatour. As if one from the Region of the Stars should look down upon the Earth, the Mountains and Hills with the Vallies would appear one flat Surface, an equal Plain, the height and lowness of the several parts being indiscernible at that immense distance.

Now in Heaven the Divine Majesty is most visible, and most awful and ador-

able. The sublimest Spirits ''cover their Faces'' before his glorious Brightness. The Prophet Isaiah had a representation of Heaven: ''I saw the Lord sitting upon a Throne high and lifted up, and his Train filled the Temple. Above it stood the Seraphims: each one had six Wings: With Twain he covered his Face, with twain he covered his Feet, with twain he did fly. And one cried to another and said, Holy, holy, holy, holy Lord of Hosts, the whole Earth is full of his Glory.''[6] They highly honour him, by the reflection of his separate and peerless Excellencies, his Almighty power, his Infinite Supremacy and Eternal Empire, in this consert of Praises. . . .

In Heaven the Saints as perfectly love God as they know him. The Love of God is the Essential Character of a Saint, that distinguishes him from the Unregenerate. Indeed, it is strange that God, who is infinitely lovely, and infinitely liberal and beneficent, should not prevail on the Hearts of all Men; But if we consider the degeneracy of Mankind, how their Minds are depraved and deceived, and their Affections are vitiated, the Wonder will cease. Carnal Men have not due Conceptions of God, and will not attentively observe his amiable Perfections. St. John tells us, ''he that loveth not, doth not know God.''[7] Knowledg is the leading Principle in the Operations of the Soul. There must be a heavenly Eye to discover the heavenly Beauty, before there can be love of it. Now Men are in ignorant darkness, and are defiled in Flesh and Spirit, and therefore cannot love God who is glorious in Holiness. Without resemblance there can be no affectionate Union which is the Essence of Love. The contrariety of Dispositions infers a contrariety of Affections. The Scripture expresses this in dreadful Colours:

---

[6]Isa. 6:2-3.

[7]Paraphrase of 1 John 4:8.

"the carnal Mind is enmity against God: the Friendship of the World is enmity with God;"[8] that is, Pride, and Covetousness, and Sensuality, which are the Lusts of the Carnal Mind, and are terminated upon worldly Things, are inconsistent with the Love of God. The Justice of God is terrible to the Consciences, and his Holiness Odious to the Affections of the Unrenewed. 'Till by Divine Grace the Understanding is enlightened and purified to have right apprehensions of God; till the Will and Affections are cleansed and changed; till there be a resemblance of God's holy Nature, and a conformity to his holy Laws, they are not capable of delightful adhering to him, which is the internal essential Property of Love.

But those who are partakers of the Divine Nature, the holy and heavenly, "taste and see how good the Lord is:" and according to the Illustrations of the Mind, such are the Impressions upon the Heart; the Love of God in their Breasts here is like smoking Flax, but in Heaven 'tis a triumphant Flame. God is the first Fair, the Original of all amiable Excellencies, in whom they shine in their unstained Lustre and Perfection. When he fully reveals himself, and displays the richest Beams of his Love and Glory, how transporting and endearing is that Sight? Our Affections that are now scatter'd on many things, wherein some faint Reflections of his Goodness appear, shall then be united in one full Current to him, "who is all in all." In Heaven the immense treasures of his grace are reveal'd: That when Man for his rebellious Sin was justly expell'd from Paradise, and under the Sentence of Eternal Death, God should not not only pardon, but prefer[9] us to the dignity of his Children, and prepare such a Glory for us, and us for such a Glory,

this will inspire the Saints with such ardent Affections, that will make them equal to the Angels, those pure and everlasting Flames of Love to God.

In Heaven we shall be with "Jesus the Mediator of the New Covenant, who is seated at the right Hand of God."[10] And how admirable will he appear to the Sense and Soul of every glorified Saint? for "we shall see the King in his Beauty." When our Saviour was upon the Holy Mount, and one vanishing Beam of Glory appeared in his Transfiguration, Peter was so transported at the sight, that he forgot the world and himself: How ravishing then will the sight of him in his Triumphant Majesty be, when we shall be transfigur'd our selves? Now while Believers are in the shadows of the earthly State, they "love their unseen Saviour" with such intense degrees of affection, as deface all the washy Colours, all the vain loves of things in this World: but when they are admitted into his shining Presence, and see him in the day of Celestial Glory; with what an extasy of Affection will they be transported?

We shall then feel the endearing Obligations our Saviour has laid upon us, who ransom'd us with so rich a Price, and purchas'd for us such an invaluable Inheritance. For in proportion as we shall understand his Greatness in himself, we shall [understand] his Goodness to us. The Eternal Son of God descended from the Heaven of Heavens to our lowly Earth; and which is more, from the Majesty he there reign'd, and was visible to the Angels, he became Man that he might die, to redeem us from the most woeful Captivity, from Death, and the sting of Death, Sin, and the strength of Sin, Law, and obtain a blessed Life and Immortality for us. O unexampled Love! "Greater love hath no Man than

---

[8]Rom. 8:7.

[9]prefer: advance.

[10]Allusion to Heb. 12:2, 24.

this, to lay down his Life for his Friend:"[11] and what is the Life of a sinful Man, a vanishing Vapour, a life mixed with Troubles and Vexation; and to lay down this for a Friend deservedly dear, is the highest expression of humane Love: but for the Son of God to lay down his Life, a Life without Sin, and without End, for Immortality was a Privilege due to his Innocence, and for Enemies, for the worst Enemies, Rebels by revolture from obedience to their Creatour and King, is a Love truly Divine, and infinitely surpassing, not only the Affections, but the understanding and knowledg of all Creatures. Briefly, he gave his Life for us, and gives himself to us, the most excellent testimonies of Love that we can receive from Love it self; and we shall love him with all the strength of our glorified Spirits. . . .

How precious and joyful will the Presence of Christ be to the Saints? 'Twas his Prayer on Earth, "Father, I will that they also whom thou hast given me, be with me where I am, that they may behold my Glory."[12] When the Saints are received into the Everlasting Kingdom, the first Object that draws their admiring regards, is Christ on the Throne. Inestimable Felicity! whether we consider him as the Son of God, in whose conspicuous Countenance all the Glory of his Father shines, or as the Saviour of Men, and the Head of the Elect, upon a double account: partly, that "he that loved us, and wash'd us from our Sins in his Blood;" after suffering all Indignites and Cruelties for our sake, has received the Reward of his meritorious Sufferings, the triumph of his Victory, being "glorified with the Father with the Glory he had before the world was:"[13] and partly because every Member shall be conform'd to him in Glory. The sight of the Face of Moses

when radiant, had no transforming efficacy, for the Light of it was not in him as its Spring, but by the derivation. But the Son of God is Light essentially, and the sight of his Glory will transform us into his Likeness. And how dear and joyful is the presence of the Saints to Christ. He then sees of the travail of his Soul, the fruit of his sharp Sufferings and bleeding Love, and is satisfied.[14] How delightful is it to him to see all his Spiritual Progeny safely brought to Heaven, and made partakers of his Glory and Joy in the everlasting Kingdom. For according to the extent of the Object, and dearness of the Affection, Joy rises. He will then present them to his Father with infinite complacency: "Behold, here am I, and the children whom thou hast given me."

The dearest Affections of Christ and the Saints in Heaven, are mutual and reflexive. In the Sacred Song,[15] the expressions of Love, Desire, and Joy, borrowed from the espousals of Solomon and his beloved Wife, are, as it were, characters in the Bark, to be understood in a spiritual Sense, of the Mystical Marriage of Christ and the Church. What endearing entercourse is there between the most perfect Lover, and his Spouse inspir'd with the same pure Flam[e]. Here amiable Perfections attract his Eye and Heart: "Thou art all fair, my love, there is no spot in thee."[16] His propriety[17] in the church is his unvaluable[18] treasure: "My vineyard which is mine, is ever before me."[19] He repeats the word "Mine," in the sweetest and most tender manner. And the Church, with the same harmonious Affections, speaks of Christ. She contemplates in a soft extasy his ever-

---

[11]John 15:13.

[12]John 17:24.

[13]Allusion to John 17:5.

[14]Allusion to Isa. 53:11.

[15]The sacred song: Song of Sol.

[16]Song of Sol. 4:7.

[17]propriety: property.

[18]unvaluable: invaluable.

[19]Song of Sol. 8:12.

satisfying beauty. "my Beloved is the chiefest of ten thousand, he is altogether lovely." She breaks forth in triumph, "My Beloved is mine, and I am his."[20] By all their expressions of joyful Love and Union, we may ascend in our Thoughts, what are the Joys of Heaven, where the Communion of Christ and the Church is entire and uninterrupted for ever. If Faith and Love of our unseen Saviour produce "a Joy unspeakable and glorious," as if Believers were wrap'd up[21] to Paradise, or Paradise descended into them, what will the sight and fruition of him? There is as great a difference in degrees between the Joy that flows from the assurance and application of Faith, and the Joy from Vision and full Possession, as between the impression of Joy the Forerunner of Christ felt, when he sprang in the Womb at the coming of our Saviour; and his ravishing Joy, when he saw Christ, and pointed him out to his Disciples, "Behold the Lamb of God, that takes away the sins of the world."[22]

---

[20]Conflation of Song of Sol. 5:10 and 5:16.

[21]Wrap'd up: rapt, carried off.

[22]John the Baptist, Luke 1:44, John 1:29.

The supream Joy of the Saints is for the Felicity and Glory of God himself. For as the holy Soul feels no more powerful motive to love God, than because he is most worthy of it, as he is God, a being of infinite Excellencies, and therefore to be loved above the dearest persons and things, even it self; so the highest Joy it partakes of is from this consideration, that God is infinitely blessed and glorious. For in this the Supream desire of love is accomplished, that the most beloved object is perfectly honour'd and pleased. In Heaven the Love of the Saints to God is in its highest Perfection, and they see his Glory in the most perfect manner, which causes a transcendent Joy to them. And this is one reason why the Saints, tho shining with unequal degrees of Glory, are equally content. For their most ardent Love being set on God, that he is pleased to glorify himself by such various communications of his Goodness, is full satisfaction to their Desires. Besides, in those different degrees of Glory, every one is so content with his own, that there is no possible desire of being but what he is.

Suggested Readings

Allison, C. F. *The Rise of Moralism: The Proclamation of the Gospel from Hooker to Baxter*. London: SPCK, 1966.

Beatty, Nancy Lee. *The Craft of Dying: A Study in the Literary Tradition of the Ars Moriendi in England*. New Haven: Yale University Press, 1970.

Brauer, Jerald C. "Conversion: From Puritanism to Revivalism." *Journal of Religion* 58 (July 1978): 227-43.

Caldwell, Patricia. *The Puritan Conversion Narrative: The Beginnings of American Expression*. Cambridge: Cambridge University Press, 1983.

Cohen, Charles Lloyd. *God's Caress: The Psychology of Puritan Religious Experience*. New York: Oxford University Press, 1986.

Coolidge, John S. *The Pauline Renaissance in England*. Oxford: Clarendon Press, 1970.

Cragg, Gerald R. *Puritanism in the Period of the Great Persecution, 1660-1688*. Cambridge: University Press, 1957.

Davies, Horton. *Worship and Theology in England from Andrewes to Baxter and Fox, 1603-1690*. Princeton: Princeton University Press, 1975.

Greaves, Richard L. *John Bunyan*. Grand Rapids: Wm. B. Eerdmans, 1969.

————— . *Saints and Rebels: Seven Nonconformists in Stuart England*. Macon: Mercer University Press, 1985.

Green, I. M. *The Re-establishment of the Church of England, 1660-1663*. Oxford: Oxford University Press, 1960.

Hambrick-Stowe, Charles E. *The Practice of Piety: Puritan Devotional Disciplines in Seventeenth-Century New England*. Chapel Hill: University of North Carolina Press, 1982.

Holifield, E. Brooks. *The Covenant Sealed: The Development of Puritan Sacramental Theology in Old and New England, 1570-1720*. New Haven: Yale University Press, 1974.

Huntley, Frank Livingstone. *Bishop Joseph Hall and Protestant Meditation in Seventeenth-Century England: A Study with the Texts of* The Art of Divine Meditation *(1606) and* Occasional Meditations *(1633)*. Binghamton: Center for Medieval & Early Renaissance Studies, 1981.

Jenkins, R. B. *Henry Smith: England's Silver-Tongued Preacher*. Macon: Mercer University Press, 1983.

Kaufman, U. Milo. *The Pilgrim's Progress and Traditions in Puritan Meditation*. New Haven: Yale University Press, 1966.

Keeble, N. H. *Richard Baxter: Puritan Man of Letters*. Oxford: Clarendon Press, 1982.

Lacey, Douglas R. *Dissent and Parliamentary Politics in England, 1661-1689*. New Brunswick: Rutgers University Press, 1969.

Lewalski, Barbara Kiefer. *Protestant Poetics and the Seventeenth-Century Religious Lyric*. Princeton: Princeton University Press, 1979.

Lovelace, Richard F. *The American Pietism of Cotton Mather*. Grand Rapids: Christian University Press, 1979.

McGee, J. Sears. *The Godly Man in Stuart England: Anglicans, Puritans, and the Two Tables, 1620-1670*. New Haven: Yale University Press, 1976.

Monk, Robert C. *John Wesley's Puritan Heritage: A Study of the Christian Life*. Nashville: Abingdon Press, 1966.

Morgan, Irvonwy. *Puritan Spirituality Illustrated from the Life and Times of the Rev. Dr. John Preston*. London: Epworth Press, 1973.

Nuttall, G. F. *The Holy Spirit in Puritan Faith and Experience*. Oxford: Basil Blackwell, 1946.

_____ . *Richard Baxter*. London: Thomas Nelson & Sons, 1965.

Petit, Norman. *The Heart Prepared: Grace and Conversion in Puritan Spiritual Life*. New Haven: Yale University Press, 1966.

Pinto, Vivian De Sola. *Peter Sterry: Platonist and Puritan*. Cambridge: University Press, 1934.

Richard, Lucien Joseph. *The Spirituality of John Calvin*. Atlanta: John Knox Press, 1974.

Richardson, Caroline Frances. *English Preachers and Preaching, 1640-1670*. New York: Macmillan Co., 1928.

Sommerville, C. John. *Popular Religion in Restoration England*. Gainesville: University of Florida Press, 1977.

Toon, Peter. *God's Statesman: The Life and Work of John Owen*. Grand Rapids: Zondervan, 1973.

Wakefield, Gordon S. *Puritan Devotion: Its Place in the Development of Christian Piety*. London: Epworth Press, 1957.

Wallace, Dewey D., Jr. ''The Image of Saintliness in Puritan Hagiography, 1650-1700.'' In John E. Booty, ed., *The Divine Drama in History and Literature: Essays Presented to Horton Davies on His Retirement from Princeton University*, 23-43. Allison Park: Pickwick Publications, 1984.

_____ . *Puritans and Predestination: Grace in English Protestant Theology, 1525-1695*. Chapel Hill: University of North Carolina Press, 1982.

Watkins, Owen C. *The Puritan Experience*. London: Routledge and Kegan Paul, 1972.

White, Helen C. *English Devotional Literature, 1600-1640*. Madison: University of Wisconsin Press, 1931.